macromedia®
DREAMWEAVER® MX
2004

training from the source

khristine annwn page

macromedia®
PRESS

Macromedia Dreamweaver MX 2004: Training from the Source

Khristine Annwn Page

Published by Macromedia Press, in association with Peachpit Press, a division of Pearson Education.

Macromedia Press
1249 Eighth Street
Berkeley, CA 94710
510/524-2178
800/283-9444
510/524-2221 (fax)
Find us on the World Wide Web at:
http://www.peachpit.com
http://www.macromedia.com

To report errors, please send a note to errata@peachpit.com

Printed and bound in the United States of America

ISBN 0-321-21919-8

9 8 7 6 5 4 3 2 1

CREDITS

Author: Khristine Annwn Page

Macromedia Press Editor: Angela C. Kozlowski

Editor: Susan Hobbs

Technical Editor: Sue Hove

Production Coordinator: Myrna Vladic

Copy Editor: Nancy Sixsmith

Compositors:
Rick Gordon, Emerald Valley Graphics
Debbie Roberti, Espresso Graphics

Indexer: Emily Glossbrenner

Cover Production: George Mattingly, GMD

BIO

Khristine Annwn Page is the Director of NorthWind Studios, a collective of artists, programmers and musicians [www.northwindstudios.com], and the editor/publisher of Crescent Magazine. She authored "Dreamweaver MX Training From The Source" and co-authored "Dreamweaver 4 Training From The Source," both published by Peachpit Press and Macromedia Press. She has taught Dreamweaver and Web Design classes at San Francisco State University's Multimedia Studies program and given training in Dreamweaver for the Reuters Digital Vision Fellowship program at Stanford University. She has worked as a Multimedia Specialist at the San Francisco Exploratorium and as a Senior Web Designer at Ideum, a company devoted to producing Web sites for museums, non-profits, and socially responsible companies. Khristine holds a BFA with a Senior Award for Excellence from Rhode Island School of Design [www.risd.edu]. She has received awards from Adobe and her artwork has been shown in galleries in Providence, RI, New York City, and Palo Alto, CA.

ACKNOWLEDGMENTS

A great many thanks to Susan Hobbs, Angela Kozlowski, Sue Hove, Robert Crooks, Patti Schulze, and the rest of the wonderful people at Peachpit and Macromedia. Thanks also to David Powers, Marja Ribbers-de Vroed, Tamara Jackson, and Scott Richards for their Dreamweaver extensions. I'd like to express particular thanks to Mary Page, Rick Page, Rich Page, Laura and Keith Schmidt, Bryon Kennedy, and the rest of my friends and family for all the support, love and encouragement.

DEDICATION
For all of my family, and in memory of my grandparents

table of contents

introduction

Macromedia's Dreamweaver MX 2004 combines powerful visual layout tools with robust text-based HTML editing features for the creation, management, and maintenance of Web sites. It gives beginners immediate access to the tools needed for creating Web pages, while allowing experienced developers who are familiar with hand-coding to work directly with the code when needed. This flexible program makes advanced techniques accessible and easy to use. The integration of powerful design, code, and interactive features provides a wealth of benefits to both beginners and advanced users.

PREREQUISITES

This book is intended to familiarize you with the Dreamweaver development environment and focuses on equipping you with the skills needed to lay out and design Web pages. Because it is geared toward beginner and intermediate users who may have little or no previous experience with Dreamweaver, coverage of advanced application building and dynamic Web site creation with the use of databases, server behaviors, and Web applications is outside the scope of this book. Those features require knowledge and understanding of dynamic design concepts and of the languages used to create these sites—including ASP, JSP, ColdFusion, and more. For those who are interested in learning about the code, Lesson 14 will get you started in the coding environment, demonstrating how to work with Dreamweaver's coding tools and pointing you to resources within the program that will enable you to learn more.

The instructions in this book are designed for Web designers, Web developers, and others interested in creating Web pages. This course assumes that you are a beginner with Dreamweaver, but are familiar with the basic methods of giving commands on a Macintosh or Windows computer, such as choosing items from menus, opening and saving files, and so on. For more information on those basic tasks, see the documentation provided with your computer.

To get the most out of this book, it is recommended that you have basic familiarity with the Web. A general understanding of standard word processing programs, such as Microsoft Word, is also helpful, although not required.

Finally, the instructions in this book assume that you already have Dreamweaver MX 2004 installed on a Macintosh or Windows computer, and that your computer meets the system requirements listed on page 5. This minimum configuration allows you to run Dreamweaver MX 2004 and open the training files included on the enclosed CD. If you do not own Dreamweaver MX 2004, a demo version is included for your use on the CD. You can complete the lessons with the trial version of the software, but the demo version functions for only 30 days, after which the program will no longer launch without a serial number. Follow the instructions in the ReadMe file to install the demo version of the software.

NOTE *After the 30-day trial period, Dreamweaver must activated over the internet or by phone in order to be used. You can learn more about activation at Macromedia's Web site: www.macromedia.com/software/activation/.*

OUTLINE

This Macromedia training course steps you through the projects in each lesson, presents the major features and tools in Dreamweaver MX 2004, and guides you toward developing the skills you need to create Web sites. This curriculum should take approximately 24 hours to complete and includes the following 17 lessons:

Lesson 1: Dreamweaver MX 2004 Basics

Lesson 2: Adding Content to a Page

Lesson 3: Working with Graphics

Lesson 4: Creating Links

Lesson 5: Designing with Tables

Lesson 6: Developing Style Sheets

Lesson 7: Using Library Items

Lesson 8: Using Templates

Lesson 9: Creating Frames

Lesson 10: Creating Forms

Lesson 11: Adding User Interactivity

Lesson 12: Managing Your Site

Lesson 13: Accessibility and Testing

Lesson 14: Editing the Code

Lesson 15: Using Find and Replace

Lesson 16: Creating Layers

Lesson 17: Extending Dreamweaver

THE PROJECT SITE

The project site that you will work on throughout the book, "Lights of the Coast," explores the history, technology, and culture of lighthouses. This is just one example of the kinds of Web sites that you can create with Dreamweaver. Because this site was developed for readers to build over the course of the 17 lessons in this book, some

2

portions are incomplete. You can see the actual "Lights of the Coast" Web site online at http://www.northwindstudios.com/lighthouse.

After performing the tasks in each of the lessons, your can continue to develop your skills by using the lessons as a guide to creating your own practice site, which provides you with the opportunity to experiment further with Dreamweaver's Web development tools.

In addition, as you browse the Web, look at other Web sites to see how the concepts and tools presented in this book are used in real-world examples.

ELEMENTS AND FORMAT

Each lesson in this book begins by outlining the major focus of the lesson at hand and introducing new features. Learning objectives and the approximate time needed to complete all the exercises are also listed at the beginning of each lesson. The projects are divided into short exercises that explain the importance of each skill you learn. Every lesson builds on the concepts and techniques used in the previous lessons.

TIP *The Tip icon indicates tips, which are alternative ways to perform tasks and suggestions to consider when applying the skills you are learning.*

NOTE *The Note icon indicates notes, which are additional background information to expand your knowledge, as well as advanced techniques you can use to further develop your skills.*

Boldface terms: New vocabulary that is introduced and emphasized in each lesson.

Text the reader types: Text that the reader types to complete the lessons is shown in a *different italicized font*.

Menu commands and keyboard shortcuts: There are often multiple ways to perform the same task in Dreamweaver. The different options are pointed out in each lesson. Menu commands are shown with angle brackets between the menu names and commands: Menu › Command › Subcommand. Keyboard shortcuts are shown with a plus sign between the names of keys to indicate that you should press the keys simultaneously; for example, Shift+Tab means that you should press the Shift and Tab keys at the same time.

Appendixes: Appendix A contains a table with special characters, regular expressions, and their meanings for use with Dreamweaver's Find and Replace feature, covered in Lesson 15. Appendixes B and C provide shortcuts for Dreamweaver commands for use on Macintosh and Windows systems, respectively.

CD-ROM: The files you need to complete the projects for each lesson are located in the DWMX2004_project folder on the enclosed CD, which can be found in the back of the book. Inside the project folder are subfolders titled with the name of the respective lesson—Lesson_01_Basics, for example—that contain the subfolders and files necessary to perform the tasks in the respective lesson. Which subfolders are included depends on the projects in the lesson. Common subfolders include **Completed**, which contains the completed files for each lesson so you can compare your work and see the end result of the project; **Images**, which contains all the images necessary for the lesson; and **Text**, which includes text documents you will import into Dreamweaver. The files you use for each of the projects are listed at the beginning of each lesson.

For additional practice with the skills you learn in each lesson, try re-creating the starting files that are provided for you in the lesson files.

MACROMEDIA TRAINING FROM THE SOURCE

The Macromedia Training from the Source and Advanced Training from the Source series are developed in association with Macromedia and are reviewed by the product support teams. Ideal for active learners, the books in the Training from the Source series offer hands-on instruction designed to provide you with a solid grounding in the program's fundamentals.

Macromedia offers the training you need to master Macromedia applications and apply them to real development tasks. Our instructor-led and online courses are geared to different experience levels to teach you the technologies and product skills you need to get your job done, whether you create user interfaces or build back-end components. And because we have our eyes on the big picture, we help you make the right decisions to allow your work to be integrated smoothly with the rest of your development team.

For more information on Macromedia Authorized Training, please visit http://www.macromedia.com/training.

Welcome to Macromedia Training from the Source. We hope you enjoy the course.

WHAT YOU WILL LEARN

You will develop the skills you need to create and maintain your own Web sites as you work through these lessons.

By the end of this course, you will be able to:

• Open Dreamweaver, create pages, and preview them in browsers

• Format text in different sizes, colors, and styles using integrated styles

• Import text from a variety of sources, including text files, Word documents, and spreadsheets

- Insert graphics and control their appearance
- Create and manage email and internal and external links throughout your site
- Learn how to make changes directly within the HTML code
- Place text and graphics within tables to achieve more control over the layout
- Make use of image rollovers and other interactive elements
- Use the Site window to manage your files and folders
- Develop library items to use the same elements quickly and repeatedly
- Create templates to set the look and feel of a site
- Make your pages accessible and redirect visitors according to the browser version they arc using
- Incorporate different types of files, such as Flash Objects and Flash Text
- Insert a background graphic or change the background colors of your pages
- Specify text attributes using cascading style sheets to gain more control over the appearance of text
- Use the extensive Find and Replace feature to make changes in single documents or throughout the entire site
- Create forms to collect information from visitors
- Test and run reports on your Web pages to verify their compatibility with multiple types of browsers
- Customize and extend Dreamweaver's capabilities to suit your needs

MINIMUM SYSTEM REQUIREMENTS: MACINTOSH

- 500 MHz Power Mac G3 processor
- Mac OS X 10.2.6 or higher
- 128 MB RAM
  (256 MB recommended)
- 275MB available disk space

MINIMUM SYSTEM REQUIREMENTS: WINDOWS

- 600 MHz Intel Pentium® III processor or equivalent
- Windows 98 SE, 2000, NT, Me, or XP
- Microsoft Data Access Components (MDAC) 2.6 or later
- 128 MB RAM
  (256 MB recommended)
- 275MB available disk space

dreamweaver mx 2004 basics

LESSON 1

Dreamweaver MX 2004 is an HTML editor that gives users visual design and editing capabilities combined with the ability to work directly with code. Dreamweaver helps speed production time for your Web sites and provides tools for the management and maintenance of those sites.

In this lesson, you'll learn the basics of Dreamweaver MX 2004 and become familiar with the program's interface and tools. You'll begin to use the main site-management features by setting up a local site for the pages that you create.

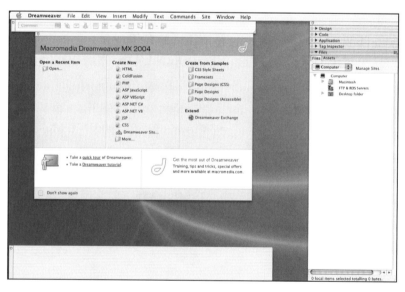

In this lesson, you'll learn about the Dreamweaver interface while setting up the site you will use throughout this book.

This lesson teaches you how to work with basic document settings to create a simple Web page as well as how to test your work in different browsers—a vital part of creating accessible Web sites.

You can find an example of the completed lesson in the Completed Project folder inside the Lesson_01_Basics folder on the CD-ROM.

WHAT YOU WILL LEARN

In this lesson, you will:

- Become familiar with the Dreamweaver interface
- Set up a new local site
- Create and save a new document
- Identify the tools
- Give your page a title
- Set a background color for your page
- Specify preview browsers and test your page

APPROXIMATE TIME

This lesson should take approximately one hour to complete.

LESSON FILES

Completed Project:

Lesson_01_Basics/Completed/introduction.htm

EXPLORING THE WORKSPACE

To get started with Dreamweaver, you need to become familiar with the interface and the initial options that are available for your workspace.

OPEN DREAMWEAVER MX 2004.

Windows Users: Dreamweaver MX 2004 provides two workspace options for Windows users: Designer and Coder. For this exercise, you should select the Designer workspace because it will be used throughout this book. The Designer workspace integrates all Dreamweaver-related windows and panels into an environment that is optimized for visually based Web site creation ideal for designers. The Coder workspace is tailored for programmers—those who want to work primarily with HTML and other languages. You can access all Dreamweaver features and tools from either workspace. You are presented with the option to select one of these workspaces the first time you open Dreamweaver on a Windows computer.

NOTE *You can switch from one workspace to the other at any time by choosing Edit > Preferences, selecting the General category, and clicking the Change Workspace button. If you change your workspace settings, Dreamweaver must be restarted for the change to take effect.*

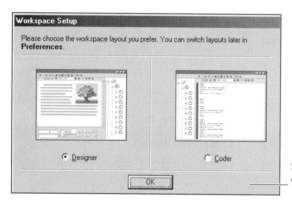

SELECTING THE DREAMWEAVER WORKSPACE (WINDOWS ONLY)

Macintosh Users: The workspace options described previously are not available on the Macintosh. The Macintosh uses a floating palette-style system that you can arrange to suit your needs. You'll learn more about customizing the Dreamweaver workspace later in this lesson and throughout the book.

START PAGE

If this is your first time opening Dreamweaver MX 2004, you should see a Start Page that provides quick links to recent documents; the option to create a new document from a variety of file types; page design samples that can give you a starting point for developing your own sites; program resources including a Dreamweaver tour and a

8

tutorial; and a link to the Dreamweaver Exchange that contains resources you use to extend the program. By default, the Start Page appears every time you open Dreamweaver unless you click the Don't show again checkbox.

NOTE *If the Start Page does not appear on startup and you want to view it, or if you don't see the Don't show again checkbox, you can adjust the display of the Start Page in the Dreamweaver Preferences. To do so, choose Dreamweaver > Preferences (Macintosh) or Edit > Preferences (Windows), select General from the Category list, and click the Show Start Page checkbox in the Document options section. A checkmark indicates that the Start Page will be displayed when the program is opened; no checkmark indicates that the Start Page will not appear. You will need to open and close a document or quit Dreamweaver and restart the program for the change to take effect.*

When you begin to create new pages or explore other options in the Get Started section, the Start Page closes on its own. Macintosh users can also close this window using the Close button in the upper left corner of the window.

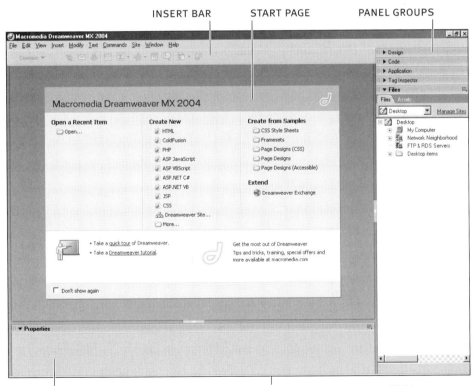

INSERT BAR   START PAGE   PANEL GROUPS

PROPERTY INSPECTOR   THE DREAMWEAVER MX 2004 INTERFACE

PREPARING TO DEVELOP YOUR SITE

Spending the time to create a thorough outline or flowchart helps you to develop your ideas, obtain a better understanding of the scope of your project, and save you time and resources down the road. A good Web site should be intuitive and create a positive, unique user experience. The creation of an effective Web site starts with defining and summarizing the reason and need for the site. Before you start work on any pages, ask yourself or your client the following questions.

Who is your audience?

Knowing your audience is vital. Defining a general user profile helps you to effectively reach your target audience. You may have multiple kinds of users; if so, develop a profile for each of them.

After you know who your audience is, you need to consider what technologies those users are likely to have. What kinds of plug-ins, browsers, and operating systems do the majority of your visitors use? The type of equipment used by your visitors is important to consider when you create a Web site that is accessible to your intended audience. For example, you wouldn't want to create a site that uses elements supported by only the most recent and up-to-date browsers if most of your audience uses older machines that can't even run those browsers.

Why is the site needed? What do you want the visitors of your site to come away with?

Consider the purpose your site will serve and how each potential user will make use of the site. What does the site need to contain to serve its purpose? Use the visitor profile(s) you created to determine possible scenarios for what visitors would do at your site. You can then determine what types of content are needed.

What content will be needed for the site?

Identifying and collecting your site assets is an important part of the preparation to design and produce a Web site. You need to gather all the content, such as text, graphics, and multimedia elements that will be used on the site. Organizing these assets enables you to create a complete and thorough Web site.

What should the site communicate?

It is essential to know exactly what you want to express to your visitors. If you don't know what you're trying to say, chances are your users won't either. Clarify the message of your site. Communication with your visitors is an integral part of maintaining an effective site, and that connection is dependent in part upon the structure of your site.

Web sites rely on structure and file management: A Web site with a poor structure can be confusing to navigate, hard to use, and difficult to maintain. To create a site that is clear, communicative, and easy for visitors to use, you need to plan out the structure and hierarchy of files and folders within your site completely before you begin to build any HTML documents.

Creating a thorough outline of the site as well as a detailed flowchart or storyboard is an important step of the planning process.

For the lessons in this book, all the work described in this section has already been done. You're now ready to begin working on the project site, "Lights of the Coast."

DEFINING A LOCAL SITE

The first step of creating a Web site—before you begin to create any individual pages—is to designate or create the folder on your computer that will contain everything within your site. This process is called defining a local site. The designated folder, known as the **local root folder**, sets the boundaries of the local site that resides on your hard disk and mirrors the remote site, which is the actual site on the Web server that your visitors will access. Defining a local site enables you to maintain the same folder hierarchy between the local and remote versions, which is crucial to creating and maintaining a functional site.

The creation of a local site, composed of the local root folder within which you set up the structure of the site's files and folders, prevents your site from storing any site files outside of the local root folder. The files on your hard disk that are outside of the local root folder cannot be transferred to the remote server . This restriction ensures that as you develop your site, you won't access files that aren't available when the site is made available online. Many Dreamweaver features, such as the potential to update all references to a file that has been moved to a different location in the site, require the definition of a local site in order to fully function. You should make a practice of always creating and working within local sites. If you don't, you may have problems with links, paths, and file management (Dreamweaver's tools for these features are covered in later lessons of this book).

The development of your site occurs in the local site on your hard disk, in which you build and initially test your pages.

NOTE *Setting up a site is not required, although it is recommended. Dreamweaver will allow you to quickly edit, connect, and transfer files without setting up a site. You'll learn more about managing your site in Lesson 12.*

1) Copy the DWMX2004_Project folder from the CD-ROM to your hard disk.

The DWMX2004_project folder will become the root folder of your local site. This folder contains all the files and folders for "Lights of the Coast," the project site you will create a portion of as you work through lessons in this book. When you begin work on your own sites, you need to create individual root folders for each of those sites.

The name of a root folder can be the name of the respective site or any name you choose. If you create multiple sites, it is helpful to use names that can be distinguished easily from one another. The name of the root folder is simply for file management purposes and is not visible to the visitors of the site.

TIP *You should save your local root folder in a location on your hard disk that is outside the Dreamweaver application folder. If you ever need to reinstall Dreamweaver, your work will be lost if you save it inside the Dreamweaver application folder.*

2) In Dreamweaver, choose Site > Manage Sites. Click the New button and choose Site from the pop-up menu.

The Site Definition dialog box opens with two tabs: Basic and Advanced. These tabs allow you to choose how you want to go through the process of defining a site. The Basic version, which is shown by default when you open the dialog box, walks you step-by-step through the process. The Advanced version gives you a number of additional options and settings to configure, and it does not include the explanatory text descriptions you see in the Basic view.

TIP *You can also create a new site directly from the Start Page by selecting Dreamweaver Site from the Create New section. The Site Definition dialog box (described previously) appears.*

For this exercise, choose the Basic tab if it is not already selected.

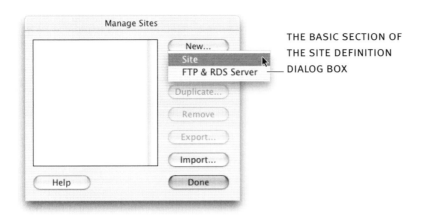

THE BASIC SECTION OF
THE SITE DEFINITION
DIALOG BOX

NOTE *If you have never defined a site in Dreamweaver, the Files panel displays a hierarchy of folders on your computer and a link to Define a Site, which opens the Site Definition dialog box. For Macintosh users, the default selection in the Site panel pop-up menu is Computer, which initially contains Macintosh HD, FTP & RDS Servers, and Desktop Folder. For Windows users, the default selection is Desktop, which initially contains My Computer, Network Neighborhood, FTP & RDS Servers, and Desktop Items. After you create a site, that site becomes the default selection. If you have more than one site, Dreamweaver displays the most recently used site in the Files panel. The Files panel is located in the Files panel group.*

Macintosh Users: Due to a bug in the Macintosh version of Dreamweaver MX 2004, the Files panel group may appear to be called Assets instead of Files. The default name of the panel group is Files, but when you expand the Files panel (as you will learn to do in lesson 12) the Files panel group will be renamed Assets. You can switch back to the default name of the Files panel group by either renaming the panel group or deleting the Dreamweaver MX 2004 Preferences. Renaming the panel group will change the name without affecting other Dreamweaver features. To do so, click the Context menu in the upper right corner of the Files (or Assets) panel group and choose Rename Panel Group. Type **Files** *into the text field and click OK. To delete the Dreamweaver MX 2004 Preferences, quit Dreamweaver, navigate to Macintosh > Users > Your User Name > Library > Preferences, delete the Dreamweaver MX 2004 Prefs file, and empty your trash. When you restart Dreamweaver, the panel group will be called Files. Please keep in mind, if you choose to delete your Dreamweaver MX 2004 Preferences, any other settings or tools that you may have changed will revert to their defaults. Neither solution will permanently change the name of the panel group — the name will change back to Assets again if you expand the files panel.*

3) In the Basic tab of the Site Definition dialog box Dreamweaver poses the question, "What would you like to name your site?" Type *Lights of the Coast* **in the Site name text field and then click Next.**

Lights of the Coast is the name of the project site you are creating in this lesson. When you create your own sites, the names that you assign can be anything that identifies them. Clear and specific site names allow you to immediately tell sites apart by name, making it easier to manage multiple sites. The site name is for your reference only and is not visible to users of your site.

NOTE *This section of the Basic site setup corresponds to the Site name text field of the Local Info category in the Advanced view. Throughout the course of defining your site, you can switch back and forth between the Basic and Advanced views if you want to see how the Advanced view appears. You'll work with the Advanced view in Lesson 12.*

4) Dreamweaver asks, "Do you want to work with a server technology such as ColdFusion, ASP.NET, ASP, JSP, or PHP?" Click the radio button for the option "No, I do not want to use a server technology." Click Next to advance to the next section.

Because you are creating pages for a static site (one that does not incorporate databases and other server technologies) in this book's lessons, you should select the No option. If at any time you need to make changes to your site setup, you can choose Site > Manage Sites, select your site in the list, and click the Edit button.

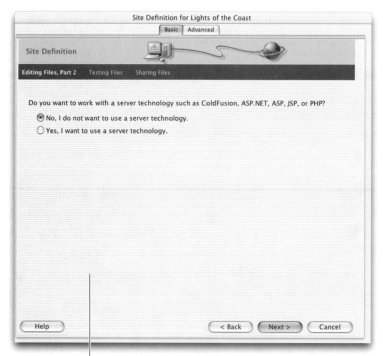

SPECIFYING SERVER TECHNOLOGY IN THE SITE DEFINITION DIALOG BOX

NOTE *This section of the Basic setup corresponds to the Testing Server category in the Advanced View, which gives you additional options that are involved with creating dynamic sites, such as choosing the server model to be used on your remote server.*

5) At the top of this section Dreamweaver asks, "How do you want to work with your files during development?" Click the radio button for the option "Edit local copies on my machine, then upload to server when ready (recommended)."

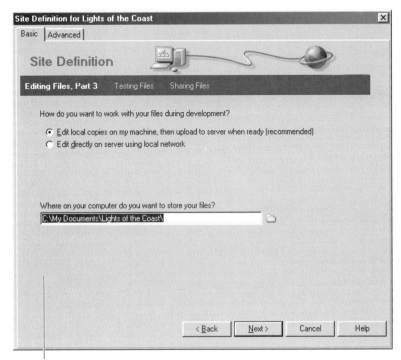

CHOOSING HOW TO WORK WITH FILES IN THE SITE DEFINITION DIALOG BOX

In this book's lessons, you will be working with files on your machine. You don't need to have access to a server.

6) Also in this section, Dreamweaver asks, "Where on your computer do you want to store your files?" Click the folder icon to the right of the text field and browse to find the DWMX2004_Project folder.

This text field allows you to specify the folder on your hard disk within which all the files for the site are stored. This folder is the equivalent of the root folder on the remote site. Dreamweaver uses this local root folder to determine the paths for documents, images, and links in your site. You will learn about paths and links in Lesson 4.

The DWMX2004_Project folder is the folder that you copied from the CD-ROM to your hard disk in step 1.

Macintosh Users: Select the DWMX2004_Project folder and click Choose.

Windows Users: Select the DWMX2004_Project folder and click Open; then click Select to choose the DWMX2004_Project folder as your root folder. The text "Select:DWMX2004_Project " appears in the lower left corner of the Choose local root folder for site Lights of the Coast dialog box to indicate that the DWMX2004_Project folder will be selected.

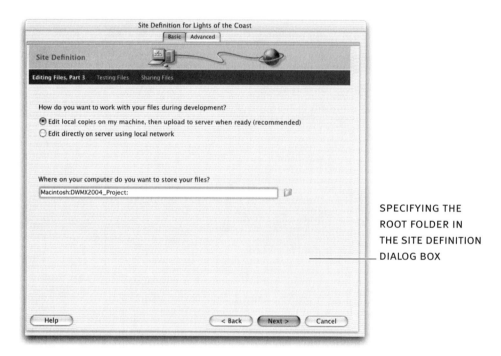

SPECIFYING THE
ROOT FOLDER IN
THE SITE DEFINITION
DIALOG BOX

The path to the root folder, DWMX2004_Project, is displayed in the text field and is relative to your hard disk.

By default, the text field initially contained the path to a folder called Lights of the Coast. Leaving that default active would create a new folder on your hard disk called Lights of the Coast that would become your local root folder. On the Macintosh, that folder would usually be created inside a folder called Sites, which would be created in the folder for your username inside the Users folder. Each time you choose a new location to store your local root folder, that location will become the default that appears in the text field when you define subsequent sites. On a Windows computer, that folder would usually be created in the My Documents folder on the C drive. In this case, however, you need to choose the DWMX2004_Project folder (containing the many files that you need to work with in this book's lessons) as your local root folder.

When you create your own sites, if you do not already have a folder, you may find it useful to allow Dreamweaver to automatically create one for you based on the name you chose for your site.

UNDERSTANDING THE ADVANCED VIEW

This section of the Basic setup corresponds to the Local root folder text field of the Local Info category in the Advanced view. The Advanced site definition view also allows you to select Refresh local file list automatically, Enable cache, specify a Default images folder and the HTTP address.

The Refresh local file list option is checked by default, causing Dreamweaver to update the site list whenever you add a new file to the site folder. If you uncheck this option, you need to refresh the local files manually whenever you make changes such as adding or deleting files.

The Enable cache is another option in the Advanced view that is checked by default. Enable cache allocates memory to store frequently used site data, improving the speed of linking and site-management tasks. Although you usually want to leave this option selected, keep in mind that re-creating the cache can slow operations on extremely large sites.

The Default images folder is an optional feature that allows you to specify the location of images in your site. The use of images in your site is covered in Lesson 3.

The HTTP address, another optional feature, is used to define the URL of your Web site. This address is used to verify absolute links. More information on links is covered in Lesson 4.

7) Click Next to advance to the next section. Below the question "How do you connect to your remote server?" choose None from the menu.

For the lessons in this book, you will work on a local site only; you do not need access to a remote server. More information about connecting to a remote server can be found in Lesson 12.

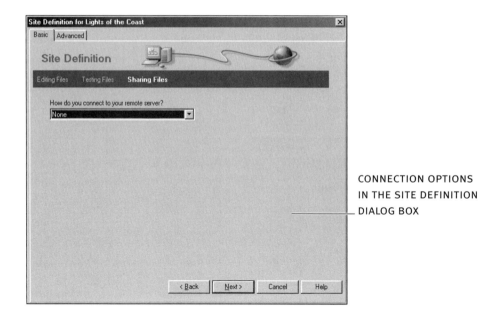

CONNECTION OPTIONS
IN THE SITE DEFINITION
DIALOG BOX

NOTE *This section of the Basic setup corresponds to the Remote Info category in the Advanced view, which gives you additional options that are involved in transferring files to a remote server.*

8) Click Next to advance to the next section. Review the information about the site you just defined and then click the Done button at the bottom of the dialog box.

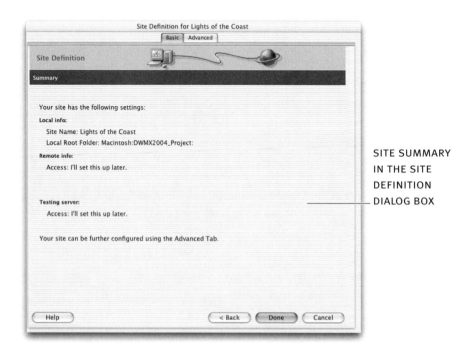

SITE SUMMARY
IN THE SITE
DEFINITION
DIALOG BOX

Because you chose the No options for the Remote Info and Testing Server sections, Dreamweaver displays "Access: I'll set this up later." for both.

When you click Done, Dreamweaver scans the files in your DWMX2004_Project folder to create the site cache. You may briefly see a dialog box as Dreamweaver completes this process. You can click the Done button to close the Manage Sites dialog box which appears.

The Files panel now displays the DWMX2004_Project folder. You'll learn more about the Files panel in Lesson 12.

CREATING AND SAVING A NEW PAGE

After you have your local site defined, you are ready to start creating your Web pages. Whenever you create a new page, the first thing you should do is save your document.

1) Choose File > New. Click the General tab in the New Document dialog box and choose Basic Page in the category list. Choose HTML in the Basic page list and click the Create button.

TIP *You can use the keyboard commands Command+N (Macintosh) or Ctrl+N (Windows) to open the New Document dialog box. If you want to bypass the New Document dialog box and open a new document immediately when using keyboard commands, choose Edit > Preferences, select New Document from the Category list, and uncheck the Show New Document Dialog on Command+N (Macintosh) or the Show New Document Dialog on Ctrl+N (Windows). This section also provides you with the option to change the default document type as well as the extension and encoding. The lessons in this book assume that you are using the defaults. Clicking the Preferences button at the bottom of the New Document dialog box also opens the Preferences dialog box.*

The New Document dialog box opens with two tabs: General and Templates. In this exercise, you create a new HTML (Hypertext Markup Language) page. The option to create a new HTML page is located in the Basic category of the General tab. These selections are the defaults and may already be selected for you.

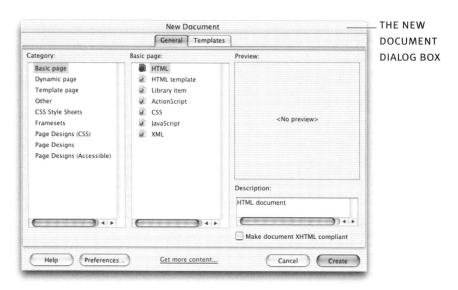

THE NEW DOCUMENT DIALOG BOX

The New Document dialog box also gives you additional options for creating a variety of page types in addition to HTML, including CSS, JavaScript, and XML; and dynamic pages that use languages such as ASP, ColdFusion, and PHP. You can access specific page types by choosing from the list of categories in the left column of the dialog box that includes Templates, CSS Style Sheets, Framesets, Table Based Layouts, and Page Designs. You won't use any of these additional page types at this time, but you should be aware of them. The contents of the middle column of the dialog box change depending upon the category selected in the left column.

NOTE *At the bottom of the New Document dialog box is an option to Make document XHTML compliant. By nature, HTML is limited, particularly in that new features are generally not backward compatible and there are a wide number of compatibility issues for cross-browser use. XHTML (Extensible Hypertext Markup Language) extends the capabilities of HTML by reforming HTML as an XML (Extensible Markup Language) language. The advantages of using XHTML include both backward and forward compatibility, operability on alternate Web access devices such as cell phones or hand-held computers, and the potential for extensibility. You should leave this option unchecked for the exercises in this book.*

After you click the Create button, a new untitled HTML document appears, and the Start Page closes automatically.

TIP *You can also create a new document directly from the Start Page by selecting the file type (such as the HTML that you are creating in this exercise) from Create New column. A new document of the type you selected appears, and the Start Page closes.*

2) Choose File > Save and locate the folder Lesson_01_Basics, in which you are going to save this file. Type *introduction.htm* **in the File Name text field at the bottom of the Save As dialog box and then click Save.**

Don't wait until you have text or graphics on the page to save—save your pages as soon as you open new documents. Provided that your file is saved first, when you import graphics or other media, all the paths that reference where those elements are located in your site will be made properly. If you don't save your document, a path name beginning with file:// is used that describes the location of the element you are inserting relative to your hard disk. If you try to insert an object without first saving the document, Dreamweaver warns you that it needs to use a file:// pathname for the element. These file:// paths do not work on remote servers because they describe the location of files specific to your computer.

TIP *You can use the keyboard commands Command+S (Macintosh) or Ctrl+S (Windows) to save your document. Always remember to save often so you won't lose a lot of work if your computer crashes for any reason.*

You can use either extension: .html or .htm. Dreamweaver automatically adds the extension .htm to the filename when you save—unless you specify the extension yourself. You can see which extension is set as the default by choosing Dreamweaver > Preferences (Macintosh) or Edit > Preferences (Windows) and selecting the New Document category. The default extension is displayed in a text box, although it is grayed-out. You can change this extension in the document-type XML file. Although either .htm or .html can be used on either Macintosh or Windows for the same type of document, they are not interchangeable—introduction.htm is not the same as introduction.html. You can save a file as either introduction.html or as introduction.htm because the extensions represent the same kind of file. You can also have both introduction.html and introduction.htm on the same server because they are recognized as two separate files. It is usually easier to stick with one or the other so you are able to make the correct links. Linking to introduction.html does not work if your file is really named introduction.htm. Links and paths will be covered further in Lesson 4.

TIP *For Macintosh users, the .htm extension appears in the Save As dialog box. For Windows users, if your system is set to automatically add the appropriate extension after you save, you do not have to include the .htm in the File Name text box.*

Throughout this book, the extension .htm is used in the examples and materials included on the CD-ROM.

THE SAVE AS DIALOG BOX

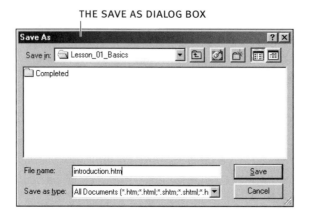

Keep in mind that naming your files for use on a Web server is a little different from naming your files for use on your hard disk. You need to know what operating system the server will be using—the most common systems are Unix, Linux, Windows NT, and Macintosh. The naming structure is different on each of these platforms. Unix, for example, is case-sensitive, which means that myfile.htm does not equal MYFILE.HTM. Using all lowercase names for your files makes naming files simpler and helps you maintain consistency. You should use only alpha characters (A–Z) and numbers (0–9) to name your files. Here are other important conventions to follow for both filenames and folder names:

• Don't ever use spaces in filenames. Use the underscore or hyphen characters to simulate a space if you need to separate words. Problems can arise because browsers substitute %20 for spaces.

• Don't use any special characters, such as %, *, >, or /. Don't use periods or commas.

• Avoid beginning your filenames with numbers.

• Keep folder and filenames as short as possible. Remember that the folder name becomes part of the URL you type to get to the page.

New documents are given a default name of Untitled-1, with the numbers increasing sequentially for every new document that is created.

TIP *The New Document and Save options are also available on the Standard toolbar, which you can open by choosing View > Toolbars > Standard. Toolbars other than the default Document toolbar appear as you add or move them only on the active document; changes are not reflected in other documents.*

EXPLORING THE TOOLS

Before jumping into the creation of any Web pages, you need to become familiar with the variety of tools and panels in the Dreamweaver MX 2004 interface that enable you to effectively produce a Web site.

1) Move the pointer over the document window and the Document toolbar. Rest the pointer over a button to see its name.

The majority of your design and coding work is done within the document window. This area is known as the "body" of the page, in which you can insert, modify, and delete the wide variety of elements that make up a Web page. As you work, the document window displays an approximation of the way your page should appear in a browser.

The filename introduction.htm (as you saved this page in the previous exercise) is shown on the title bar, displayed in parentheses after the name of the folder that contains it. By default, this page is initially titled Untitled Document. The title of the document is also shown in the Title text field on the Document toolbar. The Document toolbar, which can be shown or hidden through View > Toolbars, contains buttons and menus to provide quick access to common operations. By default, the toolbar is part of the document window. Windows users can double-click or drag the gripper area on the left edge of the toolbar to separate it from the document window, making it become an individual panel.

There are three view modes in Dreamweaver: Design view, Code view, and Split view, which shows both Design view and Code view. The buttons for these modes are located on the left side of the Document toolbar. You can see the view mode names by pausing the pointer over the buttons. At this point, the view mode you are using should be Design view. The active button is highlighted, indicating that Dreamweaver is displaying the page in that view mode. You will work with Code view and Split view in Lesson 14. If the document window is shown split into two panes with code in one pane or a single pane with code, you need to select the Design View icon located on the Document toolbar.

In the lower left corner of the document window is the Tag Selector. The Tag Selector always starts from the <body> tag, hierarchically displaying HTML tags that apply to the currently selected element. Using the HTML tags that correspond with those elements, the Tag Selector allows you to move quickly through the hierarchy of code to see what element you are working with and to easily select other elements. Getting used to working with the Tag Selector will be particularly helpful when you begin using tables to design your pages in Lesson 5.

TIP *If you can't see the Tag Selector, try reducing the size of your document. The Tag Selector can become hidden beneath the Property inspector.*

You'll become familiar with the many buttons and customizable options in the document window as you work through the lessons in this book.

2) Move the pointer over the Insert bar. Rest the pointer over a button to see its name.

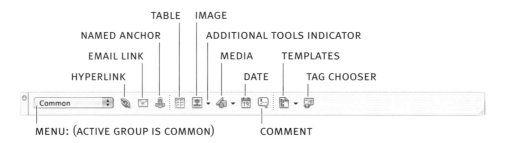

The Insert bar contains many of the objects or elements that you can add to your page, including images, tables, special characters, forms, and HTML. The elements are arranged in eight groups, according to their type: Common, Layout Forms, Text, HTML, Application, Flash Elements and Favorites. The name of the active group is displayed on the menu. The Common group is active by default. You can use the menu to switch to a different group of objects. Many of the individual objects in these groups have their own menus, indicated by a small black arrow, with additional tools, options and other closely related objects; click the object icon and black arrow once to open the menu. The last option in the Insert bar category menu is Show as Tabs, which will convert the Insert bar to show tabs at the top of the bar for each category. To switch back to the menu format, choose Show as menu from the context menu in the upper right corner of the Insert bar. Use whichever viewing method—tabs or the menu—that you prefer.

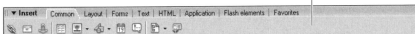

NOTE *Throughout this book, the words "objects" and "elements" are used interchangeably. Where possible, "object" is used when referring to the button, and "element" is used for the item after it appears within the document window.*

To insert an element, you can drag the object's icon from the Insert bar to the location where you want it to appear in the document window. You can also place the insertion point in your document where the element should appear and then click the object's icon in the panel. When you click the icon, the element appears in the document at the insertion point.

3) Move the pointer over the Property inspector. Rest the pointer over a button to see its name.

You use the Property inspector to view and modify the attributes of selected text, images, tables and other elements on your page. The Property inspector is contextual—the attributes that it makes available change depending on what is selected in the document window. To expand or collapse the Property inspector, click the expander arrow in the lower right corner of the panel. If the Property inspector is collapsed, there may be additional properties that are not visible until you expand the panel. Windows users can also reduce the inspector so that only the name of the panel shows in order to gain a larger viewing area.

THE PROPERTY INSPECTOR   EXPAND/REDUCE

TIP *Windows users can also resize the entire area for the Property inspector (and additional panels that later appear in that area) by dragging the arrow button on the horizontal border. Clicking the arrow button collapses the entire area; simply click the button again to reopen it. The horizontal border is not part of the Macintosh interface.*

WORKING WITH PANELS

The majority of Dreamweaver's panels are **docked**—combined in tabbed windows—within panel groups according to their functions. The default panel groups are Design, Code, Application, Tag Inspector, and Files. You can access panels from within these groups as well as from the Window menu. Panel groups let you quickly hide or access your most frequently used panels. Docking maximizes your screen area while giving you quick access to the panels you need. Each panel group can be expanded to display all the panels it contains or reduced to show only the name of the group.

If you opened Dreamweaver before, the panels are placed exactly where they were the last time you quit the program. In the Window menu, a checkmark next to an item indicates that the panel or toolbar is selected and active (visible) in the panel groups.

NOTE *As explained earlier in this lesson, a bug in the Macintosh version of Dreamweaver MX 2004 will cause the files panel group to be renamed Assets when you expand the Files panel (covered in lesson 12). For, details, please see the note that covers this topic in the Define a Local Site exercise of this lesson.*

1) Click the arrow on the Design panel group once to collapse it and twice to expand the group.

The Design panel group is located at the top of the panel groups. When the Design panel group is expanded, you will see the CSS Styles panel, which you will work with in Lesson 6. In the upper right corner of the panel you see the context menu, which is not visible when the panel group is reduced.

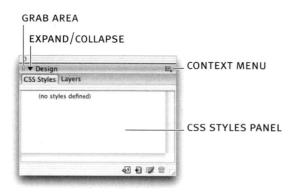

In the Window menu, a hidden panel does not have a checkmark next to the panel name. To display a hidden panel, choose the desired panel from the Window menu. If the panel you choose is in a panel group that is not currently available, both the panel and the panel group containing that chosen panel appear. If the group containing the desired panel is visible but reduced, choosing the panel from the Window menu expands the group and displays the selected panel.

There may be instances in which a panel is hidden beneath another panel or the document window. Changes in screen resolution can be one cause of this problem. If you are missing a panel and can't bring it up by choosing it from the Window menu, you might need to choose Window > Arrange Panels to reset all open panels to the default positions. The Insert bar moves to the upper left corner of the screen, the Property inspector moves to the bottom of the screen, and all other open panels move to the right of the screen.

2) Rest the pointer over the bottom of the CSS Styles panel, on the line that separates the CSS Styles panel from the Code panel group. When the pointer changes to a vertical two-arrow pointer, click and drag upward to reduce the size of the CSS Styles panel.

As you work, you may need to resize panels to show more information or provide more room for other panels and the document window.

Windows users can also resize the width of the entire area for all docked panel groups by dragging the arrow button on the vertical border. Clicking the arrow button collapses the entire docking area; simply click the button again to reopen it. The vertical border is not part of the Macintosh interface.

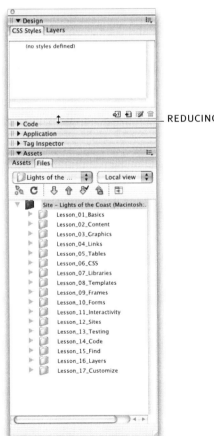

REDUCING THE SIZE OF A PANEL

After you become familiar with the Dreamweaver panels and tools, you can customize the interface by rearranging panels and reordering panel groups to make the program work with your specific needs.

NOTE *You can undock any panel group and separate it from the docking area. To undock a panel group, rest the pointer over the grab area designated by the dots on the left of the panel group. When the pointer turns to a hand (Macintosh) or a cross-hair with arrows (Windows), click and drag the panel group out of the window and release it. As you drag it outside of the docked panels, you see a ghost image of the panel group. You can rename this new window or panel group by clicking the Context Menu icon choosing Rename Panel Group. As you drag a panel group back into the docking area with other groups, you see the ghost image of the panel before you release it as well as a thick dark line at the point where the panel group appears. You can also rearrange the order of panel groups by using the grab area to move any of the groups above or below the other groups. If you want to change the organization of panel tabs by moving them into different groups, select a panel by clicking its tab and choose Group Components With from the context menu.*

The lessons in this book assume that you are using the default configuration of panels in Dreamweaver MX 2004, with no changes to the order or names of panels and panel groups.

Windows Users: Cascade, Tile Horizontally, and Tile Vertically are three options for viewing documents. If you have more than one document window open at a time, the Cascade option causes those windows to float, stacked one on top of the other, within the document window portion of the workspace. The Tile Horizontally option causes the document windows to appear stacked horizontally. The Tile Vertically option causes the document windows to appear side by side vertically. These options can be accessed from the Window menu.

Macintosh Users: The workspace options described previously are not available on the Macintosh.

GIVING YOUR PAGE A TITLE

Every HTML document you create needs to have a title. The title is used primarily for document identification. It is displayed in a browser's title bar, indicates the content of a page, and appears as the bookmark name in Favorites lists. You should choose a short, informative phrase, beginning with the site name, which is descriptive of the document's purpose. Get into the habit of adding a title to each page you create before you add text or graphics to the page. If you forget, Dreamweaver titles the file Untitled Document by default.

Type *Lights of the Coast* **into the Title text field on the document toolbar. Press Return (Macintosh) or Enter (Windows), or click in the introduction.htm document.**

TIP *If you don't see the document toolbar with the Title text field, choose View > Toolbars > Document.*

The Title text field initially displays Untitled Document—you are now replacing that placeholder title with a title for the introduction page of the project site.

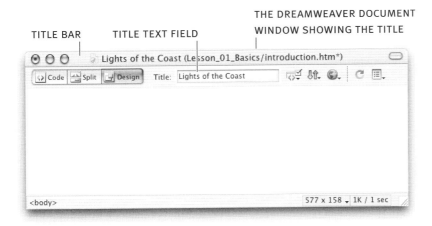

TITLE BAR   TITLE TEXT FIELD   THE DREAMWEAVER DOCUMENT
                                        WINDOW SHOWING THE TITLE

Dreamweaver gives you several reminders if you haven't titled your page. Look at the document title bar, which displays the title and the filename. If you see "Untitled Document (foldername/filename.htm)", you haven't titled your document. You'll also see "Untitled Document" in the Title text field on the document toolbar.

NOTE *You can also specify the title of your document in the title text field located in the General category of the Page Properties dialog box. To access the Page Properties dialog box, choose Modify > Page Properties.*

SPECIFYING A BACKGROUND COLOR

In Dreamweaver, you can change the background color of a page easily by using a palette of colors known as the Web-safe color palette. This palette is a collection of 216 colors that appear the same in browsers on both Macintosh and Windows. In this exercise, you access that palette from the Page Properties dialog box to change the background color for introduction.htm.

1) Choose Modify › Page Properties. Select Appearance from the Category list.

TIP *You can use the keyboard commands Command+J (Macintosh) or Ctrl+J (Windows) to open the Page Properties dialog box.*

In the Appearance screen of the Page Properties dialog box, there are no defaults displayed, even though white is the default background color for the document window in Dreamweaver. If you do not define a background color, the page uses the browser default (usually white) when a visitor views the page. Because the browser default can vary, it is recommended that you always define the background color of the page.

THE APPEARANCE SECTION OF THE PAGE PROPERTIES DIALOG BOX

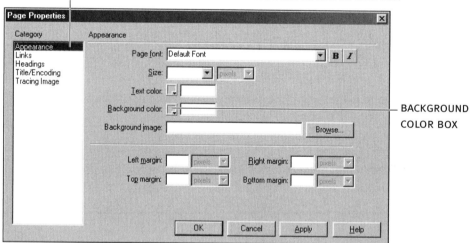

BACKGROUND COLOR BOX

2) Click the color box for the Background Color option. A color palette pops up, and the pointer changes automatically to an eyedropper. In the color palette, move the eyedropper over a color swatch.

TIP *You can also move the eyedropper over the document window and click items there, such as text and images, to match a color.*

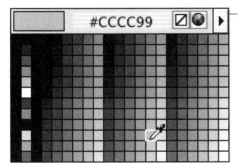

THE COLOR PALETTE

Notice that the hexadecimal equivalents for the colors are displayed at the top of the color palette as you roll over the swatches. In HTML, colors are defined in hexadecimal code using RGB: red, green, and blue. Hexadecimal is a base-16 numbering system that uses 0 through 9 and A through F. In the six-digit code used in HTML to describe color, the first two digits represent red, the second two digits represent green, and the last two digits represent blue. For example, #00FF00 has no red, a bright green, and no blue; #000000 has no red, no green, and no blue—it is black. Conversely, #FFFFFF signifies the maximum levels of red, green and blue, which combine to display white on your screen. Remember—computer screens use light to render the colors that you see. The color properties of light (which is based on an additive system) are much different from the properties of pigment used in print media (which is based on a subtractive system).

NOTE *For more colors, click the arrow located in the upper right corner of the color pop-up window and choose a color palette from the pop-up menu. Keep in mind that other palettes are not limited to cross-platform, Web-safe colors.*

3) Click the pale tan swatch that displays the hexadecimal code #CCCC99.

The pale tan color #CCCC99 is now selected as the background color for your page. You can also type the hexadecimal code directly into the text field next to the color box to change the color.

4) Click OK to close the Page Properties dialog box and return to your document. Save your file.

TIP *Clicking the Apply button allows you to view your changes without closing the Page Properties dialog box.*

The background color of your page is now the light tan color that you selected in the Page Properties dialog box.

SPECIFYING PREVIEW BROWSERS

As you develop Web pages, you need to continually test how your work appears in different browsers, such as Internet Explorer and Netscape. What you see in the Dreamweaver document window is only an approximation of how the pages will look. Every browser has differences in how it displays Web pages, and although some of these discrepancies are slight, the differences can sometimes be very significant. You may notice differences even between different versions of the same browser. The more you test your site in multiple browsers and operating systems, and make changes to your pages accordingly, the more certain you can be that visitors to the site see your pages as you intended them to appear. The Preferences in Dreamweaver enable you to specify which browsers you want to use to preview the pages in your site. To speed up the process, you can define a primary and a secondary browser, with a keyboard shortcut for each.

1) Choose File > Preview in Browser > Edit Browser List.

The Preferences dialog box opens to display the Preview in Browser preferences. Dreamweaver may automatically list one of more of the browsers that are on your computer.

NOTE *On Windows, Internet Explorer may appear as iexplore in the list.*

When you click a browser name in the browser list, the checkboxes below the list show whether that browser is the primary or secondary browser. If you have more than two browsers, it leaves both boxes unchecked to show if it is neither.

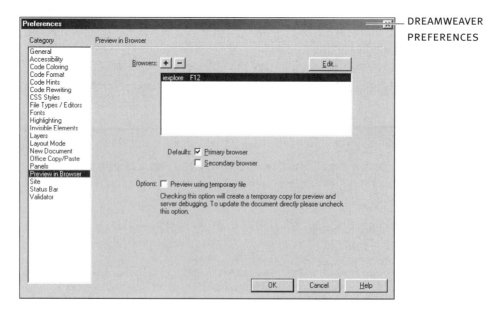

DREAMWEAVER
PREFERENCES

Alternatively, you can choose Dreamweaver > Preferences (Macintosh) or Edit > Preferences (Windows) and select Preview in Browser in the Category list, located on the left side of the dialog box, to open the same Preview in Browser Preferences dialog box. You can also use the keyboard command Command+U (Macintosh) or Ctrl+U (Windows) to open the Preferences dialog box.

2) Click the plus (+) button to add another browser to the list.

When the dialog box appears, browse your hard disk to find and choose a browser application. Check the Primary Browser checkbox if you want to launch this browser by pressing F12 when you preview your pages. Check the Secondary Browser checkbox if you want to preview your documents in this browser by pressing Control+F12 (Macintosh) or Ctrl+F12 (Windows). (You'll be previewing the pages you develop while completing the lessons in this book often, so using these shortcuts can save you time.)

Your function keys must be enabled for the preview in browser keyboard shortcuts to work. Function keys are usually enabled by default; if they are not working, check your operating system preferences. If your function keys are performing system functions, you may have to press the Fn Key to use the function keys for Dreamweaver—or adjust your system preferences.

To remove a browser from the list, select the browser name in the list and then click the minus (–) button.

To change a browser choice, select the browser name in the list. Then click Edit and locate a different browser.

3) Leave the Preview Using Temporary File option checked. Click OK when you are done adding browsers.

The Preview Using Temporary File option is unchecked by default. Checking this option will cause Dreamweaver to create temporary files when previewing pages in a browser.

4) Press F12 to preview the page in your primary browser.

PREVIEW/DEBUG IN BROWSER

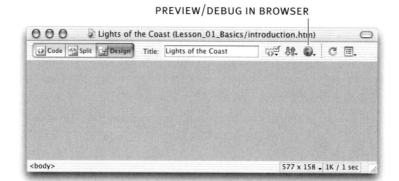

The browser defined as the Primary Browser in the Preview in Browser preferences becomes active and displays the introduction.html file in a browser window. Notice the title Lights of the Coast on the title bar of the browser.

At this point, your browser shows a blank, light tan colored page. You are ready to begin inserting content. You'll add text to this file in the next lesson.

WHAT YOU HAVE LEARNED

In this lesson, you have:

- Opened Dreamweaver (pages 8–10)

- Prepared to create a Web site, set up a local site, and defined the local root folder (pages 10–19)

- Created a new page and saved the document using the proper naming conventions (pages 19–22)

- Familiarized yourself with Dreamweaver's Insert panel, Property inspector, document window, and other tools, windows, and panels (pages 23–28)

- Given your page a title (pages 29–30)

- Defined a Web-safe background color for your document (pages 30–31)

- Specified preview browsers and used the keyboard shortcut to test your page (pages 32–34)

adding content to a page

This lesson teaches you how to import text in different file formats and how to compensate for receiving material from different operating systems. You will also learn how set document defaults, how to format text into several different types of lists, and how to use fonts and sizes to adjust text on your page. Formatting text is an important part of making your Web pages easy for visitors to read, visually appealing and inviting. Text can be a vital element on your pages; take the time to organize and format your material so that users can read through it quickly and easily.

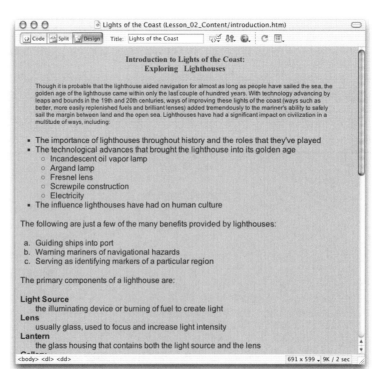

In this lesson, you'll learn how to add content to your pages and format text while creating the introduction page for the "Lights of the Coast" project Web site. You'll learn how to format text, test your pages, and use Flash Text.

You can find an example of the completed lesson in the Completed Project folder inside the Lesson_02_Content folder on the CD-ROM.

WHAT YOU WILL LEARN

In this lesson, you will:

- Place text on a page
- Create lists
- Position and format text
- Set document defaults for font and color
- Adjust font face, size, and color options
- Insert special characters and other elements
- Create and modify Flash text

APPROXIMATE TIME

This lesson should take approximately one hour to complete.

LESSON FILES

Starting Files:

Lesson_02_Content/introduction.htm

Lesson_02_Content/Text/introduction.txt

Lesson_02_Content/Text/introduction_mac.txt

Completed Project:

Lesson_02_Content/Completed/introduction.htm

BASIC TEXT FORMATTING

You can add text to the introduction.htm document by typing it directly on the page. You have a variety of basic text formatting options available to you in HTML. Most HTML formatting is extremely limited — you don't have a great deal of control over size, spacing, and alignment.

NOTE *For more specific control, you need to use CSS (Cascading Style Sheets) to define the look and placement of elements on your page. (Basic text formatting with CSS will be covered later in this lesson; additional CSS will be covered in Lesson 6.)*

1) Open the introduction.htm file in the Lesson_02_Content folder. In the document window, type *Introduction to Lights of the Coast: Exploring Lighthouses.* This starting document is similar to the one you created in Lesson 1.

The text appears in the document window as you type it. This text is the heading for your page.

2) From the Format menu on the Property inspector, choose Heading 4.
You defined the text format as a level 4 heading. The text has been formatted as a block-level element. All options chosen from the Format menu apply to an entire text block. You can't apply a heading or any other type of block-level formatting to a single word or to a portion of a text block. As a result, you don't have to select the text to apply a heading—all text contained in the text block automatically uses the formatting you select from the Format menu.

NOTE *Other block-level elements include paragraphs, lists, horizontal rules, and alignment options. You'll learn how to work with these elements throughout this lesson.*

THE PROPERTY INSPECTOR SHOWING THE
SELECTION OF HEADING 4 IN THE FORMAT MENU

Headings are displayed in larger or bolder fonts than normal body text. HTML has six levels of headings, numbered 1 through 6. Heading 1 has the largest font size, whereas Heading 6 has the smallest. Tagging a paragraph as a heading automatically generates a space around the heading, which varies according to the heading you select. You can't control this spacing unless you use CSS to control formatting.

38

Headings can be useful for splitting up your content into sections and calling attention to certain portions of the page. Users generally scan Web pages quickly and don't read everything. Taking this into account while designing your site helps you develop pages that are much easier for visitors to use. Formatting your text with headings and the other techniques used throughout the rest of this lesson enable you to differentiate between your content and create a clear visual hierarchy.

NOTE *In many documents, the first heading on the page is identical in content to the title. In multiple-part documents, the text of the first heading should be related information, such as a chapter title. The title you set for the entire page should identify the document in a wider context (including both the book title and the chapter title, for example).*

3) Press Return (Macintosh) or Enter (Windows).

You have just created another line below "Introduction to Lights of the Coast: Exploring Lighthouses" that is part of a new text block. By default, the new text block is formatted as a paragraph. Each new paragraph is its own text block. The paragraph format is generally used for regular body text and it is set apart from other text blocks by a certain amount of spacing: a blank line separates the new text block from the previous one. You can't control this spacing unless you use CSS to control the formatting.

NOTE *You can select Paragraph from the Format menu on the Property inspector or use the keyboard shortcut Command+Shift+P (Macintosh) or Ctrl+Shift+P (Windows) to set the formatting of a text block to a paragraph.*

4) Save the file.

Whenever you modify your document, notice the asterisk (*) that Dreamweaver inserts near the filename at the top of the document window. This asterisk indicates that the file has been modified but not yet saved. The asterisk disappears after you save the document. Be sure to save your documents often to prevent the loss of work.

CREATING A LINE BREAK

If you want to create a new line with no space between it and the previous line of text (a single line break in the text), you can use a line break. This technique is useful for an address line; for example, when you want a new line for each line in the address without the extra spacing that paragraphs create.

In introduction.htm, position the insertion point in the heading, just before "Exploring." Press Shift+Return (Macintosh) or Shift+Enter (Windows).

The text after the insertion point moves to the next line. A line break, not a new paragraph, has been created, so no additional spacing appears between the two lines.

NOTE *If you use two line breaks, you can simulate the appearance of a new paragraph; however, because you are not actually creating a new paragraph, you may have difficulty when you try to apply formatting styles to text that has two line breaks instead of a single paragraph return.*

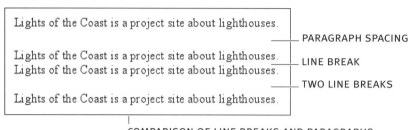

COMPARISON OF LINE BREAKS AND PARAGRAPHS

TIP *You can also insert a line break by choosing Insert > HTML > Special Characters > Line Break or by selecting the Text category on the Insert bar, clicking the Characters menu, and selecting Line Break. The line break character icon is BR because the HTML tag for a line break is <br>.*

SETTING TEXT PREFERENCES

You can add text to a page by copying and pasting from an existing document. You can easily open both Dreamweaver and the application from which you want to obtain content (such as Microsoft Office products); then copy and paste or select and drag the text or desired element into Dreamweaver.

Dreamweaver can also open files created in word-processing or page-layout applications, provided those files were saved as ASCII text files. Text files (.txt files) always open in a new window using the Code view in Dreamweaver. After you open a text file in Dreamweaver, you can copy and paste the text you need into another document.

Simple formatting, such as new lines, can be retained, but to do so you need to understand the differences between the ASCII format on different platforms. Files created in Windows use an invisible control character called a line feed (LF) to indicate a new line within the text, as well as carriage returns (CR). Macintosh computers do not use the line-feed character—only carriage returns (CR). Unix uses only the line feed character (LF).

To import text properly from ASCII files and retain the line break formatting, you need to change the Dreamweaver Line Break Type preferences to match the operating system on which the text files you want to import were created. The following exercise walks you through this process.

1) Choose Dreamweaver > Preferences (Macintosh) or Edit > Preferences (Windows) to display the Preferences dialog box and select Code Format in the Category list. From the Line Break Type menu, choose CR LF (Windows).

THE CODE FORMAT CATEGORY OF THE DREAMWEAVER PREFERENCES

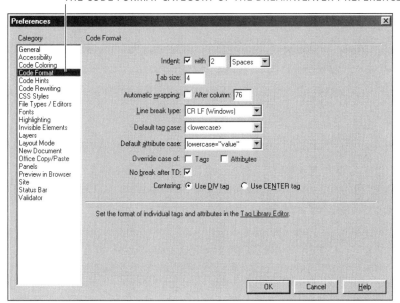

In the Line Break Type menu, your choices are CR LF (Windows), CR (Macintosh), and LF (Unix).

For Macintosh users, the default is CR (Macintosh).

For Windows users, the default is CR LF (Windows).

If you are using a Macintosh, change this setting to CR LF (Windows). If you are working in Windows, make sure the CR LF (Windows) setting is selected.

2) Click OK.

The Preferences dialog box closes.

NOTE *You can also import text into Dreamweaver by opening a Microsoft Word document that was saved as text (.txt) or HTML. To save a Microsoft Word document as HTML, open the document in Microsoft Word and choose File > Save as Web Page. There are a number of issues regarding importing HTML that has been generated by Microsoft Word. These problems and their solutions are covered in Lesson 14.*

IMPORTING TEXT

Now that your line break preferences are set, you can import text.

NOTE *This exercise uses a document that was created on a Windows computer. You set your Line Break Type preferences to work the Windows type in the previous exercise. An additional document, intro_mac.txt (created on a Macintosh computer), is provided in the Starting Files folder so that you can experiment with importing text files from different platforms. If you choose to experiment on your own with this additional file, remember that you need to adjust the Line Break Type preferences accordingly: You need to switch from CR LF (Windows) to CR (Macintosh) before opening or importing the file.*

1) Use Dreamweaver to open Lesson_02_Content/Text/introduction.txt; then select and copy all the text. In the introduction.htm file, position the insertion point on the new paragraph line you created earlier beneath the "Introduction to Lights of the Coast: Exploring Lighthouses" heading and paste the text to insert it.

You can use the Edit menu to copy and paste the text (choose Edit > Copy and/or Edit > Paste); or you can use the familiar keyboard commands Command+C (Macintosh) or Ctrl+C (Windows) to copy, and Command+V (Macintosh) or Ctrl+V (Windows) to paste.

Windows Users: By default, the document window expands into the entire space available and tabs are displayed for each document that is open. You can switch from one document to another by clicking the corresponding tab. Right-clicking a tab gives you the option to close that file. To switch to the non-tab interface and use a floating-window style layout, click the maximize button in the upper right corner of a document window—not the maximize button for the entire program. Click the maximize button on a document window again to switch back to tabs. These tabs are not part of the Macintosh interface.

THE DOCUMENT WINDOW TABS (WINDOWS ONLY)

MAXIMIZE/RESTORE

2) Save the introduction.htm file and close the introduction.txt file.

You can leave introduction.htm open for the next exercise.

INSERTING A NON-BREAKING SPACE

HTML recognizes only one standard space. A special character called a non-breaking space is used for multiple spaces. Non-breaking spaces can be used any time you need to insert more than one space between characters, words, or other elements. You can insert non-breaking spaces at the beginning of a line of text, whereas you can't begin a line with a standard space.

1) In introduction.htm, position the insertion point between the words "Exploring" and "Lighthouses" at the top of the document.

If you press the spacebar more than once, there is no change in the amount of space between the words, and only a single space remains. Multiple spaces are not recognized.

2) Press Option+Spacebar (Macintosh) or Crtl+Shift+Spacebar (Windows) twice.

TIP *You can also insert a non-breaking space by choosing Insert > HTML > Special Characters > Non-Breaking Space or by selecting the Text category on the Insert bar, clicking the Characters menu, and selecting Non-Breaking Space.*

The spacing between the words increases each time you insert a non-breaking space.

NOTE *You can allow for multiple spaces when you type by changing the preferences. Choose Dreamweaver > Preferences (Macintosh) or Edit > Preferences (Windows) and select the General category. Check the box next to Allow multiple consecutive spaces. With this option enabled, Dreamweaver uses non-breaking spaces whenever you hit the spacebar more than once.*

ALIGNING AND INDENTING TEXT

The alignment options available to you are default (no alignment), Align Left, Align Center, Align Right, and Justify. Default is the same as left.

1) In introduction.htm, position the insertion point in the heading "Introduction to Lights of the Coast." Click the Align Center button in the Property inspector.

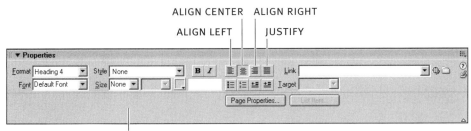

TEXT ALIGNMENT OPTIONS ON THE PROPERTY INSPECTOR

The heading is now centered. Because you inserted a line break between "Introduction to Lights of the Coast:" and "Exploring Lighthouses," both lines of text are now centered. And because the text is separated by a line break, it is still part of the same paragraph block. Any paragraph formatting that you apply to a text block, such as headings or alignments, affects everything contained within that paragraph.

2) Select the first paragraph of introduction.htm; then click Text Indent in the Property inspector.

TIP *You can also choose Text > Indent to indent the selected text.*

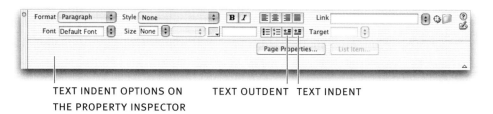

TEXT INDENT OPTIONS ON THE PROPERTY INSPECTOR   TEXT OUTDENT   TEXT INDENT

The paragraph is now indented. Indents are applied to entire paragraphs—you can't indent only the first line unless you use CSS (covered in Lesson 6). Indents can be used to set off certain portions of text from the standard body text. When you use Text Indent, the text is indented at both the left and right margins of the page. You can't control the amount of indentation because it is determined by the browser and can differ from browser to browser.

A paragraph can also be indented more than once. The margins on the left and right increase each time you indent a text block. You might indent a paragraph more than once to making it stand out from previously indented paragraphs, or when you want to increase the amount of indentation to make the indented paragraph more obvious.

Click the Text Outdent button on the Property inspector or choose Text > Outdent to remove an indent.

NOTE *If you try to indent one paragraph and nearby paragraphs become indented as well, check to see whether you are using paragraphs or double breaks. To be certain you are using a paragraph return, place the pointer at the beginning of the paragraph you want to indent. Press Delete (Macintosh) or Backspace (Windows) until you reach the end of the preceding paragraph and press Return (Macintosh) or Enter (Windows) to create a new paragraph.*

MAKING LISTS

Dreamweaver creates three basic types of lists: ordered, unordered, and definition. An **ordered list** consists of list items that are ordered numerically or alphabetically. You have the option of using Arabic or Roman numerals or upper- or lowercase letters. Ordered lists are ideal for situations in which you need to clearly organize and label items, such as presenting a list of steps. An **unordered list** is often called a **bulleted list** because each list item has a bullet in front of it. The bullet symbol Dreamweaver displays by default can be changed to a disc, a circle, or a square. Unordered lists are good for presenting information in which each item needs to be differentiated, but where labeling with numbers or letters is unnecessary, such as a list of food types. **Definition lists** are composed of terms and their definitions; these will be explored in the next exercise.

In all three list types, each item in the list needs to be contained in its own paragraph for the list to be correctly formatted.

In this exercise, you make two lists: one ordered and one unordered. You then tweak the list styles by using the List Properties dialog box. (You work with a definition list later in this lesson.)

1) In introduction.htm, select the text starting with "Guiding ships into port" and ending with "Serving as identifying markers of a particular region." Click the Ordered List button in the Property inspector.

The selected text is formatted in an indented and numbered list.

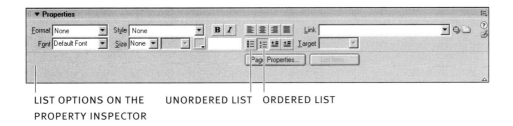

LIST OPTIONS ON THE   UNORDERED LIST ORDERED LIST
PROPERTY INSPECTOR

You can change the numbering scheme of ordered lists by modifying the list's properties. You'll do this in the next step.

2) Click any line in the list; then click the List Item button in the Property inspector.

Select only one line in the list. If you select the whole list, the List Item button is dimmed and not available for you to use. If the List Item button is not visible, click the expander arrow in the lower right corner of the Property inspector.

TIP *With the cursor in the list, you can choose Text > List > Properties to open the same List Properties dialog box.*

The List Properties dialog box opens.

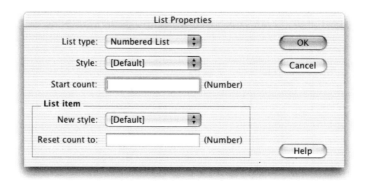

The ordered list type is known as a Numbered List in the List type menu.

3) From the Style menu, choose Alphabet Small (a,b,c). Click OK.

NOTE *Alphabet Small is an option in the Style menu only if you clicked the Ordered List icon. If you clicked the Unordered List icon, you need to change the List type menu to Numbered List before choosing the style.*

All items in the list are lettered.

NOTE *The List item area at the bottom of the List Properties dialog box contains a New style menu that you can use to change the look of a single item or several items in a list, instead of changing the organization and look of the whole list. Also available in this area is the Reset count to text field, which enables you to change the count of the list beginning with the line in which the insertion point is placed.*

Creating and modifying an unordered list is a similar process. You'll try it in the following steps.

46

4) Select the following two lines of text: "The importance of lighthouses throughout history and the roles that they've played" and "The technological advances that brought the lighthouse into its golden age." Click the Unordered List button in the Property inspector.

TIP *You can also choose Text > List > Unordered List to format the selected text as an unordered list.*

The selected text is formatted in an indented and bulleted list.

You can change the default bullet symbol of unordered lists by modifying the list's properties, just as you did with the ordered list. The appearance of bullet symbols may vary from browser to browser, and all lists use a set amount of spacing that may vary from browser to browser. You have limited options regarding the appearance of numbers/letters, bullets and list spacing—for more control over list appearances, you can make use of style sheets, which are covered in Lesson 6.

The unordered list type is known as a Bulleted List in the List type menu on the List Properties dialog box that you used in the previous step.

TIP *To remove the list formatting or switch to a different type of list, select the entire list and click the corresponding list button on the Property inspector to remove the list formatting (the Ordered List icon if it is an ordered list or the Numbered List icon if it is a numbered list) or the opposite list type to switch to that type of list.*

5) Place the insertion point at the end of the last line in the bulleted list and then press Return (Macintosh) or Enter (Windows). Type The influence lighthouses have had on human culture.

When you add text to a list, you need to use a regular paragraph return to create a new text block for the additional item. Every item in a list must be in a separate paragraph.

TIP *Pressing Return (Macintosh) or Enter (Windows) twice exits the list mode and gives you a default paragraph. If you need to create one or more new lines in the same item, use line breaks.*

6) Click any line in the bulleted list and then choose Text > List > Properties.

The List Properties dialog box opens.

NOTE *The List type menu in the List Properties dialog box contains two additional list types: Menu and Directory. These are older variations on the Bulleted list; both are similar in purpose to unordered lists and are typically displayed exactly the same as unordered lists by most browsers. It is generally recommended that you use the Bulleted list option for all unordered lists.*

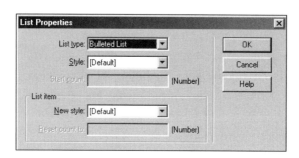

7) From the Style menu, choose Square. Click OK.

TIP *Be sure to use the Style menu—not the New style menu. If you use the New style menu in the List item area, your change will only be applied to the line of the list in which your insertion point is located.*

All items in the list now use the square bullet symbol.

NOTE *The color of numbers and bullets that is used in ordered or unordered lists is based on the document default for text color. You'll set the document defaults later in this lesson.*

MAKING DEFINITION LISTS

A **definition list** consists of a series of terms and their definitions. The word or term to be defined is left-aligned; the definition is indented and placed on the next line. There are no leading characters as there are in ordered and unordered lists.

1) In introduction.htm, select the text starting with "Light Source" and ending with "associated with the operation and maintenance of lighthouses." Choose Text > List > Definition List.

The terms are now at the left margin, and their indented definitions are on succeeding lines.

48

Your definition list should look like the following example.

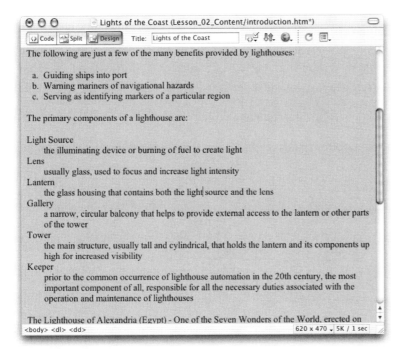

2) **Save the file and preview it in the browser.**

Now that you have put work into creating and formatting all these lists, it's a good time to save your document.

NESTING LISTS

You can create **nested lists**, which are lists within lists. Nested lists can be the same type of list as the parent list, or they can be a different type of list. An ordered list can be placed within a definition list, for example. By default, bullets are displayed as filled circles, open circles, and squares (in that order) as you nest the lists. Dreamweaver calls the bullet types bullet, circle, and square. The corresponding HTML terminology is disc, circle, and square.

Some browsers display open square bullets. Netscape 4.7 for the Macintosh displays open squares, for example, but Internet Explorer 5.0 for the Macintosh displays filled squares. In Windows, the squares are filled.

1) **In introduction.htm, add a new item to the bulleted list by placing the insertion point at the end of the line "The technological advances that brought the lighthouse into its golden age" and pressing Return (Macintosh) or Enter (Windows).**

This step adds another item after that line, at the same level.

2) To nest the item you are about to create, click the Text Indent button in the Property inspector. Type *Incandescent oil vapor lamp.*

The item indents to the next level. When you nest a list, the bullets in the nested list will appear in a different style from those in the main list. In this case, the nested list used open circles. You can change the style using the List Properties dialog box like you did earlier for the main list.

Your nested list should look like the following example.

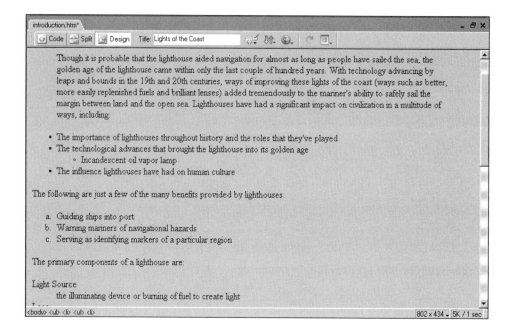

NOTE *To change an item from a nested item to a regular list, position the insertion point within the nested item, but don't select it. Click the Text Outdent button on the Property inspector.*

3) Type the following as separate items in the nested list: *Argand lamp,* *Fresnel lens,* *Screwpile construction,* **and** *Electricity.*

Just as when you indent text, you can't control or adjust the spacing of outdented text, lists, or nested lists.

TIP *If an extra line appears between the last item in the nested list and the following item in the main list, you can place the insertion point in the blank line and press Delete (Macintosh) or Backspace (Windows). The last character in the last line of the nested list may be deleted when you do this—simply retype that character.*

CHARACTER FORMATTING

You can apply a variety of formatting options to the text you create in Dreamweaver to emphasize certain points, words, or phrases. Options to set include bold, italic, and underline.

1) In introduction.htm, select the words "Light Source" in the definition list.

You will apply bold formatting to the selected text.

2) Click the Bold button in the Property inspector.

You can also choose Text > Style > Bold or click the Bold button in the Text category of the Insert bar to apply the bold format to the selected text. The keyboard shortcuts are Command+B (Macintosh) and Ctrl+B (Windows).

NOTE *When you use the Property inspector to apply bold formatting, Dreamweaver wraps the* **** *and* **** *tags around the selected text. Similarly, when you apply italic formatting, Dreamweaver wraps the* **** *and* **** *tags (em indicates emphasis) around the selected text. Dreamweaver uses strong and emphasis tags, which are referred to as logical markup, because they affect content in both conceptual and visual appearance, instead of bold and italic tags (***<b>***,* **<i>***), which are referred to as physical markup because they affect only visual appearance. Logical markup is more flexible and accessible to a wider audience.*

You can apply italic formatting in the same way.

BOLD   ITALIC

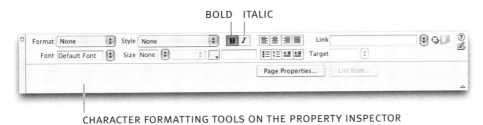

CHARACTER FORMATTING TOOLS ON THE PROPERTY INSPECTOR

TIP *Be careful of using the underline formatting on your Web pages. One of the ways a link is designated on a Web page is with an underline. Using the underline style for text other than links can potentially confuse your visitors.*

3) Repeat the bold formatting on the other terms in the definition list.

Many times, you may need to repeat the most recent action, such as the formatting you set on another paragraph or other selected text. The Redo command reduces that task to a simple keystroke. The first two items listed in the Edit menu are the Undo and Redo commands. You'll want to remember their keyboard shortcuts:

Undo: Command+Z (Macintosh) and Ctrl+Z (Windows)

Redo: Command+Y (Macintosh) and Ctrl+Y (Windows)

51

You can use the History panel to speed up actions that you repeat often by selecting a series of actions in the panel and clicking the Save selected steps as command button in the lower right corner of the panel or by choosing Save As Command from the context menu on the upper right corner of the panel. If you want a quick way to insert often-used bits of code, you should use Snippets (covered in Lesson 14).

NOTE *Due to a Dreamweaver bug in both Macintosh and Windows, the Redo command will not work for reapplying bold or italic formatting. You should continue to use the Property inspector or the keyboard shortcut Command+B (Macintosh) or Ctrl+B (Windows) to apply the bold formatting to the remaining terms. This bug also applies to repeating a bold or italic action through the History panel. You may need to use the Undo command as many times as is necessary to remove the code generated by redoing bold or italic. The code created when using Redo to repeat bold formatting is* `<span body="bold">` *and* `</span>`*. The code created when using Redo to repeat italic formatting is* `<span mm:togglevisibility="italic">` *and* `</span>`*. These tags are incorrect and should be removed from your document. You can use the Undo command to remove these tags or you can delete the tags from the code yourself. You will learn to work with the code in Lesson 14.*

CHANGING THE FONT

To make your page more interesting and easier to read, you can change the fonts that are used to display text. Although a great deal of information is available concerning how type is used for print, not all of that knowledge translates to the Web.

Generally, sans-serif fonts are easier to read on computer screens than serif fonts. Typically, serif fonts are used in print media because the serifs (the small strokes or flares on the ends of the lines) make characters easier to recognize. However, on a computer screen, those same serifs can actually make it more difficult to discern letterforms, particularly when large amounts of text are involved or when the text in question uses a relatively small font size. It is also important to consider that the way type flows on a page can vary from user to user.

To define font options, Dreamweaver uses integrated CSS styles instead of the older method of using font tag attributes. You'll learn more about CSS in Lesson 6.

You can change the font for the entire page or for selected text on the page, as you will see in the following exercise.

1) In introduction.htm, choose Modify > Page Properties and select Appearance from the Category list. From the Page font menu, choose Arial, Helvetica, sans-serif. Click OK to close the Page Properties dialog box.

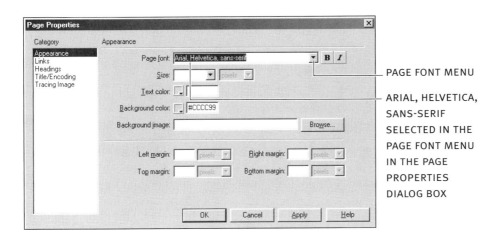

PAGE FONT MENU

ARIAL, HELVETICA,
SANS-SERIF
SELECTED IN THE
PAGE FONT MENU
IN THE PAGE
PROPERTIES
DIALOG BOX

All the text on the page is now formatted in the font you chose: Arial, Helvetica, sans-serif. Any additional text that you might add to the page in the future will be formatted in the same font.

NOTE *The Page Properties dialog box generates an internal CSS style to redefine a set of tags (body, td, th) with the selected font attributes. Internal CSS styles are covered in Lesson 6.*

The font combinations that are listed in the Page font menu of the Appearance category on the Page Properties dialog box instruct the browser to change the text to a font in that group, depending on which fonts are installed on the visitors' computers. If the first choice in the font group is not available, the browser attempts to use the second choice. If the second font is not available, it uses the third font. If none of the fonts in the combination is available on the user's computer, the text is displayed in the browser's default font.

2) Select the text "Introduction to Lights of the Coast: Exploring Lighthouses" at the top of the page. From the Property inspector's Font menu, choose Times New Roman, Times, serif.

The font you chose for the header overrides the default font set for the page. The font combinations available to choose from in the Font menu on the Property inspector are the same as the font combinations that were listed in the Page Font menu of the Appearance category on the Page Properties dialog box.

FONT MENU

TIMES NEW ROMAN, TIMES, SERIF SELECTED IN
THE FONT MENU ON THE PROPERTY INSPECTOR

NOTE *A number of formatting options can be applied directly in the document window to selected text if you right-click (Macintosh and Windows) or Control+click (Macintosh single button mice) to access the context menu.*

For visitors to your site to see the text displayed in the fonts that you chose, those fonts must be installed on their computers. Don't assume that all fonts are loaded on everyone's computer. Any fonts not included with the basic operating system are potentially not on your visitors' machines. In addition, the availability of fonts is not the same on the Macintosh as it is on Windows. The fonts specified in Dreamweaver's default font sets are generally available on most computers, both Macintosh and Windows.

TIP *If you want to use a special font that may not be installed on a visitor's computer, it is recommended that you create a graphic to use in place of the text. This technique is often used for headers, titles, and so on. Graphics are not recommended for large amounts of text.*

The font combinations (such as Arial, Helvetica, sans-serif) are useful, but they may not always include the specific fonts you want to use. You can change the font combination by choosing Edit Font List from the Property inspector's Font drop-down menu or by choosing Text > Font > Edit Font List to display the Edit Font List dialog box.

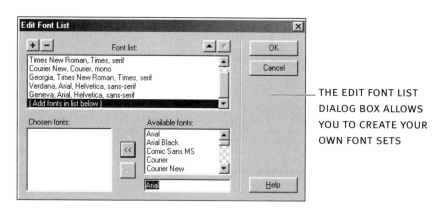

THE EDIT FONT LIST DIALOG BOX ALLOWS YOU TO CREATE YOUR OWN FONT SETS

Using the Font List dialog box, you can make a number of changes to font sets:

• **To add fonts to an existing combination:** Select the font combination you want to modify in the Font list and select the font you want to add in the Available fonts list; then click the left directional button located between the Chosen fonts list and the Available fonts list to add the font to the Chosen fonts list.

- **To remove fonts from an existing combination:** Select the font combination you want to modify and select the font you want to remove from the Chosen fonts list; then click the right directional button located between the Chosen fonts list and the Available fonts list to remove the font from the Chosen fonts list.

- **To add a font combination:** Select the Add fonts in list below choice in the Font list. For additional font combinations, click the plus sign (+) button in the upper left corner of the dialog box and then select the new Add fonts in list below choice from the Font list.

- **To remove a font combination:** Select the font combination you want to remove from the Font list and click the minus sign (–) button in the upper left corner of the dialog box.

- **To add a font that is not installed on your system:** Type the font name in the text field below the Available fonts list and click the directional arrow to add it to the combination. Adding a font that is not installed on your system is useful; you can specify a Windows-only font when you are authoring on a Macintosh, for example. Be sure to use the exact font name.

- **To change the order of the font combinations:** Select a font combination and click the directional arrow buttons in the upper right corner of the dialog box.

The Available fonts list in the Edit Font List dialog box contains the fonts that are installed on your computer.

3) Save the file and preview it in the browser.

The text now displays with the fonts you selected in your browser, depending on which fonts are installed on your computer.

TIP *You can remove font settings and return the type to its default setting by first selecting the text that uses the font you want to remove. In the Property inspector, choose Default Font from the Font drop-down menu or choose Text > Font > Default Font.*

CHANGING THE FONT SIZE

In HTML, the available options for adjusting font sizes are limited. The size of text is specified as an attribute of the <font> tag (the portion of HTML code that defines the properties of text) and is based on a system of relative and absolute sizes. If you are accustomed to developing print media such as magazines or brochures, you may be frustrated by the lack of typographic control. HTML font attributes offer a bare minimum of control over text appearance, whereas the use of CSS allows Web developers to create text-based pages with much greater precision.

The outdated HTML <font> attributes, including size, are no longer available in Dreamweaver. Instead, there is a variety of presets, including numeric values at set intervals ranging from 9 to 36, relative values ranging from xx-small to xx-large, and options for smaller and larger. All these options use CSS to define text size. Using Dreamweaver, you can achieve a great deal of control over the text on your pages through the use of these integrated CSS features. You'll learn about more advanced CSS functionality in Lesson 6.

NOTE *There is a dramatic difference between font sizes on a Macintosh and on Windows. Macintosh computers display text approximately 25 percent smaller than the same text on Windows computers—text on a Macintosh computer is three-quarters the size of text on Windows. Users can also change the font size, which may affect your page design. Test and design your pages accordingly, taking these potential variations into account for a flexible Web site that functions correctly for a wider number of visitors.*

Select the first indented paragraph near the top of the page. From the Property inspector's Size menu, choose 12. Leave the measurement at the default: pixels.

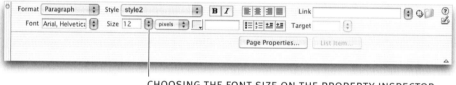

CHOOSING THE FONT SIZE ON THE PROPERTY INSPECTOR

The text size of the paragraph decreases slightly and appears somewhat smaller than the rest of the text on the page that is not formatted with a size. Every time you choose a size that's used for the first time on your page, Dreamweaver creates a new style that is listed in the Style menu on the Property inspector. All subsequent text defined at that size will use the same style. These styles have generic names that are generated automatically in a numeric order: style1, style2, and so on. New styles are created for each unique combination of font face, size, and color formatting.

TIP *You can also set a default text size for the document in the Appearance section of the Page Properties dialog box.*

If no size is specified for the selected text, "None" is displayed in both the Size and Style menus. Browsers display text that has no size definition at the default size that is equal to the value 14 in the Size menu (although it might vary from browser to browser depending on user preferences).

TIP *You can remove font size settings and switch back to the default setting by first selecting the text that you want to change. In the Property inspector, choose None from the Style menu or choose Text > CSS Styles > None.*

You can't type a value into the Size menu; you must select one of the preset choices. If you want to use sizes other than those listed, you need to create additional text styles, which can be done easily directly from the Style menu. You'll learn how to create additional styles and work with CSS in Lesson 6.

The numeric font size options that are available in the Size menu may be familiar to you because they are similar to the standard sizes that can be found in word-processing programs.

The following table compares the values that are now available in the Size menu to the standard HTML <font> tag size options.

FONT SIZE COMPARISON: HTML AND CSS

HTML Text Sizes: Relative	HTML Text Sizes: Absolute	Numeric Values* in the Size Menu (CSS-based)	Relative Values in the Size Menu (CSS-based)
		9	
−2	1	10	xx-small
−1	2	12	x-small/smaller
None (default)	3	14	small
+1	4	18	medium/larger
+2	5	24	large
+3	6		x-large
		36**	
+4	7		xx-large

Using the default setting, pixels, in the measurement menu
**This numeric value is slightly larger than x-large (6), and slightly smaller than xx-large (7).*

NOTE *The HTML <font> tag defines text sizes as either absolute (1 to 7) or relative (+1 to +7 and -1 to -7). Selecting an absolute number (1 is smallest, 7 is largest) sets the size. The default base size for text in a browser is 3. Picking a positive or negative number makes the font size relative to the base size of the font. The positive number +1, for example, makes the font size one size larger than the base size. If you choose +3 for the font size, you are effectively changing the size to 6 (3 + 3). The largest size for the font is 7 and the smallest is 1. Any HTML font size larger than 7 displays as 7; for example, if you set the font size to +6, 3 + 6 is larger than 7, but the font still displays only at the 7 size. These are limitations of the HTML <font> tag and do not affect CSS, which is a far more flexible and versatile method for defining text specifications.*

SPECIFYING FONT COLOR

When you change the background color of a page, as you did in the previous lesson, you might also need to change the color of the text that is displayed to avoid viewing problems. Black text doesn't display on a black background, for example. When choosing a color scheme for your document, try to select combinations of colors that work well together and have enough contrast between them. Colors that are too similar to each other can be very hard to view, as can complementary colors, especially on a computer screen. In the following steps, you'll change the default font color in the introduction.htm document.

1) Choose Modify > Page Properties and then select Appearance from the Category list.

The Page Properties dialog box appears with a number of choices that allow you to adjust a wide variety of document settings.

2) Click the color box for the Text color option.

A color palette pops up, similar to the one that you used to pick the background color for the document in the previous lesson.

3) Select the dark reddish-black color with the hexadecimal code #330000 and then click OK.

THE APPEARANCE SCREEN IN THE PAGE PROPERTIES
DIALOG BOX SHOWING THE WEB-SAFE COLOR SWATCHES

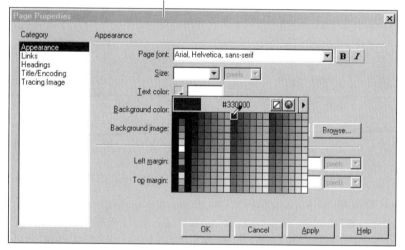

You can either type the hexadecimal color code into the text field or you can click to select the color from the swatches. After you click OK, the Page Properties dialog box closes, and you return to your document.

NOTE *Dreamweaver provides a variety of preset Web-safe color schemes that you can choose from. Choose Commands > Set Color Scheme to open a dialog box in which you can select background colors in the left column, and text and link colors in the middle column. The right column displays a preview of the selected combination. Click the Apply button to view the color settings in your document without closing the dialog box. Click OK to accept the change, close the dialog box, and return to your document.*

4) Select the text "Introduction to Lights of the Coast: Exploring Lighthouses." Click the Text Color Picker button in the Property inspector.

The Web-safe color palette appears.

5) Choose a dark blue color (#003366).

TIP *Sometimes when you apply text formatting of font, size or color, the fields for these options on the Property inspector may appear to be blank. If this happens, you can refresh the Property inspector by clicking in the document window outside of the text to which you applied formatting. Then click back in the text to which you applied the formatting and the text fields will show the formatting values you applied.*

The Color palette closes automatically after you click a color, and Dreamweaver applies the color immediately. Similar to font face and size options, font color is defined using integrated CSS styles. By applying a color, you modified the style that was created when you applied a font face to the selected text. You can see the name of the style listed in the Style menu on the Property inspector. The number of your style may differ from those shown here if you have created any additional styles by experimenting with font face, size, or color attributes.

THE STYLE MENU ON THE PROPERTY INSPECTOR

You can access the Colors dialog box by choosing Text > Color. Windows users can use the dialog box to pick colors from the color spectrum and slider, can use 48 basic color squares, or can create their own custom colors. Macintosh users can use the dialog box to choose between several different methods of selecting color and defining custom colors, including the Color Wheel, Color Sliders, Color Palettes, Image Palettes (Spectrum), and Crayons. Hexadecimal color codes can also be typed directly into the color text field, alongside the Text Color picker on the Property inspector.

59

NOTE *You can keep track of the hexadecimal colors used in your sites through the Assets panel. The Assets panel is located in the Files panel group. (On the Macintosh, due to a bug mentioned earlier in this lesson, the Files panel group may be renamed Assets.) You can also open the Assets panel by choosing Window > Assets. To access the color assets, click the Colors icon in the left column the Assets panel. Radio buttons across the top of the Assets panel give you two options for viewing colors: Site and Favorites. Clicking the Site list radio button shows the colors that have already been used within the "Lights of the Coast" project site or your current active site. You don't see colors in the list if you haven't used any colors in your site. If you have defined colors, but do not see them listed, click the Refresh Site List button in the lower right corner of the panel. You will see colors in this list that you have not yet used because there are colors used throughout documents in other lesson folders in the Lights of the Coast project site. To ensure that the colors you use are consistent across your site, you can save commonly used colors in the Assets panel as Favorites. To save a favorite color, select the desired color from the Site list and click the Add to Favorites button in the bottom right corner of the Assets panel. Dreamweaver displays a dialog box informing you that the color has been added to your favorites. You need to click the Favorites radio button at the top of the Assets panel to see the favorites list.*

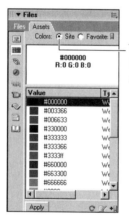

THE SITE LIST ON THE ASSETS PANEL SHOWING THE COLORS THAT HAVE BEEN USED IN THE SITE

ADDING SPECIAL CHARACTERS

When you work in Dreamweaver, you sometimes need to use characters that you can't access directly from the keyboard. These special characters have specific HTML codes or alternative keyboard commands that might be difficult to remember.

1) Place the insertion point on a new line at the very bottom of the introduction.htm document.

Web pages often have footers with copyright information at the bottom. These footers also tend to contain text links to the main sections of the site and sometimes contain contact information.

2) Choose Text from the Insert bar. Click the Characters menu and click the ©
(copyright) character to insert it on the new line at the bottom of the document.
Type *2003, Lights of the Coast* **to the right of the copyright character.**

Like other menus on the Insert bar, the icon that represents the Characters menu
will change based on what item was last selected in the menu.

Macintosh Users: If you do not see the Characters icon/menu in the Text category
of the Insert bar, you may need to enlarge the Insert bar. To do so, click and drag
the lower right corner to extend the bar horizontally.

THE TEXT CATEGORY ON THE INSERT BAR   CHARACTERS MENU

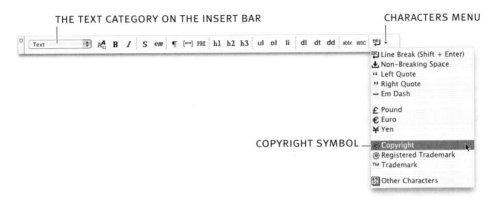

COPYRIGHT SYMBOL

The © (copyright) character is inserted on the new line when you click the icon in
the characters menu.

NOTE   *Although the Characters menu in the Text category of the Insert bar gives you*
quick access to many of the most common characters you may need, it doesn't provide an all-
encompassing list. If the character you want to use isn't available in the Characters menu, you
can still find it by clicking the Other Characters option at the bottom of the menu or by choosing
Insert > HTML > Special Characters > Other. When you select a character in the Insert Other
Character dialog box, the corresponding HTML code appears in the text field at the top left
corner of the dialog box. After you click the character that you want to use, click OK.

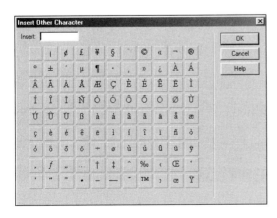

ADDING HORIZONTAL RULES

A **horizontal rule** is a line that goes across the page and provides a visual division between sections of your content. In this exercise, you will add a horizontal rule above the copyright information.

1) Place the insertion point at the very beginning of the copyright line you created in the previous exercise. From the HTML category on the Insert bar, click the Horizontal Rule button.

HORIZONTAL RULE

TIP *You can also click in the document and choose Insert > HTML > Horizontal Rule.*

After you insert the horizontal rule, it is selected in the document window. It is placed just above the copyright information, which drops down to a line below the horizontal rule.

NOTE *If the Insert bar is not visible, choose Window > Insert.*

2) With the horizontal rule still selected, type *70* in the W (width) text field on the Property inspector. Choose % from the menu to the right of the value you just typed.

THE HORIZONTAL RULE ATTRIBUTES ON THE PROPERTY INSPECTOR

The horizontal rule extends across 70 percent of the browser window regardless of the browser width. The rule is displayed as a thin bar on the page.

NOTE *Choose pixels from the menu to specify an absolute width. If you choose this option, the rule is not resized when users resize the browser window.*

3) With the horizontal rule still selected, uncheck the Shading box in the Property inspector. Type *1* in the H (height) text field.

Deselecting the Shading checkbox displays a solid bar. The horizontal rule is 1 pixel high.

You can also choose to align the bar horizontally by choosing left, center, or right from the Align menu. The default alignment for horizontal rules is centered. For this exercise, you should use the default alignment.

4) With the horizontal rule still selected, click the Class menu on the Property inspector. From the Class list, select the style that was created when you applied the dark blue color to the header text at the top of the page earlier in this lesson. Save the file and preview your document in the browser.

The names of the styles that are used in your document are displayed in the font faces and colors defined for those styles. The name of the style you select should be style1, although the number may differ if you created any additional styles by experimenting with font face, size, or color attributes. Although the color of the horizontal rule may still appear as the default gray in Dreamweaver, you should see a dark blue color used for the horizontal rule in the browser.

Notice how the horizontal rule appears in the browser. You can modify it by selecting it and adjusting the attributes in the Property inspector. The horizontal rule has a set amount of space above and below the line; you can't control the amount of spacing.

ADDING A DATE AUTOMATICALLY

Sometimes, you may need to keep track of the date you last modified a page on your site or you may want your visitors to see when the information on your page was last updated. Dreamweaver lets you place a date and time on your pages to track this information. Dreamweaver can update the date and time automatically every time you save, so you don't have to do it manually.

NOTE *This date is not a dynamic date that changes according to the date and/or time a user accesses the page. This date simply tells your users when your pages have been updated. Dynamic dates are often generated with JavaScript. You can learn more about JavaScript in Lesson 11.*

1) Place the insertion point at the end of the copyright information line, insert a line break and type *Updated:*.

This information is often shown in the upper right corner of news sites or displayed at the bottom of a page on other informational sites.

2) Select the Common category on the Insert bar and click the Date button to place the current date on the page.

THE COMMON CATEGORY
OF THE INSERT BAR   DATE

TIP *You can also choose Insert > Date to open the Insert Date dialog box.*

The Insert Date dialog box opens.

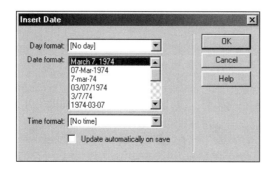

3) From the Day format menu, choose the Thursday option. From the Date format menu, choose March 7, 1974. From the Time format menu, Macintosh users should choose 9:18 PM and Windows users should choose 10:18 PM. Check the Update automatically on save checkbox to update the date on your page each time you save your document. Click OK.

The current day, date, and time are displayed, and this information changes every time you save the document. Thursday is used as an example in the Insert Date dialog box of how the day will appear in your document. The date and time are also examples.

NOTE *If the date is set to update automatically, you can change the format at any point after inserting the date. To change the date format, click the date in your document and click Edit date format in the Property inspector. The Insert Date dialog box opens. Make the appropriate changes and then click OK. Your changes are applied to the document. The format of dates that do not update automatically can't be edited through the dialog box—to update such dates, you will have to delete and re-insert the date or change the text yourself in the document window.*

ADDING FLASH TEXT

When you add a heading to your page, your options are to use text and format it as a heading tag, or to create a graphic and insert it into the page (you'll learn more about using graphics in Lesson 3). Text formatted as a heading loads quickly because it is text, but your font and size choices are limited. Using graphics as headings solves the font-choice problem, but you may not have access to a graphics program or you may just not have enough time to create the graphic you need.

Flash text provides the best of both these options. You can use any font you choose and create the text directly within Dreamweaver. The text you create is saved as a small Flash file—these files use the extension .swf.

NOTE *Although creating and working with Flash text is quick and easy, you should always consider whether your audience is likely to have the correct plug-ins before adding it to your site.*

1) Position the insertion point on a new blank paragraph line above the list that begins with "The Lighthouse of Alexandria (Egypt)". Click the Media menu on the Common category of the Insert bar and select the Flash Text option from the menu.

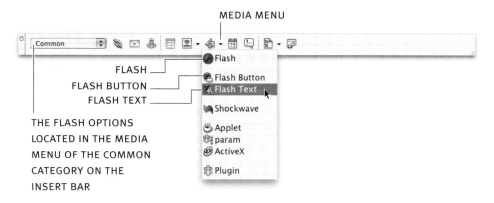

Make sure that you don't click the Flash or Flash Button options. This exercise deals with creating Flash text. The Flash option enables you to insert Flash movies into your page, whereas the Flash Button option lets you create buttons.

The Insert Flash Text dialog box appears.

2) Make the following changes.

- From the Font menu, choose Comic Sans MS. If Comic Sans MS is not available on your machine, choose another font.

- In the Size text field, type **22**.

- Use the Color box to choose a dark red color.

- In the Text window, type *Some of the world's most notable lighthouses include:*.
- For Bg color, type **#CCCC99** or use the eyedropper and click the background in the document window.

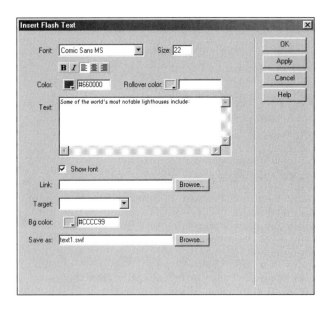

3) In the Save as text field, type *notable.swf* and click OK.

The Insert Flash Text dialog box closes.

NOTE *Initially, a default filename is automatically included in the Save as text field. This default name is generated with a numeric identifier: text1.swf, text2.swf, and so on. It's recommended that you replace the generic name with one that is descriptive of the Flash text file you are creating. The default location to save the Flash text is in the same folder as the HTML file into which you are inserting the Flash text, although you can save it into another folder (such as an images folder or a media folder) if you prefer.*

The Flash text appears in your document. The Property inspector reflects the attributes of the notable.swf Flash text file.

4) In the document window, select the Flash text and resize it by dragging one of the handles.

It doesn't matter what size you make the Flash text. Because the text is vector-based Flash text and not normal body text or a bitmap graphic, you can resize it directly in the document window. You can increase or decrease the image size without concern about loss of image quality.

Resizing graphics (discussed in Lesson 3) within Dreamweaver is not recommended. But you can resize the Flash text image that you create because it is a vector graphic.

66

Vector graphics retain the integrity of the image when scaled; bitmap graphics (such as GIFs and JPEGs) do not.

TIP *Hold down the Shift key to constrain the proportions while you resize the Flash text.*

5) Save the file and preview it in the browser.
The text appears as it did in Dreamweaver.

NOTE *You can also set a link and rollover color on Flash text. The Play button on the Property inspector will enable you to see such effects directly within Dreamweaver. You'll work with links in Lesson 4 and with rollovers and other interactive elements in Lesson 11.*

MODIFYING FLASH TEXT

Changing Flash text objects within Dreamweaver is easy. You might need to change these text objects if you have to rephrase the text, use a different font, or otherwise adjust the content.

1) In the document window, double-click the Flash text.

TIP *If you can't select the text, first click Stop in the Property inspector.*

The Insert Flash Text dialog box opens.

2) Change the options to your liking and then click Apply to see the results of your changes. When you finish, click OK to close the Insert Flash Text dialog box.
The edited Flash text is refreshed on the page, and the .swf file is updated.

WHAT YOU HAVE LEARNED

In this lesson, you have:

- Learned how to set text preferences and import text in different ways (pages 38–43)
- Positioned text by using paragraphs, breaks, and alignments (pages 43–44)
- Created three list types and modified their properties (pages 45–50)
- Applied text formatting of style, size, and color by using Page Properties and the Property inspector (pages 51–60)
- Customized font combinations and settings (pages 51–60)
- Added special characters to the page (pages 60–61)
- Added a date to the page and set it to update every time the page is saved (pages 63–64)
- Created and edited Flash text (pages 65–67)

working with graphics

LESSON 3

Graphics and multimedia elements play a significant part in capturing the attention of your audience and effectively communicating the intended message of your Web site. In this lesson, you will create Web pages that incorporate graphics, as well as Flash and QuickTime Movies. In the process, you'll learn about different graphic file formats, how to control their appearances in an HTML document, and how to combine them with text.

The features in Dreamweaver MX 2004 give you a great deal of control over the graphics and other multimedia elements used in your site. They enable you to modify

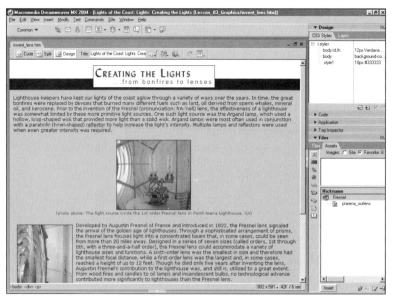

In this lesson, you'll create a page similar to this one while you learn to incorporate graphics with text on your pages.

image properties quickly within Dreamweaver, as well as immediately open images within an external image editor. The Assets panel simplifies the management of graphics by allowing you to create catalogs of all the images used in your site or of images that you need to have available.

If you want to view the final result of this lesson, open invent_lens.htm in the Completed folder within the Lesson_03_Graphics folder.

WHAT YOU WILL LEARN

In this lesson, you will:

- Identify graphics formats and explore their differences
- Insert graphics into a page
- Modify the properties of your images
- Change the positioning of graphics on a page
- Give your images names and `<alt>` attributes
- Use the Assets panel to manage graphics
- Wrap text around an image
- Make use of image placeholders
- Use basic image editing tools to adjust graphics
- Align text with an image
- Insert buttons and animations from Macromedia Flash
- Develop a slideshow using the Image Viewer
- Incorporate a QuickTime movie in a page

APPROXIMATE TIME

This lesson should take approximately two hours to complete.

LESSON FILES

Media Files:

Lesson_03_Graphics/Images/bkg_inside_tan.gif

Lesson_03_Graphics/Images/invlens_header.gif

Lesson_03_Graphics/Images/ptarena_lens.jpg

Lesson_03_Graphics/Images/ptarena_outlens.jpg

Lesson_03_Graphics/Images/ptarena_belowlight.jpg

Lesson_03_Graphics/Images/LenseDemoY.swf

Lesson_03_Graphics/Images/ptarena_prisms.jpg

Lesson_03_Graphics/Images/cabrillo.mov

Lesson_03_Graphics/Images/arena_photo.jpg

Lesson_03_Graphics/Images/bonita_photo.jpg

Lesson_03_Graphics/Images/bridge_photo.jpg

Lesson_03_Graphics/Images/fort_photo.jpg

Lesson_03_Graphics/Images/montara_photo.jpg

Lesson_03_Graphics/Images/pigeon_photo.jpg

Lesson_03_Graphics/Images/reyes_photo.jpg

Lesson_03_Graphics/Images/pt_cabrillo_header.jpg

Starting Files:

Lesson_03_Graphics/Text/invent.txt

Lesson_03_Graphics/Text/lens_demo.txt

Lesson_03_Graphics/cabrillo.htm

Lesson_03_Graphics/lightshow.htm

Completed Project:

Lesson_03_Graphics/Completed/invent_lens.htm

Lesson_03_Graphics/Completed/lens_demo.htm

Lesson_03_Graphics/Completed/cabrillo.htm

Lesson_03_Graphics/Completed/lightshow.htm

USING A BACKGROUND GRAPHIC

In this exercise, you add a background graphic to a new document that you'll work with for the rest of this lesson. A background graphic is generally a small graphic that tiles across your page by repeating itself to the extent of the width and height of the browser window. A tiled background graphic has no effect on the appearance of scrollbars (or lack thereof) on your page. You can define both a background color and a background graphic for your pages. On slow connections, or in older slower browsers, you may see the background color displayed first—a good reason to set a background color even if you plan on using a background image. After the background graphic loads, it remains onscreen, overriding the background color.

1) Create a new HTML file by clicking HTML in the Create New column on the Start Page and save it as invent_lens.htm in the DWMX2004_Project/Lesson_03_Graphics folder. Type *Lights of the Coast: Lights: Creating the Lights* **into the Title text field on the Document toolbar.**

In this step, you create, save, and title a new document as you learned to do in Lesson 1. The document you create in this lesson is part of the Lights section of the Lights of the Coast project Web site. To indicate this to viewers as well as its place within the site, you give the page a title that starts with the name of the site, gives the name of the section the document is in, and finally gives the name of the document itself. This naming method makes it very clear what page is being shown in the browser and where this page is located in the site.

2) Choose Modify › Page Properties and select the Appearance category. Type *#CCCC99* **in the Background color text field and then type** *#000000* **into the Text color text field to set the default font color to black.**

TIP *Use the keyboard shortcut Command+J (Macintosh) or Ctrl+J (Windows) to access the Page Properties dialog box quickly.*

It is best to apply these general document settings before you begin laying out your pages. You can always modify them later, but it helps to see the document with the colors and settings it will use.

3) Click the Browse button next to Background image text field. Locate the bkg_inside_tan.gif graphic in the Images folder of the Lesson_3_Graphics folder. Click Choose (Macintosh) or Select (Windows) to designate the image as the background for the page and click OK to close the Page Properties dialog box.

THE PAGE PROPERTIES DIALOG BOX DISPLAYING
THE SELECTION OF A BACKGROUND IMAGE

Your changes are applied to the document, and you see the background image tiling in the document window. The bkg_inside_tan.gif image tiles across the page, creating horizontal bands of white, black, and tan. Background images tile both horizontally and vertically. If this page became longer than the background image you would see the white and black bars repeating. You can create a background graphic in an image editor such as Macromedia Fireworks.

TIP *If you are considering several background images, you can click the Apply button to see the background image displayed on your page without closing the Page Properties dialog box.*

If you want to delete a background graphic, you need to open the Page Properties dialog box and delete the filename in the Background text field. For this lesson, however, you should leave the background image in the document.

A pathname, or path, describes the location of a file. If you have not yet saved your file when you add a background image, the entire pathname for the graphic relative to your hard disk displays in the text field. You see an alert informing you of this and advising you to save your page. Until you save your file, Dreamweaver has no way to make these kinds of references, so a pathname based on the location of the image on your hard disk is substituted instead of a valid link. When you save your file, the pathname updates and changes to the location of the graphic relative to your document. It is always best, however, to save your file before importing any graphics—even background images. Pathnames that are relative to your hard drive don't work on the remote server; if you insert graphics without first saving your page, you run the risk of having "broken" images.

NOTE *If the image you select in the Select Image Source dialog box is outside of your local site, Dreamweaver displays an alert and gives you the option to copy the file into your site. The pages and elements (HTML, images, mulimedia,and so on) that you use in your site will usually be located in your local root folder. You can also use elements that do not exist in your local root folder but are in a location on the Internet, whether on your own site or elsewhere, through the use of absolute paths (covered in Lesson 4)—a technique that is often used for advertising banners. Because such items do not display in the Dreamweaver document window, you need to preview your page(s) in the browser to view them.*

PLACING GRAPHICS ON THE PAGE

The most common and widely supported graphic formats on the Web are GIF (Graphic Interchange Format) and JPEG (Joint Photographic Experts Group). When deciding whether to save a graphic as a GIF or a JPEG, aim for the highest image quality and the lowest possible file size.

As a general rule, you should use GIFs if the artwork has large areas of solid, flat colors and little or no blending of colors. GIFs works well with text, vector graphics, images with a limited number of colors, and very small image dimensions. GIF images can be saved, at maximum, using 8-bit color mode in which only 256 colors can be represented. GIF files tend to load faster, have more optimization options, and support transparency and animation.

You should usually choose JPEG for photographic images or images with a large tonal range. The JPEG format handles blending of colors very well and can produce much higher quality photographic images at a fraction of the size of a GIF. JPEG saves the image in 24-bit mode, retaining all the colors and using a lossy form of compression in which redundant data is lost. The lower the quality of a JPEG, the more information is lost about the image through this discard of data.

NOTE *A third graphic format, PNG (Portable Network Graphic), is also used on the Web. The PNG format combines features of both JPEG and GIF. PNG files are lossless, can compress better than GIF files and can retain all colors like a JPG. PNG does not support animation. PNG is not supported by older browsers.*

In this book, all the images you work with have already been saved for use on the Web as GIFs and JPEGs. You do not need to save or optimize any graphics.

1) Place the insertion point in the first line of the document. Click the Images menu button on the Common category of the Insert bar; then select the Image option.

The Select Image Source dialog box opens, which allows you to insert a graphic into the page. An alternative method is to choose Insert > Image.

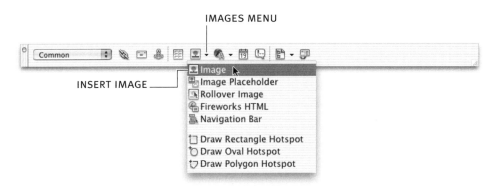

TIP *For Windows users, the Preview images checkbox provides a useful option that enables you to see a thumbnail of the images you click as you browse. When this option is selected, images are displayed in the Select Image Source dialog box along with their dimensions, file size, and approximate download time. On the Macintosh there is no Preview images checkbox; you see the image preview along with dimensions, file size, and approximate download time in the right pane of the Select Image Source dialog box after you select an image.*

2) Locate the file Lesson_03_Graphics/Images/invlens_header.gif.

The Select Image Source dialog box contains a variety of options. You can specify the folder from which you want to pick an image using the From (Macintosh) or Look in (Windows) menu or the display of files and folders below. Macintosh users have a hierarchical view enabling users to scroll through different levels of files and folders; Windows users have a Files of type menu that can be used to limit the view to specific kinds of files, and a File name text field that displays the name of the selected file (minus extension).

The URL text field displays the path that will be used by the document to access the selected image. Below the URL text field, is the Relative to menu—set to Document by default, the Relative to option lets you choose how Dreamweaver references images: with **document-relative** (the Document option) or **site root-relative** (the Site (Macintosh) or Site Root (Windows) option) references. In document-relative referencing, Dreamweaver constructs the path to the image based on the relative location of your HTML document to the graphics file. When Document is selected in the Relative to menu, the filename of the document into which you are inserting the image appears to the right of the menu—in this case you will see invent_lens.htm. Site root-relative referencing constructs the path to the image based on the relative location of the selected image to the site root, also known as the top level of the local root folder. If Site (Macintosh) or Site Root (Windows) is selected, the name of the site will appear to the right of the menu. Generally, you should use document-relative links and paths. If you have an extremely large site or plan to move pages frequently, you might want to use site root-relative referencing. Throughout the course of this book, you should use only document-relative paths for images.

You also have several additional options in the Select Image Source dialog box that are intended for use with dynamic sites. In the Select file name from section, Macintosh users have a Data Sources button and a Sites and Servers button; Windows users have two radio buttons, File system and Data sources, as well as a Sites and Servers button. The File system option is the default view on both Macintosh and Windows for this site and others similar to it that do not use a server technology (such as ColdFusion, ASP, JSP or PHP). The Data Sources and Sites and Servers options are used for dynamic sites in which a document executes on an application server. You do not need to use these options in the lessons contained in this book because you are not creating a dynamic, data-driven site.

For Macintosh users, a Go to text field appears near the bottom of the Select Image Source dialog box—this is an OS X system feature. You can use this text field to type in the Unix path to a location from which you would like to select an image. When you type in a location, the panes showing the folders and files will refresh to the location you designated. To jump to a location using this feature, you need to understand the file structure of Unix system, on which OS X is based.

3) Click Choose (Macintosh) or OK (Windows).

The image appears in the document window.

*This image was saved as a GIF to maintain crisp lines for the text. As a JPEG, the same image would show JPEG **artifacts** (small, blocky squares where redundant data is discarded, which are more common in areas of solid flat color) in the white background if saved to approximate the small file size of the GIF. If the image were to be saved as a higher-quality JPEG to achieve the same image quality as the GIF, it would have a much larger file size. In this case, GIF was the best option.*

RESIZING AND REFRESHING GRAPHICS

When you import a graphic, the width and height of the image are shown in the Property inspector and placed into the code automatically, giving the browser the information it needs to define the layout of the page. This important option can make a difference in the loading speed of your graphics.

1) With the invlens_header.gif image selected, use the Property inspector to change the width in the W text field to 220 pixels and the height in the H text field to 38 pixels.

You will need to either press Return (Macintosh) or Enter (Windows), or click in the document window to apply the change and refresh the view.

The new width and height attributes of the <img> (image) tag to make this graphic appear in smaller dimensions without making the actual graphic file smaller. Notice that the file size of the selected image that is displayed in the Property inspector does not change. There are many important advantages of restricting all image adjustments to being performed within an image editor, including sharpness, image quality and file size. If you were to reduce the same image in an image editor and re-optimize it for the Web, the file would be smaller in file size and higher in image quality.

NOTE *File size is an especially important consideration for Web pages. The smaller the file size, the quicker your images load. And the quicker your pages load, the more likely your visitors will wait around long enough to see your site.*

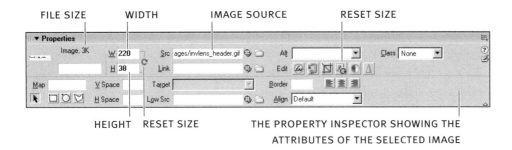

FILE SIZE   WIDTH   IMAGE SOURCE   RESET SIZE

HEIGHT   RESET SIZE   THE PROPERTY INSPECTOR SHOWING THE
ATTRIBUTES OF THE SELECTED IMAGE

2) Click one of the selection handles—the black squares—on the border of the selected image. Drag to resize the image and make it larger than the original size.

The width and height specifications update automatically. Notice that the new dimensions are displayed in bold. This bold formatting is an indicator that the graphic has been resized. At times, you may resize a graphic accidentally, and the bold numbers will clue you in to that change.

TIP *Hold down the Shift key while you drag the image's selection handles to constrain the proportions of the image.*

Notice that when you scaled the image larger, the image quality diminished. Images display in browsers at screen resolution, which is 72 dpi. This resolution is not high enough to display an image at a size that is larger than the actual size of the graphic—another reason to always adjust the image size in your image-editing software (such as Macromedia Fireworks or Adobe Photoshop) to ensure that you have the smallest file size possible.

3) In the Property inspector, click the Reset Image to Original Size button that is located just to the right of the W and H text fields.

The refresh icon indicates the Reset Image to Original Size button. It is in the center of lines connecting the W and H text fields. The refresh icon and connecting lines gives you another indication that the dimensions of the image have been altered. The image resets to the original size of the graphic. Notice that the width and height numbers revert to plain text, indicating that the image is set at the original size.

NOTE *When using very large images or images that are located on other servers, you can provide a visual clue to viewers by using a low source image. By defining a low source, you are choosing a lower-quality image that will appear first. The higher-quality image will appear in its place when the download is complete. When an image is selected, the Property inspector provides a Low Src text field for defining a low source image. Click the Browse for File Folder icon next to the field to choose an image. This technique is sometimes used when you know the final image will be large in file size and therefore take longer to download than a user might expect, or if the image is being obtained from a source that may experience frequent slow downs or lags. Low source images used in such situations often depict "loading" or similar messages.*

POSITIONING GRAPHICS

When you place an image directly in the body of a document, you have a limited number of options for positioning it. The following exercise shows a method for creating an alignment that uses <div> tags—containers that specify the alignment of everything between the opening and ending tags. You will learn about other ways to position images later in this lesson.

1) In invent_lens.htm, click the invlens_header.gif image to select it. In the Property inspector, click the Align Center button.

If you don't see the Align Center button, click the expander arrow in the lower right corner. The image is centered on the page.

IMAGE ALIGNMENT OPTIONS ON THE PROPERTY INSPECTOR

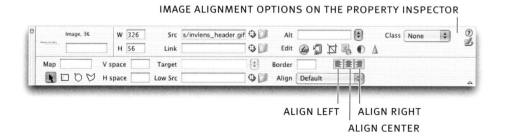

ALIGN LEFT   ALIGN RIGHT
ALIGN CENTER

TIP *The Align Center button is not the same as the Align menu that you will see below the three alignment buttons.*

2) Insert a paragraph break after the page-title graphic by clicking off of the image and pressing Return (Mac) or Enter (Windows). Copy and paste the text from invent.txt into the new paragraph line. Select all the text and click the Align Left button on the Property inspector to set the alignment to the left.

You can copy and paste the text from invent.txt into the invent_lens.htm document just as you did in Lesson 2. The invent.txt is located in Text folder of the Lesson_03_Graphics folder.

When you work with multiple elements, you must put them in separate paragraphs to give them different alignments. You can't center part of a paragraph and align the rest left. When you insert text directly below an image, for example, you need to use a regular paragraph break—press Return (Mac) or Enter (Windows)—between the image and the text if you want to apply different alignments. If you use a line break (by pressing Shift+Return on the Macintosh or Shift+Enter in Windows) to separate them, or do not use any separation at all, any alignment you apply affects both the image and the text because they would be considered part of the same paragraph block.

3) Set the following text options using the Appearance section of the Page Properties dialog box: The Page Font combination should be Verdana, Arial, Helvetica, sans-serif; and the Size option should be set to 12 pixels.

You can save this file and preview it in the browser.

ADDING A BORDER AROUND AN IMAGE

At times, you need to set an image apart from the background to make it stand out. One way to create this effect is to place a border around the image. A border can draw attention to an image, and it can continue a stylistic look throughout a site. At times, a border can also indicate a link.

In invent_lens.htm, click the invlens_header.gif image to select it; then, in the Border text field of the Property inspector, type *1*.

Dreamweaver adds a 1-pixel border around the image. The border setting uses pixel-based measurement.

You can set the width of the border to any number you want. The border color will be the same as the default text color that was specified in Page Properties dialog box.

THE BORDER OPTION SET TO 1 FOR THE SELECTED
IMAGE IN THE PROPERTY INSPECTOR

NOTE *When you start assigning links to images in Lesson 4, the border color will be the same as the default Link Color specified in Page Properties.*

ASSIGNING NAMES AND ALT TEXT TO IMAGES

Image names and alt (alternative) text for images are important, although largely invisible, parts of Web pages. It is generally a good practice to assign names and alt text because they help both you and the users of your site. Image names are used in scripting to identify the object and alt text provides additional information about the image to users. You'll work with both in the following exercise.

1) Select the invlens_header.gif image and type *header* **in the image name text field in the Property inspector.**

The image name text field is not labeled in the Property inspector. It is located in the upper left corner, directly under the size of the image.

The name you assign to the image is an internal name, used mainly for functions such as Behaviors (covered in Lesson 11). Although naming your images is not essential, doing so is good practice. You should keep image names short, enter them in lowercase, and avoid using spaces or special characters.

2) Type *Creating The Lights…from bonfires to lenses* **in the Alt text field.**

The Alt option lets you specify text that are displayed if users have graphics disabled, if their browsers are not capable of displaying graphics, or if a particular image fails to load. In this case, the text you typed is the same text shown in the image. Alt text is an attribute of the <img> tag that defines images. You can learn more about HTML tags and their attributes in Lesson 14.

You must add alt text to any graphics that are critical for site navigation. Adding alt text to other images is also useful because if users have graphics disabled or are using a text-only browser, they can see some of the information they are missing. Additionally, people who have vision disabilities use various programs, often called readers or speech synthesizers, which relay content on Web pages audibly. In these cases, the alt text of an image is spoken so that the user will know what the image is.

The more descriptive and detailed your alt text is, the more useful it is for these users. You'll learn more about Web accessibility and developing accessible sites in Lesson 13. Further, alt text is displayed briefly in Internet Explorer when the user moves the pointer over the graphic.

Often, you may have graphics that serve a strictly visual function and do not display words or other imagery that are important to the content of your page. These design elements can make it more difficult for users with vision disabilities to use your site if they are labeled inappropriately with alternative text. For these types of images, you should click the menu button to the right of the Alt text field in the Property inspector and select <empty>. Avoid setting irrelevant alternative text—it does more harm than good.

INSERTING AN IMAGE FROM THE ASSETS PANEL

The Assets panel provides you with the ability to organize the components of your site from within Dreamweaver. You can use it to view and catalog a wide variety of media and page elements.

For example, it may be difficult to manage all your images, especially if you are working on a large site. The Assets panel gives you a way to keep track of those images.

NOTE *Because of a bug described in Lesson 1, the Files panel group may be called Assets instead of Files. For details, read the note on this topic in the Define a Local Site exercise of Lesson 1.*

1) Select the Assets panel from the Files panel group. Click the Images button located at the top of the column of buttons on the left side of the Assets panel.

TIP *If the Assets panel or Files panel group is not visible, you can choose Window > Assets to open the Assets panel within the Files panel group.*

The other buttons along the left side of the Assets panel represent different types of assets that may be available to your site, including colors, which you learned to apply in Lesson 1 (background page color) and Lesson 2 (font colors) using the Page Properties dialog box and the Property inspector.

You can work with the Assets panel in two ways: You can view it with the Site list, which gives you a complete list of the images in your site; or view it with the Favorites list, which shows only the images that you marked as Favorites. Both views allow you to add a selected image to your page.

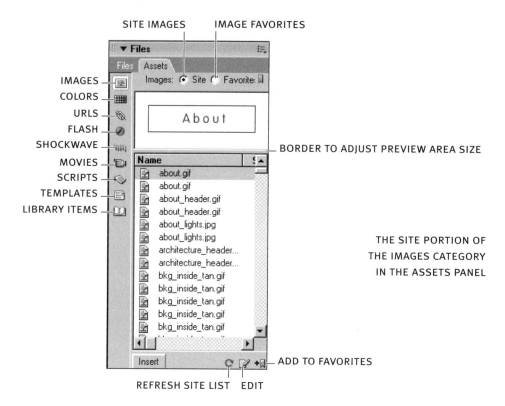

2) **Click the Site button at the top of the Assets panel if it is not already selected (as it should be by default).**

NOTE *In the Lights of the Coast project site you will see multiple copies of most images listed in the Images portion of the Assets panel because the are several copies of each image in the site. The Completed folders contain image folders that are duplicates of the image folders contained within each of the lesson folders. Additionally, some images may be listed more than twice if they are used in more than one lesson. In your own sites, you will not have this situation unless you have multiple image folders that contain several of the same images. Spacer GIFs and navigation images are sometimes contained in several image folders. Usually it is not necessary to have multiple copies of an image because you can use images from any location in your site. In fact, multiple images may not be desirable—if you update an image you may need to make changes on a number of files if you have multiple copies of the same image.*

All images within the site are shown in the Site Assets window. The images appear in this window automatically, whether or not they are used in any document. It may take a few seconds for the panel to create a catalog of the image assets available for your site.

NOTE *If you didn't enable cache for your site when it was created, Dreamweaver will prompt you to click the refresh button on the Assets panel in order to enable and create the cache. Cache is enabled by default and is automatically created unless you uncheck the Enable Cache box in the Site Definition dialog box for your site.*

If you add a new asset to your site, it might not appear in the Assets panel immediately. To update the panel to match all the images in your site, you need to refresh the site catalog. To do so, click the Refresh Site List button in the lower right corner of the Assets panel.

3) Insert a new paragraph line after the first paragraph by pressing Return (Macintosh) or Enter (Windows). Find the ptarena_lens.jpg graphic in the Assets panel that is located in the Lesson_03_Graphics/Images folder and drag it to the document between the first and second paragraphs.

Expanding the Assets panel horizontally will allow you to see the Full Path column, which you can use to determine where the images are located. On the Macintosh you can expand the panel by clicking and dragging the lower right corner to the right— you may need to move the panel or panel groups to the left first so that you have room to expand the panel. On Windows you can click the vertical bar separating the panels from the rest of the interface and drag it to the left.

TIP *Alternatively, you can place the insertion point in the document, select the image in the Assets panel, and click the Insert button.*

The image appears in the document window.

As you select images in the Assets panel, you'll see a thumbnail preview at the top of the panel. You can enlarge the thumbnail by increasing the available preview area (place the cursor over the lower border of the viewing area and drag to resize) and/or enlarging the whole Assets panel. You can easily select an image from the Assets panel and click the Edit icon to open the image in your default image-editing program.

Clicking the column headers will reorder the list of images. For example, clicking the Name column header will reorder the images alphabetically in ascending (indicated by an upwards-facing arrow) or descending order (indicated by a downwards-facing arrow). You can use the other column headers to sort by Size, Type, and Full Path. You may need to scroll to the right to see the other columns. If you see an ellipse (…) in a column or column header, you will have to expand the panel to view the contents of that column. After the Assets panel is in focus—click an image in the list to bring it into focus—you can type the first letter (or the first several letters in quick succession) of the file that you are looking for to select it.

NOTE *This photographic image was saved as a JPEG. The same image would appear posterized (rough gradations, with jagged edges to colors causing noticeable pixelation) if saved as a GIF image because all the different shades would be mapped to only a few colors. In this case, JPEG was the best option.*

4) Select the image you just inserted. In the image-name text field of the Property inspector, type lightsource. **In the Alt text field, type** Point Arena Light Source Photo. **Define a border of 1 pixel.**

Giving names and alt text to your images as you insert them saves you time and make it easier to work with them in Code view later, if necessary.

5) Center the ptarena_lens.jpg image. Create a line break after the image and type the following: (photo above: The light source inside the 1st order Fresnel lens in Point Arena Lighthouse, California).

TIP *Use the Align Center button on the Property inspector to center the image, as you did earlier in this lesson.*

Providing captions for your images helps viewers understand them in the proper context. The caption is centered because it is considered to be in the same paragraph block as the image above.

6) Select the caption and use the Property inspector to apply formatting to the text: the size should be 10 pixels and the color should be #333333.

In this case, you fade the text and make it smaller in order to subtly differentiate it from the body text of the document.

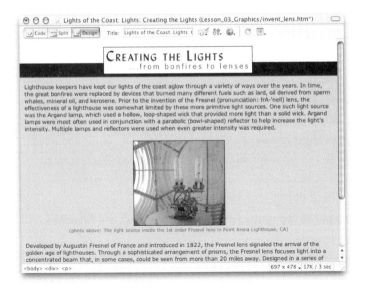

At this point, your document should look similar to the example above.

MANAGING IMAGES WITH THE FAVORITES LIST

Placing images that you use repeatedly in the Favorites list can be a time-saver. You can add any image contained within the site to your Favorites list. Each site has its own Favorites list. This list is empty when you start using Dreamweaver. In the following exercise, you'll add an image from the Site category to your Favorites list and then organize that list.

1) In the Assets panel's site list, select ptarena_outlens.jpg and click the Add to Favorites button, located in the lower right corner.

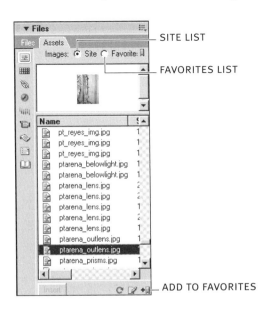

85

A dialog box appears to let you know that the selected assets have been added to this site's Favorites list. Choose OK to acknowledge the message and close the dialog box.

TIP *You can use an alternative method to add an image to the Favorites list. Select an image in the Files panel and use the context menu in the upper right corner of the panel to choose Add to Favorites. Yet another method is to make an image in your document window a favorite. To do this, Control-click (Macintosh) or right-click (Windows) the image and choose Add to Image Favorites from the context menu that appears. This context menu contains a wide variety of options and also works for other elements such as links and Flash objects.*

2) Use the Images options at the top of the Assets panel to select the Favorites radio button.

The Assets panel now displays the list of favorites, with the image you added in the previous step.

PREVIEW AREA

CONTEXT MENU

NEW FAVORITES FOLDER

THE FAVORITES LIST IN THE IMAGES CATEGORY ON THE ASSETS PANEL

As you begin to manage your images through the Assets panel, you probably will need to remove as well as add images. When an image is selected in the Favorites list, the Add to Favorites button becomes the Remove from Favorites button. Clicking Remove from Favorites causes the selected image to disappear from the list.

NOTE *In both the Site and Favorites lists in the Images category you can use the context menu to find the location of a particular image within your site. To do so, select and image and choose Locate in Site from the context menu. The Files panel becomes active, with the image selected in the site structure.*

3) Click the icon for New Favorites Folder at the bottom of the panel. In the name text field of the folder that appears, replace the default name of untitled with `Fresnel` **and press Return (Macintosh) or Enter (Windows).**

You can organize your images in folders to make them easy to locate.

TIP *You can also select the New Favorites Folder option from the context menu. This option is available only in the context menu when you are viewing the Favorites section of the Images category.*

4) Drag the ptarena_outlens image into the Fresnel folder.

You can double-click the small folder icon to see the contents of the folder and double-click again to collapse the folder. Images contained within a folder will appear below and slightly indented from the folder.

NOTE *When moved into a folder, files shown in the Favorites list will indent slightly to indicate they are contained within the folder. Because of a bug, the indentation may not appear on the Macintosh—if this is the case, you can collapse or expand a folder to check if the image was moved to the folder.*

Images in the Favorites list are listed by their nicknames (with no extensions such as .jpg or .gif—you can determine the kind of image file by looking in the Type column), which Dreamweaver assigns automatically based on the image's filenames. You can change these nicknames in the Favorites list by clicking the name, pausing, and clicking again. A border appears around the text field, and the name is highlighted. Start typing to replace the highlighted text. Don't double-click—double-clicking an image in either the Site list or the Favorites list cause the image to be opened in a graphical editor if one is defined, such as Adobe Photoshop or Macromedia Fireworks.

When you create a Favorites list, a folder called _notes is added to your site. You will not see this folder in the Files panel in Dreamweaver, although you will see it in the Finder (Macintosh) or through My Computer (Windows). This folder contains images.dfv, which is the file that tracks your Favorites list.

NOTE *If you need to delete a folder that you created in the Favorites list, select the folder and then click Remove from Favorites at the bottom of the Assets panel.*

WRAPPING TEXT AROUND IMAGES

Basic layout options in HTML include wrapping text around images. The following exercise demonstrates how to create a text wrap. You can use the same procedure to align images with other elements, including other images.

1) In invent_lens.htm, place the insertion point at the beginning of the second paragraph and insert ptarena_outlens.jpg.

The image is placed in the document and appears in the default position, with the first line of the text starting at the baseline of the image.

2) Select the ptarena_outlens.jpg graphic in the document window and choose Left from the Align menu in the Property inspector.

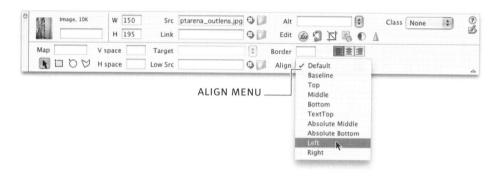

ALIGN MENU

The image is aligned left. The text on the right wraps to the bottom of the ptarena_outlens.jpg graphic and then returns to the left margin of the window. By changing the Align attribute, you can wrap multiple lines of text around the image. The Align menu contains several options for images, including Top and Text Top. Remember, the only options for wrapping text are Left or Right. The other options are for the placement of a graphic next to a single line of text. Default is the same as no alignment.

When you choose the Right option from the Align menu, Dreamweaver places an image-anchor symbol at the point where the image was inserted. You may not see the symbol if the visual aid element isn't turned on. If you don't see the symbol, choose View > Visual Aids > Invisible Elements and check the Anchor points for aligned images box. This symbol indicates where the HTML tag for the image is in relation to the text. The anchor needs to be at the beginning of the text for the text wrap to work properly. The symbol will not be visible in the browser.

NOTE *Although you should be able to move this anchor to a new location, a bug on both Macintosh and Windows makes it impossible to drag and reposition the anchor points.*

3) Give the ptarena_outlens.jpg image a border of 1 pixel by typing *1* into the border text field on the Property inspector. Save the file and preview it in the browser.

Keep in mind that whenever you select an alignment option (except for Default) the image is offset slightly from the original position. You can't control or get rid of this offset. The amount of offset varies from browser to browser, but usually is only a couple of pixels and not noticeable. The offset may be a problem, however, if you are trying to align images in tables (you'll learn to work with Tables in Lesson 5), in which case you will need to use other methods to control the placement of your images.

The amount of text that wraps around the image depends on the size at which the text displays in the browser window, the amount of text, and how big the browser window has been opened. When you resize the window (whether in Dreamweaver or a browser), the way the text wraps around the image changes. Keep in mind that what you see in the Dreamweaver document window is only an approximation of what will be seen in the browser.

ADJUSTING THE SPACE AROUND AN IMAGE

When you wrap text around graphics, you may also need to adjust the space around the image. Initially the text in your document will be very close to the image, which may make it difficult to read. Creating a certain amount of open space will help the visual layout of your page. You can add vertical space (V Space) and horizontal space (H Space). The space settings use a pixel-based measurement.

1) In invent_lens.htm, click the ptarena_outlens.jpg image to select it.

Right now, the text is very close to the edge of this graphic. The page would look better and the text would be easier to read if space were added around the image.

2) In the Property inspector, type *10* in the H Space text field and press Return (Macintosh) or Enter (Windows).

This setting creates 10 pixels of space on the left and right sides of the image. You can't add space on only one side.

3) Type *6* in the V Space text field and press Return (Macintosh) or Enter (Windows).

This setting creates six pixels of space at the top and bottom of the image. You can't add space on only one side.

INSERTING AN IMAGE PLACEHOLDER

You have the option to insert an image placeholder if you do not have the final image. A placeholder can be inserted and used to approximate how the final graphic will appear on the page in combination with text, tables, or other elements.

1) Place the insertion point on a new paragraph line after the second paragraph of body text. In the Common category of the Insert bar, click the Images menu and select the Image Placeholder option.

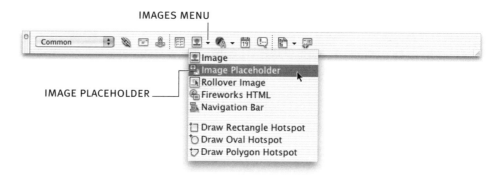

The Image Placeholder dialog box appears.

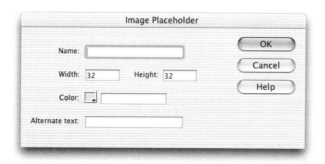

NOTE *The default width and height for an image placeholder is 32 × 32 pixels.*

2) In the Name text field, type *belowlight*. **Set the width to 250 and the height to 195. Click the color box and use the swatches to pick black; then type** *below the light source* **in the Alternative text text field. Click OK.**

The image placeholder appears in the document window. It is black and displays the image name and the dimensions.

If you have Fireworks installed and set as the default editor for your image files, you can select the placeholder image in the document window and click the Create button on the Property inspector to open a Fireworks document at the size you specified for the placeholder. When you save that document, the name you used for the placeholder image is automatically assigned in the Fireworks Save As text field.

When you preview your page in a browser, the image placeholder displays a broken image icon along with the alt text within a box with the dimensions and color you defined in the Image Placeholder dialog box. To replace this, you need to swap the image placeholder with the intended image, as described in the next exercise.

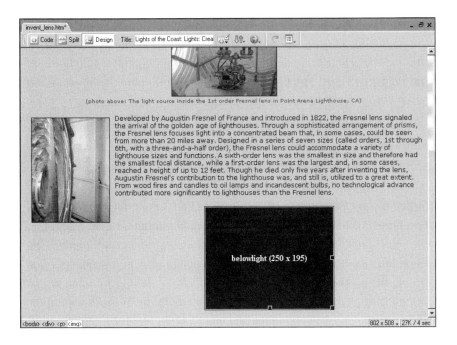

You page should now look similar to the previous example.

The position of the image placeholder in your document may be slightly different that the example shown here. If the text that wraps around the image doesn't reach the bottom of the image, any object below the text will continue in the same alignment, regardless of whether those objects are in separate paragraph blocks. This variation is due to the difference in text appearance between the Macintosh and Windows operating systems, Depending on your system and how wide your document window is, the image placeholder may appear to be wrapping around the aligned image, or it may appear below the image. You can see the difference by increasing or decreasing the width of your document window. To change the width of the document window, Windows users need to either switch to the non-tabbed interface by clicking the document window maximize button, or by collapsing/expanding the area available for the panels.

REPLACING AN IMAGE PLACEHOLDER

After you have created the final graphic or received the necessary image from your client, you need to replace the image placeholder you used to approximate the graphic.

TIP *You can also use this same technique to replace one image with another.*

1) Double-click the image placeholder in the document window.

The Select Image Source dialog box opens.

2) Select the ptarena_belowlight.jpg from the Lesson_03_Graphics/Images folder and click Choose (Macintosh) or OK (Windows).

The image replaces the placeholder in the document window. The name and alt text that were assigned to the image placeholder are now applied to the image.

SETTING IMAGE EDITING PREFERENCES

As you create Web pages with Dreamweaver you may find that you need to modify the images that you are using. For extensive editing you will need to open and adjust the image in an external image editing program. Dreamweaver makes this process easy by providing a quick way for you to open the image in a program you specify.

1) Choose Dreamweaver Preferences (Macintosh) or Edit > Preferences (Windows) and select File Types/Editors in the Category list of the Preferences dialog box.

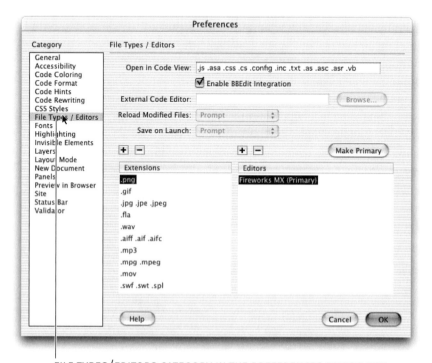

FILE TYPES/EDITORS CATEGORY IN THE PREFERENCES DIALOG BOX

You can use this dialog box to assign different external programs as the default editors according to the file extensions.

NOTE *Production with Dreamweaver MX 2004, Flash, and Fireworks can be integrated through what is known as* **roundtrip editing***, a feature that makes it possible for file updates to be transferred between the programs. For this feature to function, Fireworks must be the default image editor.*

2) Select .gif in the Extensions list. Click the plus (+) button above the Editors list and select an image-editing program such as Fireworks. With the program selected in the application list, click the Make Primary button to set the program as the default editor for all GIF files.

Tip: To specify an editing program, be sure to use the buttons above the Editors list. The buttons above the Extensions list are for adding other extensions.

If you do not have an image-editing program, you can skip this step.

If you do have an image-editing program, you should repeat this step for JPEG and PNG files.

NOTE *A trial version of Fireworks is also provided on the CD-ROM.*

3) Select the invlens_header.gif image.

The Property inspector for images features an Edit button (which looks like a Fireworks icon) in the top half and right side of the panel as well as an option to Optimize in Fireworks. The Edit option provides a quick way to open and modify your images in an external image editor, provided you have defined a default image editor, as detailed in the previous step.

EDIT IMAGE IN AN EXTERNAL IMAGE EDITING
PROGRAM (SPECIFIED IN PREFERENCES)

BASIC IMAGE EDITING

Several basic image-editing functions are available directly within Dreamweaver, enabling you to alter images without the need for an outside editor. Although you need an external image editor to initially create the graphics for your site or to make major changes, you can now make a variety of modifications—including cropping, adjusting the contrast, and sharpening—right in the Dreamweaver document window using the integrated Fireworks image editing features.

1) Select the ptarena_belowlight.jpg image.

The Image editing options appear on the Property inspector.

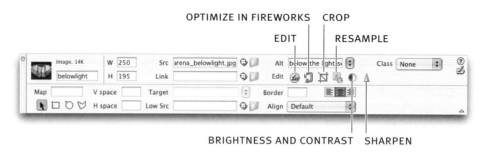

2) Click the Crop tool on the Property inspector.

An alert box informs you that the operation will change the actual image file on your disk. You can click the Don't show me this message again dialog box to avoid seeing this message again. Click OK to continue.

A selection area appears inside the image, indicated by a solid black line (Macintosh) or a dashed line (Windows). Grab handles are located in the corners and centers of each side of the selection area. The selection area may be difficult to see on dark images. By default, the selection area is slightly smaller than the image and has approximately the same proportions. The area within the selection is clear; the area outside the selection is grayed-out to show that it will be cropped. The cursor, when placed in the center of the selection area, turns into a hand (Macintosh) or a cross-hair with arrows (Windows) so that you can click and drag to move to selection area. You can click the cursor on any of the handles and drag to reduce or enlarge the size of the selection area.

3) Adjust the size of the crop area so that it is about three quarters the size of the original image and then press Return (Macintosh) or Enter (Windows) to crop the image.

TIP *You can also double-click inside the selection area or click the crop icon on the Property inspector to apply the change. To cancel the crop, click elsewhere in the document window outside of the image.*

The image is now cropped to the area that you selected. You may notice that the file size of the image is reduced; how much depends on the amount of the image that you cropped. The original size of the ptarena_belowlight.jpg image was approximately 14 KB. The image size is given near the upper left corner of the Property inspector when the image is selected.

NOTE *If you alter an image using Dreamweaver's Image tools, all instances of that image in your site will change. If this is not what you intend, you may want to make a duplicate of the image and perform your adjustments on the copy. If you make a crop and decide you don't like it, you can revert back to the original image by using Dreamweaver's undo command. Choose Edit > Undo Crop or use the keyboard command Command+Z (Macintosh) or Ctrl+Z (Windows) to switch back to the original image.*

4) With the ptarena_belowlight.jpg image selected, click the Brightness and Contrast tool on the Property inspector. Change the brightness to +25 and click OK.

The alert informs you that the image file will be changed. Click OK to continue.

The Brightness/Contrast dialog box appears with one slider for Brightness and one for Contrast. The sliders range from –100 to +100 with the center and default being 0. You can type any value within the range into the text fields, or you can click and drag the sliders. Moving a slider to the left into the negative numbers decreases the brightness or lowers the contrast; moving a slider to the right into the positive numbers increases the brightness or heightens the contrast.

The Preview box is checked by default—this allows you to immediately see the effects of your adjustments in the Dreamweaver document window.

NOTE *The brightness change you apply in this step is fairly drastic so that you can clearly see the effect upon the image. Take care with using this option because it can severely affect the quality of an image if over-used.*

5) With the ptarena_belowlight.jpg image selected, click the Sharpen tool on the Property inspector. Adjust the slider value to 2 and click OK.

The alert informs you that the image file will be changed. Click OK to continue.

The Sharpen dialog box uses one slider with a range of 0 to 10 and, like the Brightness and Contrast feature, has a Preview option turned on by default.

You can repeat this function if necessary. Take care when using this option because it can severely affect the quality of an image if over-used. Extreme sharpening may cause the image to appear pixilated.

NOTE *The additional image editing options on the Property inspector include Edit, Optimize in Fireworks, and Resample. You must have Fireworks installed to take advantage of the option to optimize files. The Optimize Images dialog box allows you to make a wide variety of changes including switching the format of images, adjusting the quality (JPEGs), and adjusting the color palette (GIFs). Keep in mind that you can lower the quality of an image and reduce its file size, but you can't increase the quality. To obtain a better image, you need to use original source files. The Launch External Editor opens in whichever editor you defined as Primary in the Preferences, which you set earlier in this lesson. The Resample tool gives you the option of increasing or decreasing the resolution of your images. It is always better to start with a higher resolution file and decrease the resolution to the desired size, rather than increasing a low-resolution file. Even when increasing the resolution, you can't add quality to an image that isn't there to begin with. Web resolution is 72ppi (pixels per inch).*

ALIGNING AN IMAGE RELATIVE TO A SINGLE LINE OF TEXT

Many times, you'll want to control the placement of an image in relation to a single line of text that appears near it. You can change the relative location of the image to the text by using alignment options. The seven options discussed in the following exercise work well to align a single line of text near a graphic.

TIP *The options used in this exercise don't work for wrapping multiple lines around a graphic. To wrap multiple lines, you need to choose either the Left or Right alignment options, as demonstrated in the Wrapping Text Around Images exercise earlier in this lesson.*

1) Position the insertion point to the right of the belowlight graphic and type Point Arena, California. **Select the text and change the size to 10 pixels and the color to #333333.**

TIP *Because you've already used this font size and color combination for a previous caption, you can quickly apply the formatting by selecting the text and choosing the style that was created for the previous caption. The style should be style1, unless you've created any additional styles by applying text formatting to other portions of the document.*

Initially, the text is aligned with the bottom of the graphic and is too close to the graphic.

2) Select the belowlight graphic, and add a 1-pixel border to it. In the Property inspector, type _10_ in the H Space text field.

The graphic and text move apart, and a thin border appears around the image.

3) From the Align menu, choose Absolute Middle.

This option aligns the baseline of the text with the middle of the image.

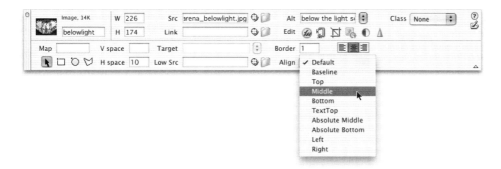

The options for aligning an image to a single line of text are as follows:

- Baseline: Aligns the bottom of the image with the baseline, or bottom line, on which the text sits. This option normally is the browser default.

- Top: Aligns the image with the top of the tallest item in the line. That item may be text or a larger image.

- Middle: Aligns the baseline of the text with the middle of the image.

- Bottom: Aligns in the same way as Baseline.

- Text Top: Does what you would expect Top should do, which is to align the image with the top of the tallest text in the line. (This option usually, but not always, is the same as Top.)

- Absolute Middle: Aligns the middle of the image with the middle of the text line or the largest item in the line.

- Absolute Bottom: Aligns the bottom of the image with the lowest point of the text line.

4) Save the file and preview it in the browser.

You can also use these options to position images relative to other images; you're not limited to using text.

ADDING FLASH BUTTONS

You can achieve special effects by using Flash objects such as text, buttons and movies. Because Flash graphics are vector-based, their file sizes are very small, which helps them load quickly in the user's browser. Similar to Flash text, which you worked with in Lesson 2, you do not need to have Flash to create Flash buttons—you can develop them directly in Dreamweaver.

Flash buttons have several states, depending on the position of the pointer and whether the mouse button has been clicked. The first state is the appearance of the button when the pointer is not on it. The second state occurs when the pointer is on the button, but the mouse button has not been clicked. The third state occurs when the pointer is on the button and the mouse button has been clicked. You can create and maintain Flash buttons in Dreamweaver from a set of pre-made button styles.

1) In the invent_lens.htm document window, position the insertion point on a new paragraph line under the ptarena_belowlight.jpg image and its caption.

You'll insert a Flash button on this page.

2) From the Common category of the Insert bar, click the Media menu and select the Flash Button icon.

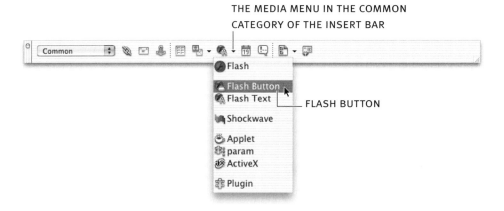

THE MEDIA MENU IN THE COMMON
CATEGORY OF THE INSERT BAR

FLASH BUTTON

The Insert Flash Button dialog box opens.

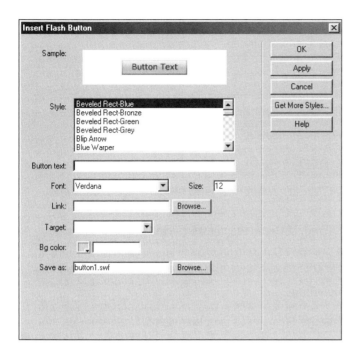

3) In the Style list, scroll down and select Glass-Silver. In the Button text text field type *Main***. Leave the Font and Size at their defaults: Verdana and 12 respectively.**

A sample area at the top of the dialog box shows a preview of the button style. You can move the mouse over this sample image to see how it will function.

You can edit these settings later, if necessary. The next exercise shows you how.

NOTE *In this exercise, you are leaving the optional Link text field blank. You'll learn how to create links in Lesson 4.*

4) Click the Bg color box. When the cursor turns into an eyedropper, click anywhere on the tan background color of the document window to select that color.

The background-color hexadecimal code #CCCC99 appears in the Bg color text field. This code represents the background color that will be used for the button. To make the button appear seamlessly on your page, you select the same color as was used for the background of the page.

5) In the Save as text field, type main-button.swf**; then click OK at the upper right of the dialog box.**

You should always name your Flash buttons. If you don't, Dreamweaver automatically assigns generic names.

TIP *The preview does not change dynamically as you alter the settings; it only shows the button style. If you want to view the button as you make changes, you need to click the Apply button so that you can see the changes in the document window.*

The Insert Flash Button dialog box closes, and a button with the specifications you set appears in the document. Because you just inserted the button, it is selected.

6) With the button still selected, click the Play button in the Property inspector.

Clicking Play allows you to see the Flash button effects in the document window. The button appears as it will in a browser, and the selection handles disappear. The Play button becomes a Stop button.

FLASH BUTTON PROPERTIES IN THE PROPERTY INSPECTOR

7) In the document window, move the pointer over the Main button; then click the button.

The button changes to its rollover state when the pointer is moved over it. The button changes to its clicked state when clicked.

8) Click Stop in the Property inspector. Save the file and preview it in the browser.

The button changes states just as it did in Dreamweaver, depending on the pointer position and mouse click.

MODIFYING FLASH BUTTONS

You can easily change many of the button attributes at any time.

1) In the document window, double-click the Flash button you created.

The Insert Flash Button dialog box opens.

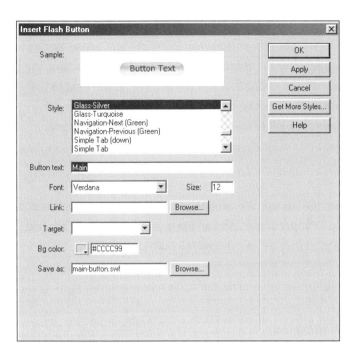

2) Make changes in the Flash button settings. Set the options however you want.

Change the font to Arial, for example.

3) Click Apply to see the changes. Click OK when you finish.

You can add your own template buttons to those in the Style list by using Flash to create .swt Generator Template files outside Dreamweaver. To add these files to Dreamweaver, you need to open the Dreamweaver program folder and place them in the Configuration > Flash Objects > Flash Buttons folder.

ADDING FLASH ANIMATIONS

Using Macromedia Flash, you can create vector-based graphics, animations and movies. Unlike bitmap graphics such as GIFs and JPEGs, which you've used so far in this lesson, vector graphics use geometric formulas to create the images and objects that you see.

You can add Flash animations to your documents as easily as you can add any bitmap image, provided that the animation already exists. You can't create these kinds of animations directly within Dreamweaver—you must use Flash. For this exercise, an animation that was created in Flash is provided for you.

1) Create a new document and save it as lens_demo.htm in the Lesson_03_Graphics folder. Set the title as *Lights of the Coast: Lights: Refraction.* **Choose Modify › Page Properties, select the Appearance category and set Page font to Verdana, the text Size to 14, and the Text color to #000000. Click the Browse button next to the Background image text field and select bkg_inside_tan.gif from the Lesson_03_ Graphics/Images folder; then click OK to close the Page Properties dialog box.**

You have saved the document and set the page properties as you learned in Lessons 1 and 2.

2) Open lens-demo.txt from the Lesson_03_Graphics/Text folder. Copy the text and paste it into the lens_demo.html document. Add an extra paragraph above the text (animation above: how the prisms of a Fresnel lens refract light) and place the insertion point on the new line.

Be sure to use a paragraph return and not a line break. You need a new text block.

NOTE *The additional paragraph breaks between the two lines of header information at the top of the document and the first paragraph help to prevent the black bar of the background from obscuring the text in the first paragraph.*

3) In the Assets panel, click the Flash button in the left column and select the Site list view.

The Flash assets appear in the panel. The Site and Favorites lists for Flash assets work the same way as they do for image assets. You can use the same techniques to manage and organize Flash files as you do to manage and organize images.

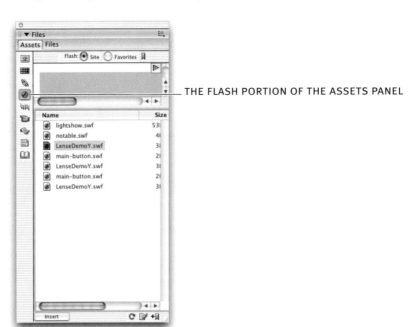

THE FLASH PORTION OF THE ASSETS PANEL

4) In the Site list, select the first LenseDemoY.swf; then click the Insert button at the bottom of the Assets panel.

The Flash animation is placed on the page.

5) In the Property inspector, make sure the boxes for Loop and Autoplay are checked. Click Play to view the animation in Dreamweaver.

To view animation files in Dreamweaver, click Play. Click Stop when you are done testing.

THE PROPERTY INSPECTOR DISPLAYS THE PARAMETERS
THAT YOU CAN SET FOR A FLASH MOVIE

6) Click Stop on the Property inspector, Save the file and preview it in the browser.

Autoplay causes the Flash animation to begin playing as soon as the page is loaded into the browser. The animation plays repeatedly because you chose Loop in the Property inspector.

INSERTING AN ACCESSIBLE IMAGE

It is important to create sites that are accessible to people with disabilities. Dreamweaver's accessibility tools make it easier for Web developers to comply with accessibility standards such as Section 508 of the Rehabilitation Act. You'll learn more about accessibility in Lesson 7.

1) Choose Dreamweaver > Preferences (Macintosh) or Edit > Preferences (Windows).

The Preferences dialog box opens.

2) From the Category list, choose Accessibility. In the list of objects displayed on the right, check the box for images. Click OK to close the Preferences dialog box.

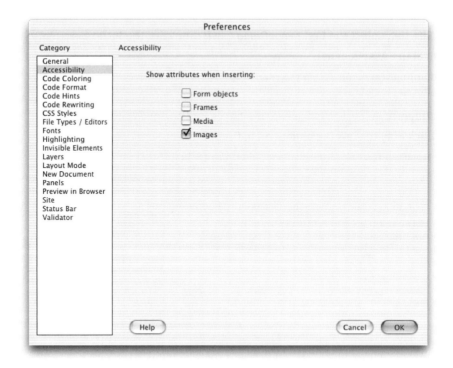

Dreamweaver's image accessibility authoring options are now enabled.

3) Create a new paragraph between the caption for the Flash animation and the caption below it for the Prism image that you will insert in the following step. Select the Image option from the Images menu in the Common category of the Insert bar.
The Select Image Source dialog box opens.

4) Choose ptarena_prisms.jpg from the Lesson_03_Graphics/Images folder and click Choose (Macintosh) or OK (Windows).
The Image Tag Accessibility Attributes dialog box opens, which prompts you to enter Alternate Text and a Long Description.

5) In the Alternate text field type *Prisms*. **Leave the Long Description field as is and click OK.**

TIP *You can click the Cancel button on the Image Tag Accessibility Attributes dialog box if the image accessibility option is turned on but you want to bypass it.*

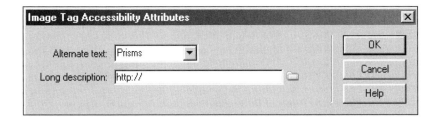

The Alt text field on the Property inspector displays "Prisms."

Long descriptions are not displayed on the Property inspector. Because you did not define a long description for this image, no tag has been created for it. A long description is usually text-based content that serves as a substitute for its respective image. Long descriptions are used by those who can't view images and are using an alternative method of accessing the page, such as a screen reader. It is meant to be longer and more definitive than the Alt text. For full accessibility, you should create long descriptions whenever the Alt text does not adequately and completely serve to stand in for the visual element.

NOTE *You can set a default folder for your images in the Local Info category of the Advanced tab on the Site Definition dialog box. If you choose a folder, Dreamweaver opens the Select Image Source dialog box to the directory you choose. You are not limited to storing only images in that folder; it simply becomes the default location for images that you import into your site.*

6) Choose Dreamweaver > Preferences (Macintosh) or Edit > Preferences (Windows). In the Accessibility category, uncheck the box for images. Click OK to close the Preferences dialog box. Save and close the document.

The accessibility option for images is turned off.

USING THE IMAGE VIEWER

Flash Elements are a new feature in Dreamweaver MX 2004 that enable you to quickly add interactivity to your pages. The Image Viewer Flash Element creates a slide show interface that you can use to present a series of images. This interactive presentation format, which can be configured easily within Dreamweaver, gives you a variety of options including the ability to set captions and links for each image in the slide show.

NOTE *The Image Viewer is the only Flash Element that Dreamweaver MX 2004 initially contains. Additional Flash Elements may be created in the future by Macromedia or third-party developers and made available through the Dreamweaver Exchange. You'll learn more about extending Dreamweaver in Lesson 17.*

105

1) Open lightshow.htm from the Lesson_03_Graphics folder. Choose the Flash Elements category on the Insert bar and click the Image Viewer button.

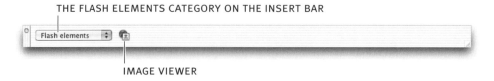

THE FLASH ELEMENTS CATEGORY ON THE INSERT BAR

IMAGE VIEWER

The Save Flash Element dialog box opens.

2) Type *lightshow* into the Save as text field and save the file into the Lesson_03_Graphics folder.

The Image Viewer Flash Element file is saved and Dreamweaver automatically adds the required .swf extension.

The Image Viewer appears in the document window as a large gray placeholder with the Flash icon in the center.

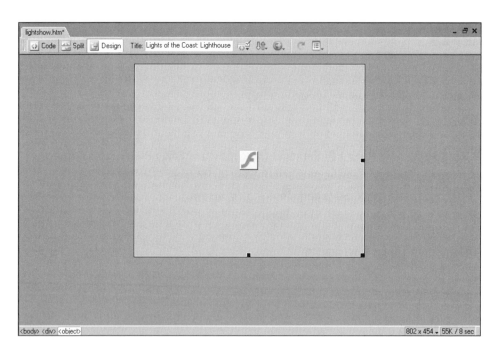

3) Click the Play button on the Property inspector.

THE ATTRIBUTES OF THE IMAGE VIEWER ON THE PROPERTY INSPECTOR

The Image Viewer now appears in the document window with default settings. A control bar is located at the top of the Image Viewer, which contains a blank area to the left for a title; a text field that displays the number of the current image and allows the user to type in a number and jump to a different image; and three buttons—Back, Play/Stop, and Forward. Below the control bar is the image area.

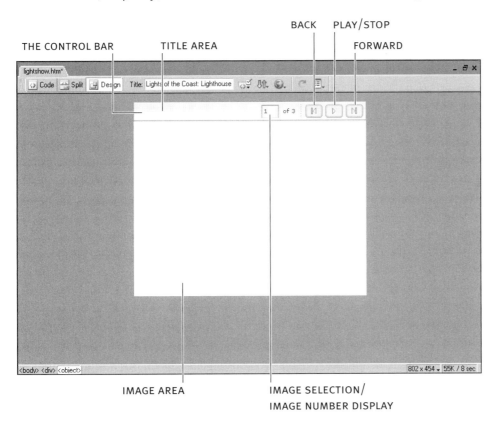

BACK   PLAY/STOP

FORWARD

THE CONTROL BAR   TITLE AREA

IMAGE AREA   IMAGE SELECTION/
IMAGE NUMBER DISPLAY

4) In the Tag inspector, click the Color picker for frameColor and choose the #666666 gray.

You will do the majority of the configuration for the Image Viewer in the Tag inspector. The Tag inspector opens automatically when the Image Viewer is inserted and displays the initial default settings for this Flash Element. When the Image Viewer is selected the title of the Tag inspector panel will be Tag <object>.

TIP *If the Tag inspector is collapsed, click the Expand/Collapse button to the left of the name to expand it. If you do not see the Tag inspector, choose Window > Tag Inspector.*

TAG INSPECTOR PANEL GROUP

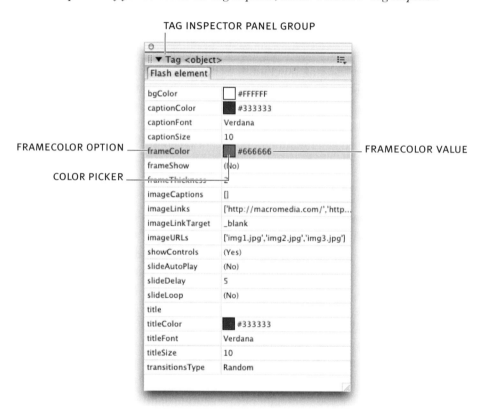

The frameColor option determines the color of the border that outlines the Image Viewer. The control bar uses several different shades of gray, and the #666666 gray color matches the darker shades. After you select a color the Flash Element may automatically switch back to the placeholder image in the document window. In the following steps you'll continue to configure the Image Viewer before making it visible in the document window again.

108

5) In the Tag inspector, click the (No) value for the frameShow option to make menu buttons available. Click the menu that appears and select (Yes).

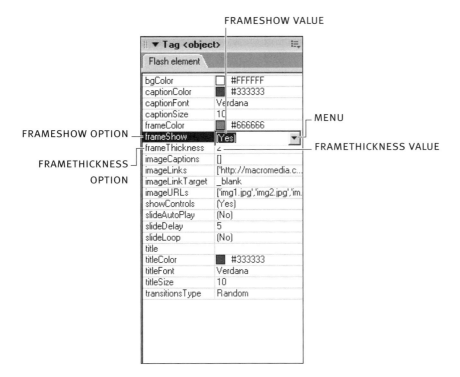

FRAMESHOW VALUE

FRAMESHOW OPTION

MENU

FRAMETHICKNESS OPTION

FRAMETHICKNESS VALUE

The frameShow option turns the border option on for the Image Viewer.

6) In the Tag inspector, click the value field for frameThickness and change it to *1*; then press Return (Macintosh) or Enter (Windows) to apply the change. Click the Play button on the Property inspector to see the Image Viewer again in the document window.

The border is now set to a width of one pixel and you can see the gray outline around the Image Viewer.

The background color of the Image Viewer, defined by the bgColor option in the Tag inspector, is set to white by default. You should leave the background color set to white for this exercise.

7) Click the value field for the imageURLs option in the Tag inspector; then click the Edit Array Values button that appears at the right of the text field.

The imageURLs option defines the images that the Image Viewer will contain. You need to use this option to specify the location of the images.

NOTE *A series of values in Flash Elements is called an array. The Image Viewer uses arrays for the image, caption and URL options.*

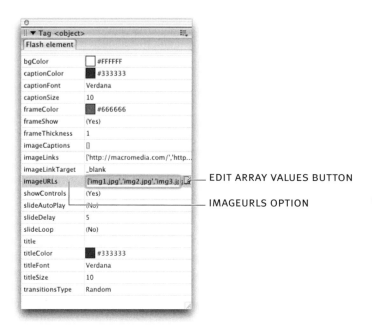

EDIT ARRAY VALUES BUTTON

IMAGEURLS OPTION

The Edit 'imageURLs' Array dialog box opens with three default images defined. Because there are no images with these file names in the Lights of the Coast project site, these default images are not functional.

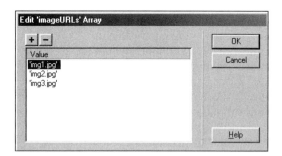

8) Select the first image in the list and click the folder that appears to the right of it. Use the Select File dialog box to browse to the Lesson_03_Graphics/Images folder and select arena_photo.jpg.

The values, which are the paths to the images, will be contained in single quotes—these quotes must be included for the Image Viewer to work properly.

9) Repeat step 8 to replace the second and third default image values with the bonita_photo.jpg and bridge_photo.jpg images. Click the plus (+) button to another value field and select the fort_photo.jpg image. Continue to add additional value fields and set their sources to montara_photo.jpg, pigeon_photo.jpg, and reyes_photo.jpg. Click OK to close the Edit 'imageURLs' Array dialog box.

TIP *You can also press the Tab key to create add another item to the list when the insertion point is in the last value.*

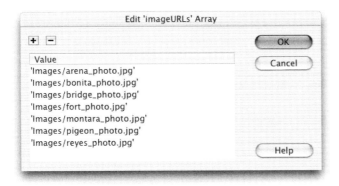

You now have seven images defined in the Image Viewer.

10) Click the value field for the imageCaptions option in the Tag inspector; then click the Edit Array Values button that appears at the right of the text field. Type *"Point Arena"* **in the Value text field. Press Tab or use the plus (+) button to insert additional value fields while adding the following captions:** *"Point Bonita"*, *"Golden Gate Bridge"*, *"Fort Point"*, *"Point Montara"*, *"Pigeon Point"*, *"Point Reyes"*. **Click OK.**

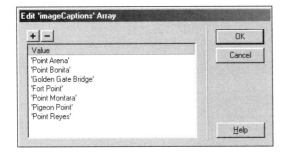

Similar to the image values, the captions must contained in single quotes for the Image Viewer to work properly.

When creating captions you need to add caption text in the same order that the images were added. If your image and captions are not listed in the same order, your captions may not match up correctly with their corresponding images.

NOTE *You can control the color, font face and size of the captions using the captionColor, captionFont, and captionSize options on the Tag inspector, respectively. For this exercise you should leave the caption formatting options at their default settings.*

11) Click the value field for the title option in the Tag inspector; then type *Lighthouses* **into the text field and press Return (Macintosh) or Enter (Windows). Click the Play button on the Property inspector to see the Image Viewer again in the document window.**

The title is placed in the space on the left of the control bar.

NOTE *You can control the color, font face and size of the title using the titleColor, titleFont, and titleSize options on the Tag inspector, respectively. For this exercise you should leave the title formatting options at their default settings.*

By default, the transitions between images are set to Random. You can modify the transition effect and choose a single transition by clicking the transitionsType value text field and choosing an option from the menu. Leaving the transition value set to Random for this exercise will allow you to see the different transition effects when you preview the page in a browser or use the control bar buttons to view the images in Dreamweaver.

Your document should now look similar to the following example.

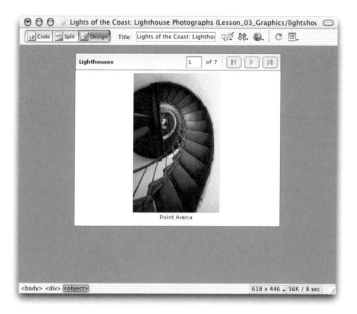

112

> **NOTE** *Also by default, the first three images are linked to http://macromedia.com. You can add, change or remove links by clicking the imageLinks value text field and then clicking the Edit Array Values button. The Edit 'imageLinks' Array dialog box is similar to the ones you used to set the images and captions. Each URL must be contained by single quotes. Just like when adding captions, you need to take care to add links in the same order of the images so that the links correspond with the appropriate images. Targets define where the links will be opened and can be set through the imageLinkTarget option, the default is _blank which causes the links to open in a new window. Links are covered in Lesson 4.*

12) Use the Property inspector to change the width of the Image Viewer by typing *300* into the W text field. Press Return (Macintosh) or Enter (Windows) to apply the change.

The size of the Image Viewer in the document window is reduced.

13) Click off of the Image Viewer in the document window to deselect it. Save the document, preview it in the browser, and test the Image Viewer.
You must deselect the Image Viewer to save the document. You can close the lightshow.htm document when you are done viewing it in the browser.

USING THE WEB PHOTO ALBUM

Dreamweaver also provides a feature that creates a Web Photo Album from a folder of images. This provides you with a quick way to take a folder of images and batch process thumbnails and large images for use on a Web site—without altering the original images. The Web Photo Album creates a page that contains thumbnails and links to larger copies of the images. To use this command, you must have Fireworks installed on your computer. A trial version of Fireworks MX 2004 is included on the CD-ROM that accompanies this book.

To create a Web Photo Album, open a new HTML document. Although Dreamweaver will not use this page in creating your Web Photo Album, it is necessary to have a document open in order to access the Web Photo Album command. Choose Commands > Create Web Photo Album. In the Create Web Photo Album dialog box, type Lighthouses in the Photo album title text field—a title is required but you can leave the Subheading info and Other info text fields blank. Click the Browse button to the right of the Source image folder text field and Choose (Macintosh) or Select (Windows) the lights_photos folder, which is located at: Lesson_03_Graphics/Images/lights_photos. Click the Browse button to the right of the Destination folder text field and Choose (Macintosh) or Select (Windows) the light_album folder located in the Lesson_03_Graphics folder. The light_album folder is currently an empty folder, when you are done it will contain all files related to your Web Photo Album. The Thumbnail size menu gives you a choice between 5 preset sizes; the default size is 100x100. Your source images do not have to be square—nor will they be resized into a square. When you have a series of images of varying sizes, as is the case with the photographs in the lights_photos folder, the largest dimension will be set to the size selected in the Thumbnail size menu and the other dimension will be sized proportionately. The Show filenames option, which is checked by default, will show the image filenames beneath the thumbnails. When the Web Photo Album is created, the thumbnails (and corresponding filenames if you selected that option) will be arranged in a table. The Columns option lets you choose how many columns will be used. The Thumbnail format and Photo format menus let you choose how the images will be saved. The JPEG format is recommended for photographs, although when the size is below 100 pixels the GIF format often achieves better results in file size and image quality—even for photographic images. If you choose to use a very small thumbnail size you may wish to use the GIF format. The Scale option only applies to the large versions of the photographs and allows you to adjust their sizes in relation to the originals. If you want those large versions of each photograph to be placed into their own HTML documents, leave the Create navigation page for each photo turned on.

After you are done adjusting the Web Photo Album options, click OK. Fireworks will open automatically (if you are using a trial version, you may have to click the Try button), and begin the batch process. Let Fireworks continue uninterrupted. After the image processing is done, Dreamweaver will display an alert: Album created. Click OK and the index page containing your Web Photo Album will open automatically.

Dreamweaver places all of the resulting files in the light_album folder that you specified. Those files includ: an images folder that contains large versions of the photographs; a thumbnails folder that contains the thumbnail versions of the photographs; an index.htm page that contains the table of thumbnails and links; and—if the Create navigation page for each photo option was checked—a folder called pages that contains an HTML file for each large image with Previous, Home and Next links. Your original folder of photographs is unchanged. Preview your new photo album page in the browser and test it. You may want to use CSS (covered in Lesson 6) to control the format and appearance of the resulting pages. You can use the Find and Replace feature (covered in Lesson 15) to quickly affect all of the Web Photo Album files. You can also apply site layout and navigation by applying a Template to the files (Templates are covered in Lesson 8).

EMBEDDING QUICKTIME MOVIES

QuickTime is a popular, widely used format for video on the Web that is available for both Macintosh and Windows. QuickTime movies can be straightforward videos, or they can include interactive elements including Flash and JavaScript. In this exercise you'll insert an interactive QTVR (QuickTime Virtual Reality) movie: a 360° panorama of Point Cabrillo Lighthouse. You can insert QuickTime movies as easily as you can insert Flash movies.

1) Open cabrillo.htm from the Lesson_03_Graphics folder and place the insertion point on the blank line below the Point Cabrillo header. Select the Common category on the insert bar, click the Media menu, and choose the Plugin option.

Dreamweaver treats QuickTime movies as plug-ins.

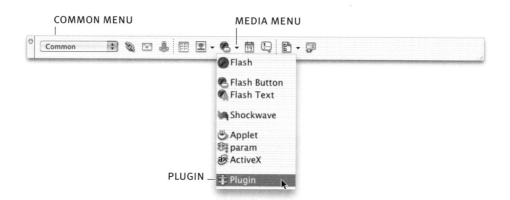

The Select File dialog box opens, enabling you to choose the plug-in.

2) Locate the file Lesson_03_Graphics/Images/cabrillo.mov and click Choose (Macintosh) or OK (Windows) to select it.

The plug-in is embedded into the page using the <embed> tag, at a default size of 32x32 pixels and appears in the document window as a gray square with a plug-in icon in the center.

3) With the plug-in selected, use the Property inspector to change the width to 320 and the height to 256.

116

The standard dimensions of small QuickTime Web movies that are made for the Web are 320 pixels wide by 240 pixels tall. The QuickTime controller is 16 pixels tall, so you need to add 16 pixels to the height of the movie. Sometimes when you insert movies, they may appear cropped or the controller may seem to be missing. In these cases, try enlarging the amount of space allotted to the movie by increasing the width and height. When inserting your own movies, be sure to obtain the correct dimensions of the movie and add an additional 16 pixels for the controller.

4) With the plug-in selected, click the Parameters button on the Property inspector.
The Parameters dialog box opens.

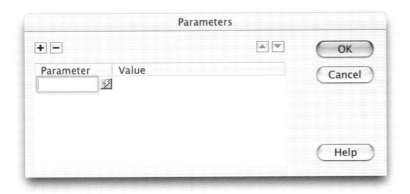

5) Click in the Parameter column and type *controller* **into the text field. Macintosh users should press Tab once; Windows users should press Tab twice. Type** *true* **and click OK.**

Parameters define the properties of the movies. Specifying a controller parameter with the value as true will include the QuickTime controller beneath the movie. You can set the value to either true or false. In the case of the controller, true will turn the controller on while false will turn it off. If you do not specify the controller parameter with a value of true, your visitors may not see a controller.

TIP *Another parameter that you can set is autoplay, which will define whether your movies start after the page is loaded or are dependent upon the visitor pressing Play. To define this parameter, you would need to add an item to the Parameters list, type autoplay in the parameter text field and type either true or false into the corresponding value text field.*

6) Click in the document window outside the plug-in to deselect it. On a new line below the plug-in type *Click in the image and drag to see the panoramic view.* **Create a line break and type** *Press Shift to zoom in, Control to zoom out.*

It's always a good idea to let your visitors know how to use the materials that you include on your Web site. The default text for this page has already been set to a light gray.

You can click the Play button on the Property inspector to view the movie in the Dreamweaver document window, or you can preview the page in the browser. You must have the QuickTime player installed on your machine to view QuickTime movies. You can obtain the free QuickTime player at Apple's Web site: http://www.apple.com/quicktime

You can save and close the cabrillo.htm file.

NOTE *An extension called fiXMovie, available on the Dreamweaver Exchange Web site, makes the process of inserting QuickTime movies even easier and fixes an issue with QuickTime movies in older versions of Explorer. You'll learn more about extending Dreamweaver in Lesson 17.*

WHAT YOU HAVE LEARNED

In this lesson, you have:

- Placed JPEG and GIF images on the page (pages 71–76)
- Resized images and reset them to their original dimensions (pages 76–78)
- Positioned images (pages 78–79)
- Added a border around an image (page 79)
- Assigned names and <alt> tags to images (pages 80–81)
- Used the Assets panel to manage images in the site (pages 81–87)
- Wrapped text around images (pages 88–89)
- Adjusted the space around images (page 89)
- Inserted an image placeholder (pages 90–93)
- Cropped an image (pages 94–95)
- Adjusted the brightness and contrast of an image (pages 95–96)
- Aligned images relative to text (pages 96–97)
- Added and modified Flash buttons (pages 98–101)
- Added Flash animations (pages 101–103)
- Inserted images with accessibility options (pages 103–105)
- Used the Image Viewer to create a slideshow (pages 105–113)
- Incorporated a QuickTime Movie on your page (pages 115–118)

creating links

LESSON 4

The power of HTML (Hypertext Markup Language) comes from its capability to connect text and images with other documents through links that are not sequential or linear. The browser may highlight these regions (usually with color or underlines) to indicate that they are links.

A link in HTML has two parts: the name and path (or URL—Uniform Resource Locator) of the file to which you want to link and the text or graphic that serves as the clickable area. When the user clicks a link, the browser jumps to the linked document. In some browsers, the path of the link is displayed in the status area of the browser window (located in the lower left part of the window) when the pointer is positioned over the link. Links can direct the user to other HTML files, images and other media, and downloadable files.

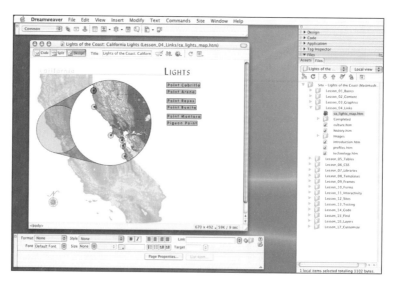

In this project, you will create text and graphic links to pages within this site as well as to other Web sites.

To see an example of the finished pages, open Lesson_04_Links/Completed/intro.htm for the text and graphic links, profiles.htm for the named anchors, and ca_lights_map.htm for the image map.

WHAT YOU WILL LEARN

In this lesson, you will:

- Specify link colors according to the link state
- Create text and graphic links
- Use anchors to jump to different parts of the page
- Create image maps to set multiple links in the same image
- Create email links

APPROXIMATE TIME

This lesson should take about one hour to complete.

LESSON FILES

Media Files:

Lesson_04_Links/Images/bkg_inside_tan.gif
Lesson_04_Links/Images/light_resources.gif
Lesson_04_Links/Images/more_lights.gif
Lesson_04_Links/Images/CAmap_full.gif

Starting Files:

Lesson_04_Links/intro.htm
Lesson_04_Links/profiles.htm
Lesson_04_Links/ca_lights_map.htm

Completed Project:

Lesson_04_Links/Completed/introduction.htm
Lesson_04_Links/Completed/profiles.htm
Lesson_04_Links/Completed/ca_lights_map.htm
Lesson_04_Links/Completed/culture.htm
Lesson_04_Links/Completed/history.htm
Lesson_04_Links/Completed/technology.htm

SPECIFYING LINK COLOR AND FORMAT

You can specify the default color of text links on your page to be consistent with the set of colors you have chosen to use in your document. The colors you select should contrast (but not clash) with the background so the links can be read clearly. Choosing a link color that stands out from the regular body text in the document enables viewers to spot the links easily. The default link properties for your document are specified through the Page Properties dialog box.

NOTE *Dreamweaver controls the appearance of links through the use of Cascading Style Sheets (CSS) to set color, font face, and font size properties that apply only to links. A CSS link style is known as a* **pseudoclass**, *which is a type of style that is applied in only specific circumstances such as links. CSS is covered in Lesson 6.*

1) Open the introduction.htm document, located in the Lesson_04_Links folder. Choose Modify > Page Properties and select the Links category.

For this exercise, you should leave the Link Font on the default selection (Same as Page Font). With this setting, the links on your page inherit the properties of the styles that have already been set for your document.

NOTE *If you have used a different style for the text in which a link is located, the link inherits the properties of that style instead of the default document styles.*

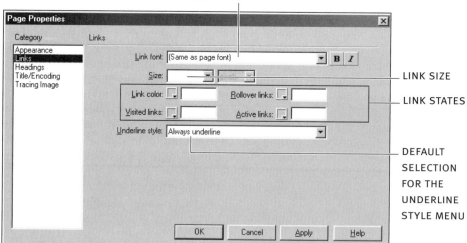

There are different states of a link, such as links that haven't been clicked and those that have. You can apply formatting for each state of a link. You have the option to define colors for up to four different link states based on a user's actions.

NOTE *CSS link styles control the link tag (<a>) with specific attributes for the different states that can be applied to it. The different states of the <a> tag are activated when a user performs an action such as clicking the link.*

Link Color: The initial color of a link, prior to the link being clicked. The standard default browser color for a link is blue. (This state is defined by the CSS selector a:link.)

Visited Links: The color that a link changes to when a user clicks the link. The standard default browser color for a visited link is purple. (This state is defined by the CSS selector a:visited.)

Rollover Links: The color to which a link changes as a user pauses the pointer over the link. This serves as an additional indicator that the item is clickable. No rollover is used if this is left blank. (This state is defined by the CSS selector a:hover.)

Active Links: The color of the link when the mouse is being pressed on it. Active links can serve as an interactive indicator to the visitor that the link is being clicked, although as a result of the growing speed with which users access the Web, the Active link is no longer as prominent as it used to be. No active color is used if it is left blank. (This state is defined by the CSS selector a:active.)

2) Use the text fields next to the color boxes to select the colors for your links by typing in *#333366* **for the Link color,** *#3333FF* **for the Rollover Links color,** *#333333* **for the Visited Links color and** *#333366* **for the Active Links color.**

When you know the hexadecimal values of your colors, you can enter the numbers directly in these text fields. Dreamweaver automatically fills in the color box with the matching color swatch. On the other hand, if you choose a color swatch from the palette, Dreamweaver automatically fills in the text field with the hexadecimal value. You can click the color box to bring up the palette, as you did in Lesson 2, and the hexadecimal value displays at the top of the palette as you roll over the color swatches. As always, you can use the color picker to select any color on the page by mousing over the page and clicking to select the color. This allows you to easily match existing colors.

Consider the standard link colors when you select the colors for your link. It may be confusing for visitors if, for example, you decide to use a purple similar to the visited link color as your standard link color. Taking what have become standard Web conventions into consideration, and understanding what your viewers' expectations are, is important when designing your site.

The number sign (#), also known as a pound sign, indicates that what follows is a hexadecimal value and not a named color (such as black, white, red, and so on).

TIP *You can type any valid color name into the text fields, and Dreamweaver displays the corresponding color swatch. Although color names are a quick way to specify color, they are not as specific as hexadecimal values. Although Dreamweaver uses the standard color values associated with color names, hexadecimal values are a more accurate way to define your colors.*

Although Dreamweaver accepts a value without the number sign, it is best to include it. When you use the color box to select a swatch, notice that the number sign is included.

The last option in the Links section of the Page Properties dialog box is to define the Underline style to be used on your page. For this exercise, you should leave the menu selection on the default, Always Underline. The other options in this menu are Never underline, Show underline only on rollover, and Hide underline on rollover. You can use the Never underline option to remove the default underline that appears on all links; however, remember to consider the expectations of your visitors when creating Web sites. Many users have become accustomed to the conventional underlined appearance of links. If you remove the underlines, your users might overlook the links and miss the information. Conversely, if you underline other words in your text, users might try to click them, expecting links.

3) Click OK to close the Page Properties dialog box and return to your document. Save the introduction.htm file.

The default link colors for your page are now the colors you specified. You will see the colors after you begin to create links.

Keep the document introduction.htm open. It contains all the text and graphics you need to create links in the following exercises.

CREATING HYPERTEXT LINKS

Hypertext links give you the ability to direct the visitor to other documents within your Web site or to any other page on the Web. Links made within the same site are called **relative links**. Relative links may connect to files in any number of locations within the folder structure of a single site. There are a variety of ways to create such a link. The following exercise demonstrates these methods.

Remember that it is important to save new documents before you create any links. This tells Dreamweaver where your document is and allows it to determine the link paths. Dreamweaver needs to determine the location of the linked file in relation to your hard drive. If you try to create a link without saving your document for the first time, these paths begin with file:// and they do not work on remote sites. Although Dreamweaver updates the links when you do save, it is better to avoid the chance of problematic paths.

1) In the introduction.htm document window, select the word "History" in the first line of the bullet list near the top of the page.

You will create a link from this term to a page concerning the history of lighthouses.

When creating sites, choose the language that you use to indicate links carefully. Avoid using the phrase "click here" because it is unclear and can cause multiple problems including navigational difficulties. For example, visitors with vision disabilities may not be able to distinguish the links and may have a particularly hard time navigating as a result. In addition, when users skim pages looking for links of interest, they usually watch for the underlines that indicate links. Finding "click here" instead of a clear description can make this process more difficult. Always be specific when creating phrases that contain links. For example, when directing readers to a document in which they can learn about the history of lighthouses, you might want to use "learn more about lighthouse history" (where "lighthouse history" is linked) in which the actual link is more descriptive and informative instead of "click here to learn more about lighthouse history" (where "click here" is linked). Bullet lists with specific terms such as the one you are using in this exercise also serve the need for clarity and can work for links.

2) In the Property inspector, click the Browse for File button to the right of the Link text field.

The Select File dialog box opens.

3) Select the history.htm file in the Lesson_04_Links folder, and click Choose (Macintosh) or OK (Windows).

The filename history.htm appears in the Link text field, and the text you selected in the document is marked as a link. The link is underlined and appears in the color you chose for your links in the first exercise of this lesson.

NOTE *You can easily override the page's default link color for individual links by selecting the text that is linked and choosing a color from the Property inspector. Dreamweaver automatically creates a new style for that color.*

This link is an example of a document-relative path, which is the best option to use for local links in most Web sites and the type that is used throughout this book. A **document-relative path** omits the part of the absolute URL that is the same for the current document and the linked document, leaving only the portion of the path that differs. The path to the linked document is determined in relation to the location of the document as the starting point. A path to a file in the same folder, for example, is expressed as name_of_file.htm. A path to a file in a subfolder would look like 'name_of_folder/name_of_file.htm.

On the other hand, a **site root-relative path** is determined in relation to the root folder of the site as the starting point and has no bearing on where the current document is located. The linked document is specified according to its location within the structure of the site.

4) Repeat steps 1 through 3 to link the word "Technological" in the next line of the bulleted list to technology.htm, and the word "culture" in the last line of the bulleted list to culture.htm.

When you know the names of the files, you can type them directly in the Link text box instead of browsing to find them, however, letting Dreamweaver write the links will reduce the chance of typos.

TIP *If you need to use the same links multiple times, you can save time by choosing recently used links from the menu to the right of the Link text field on the Property inspector.*

Editing the destination of a link is a simple process: Click anywhere inside an existing link and make the desired changes to the value in the link text field on the Property inspector. You do not need to select the entire link because Dreamweaver prevents links from becoming nested—a link can't be placed inside of another link. Text that you choose to apply a link to is defined by the HTML tags that surround or contain it; therefore, any change you make to the link is automatically applied to all the text contained within the link (between the opening and closing portions of the <a> tag that denotes links of all types). You'll learn more about HTML tags in Lesson 14.

5) Save the file and preview it in the browser.

The three links you just created should take you to the corresponding pages. Always test your links to be sure they go to the correct locations!

TIP *You can preview your document in the browser by pressing the F12 key to open a window of the primary browser that you defined in Lesson 1.*

UNDERSTANDING LINKS AND FILE STRUCTURE

The links that you create depend on the file and folder structure of your site. It is good to understand how the paths work when creating links. The following illustration is an example of a possible site structure.

ROOT FOLDER

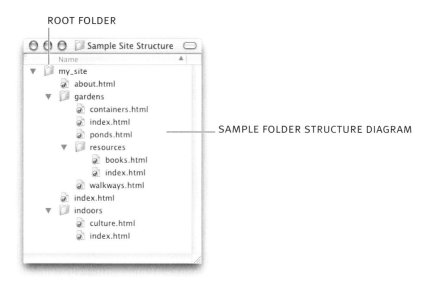

SAMPLE FOLDER STRUCTURE DIAGRAM

You may notice when you create a link to any document that exists above the folder in which the current document is located, the path for the link will include the characters **../** preceding the filename. ../ is a command that tells the browser to go up one folder level from the current location. Each instance of ../ indicates moving up one folder level; you may have something similar to ../../filename.html to link to a document that is located two folder levels above the current directory. For instance, in the previous example, the path of a link from the books.html page to the about.html page would be ../../about.html. You do not need to use the ../ characters unless you are inserting links by typing them directly into the link text field. If you are not sure of the proper path, you should browse to select the desired file. Dreamweaver determines the appropriate path for you.

You'll also notice that there are multiple index.html files in the preceding sample site structure. The filename **index** is a standard name for the default file of a folder or directory on many servers. These default files do not need to be specified in the URL. The visitor is automatically taken to the default file of a folder if no file is specified. In the previous example, a user could simply type the domain name followed by /gardens to get to the index page inside of the gardens folder. Other common names for default files include default.html and home.html. Many types of extensions can be used, but your server may need to be configured to recognize index files with extensions other than .html or .htm.

When you link to a document that exists in the same folder as the current document, the path for the link will be the name of the linked document. When you link to a document that exists in a folder inside the one in which the current document is located, the path for the link includes **foldername/** preceding the filename. foldername/ tells the browser to look in the specified folder, and that folder is located inside of the current directory.

As you develop your site, you may find it necessary to move files or even entire folders to different locations. Using the preceding example, suppose you move containers.html into the indoors folder. Any links or other paths that are included in the containers.html document need to be updated, as do any links from other files to that document. If those paths are not updated, the paths are "broken"—links and images no longer work. As you move files, Dreamweaver automatically updates the paths for all links, images, and other media in your site as long as you make all changes within the Dreamweaver Files panel. If you make any changes outside of Dreamweaver, such as through the Macintosh Finder or Windows Explorer, Dreamweaver has no way to track or maintain your files. You'll work more with site structure in Lesson 12.

CREATING GRAPHIC LINKS

You can also use images to link to documents within your site, as well as to sites other than your own. This exercise shows you how to create an external link. You can use the same techniques you used in the preceding exercise to link images to files on your site.

1) Below the list of notable lighthouses in the introduction.htm document, click the Lighthouse Resources graphic to select it. Type *links.htm* **in the Property inspector's Link text field.**

This link is a relative path, just like the text links you created to history.htm, technology.htm, and culture.htm in the previous exercise. You can use graphics to provide links just as easily as text.

The links.htm files does not exist in the Lesson_04_Links folder. You can use this method to insert links for pages that have not yet been created.

2) Below the graphic you just linked, click the More Lighthouses graphic to select it and type *http://www.pbs.org/legendarylighthouses/index.html* **in the Property inspector's Link text field. You must type the complete URL.**

LINK TEXT FIELD

This link is an **absolute path**, which provides the complete URL of the linked document, usually located on a different Web site. You must use an absolute path to link to a document that is located outside of your local file structure or to anything that is outside of the root folder. An absolute link begins with http:// (HyperText Transfer Protocol) to indicate that the user is connecting to a Web server. The remainder of the absolute link specifies the address of the linked site. All links to documents that exist on external Web sites are absolute links.

TIP *If a URL is long or complex, you can go to that site in your browser, copy the URL, and then paste it into the Link text field.*

3) Save the file, and preview it in the browser.

Notice that when you roll over the graphics at the bottom of the page, you see the hand indicating that they are linked. The link locations will appear in the browser's status bar as you roll over the links.

NOTE *When you attach a link to an image, if you have not specified the image border in the Property inspector, Dreamweaver applies a default border of 0 pixels. If you do define a border, the color is the same as your page's default link color. You can change the color of the border by using CSS. You work with CSS in Lesson 6.*

TARGETING LINKS

Whenever a user clicks on a link, the linked page usually replaces the current browser page. This is the standard link function, which has been used for all links in this lesson up until this point. The instruction to a browser in regards to where the link will appear is known as the **target**. There are a number of different targets that you can use with your links. At times, you may want to display the new browser page in a different window. If you link to a site outside your site, for example, you may be leading users out of your site if the new site replaces yours in the browser window. If users haven't bookmarked your URL, they might not remember how to return to your site. When an outside link opens a new browser window, the original page remains in the first window.

1) In the introduction.htm document, select the More Lighthouses graphic. From the Property inspector's Target menu, choose _blank.

_BLANK SELECTED FROM THE TARGET MENU

Dreamweaver provides you with a number of target options to change where the linked page is to be displayed. Targets other than _blank are used with frames. You will learn about frames in Lesson 9. The additional targets are as follows:

- **_blank:** Loads the linked document into a new unnamed browser window.
- **_parent:** Loads the linked document into the parent frameset or window of the frame that contains the link.
- **_self:** Loads the linked document into the same frame or window as the link. This target is the same as the default, so you usually don't have to specify it.
- **_top:** Loads the linked document into the full browser window, thereby removing all frames.

2) Save the file and preview it in the browser.

When you click the lower graphic, the linked page opens in a new browser window. You can close this file.

NOTE *Be careful when using link targets to open new browser windows. Each new window can increase the RAM requirements on the user's computer. Besides taxing a machine's memory resources, multiple windows may annoy or confuse your visitors.*

INSERTING AND LINKING TO NAMED ANCHORS

When a document is long or has many sections, you may need to create a series of links that will jump the user to specific places within the document. This technique eliminates the need for the viewer to scroll through long passages of text. A **named anchor** marks the place in the page to which a link jumps. In this exercise, you insert and link to a named anchor. You also learn another method of selecting link files using the Point To File icon.

1) Open profiles.htm from the Lesson_04_Links folder. Choose Modify > Page Properties and select the Links category of the Page Properties dialog box. Set the same default link colors that you used for the intro.htm document in this lesson's first exercise.

Recall the links color's hexadecimal value was #333366,, the rollover links color was #3333FF, the visited-links value was #333333, and the active links color was #333366.

TIP *Keep your link colors the same throughout your site. Randomly changing link colors can be confusing for visitors.*

This file contains a large amount of text that requires the visitor to scroll to see the entire document.

2) Position the insertion point before the text "Name: Pigeon Point Light" at the bottom of the document. Click the Named Anchor button in the Common category of the Insert bar.

NAMED ANCHOR

The Insert Named Anchor dialog box opens.

TIP *You can also insert a named anchor by choosing Insert > Named Anchor, or by using the keyboard commands Option+Command+A (Macintosh) or Ctrl+Alt+A (Windows).*

3) Type *pigeon* **in the Anchor name text field; then click OK.**

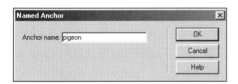

Don't use spaces, punctuation, or special characters (such as copyright symbols, number signs, and so on) in the name. There should never be more than one named anchor with the same name in the same document; otherwise, the browser cannot jump the user to the correct named anchor.

A yellow icon appears on the page to represent the named anchor. The icon may be selected when it first appears on the page—selected anchor icons are blue. This icon is an invisible element that doesn't appear in the browser.

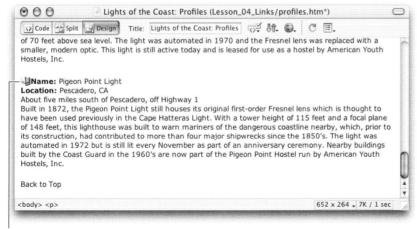

A NAMED ANCHOR ICON IN THE DOCUMENT WINDOW

131

TIP *If you can't see the Named Anchor icon, make sure that the Invisible Elements option is turned on by choosing View > Visual Aids > Invisible Elements. When you insert a named anchor, a dialog box may open to warn you that you won't see the anchor unless the Invisible Elements option is turned on. Named anchors must also be checked in the Invisible Elements category of the Preferences. You can determine which options have been turned on by choosing Edit > Preferences and selecting the Invisible Elements category. The Named anchors box should be checked. The lessons in this book assume that you are using the default configuration.*

4) Select the text "Pigeon Point" from the list of lighthouses at the top of the document.

This text will act as a navigational element by jumping the user to the corresponding section of the page. You will make this text a link that references the named anchor you created near the bottom of this page in the preceding steps.

5) Type *#pigeon* in the Link text field of the Property inspector.

LINKING TO A NAMED ANCHOR

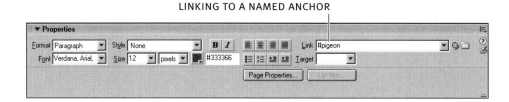

The number sign (#) is required to tell the browser that this link is internal—it takes the user to a location on the same page.

Make sure that the name you type after the number sign is exactly the same as the anchor name. You should follow the naming guidelines from Lesson 1 when you name your anchors. Named anchors are case-sensitive, even though many browsers accommodate a case change. For example, if you name your anchor "pigeon" and then type **#Pigeon** in the Link text field, your link might not work consistently in all browsers.

Pigeon Point is now linked to the Pigeon Point profile section near the bottom of the page. Now you will repeat the process for Point Cabrillo.

6) Add another named anchor before the "Name: Point Cabrillo" text and name it *cabrillo.*

You have created a second anchor.

7) Select the words "Point Cabrillo" in the list of lighthouses at the top of the document. Drag the Point to File icon (located next to the Link text field in the Property inspector) to the cabrillo named anchor you just made. Release the mouse button when the pointer is directly over the named anchor.

When you first click the Point to File tool, the Link text field initially contains instructional text that will be replaced with the link that you choose. Using the Point to File icon to create links may help prevent typing errors.

NAMED ANCHOR   SELECTED TEXT TO BE LINKED

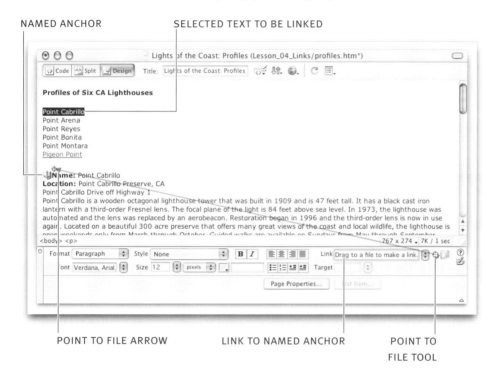

POINT TO FILE ARROW   LINK TO NAMED ANCHOR   POINT TO
                                                       FILE TOOL

8) Insert named anchors and links to them for the remaining navigational headings and their corresponding sections of the document. For the anchor names, type *arena*, *reyes*, *bonita*, **and** *montara* **for their respective lighthouses.**

You can edit the names of any anchors you create by clicking the named anchor. The Property inspector changes to show that a named anchor is selected. You can change the name in the Property inspector's Name text field.

9) Insert a named anchor at the very top of the page in front of the text "Profiles of Six California Lighthouses" and name it *top*. **Select the text "Back to Top" that is located at the bottom of the page and type** *#top* **in the Link text field on the Property inspector.**

In long documents, it is a common practice to include links at the end of every section to a named anchor at the top of the page or to a navigational table of contents. This common anchor is usually called **#top**. When you provide this type of a link, users don't need to scroll back up to the top of the page if they want to continue using those links to jump to other sections. Any number of links on the page can reference the same named anchor.

NOTE *Viewing problems, such as a link to a named anchor jumping to the wrong area or simply not working, may occur if that named anchor is located inside of a link. To avoid this problem, any attempts to move or insert a named anchor inside of a link causes Dreamweaver to automatically end the link just before the named anchor and create a second link to the same destination immediately after the named anchor (which ends at the same point where the original link ended). In these cases, the named anchor is actually sandwiched between two separate links that have an identical value. As a result, placing the cursor at the beginning of the linked text and making a change to the link value changes only the first instance of the link; you need to remember to duplicate any changes that you make to the second instance of the link that occurs after the named anchor.*

10) Save the file and preview it in the browser.

The navigational terms at the top of the page now link to their corresponding sections. You can close the profiles.htm file.

TIP *Named anchors may not work as expected if they are placed inside tables or layers. For best results, keep named anchors outside of tables and layers. You'll learn to create tables in Lesson 5 and layers in Lesson 16.*

In steps 6 and 9 of the following exercise, you will continue to use named anchors and learn how to link to a particular section in another document.

CREATING IMAGE MAPS

Earlier in this lesson, you experienced how easy it is to apply a link to an image. The user can click any part of the image to go to the linked page. You also have the option of dividing the image into several linked areas called **hotspots** by using an **image map** to place individual hotspots on the image. These hotspots are not limited to rectangles; they can have other shapes. In the following exercise, you will add a rectangular hotspot and a circular hotspot.

The example you use to create an image map in this exercise happens to be a map of California. Conceptually, image maps work quite well when applied to geographical maps; however, you can apply an image map to any image regardless of what that image represents.

1) Open ca_lights_map.htm from the Lesson_04_Links folder. Select the map graphic.

This large image is a geographical map that shows the locations of six California lighthouses and lists the names of each to the right of the map. The graphic needs to be divided into 12 hotspots: six spots for the locations and six for the names.

2) In the Property inspector, type *californiamap* **in the Map text field.**

Don't use spaces or special characters in the name. You can have several image maps on one page, but each map on that page must be uniquely named. If you fail to name your maps, Dreamweaver creates automatic sequential names for each (Map1, Map2, Map3, and so on.). Such generic names do not provide any identifying information about the image map or the graphic that it is applied to. On the other hand, the name you are using in this exercise, californiamap, suggests that the image map is a map of California. By creating your own names in the Map text field, you can use names with distinct meanings. Short, concise, and specific names serve you best.

MAP TEXT FIELD   EXPANDER ARROW

TIP *If you don't see the Map text field, click the expander arrow in the lower right corner of the Property inspector.*

3) Select the Rectangular Hotspot tool below the map name in the Property inspector. Click and drag one square around the words "Point Cabrillo" and "Point Arena."

A translucent blue-green area with handles appears around the names on that portion of the image, and the Property inspector displays the hotspot properties. Dreamweaver automatically places a null link (#) in the Property inspector's Link text field. Do not delete this character unless you immediately replace it with a link—it serves as a placeholder link to indicate that the area is clickable.

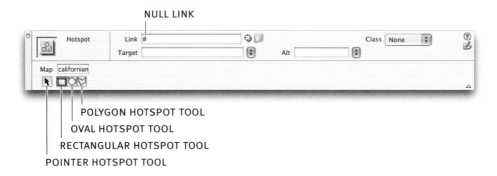

NULL LINK

POLYGON HOTSPOT TOOL
OVAL HOTSPOT TOOL
RECTANGULAR HOTSPOT TOOL
POINTER HOTSPOT TOOL

NOTE *If the client-side image maps option is enabled in the Invisible Elements category of the Preference dialog box, when you create one or more image maps, a map icon appears, usually at the bottom of the document. The map icon looks similar to the Named Anchor icon, and it is visible only in Dreamweaver—it does not appear in the browser. You can turn the visibility of the hotspot regions on and off through the View > Visual Aids menu. The Client-Side image maps option for Invisible Elements is off by default.*

4) Select the Pointer Hotspot tool below the Map text field on the Property inspector. Resize the hotspot you created in step 3 by dragging a handle until the hotspot encompasses only the name "Point Cabrillo."

The hotspots you create are easy to edit—you can resize, move, or delete them at any time.

To move the hotspot, position the pointer inside the hotspot and drag. After the hotspot is selected with the Pointer Hotspot Tool, you can also adjust the position of hotspots using the arrow keys.

Holding the Shift key down at the same time causes the arrow keys to affect the size of the hotspot.

To delete the hotspot, select it and press Delete (Macintosh) or Backspace (Windows).

5) In the Property inspector, type `Point Cabrillo` **in the Alt text field.**

The hotspot <alt> text serves a similar purpose as <alt> text for an image; it gives an indication to where this hotspot will link.

6) Type `profiles.htm#cabrillo` **in the Property inspector's Hotspot Link text field.**

136

Be sure to replace the original number sign (#) in the Link text field with the link you have typed in.

INSERTING A LINK TO ANOTHER PAGE THAT INCLUDES A NAMED ANCHOR

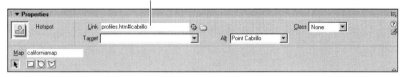

In the previous exercise, you created a named anchor in the Point Cabrillo section of the profiles.htm file. Now you are making this region of the California map graphic point directly to the Point Cabrillo section, instead of linking to the top of the page as it would if you had made the link profiles.htm. The use of anchors to link to specific portions of other pages helps your site to be more functional, directing your viewers to what they are looking for immediately and reducing the amount of time they have to spend scrolling through long documents. The more functional and easy to use your site is, the more likely it is that you will have new and repeat visitors.

NOTE *You can also create links that include named anchors to other pages using the Point to File tool, which you used in the previous exercise to create links within the same document. For example, with both profiles.htm and ca_lights_map.htm open, you can select a hotspot in ca_lights_map.htm, click the Point to File icon to the right of the Link text field, and point to the desired named anchor in profiles.htm.*

7) In the Property inspector, select the Oval Hotspot tool. In the ca_lights_map.htm document, drag a circle around the topmost target-style circular dot located on the detail of the California.

You have created a circular hotspot around Point Cabrillo. If needed, adjust the placement of the circular hotspot by using the Pointer Hotspot tool to move it or by using the arrow keys to move it after it is selected.

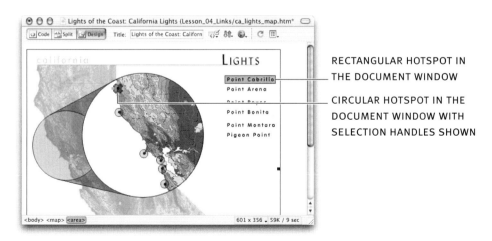

RECTANGULAR HOTSPOT IN THE DOCUMENT WINDOW

CIRCULAR HOTSPOT IN THE DOCUMENT WINDOW WITH SELECTION HANDLES SHOWN

NOTE *If two or more hotspots overlap each other, the first one you create takes precedence over any subsequent hotspots that overlap it.*

8) Type `Point Cabrillo` **into the Alt text field on the Property inspector. In the Link text field, replace the number sign (#) with** `http://www.pointcabrillo.org` **and choose _blank from the Target pop-up menu to have the link open in a new browser window.**

You have directed the circular region to open the link in a new, unnamed browser window. The hotspot must be selected to modify the link, target, or alt text.

TIP *You can also use the Polygon Hotspot tool to click multiple points around any area with a more complicated shape for which you want to create a hotspot. When you use the Polygon tool, each click creates a point. A line connects each subsequent point to the preceding point. As you click, you'll see the translucent hotspot area begin to form. You can continue clicking until you have the shape you want. You do not need to "close" the shape by clicking back on the original point. The more points that a polygon shape uses to define the hotspots, the more code is necessary in the document to describe those areas.*

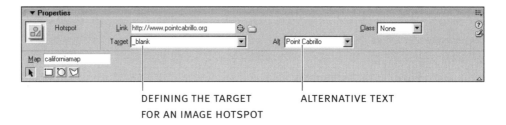

DEFINING THE TARGET   ALTERNATIVE TEXT
FOR AN IMAGE HOTSPOT

When you finish working with the image map, you can use the Pointer Hotspot Tool to click outside the hotspot to another area of the image. Clicking outside the image map on to a different portion of the image resets the Property inspector to display image properties.

9) Use the Rectangular Hotspot tool to create clickable areas for the five remaining lighthouse names, displayed to the right of the map. Apply the following attributes for each lighthouse:

For Point Arena: Alt text—`Point Arena;` link—profiles.htm#arena

For Point Reyes: Alt text—`Point Reyes;` link—profiles.htm#reyes

For Point Bonita: Alt text—`Point Bonita;` link—profiles.htm#bonita

For Point Montara: Alt text—`Point Montara;` link—profiles.htm#montara

For Pigeon Point: Alt text—`Pigeon Point;` link—profiles.htm#pigeon

Remember to replace the original number signs (#) in the link text fields with the links given previously. If you leave the original number sign in, the link does not work. You must, however, include the number signs that are in the links themselves.

Each lighthouse name now links to a corresponding section of the profiles.htm document.

TIP *You can hold down the Shift key while using the Rectangular Hotspot tool to constrain the proportions to a square.*

10) Save the file and preview it in the browser.
Test the links on the image map you have created. You can close the ca_lights_map.htm document.

NOTE *If you copy an image map and paste it into another document, Dreamweaver retains the links and hotspots.*

INSERTING EMAIL LINKS

Providing a linked email address makes it easy for your visitors to contact you from a Web page. You should always include some method of contact that allows visitors to correspond or interact with someone in your organization. There are two ways to insert an email link in Dreamweaver. You can either insert both the text and the email address for the link at the same time, or you can add a link to text that already exists on the page. You learn to do both in this exercise.

1) Open introduction.htm. Click at the beginning of the sentence "Some of the world's most notable lighthouses include:" and press Return (Macintosh) or Enter (Windows) to create a blank paragraph below the definition of Keeper. Place the cursor on the new paragraph line that was created.
You will insert an email link here, below the definition list for lighthouse components.

2) Click the Email Link button in the Common category of the Insert bar, or choose Insert > Email Link.

EMAIL LINK

NOTE *The Insert bar should be open by default. If it is not visible, choose Window > Insert to open the panel or Window > Arrange Panels to reset the panels to their default positions.*

The Insert Email Link dialog box appears, displaying options for text and email.

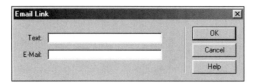

3) In the Text text field, type *Suggest more lighthouse terms*. **In the Email text field type your email address; then click OK.**

The text appears on the page as a link. The Property inspector shows the email address in the Link text field when you place the insertion point within the link.

4) At the bottom of the document, select the text "Lights of the Coast" located to the right of the © symbol.

If you select text that is already on the page and then open the Insert Email Link dialog, the selected text appears in the Text text box.

Contact information commonly appears at the bottom of a page, often near copyright information.

5) In the Link text field of the Property inspector, type *mailto:* **immediately followed by your email address. Make sure that you type the colon and do not leave a space between the colon and your email address.**

INSERTING AN EMAIL LINK USING MAILTO:

When you are applying a link to text that is already on the page, you can still use the Email Link dialog box. With the text to which you want to apply an email link selected in the document window, it appears in the Text text field of the Email Link dialog. You can make modifications to that text through the dialog, or leave it as is.

You can save and close the introduction.htm file.

WHAT YOU HAVE LEARNED

In this lesson, you have:

- Specified the default colors of links, visited links, and active links to match the colors of graphics used in the page (pages 122–128)

- Created text and graphic links to pages within the site as well as to other sites (pages 128–129)

- Targeted a link to open in a new window (pages 129–130)

- Inserted named anchors for each section of a document and linked the corresponding titles of those sections to each named anchor (pages 130–134)

- Created image maps with multiple hotspots of different shapes and sizes, learned how to edit the hotspots, and specified their links (pages 135–139)

- Created email links automatically using the Insert bar and manually using the Property inspector's Link text field (pages 130–140)

designing
with tables

LESSON 5

One way to quickly build basic Web pages is to place content such as text and images directly into a document, as you did in the first four lessons of this book. It is a simple and straightforward way of presenting information; however, it is a method with very limited options. You can wrap text around an image; align text or images to the left, center, or right of a page; and create indented blocks of text—but you can't do much more in regards to layout and placement of those elements.

CSS (cascading style sheets) is one answer to this dilemma. It provides a wide number of layout choices and appearance options while giving designers and developers a great deal of control over the look and feel of the entire site. CSS is covered in Lesson 6.

Another means to gain control over the placement of elements on your pages is to use tables. Tables allow you to present information in an organized manner; they contain rows and columns that intersect to form cells in which you can place content. Cells

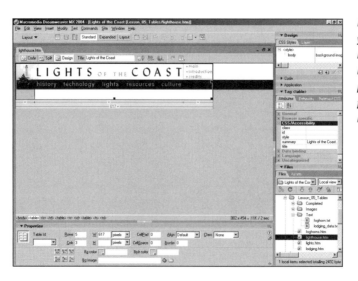

In this lesson's exercises, you will create tables to hold text and graphics and learn how to lay out your pages with consideration for the constraints of your users' viewable area.

can then be merged to create larger cells. The arrangement of content within tables enables you to construct pages with a greater degree of design precision. Using tables, you can place objects in specific locations on a page and create more complex visual arrangements. In this lesson, you will create several different pages. You will use combinations of tables to develop layouts that are far more compelling visually than the same information would be without the use of tables to display the content.

If you want to view the final result of this lesson, open foghorns.htm, lodging.htm, lights.htm, and lighthouse.htm in the Completed folder within the Lesson_05_Tables folder.

WHAT YOU WILL LEARN

In this lesson, you will:

- Learn how to create tables to control the layout of your pages
- Modify the table properties, including border, background, spacing, color, alignment, and size
- Create accessible tables
- Import tabular data from spreadsheets
- Modify a table by adjusting rows and columns
- Sort a table
- Export a table
- Determine the optimal size of your layout
- Create your page design using Layout mode
- Import a tracing image

APPROXIMATE TIME

This lesson should take about two hours to complete.

LESSON FILES

Media Files:
Lesson_05_Tables/Images/…(all files)

Starting Files:
Lesson_05_Tables/Text/lodging.htm

Completed Project:
Lesson_05_Tables/Completed/foghorns.htm
Lesson_05_Tables/Completed/lodging.htm
Lesson_05_Tables/Completed/export_lodging.txt
Lesson_05_Tables/Completed/lighthouse.htm
Lesson_05_Tables/Completed/lights.htm

CREATING A TABLE

A table is one of the primary layout tools used in designing a Web site. All content in a table is always contained within a cell, and every table has one or more cells. A cell is the area created by the intersection of a **row** and a **column**.

Dreamweaver MX provides a variety of tools and options for creating tables. These tools are available through three viewing modes: Standard, Layout, and Extended. Each visual editing mode offers a different perspective on table design and structure while enabling you to create and edit tables.

In this exercise, you will begin to create a page in the "Lights of the Coast" project site using the Standard mode.

NOTE *In HTML, tables were originally meant as a method to organize information—they were not intended to be a design tool. Over the years, as Web designers worked to develop more visually appealing and functional Web sites, the table has become a primary tool for layout. As a result, the contents and structure of Web pages have become more dependent upon one another. CSS, which you'll learn about in Lesson 6, gives designers the ability to separate the content from the structure of Web pages. This can be beneficial in terms of increasing accessibility and flexibility, decreasing download time, and decreasing the amount of time that is needed to create and maintain pages. Whether you use tables or CSS to control the layout of your Web pages will depend on a number of factors including browser support, how your pages display across different platforms and browsers, and the desired layout. CSS support is becoming more widespread, but it may not yet enable you to create the layout you want. You'll need to consider the requirements of your Web site, weigh the options of using CSS and/or tables, test your pages with both, and choose a layout method(s) accordingly.*

1) Open lodging.htm from the Lesson_05_Tables folder.

This page already has an image and text at the top of the page, as well as basic document formatting including a default font face, a default font size, a background color, and a title. You learned the techniques to apply these properties in Lesson 1 and Lesson 2.

2) Choose the Layout category on the Insert bar and verify that the Standard mode button is selected.

The Standard Mode option should be active by default—a highlighted button indicates the active mode. If Standard mode is not the active table mode, click the Standard button.

TIP *You can also check the mode or switch to another by choosing View > Table Mode—a checkmark next to a mode in the menu indicates that mode is active.*

STANDARD   LAYOUT

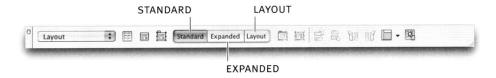

EXPANDED

3) Place the insertion point in a new paragraph after the text that is already on the page and click the Table button in the Layout category on the Insert bar.

TIP *The Table button is also available in the Common category on the Insert bar. Alternatively, you can choose Insert > Table or use the keyboard shortcut Option+Command+T (Macintosh) or Ctrl+Alt+T (Windows) to open the Table dialog box.*

TABLE

The Table dialog box opens.

The Table dialog box is split into three sections: Table size, Header, and Accessibility. The Table size section contains these options:

- **Rows:** The number of table rows. The Dreamweaver default is 3 if you have not previously created a table.

- **Columns:** The number of columns. The Dreamweaver default is 3 if you have not previously created a table.

- **Table width:** The width of the table in pixels or as a percentage of the browser window. Tables specified in pixels are good for a precise layout of text and images. Tables specified in percentages are an ideal choice when the proportions of the columns are more important than their actual widths. The Dreamweaver default is 200 pixels if you have not previously created a table.

- **Border thickness:** The width of the table border. The Dreamweaver default is 1 if you have not previously created a table.

- **Cell padding:** The amount of spacing between the cell content and the cell walls. If you leave this option blank, cell padding defaults to 1 pixel. If you don't want cell padding, be sure to type *0* in the text field. The Dreamweaver default is blank if you have not previously created a table. To the right of the text field is a small table that uses blue shading to illustrate cell padding.

- **Cell spacing:** The amount of spacing between table cells, not including the border. If you leave this option blank, cell spacing defaults to 1 pixel. If you don't want cell spacing, be sure to type *0* in the text field. The Dreamweaver default is blank. if you have not previously created a table To the right of the text field is a small table that uses blue shading to illustrate cell spacing.

These properties can all be changed at a later time—the options in the Table size section are all available on the Property inspector when a table is selected in the document window. The default values of these options may be different if you have already used the Table dialog box, in which case the values will be the same as the last values you specified for a table.

TIP *A number of table properties can also be adjusted through the Tag inspector—in a default configuration the Tag inspector is located between the Application and Files panel groups. You can access the Tag inspector by choosing Window > Tag Inspector.*

The Header section contains four different placement options for headers: None, Left, Top and Both. A header is essentially a row or column title that is used to label your content. Headers are most often used for data tables (those that function much like spreadsheets) as opposed to design/layout tables (those that are used to arrange and position visual elements for design purposes). The header option uses the scope attribute to make the information that is placed in header rows or columns act as identifiers for each of the cells in their respective rows or columns. For example, if you use the top header option and type *Order* in the top cell of the first column, the remaining cells in that column are prefaced verbally by the word "Order" when read aloud by a screen reader (a type of browser used by visitors with vision disabilities or situations that prevent them from using a standard browser) to indicate the contents of those cells. This option is also available through the Property inspector and can be modified at a later time.

It is important to continually consider how accessible your pages will be to your visitors. The goal of creating accessible pages is to develop content that is functional for the widest possible audience, including those with disabilities. You will learn more about accessibility in Lesson 13. Dreamweaver makes it easy to include accessible features from the beginning through the Accessibility section, which includes the following options:

- **Caption**: When you define a caption, it is displayed to all users and can be aligned to the top, bottom, left, or right of the table. If you leave this option blank, no caption is inserted. This option is available only in the Table dialog box. If you want to add this feature at a later time, you need to do so by editing the HTML code, covered in Lesson 14.

- **Summary**: A table summary is not displayed on the page; it is read by screen readers and is used to explain the purpose and context of the table. The summary should provide a concise and descriptive, but fairly brief, synopsis of the material contained within the table. It should indicate what the content of the table is. If you leave this option blank, no summary is inserted. This option can be modified at a later time through the CSS/Accessibility portion of the Attributes tab, which is located in the Tag inspector.

5) Type *2* in the Rows text field and *6* in the Columns text field. Change the Table width to *600* pixels, leave the Border thickness set to 1, and leave the Cell padding and Cell spacing text fields blank. In the Header section select Top. In the Accessibility section, type *Staying at a Lighthouse: Accommodation Information* in the Caption text field and choose top from the Align caption menu. In the Summary text field, type *Accommodation information for a variety of lighthouses. Each entry includes the lighthouse name, its location, price per night, contact information, the availability and whether the lens is operational*. Click OK to close the dialog box.

A table with the properties you specified appears on the page and is automatically selected. A table header—the light gray bar—is attached to the top of the table. Vertical green lines indicating the left and right boundaries of the table are displayed on the sides of the bar. A green line, with the width value of the table and a menu arrow both shown in the center, spans the topmost portion of the bar. At the portion of the bar closest to the table, a series of shorter green lines, each with its own menu arrow, indicates the widths of the columns. The table header disappears whenever you click outside of the table and reappears whenever the table is active or selected. The table header may obscure nearby content above the table. If the table is the first item in your document, the table header may be attached to the bottom of the table. You cannot control where the bar appears.

TIP *You can turn the table header visual aid on or off by selecting View > Visual Aids > Table Widths. A checkmark indicates that the option is turned on; no checkmark indicates that the option is off. You can also turn all visual aids on and off through the same menu or with the use of a keyboard shortcut—Command+Shift+I (Macintosh) or Ctrl+Shift+I (Windows). The following exercises assume that you have visual aids, including the table header, turned on.*

TABLE WIDTH BAR   TABLE WIDTH TABLE MENU

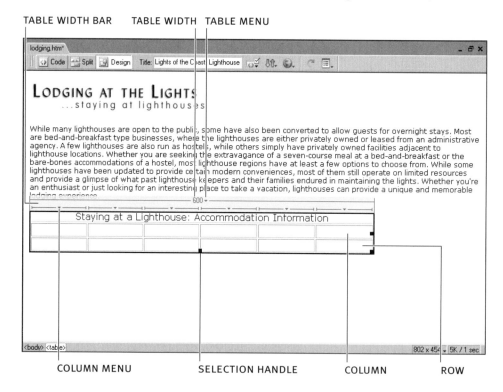

COLUMN MENU   SELECTION HANDLE   COLUMN   ROW

A solid black outline, with selection handles on the bottom and right sides, surrounds the table and the caption, indicating that the table is selected. The two rows and six columns are shown with a gray border, which does not surround the caption. You can see the spacing between the cells as a result of the default cell padding that is applied because the Cell spacing option was left blank.

6) Click in the first cell of the top row and left column. Type *Name* **in the cell; then press Tab to move to the next cell. Type** *Location* **and press Tab. Type** *Price* **and press Tab. Type** *Phone* **and press Tab. Type** *Availability* **and press Tab. Type** *Lens* **in the last cell.**

As you type and jump to other cells, the table may automatically shift the widths of the columns.

You can use the Tab key or the arrow keys to move between cells. Tab is the quickest method to jump to the next cell to the right or down to the next leftmost cell if you are at the end of a row. If you move to a cell that already has content in it, that content is selected when you press Tab.

Because the top row is the header row, the text that you type is centered and rendered in bold (a default property of headers). You can use the text-formatting options that you learned in Lesson 2 to apply additional formatting. For this exercise, leave the headers as they are.

HEADER ROW

7) Place the insertion point on the blank paragraph line below the table.

TIP *If you do not have a blank paragraph line below the table, click after the table and press Return (Macintosh) or Enter (Windows)*

When you click outside the table, the columns may shift slightly, changing their widths. The insertion point is now in a new paragraph.

You can enter the data for the table by typing directly into the cells. In the next exercise, however, you will use another method to fill the table with the content.

IMPORTING DATA FROM SPREADSHEETS

If you have text in a spreadsheet or even in a Microsoft Word table, you can easily insert that content into Dreamweaver documents. To do so, you need to save a document from Microsoft Word as a tab- or comma-delimited file to make it compatible with Dreamweaver. You can also use tab- or comma-delimited files that have been created using spreadsheet programs such as Microsoft Excel. In this exercise, the text file has already been created for you.

1) With the insertion point on the new line that you created in the previous exercise in the lodging.htm document, click the Tabular Data button in the Layout category on the Insert bar.

TIP *You can also choose Insert > Table Objects > Import Tabular Data to open the same dialog box.*

The Import Table Data dialog box opens.

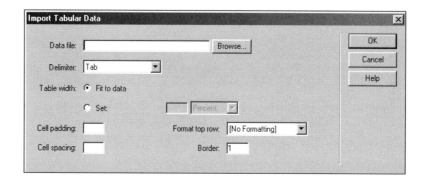

2) Click the Browse button to the right of the Data file text field and choose lodging_data.txt from the Lesson_05_Tables/Text folder. Leave Tab selected in the Delimiter menu. For Table width, choose Set, type *600* in the text field, and choose Pixels from the menu. Leave both Cell padding and Cell spacing blank. You should leave Format top row set to (No Formatting), which is the default, and leave Border set to 1. Click OK when you are done.

NOTE *If Set is selected in the Table width section when you open the Import Tabular Data dialog box, the table width text field for specifying size may be grayed-out. If this happens, try switching to the Fit to data option and then switch back to Set.*

A table is built for you according to the options you just selected, and the data from the tab-delimited lodging.txt file that you are importing has been inserted into that new table.

You can also use a variety of other delimiters, including semicolons and colons, but tabs and commas are the most widely used. Choosing Other from the Delimiter menu displays a text field in which you can type the delimiter of your choice.

When the second table is selected, the gray bar of the table header may overlap and obscure the lower portion of the first table. Click outside the tables and the table header will disappear.

COPYING AND PASTING TABLE CELLS

You now have two tables: the first table contains the titles for each column and the second table contains the data. Now you need to combine the two tables. You can copy and paste multiple table cells at the same time, which preserves the cell's formatting if there is any, or you can copy and paste only the contents of the cell.

Cells can be pasted at an insertion point or by replacing a selection in an existing table. If you want to paste multiple table cells, the contents of the Clipboard (a system feature on both Macintosh and Windows—the Clipboard is not a part of Dreamweaver) must exactly match the structure of the table or the selection in the table that the pasted cells will replace. You can copy one cell and paste it to replace a selected cell, but you can't copy two cells and paste them to replace a single cell. The number and orientation of the cells that you copy must match the number and orientation of the cells you plan to replace.

1) In the lodging.htm document, select all the cells in the second table by clicking the upper left cell and dragging across the cells to the lower right cell.

The selected cells are now outlined with black borders. Selecting the cells in this manner selects the cells themselves, not the entire table.

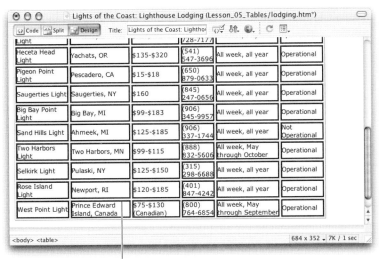

BLACK BORDERS SHOW WHICH CELLS ARE SELECTED

2) Choose Edit > Copy.

TIP *You can also use the keyboard shortcuts Command+C (Macintosh) or Ctrl+C (Windows).*

To be cut or copied, the selected cells must form a rectangle. For example, you can't select six cells in the top row and four cells in the bottom row.

3) Click once inside the first cell of the second row in the top table.

You may need to click a visible portion of the top table first or click in an area of the page that is outside both tables to show the bottom row if the table header of the second table obscures it.

This empty cell is where the copied cells will be pasted.

4) Choose Edit > Paste.

TIP *You can also press Command+V (Macintosh) or Ctrl+V (Windows) to paste the contents of the Clipboard—the cells you copied in step 2.*

All the cells from the second table are inserted into the first table. Your first table will now look like the following example.

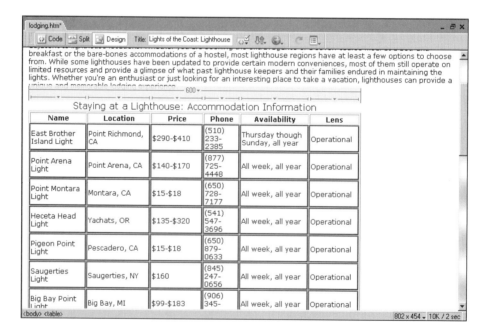

Click outside the table to deselect the cells.

NOTE *If you are pasting entire rows at the end of a table (as in this exercise), the rows are added to the table. If you are pasting to replace one or more cells, the contents of the selected cell(s) are replaced if the Clipboard contents match the structure of the selected cell(s). If you are pasting outside a table, the rows, columns, or cells are used to define a new table.*

If you need to remove the contents of cells, but want to leave the cells themselves intact, select one or more cells (but not an entire row or column); then choose Edit > Clear or press Delete. If you need to remove an entire row, drag across all the cells in the row to select it, and press Delete.

SELECTING A TABLE

Now that all the content from the second table is in the first table, you no longer need the second table. To delete it, you need to select the table first. Dreamweaver provides several methods for selecting a table. You will find that some methods are easier to use than others, depending on the complexity of the table structure.

1) In the lodging.htm document, select the second table by positioning the pointer anywhere inside the table and then selecting the `<table>` tag in the Tag Selector on the lower left corner of the document window.

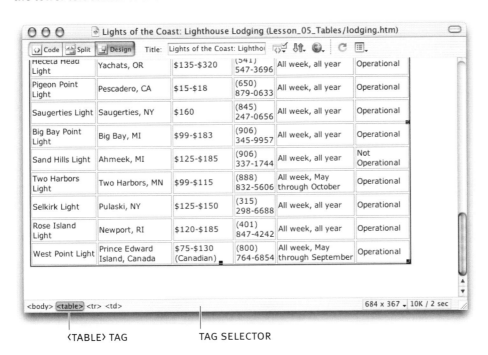

⟨TABLE⟩ TAG   TAG SELECTOR

TIP *You can also select a table by clicking the upper left corner of the table or anywhere on the right or lower edge. The pointer shows a table icon next to the pointer arrow when you are close to the edge. Wait until you see the pointer before you click. Another way to select a table is to click inside the table and choose Modify > Table > Select Table. You can also click the horizontal green table width line that spans the gray bar to select the table.*

Selection handles appear around the table when it is selected and a black border surrounds the entire table—there are no black borders around any of the individual cells.

NOTE *If the insertion point is inside the table and the table itself is not selected, you can see the <tr> and <td> tags in the Tag Selector in addition to the <table> tag. The tag <tr> represents the table row. The tag <td> represents the table data, otherwise known as a cell. Selecting a <td> tag selects the corresponding cell and enables you to make changes to that cell in the Property inspector. You'll learn more about tags in Lesson 14.*

2) With the table selected, press Delete (Macintosh) or Backspace (Windows) to remove the second table.

The second table is gone.

TIP *When the pointer is inside a cell, the keyboard shortcut Command+A (Macintosh) or Ctrl+A (Windows) selects the cell. Using the keyboard shortcut a second time selects the entire table.*

SELECTING AND FORMATTING TABLE CELLS

You can easily select a row, a column, or all the cells in the table. Earlier in this lesson, you selected **contiguous cells**—that is, cells that adjoin or touch one another. You can also select noncontiguous cells—those that do not touch—in a table and modify the properties of those cells. You can't copy or paste noncontiguous cells. The following steps demonstrate various selection methods.

You can change several options for each cell, either on an individual basis or for multiple selected cells. These options include background color and alignment.

1) In the lodging.htm document, select noncontiguous cells in the top row of the remaining table by holding down Command (Macintosh) or Ctrl (Windows) and clicking the first cell, which contains the text "Name." Continue to hold down the Command or Ctrl key; click the cell containing the text "Price" and also the cell containing the text "Availability."

When you hold down the Command or Ctrl key as you move the pointer over a cell, an outlined square may appear next to the pointer arrow to indicate you are selecting cells.

All three noncontiguous cells should now be selected, as shown by the black borders around the individual cells.

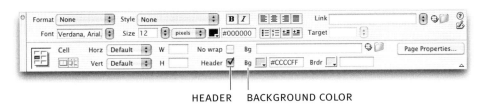

Name	Location	Price	Phone	Availability	Lens
East Brother Island Light	Point Richmond, CA	$290-$410	(510) 233-2385	Thursday though Sunday, all year	Operational
Point Arena Light	Point Arena, CA	$140-$170	(877) 725-4448	All week, all year	Operational
Point Montara Light	Montara, CA	$15-$18	(650) 728-7177	All week, all year	Operational
Heceta Head Light	Yachats, OR	$135-$320	(541) 547-3696	All week, all year	Operational
Pigeon Point Light	Pescadero, CA	$15-$18	(650) 879-0633	All week, all year	Operational
Saugerties Light	Saugerties, NY	$160	(845) 247-0656	All week, all year	Operational

2) Type the hexadecimal code *#CCCCFF* **into the Bg color text field on the Property inspector.**

HEADER   BACKGROUND COLOR

The color of the cell changes to the color you selected. You may need to click outside of the table for the change to be applied.

You can change the background color of single cells, multiple cells, or the entire table, depending on what you select. In this step, you changed multiple cells at the same time.

155

Notice that the Header option on the Property inspector is checked. Earlier in this lesson you set the header row to top—all cells in this row are formatted as headers. You should leave this option checked for all cells in the top row.

NOTE *To change the background color of the entire table, select the table and use the Bg color box on the Property inspector to choose a color for the table, or type the desired hexadecimal code into the corresponding text field.*

3) Select the noncontiguous "Location," "Phone," and "Lens" cells; change their background colors to #9999CC.

You can also apply a background image to single cells, multiple cells at once, or entire tables. The background image option is also available in the Property inspector, directly above the background color option.

NOTE *A background images applied to an entire table may not display as expected if the table has multiple cells or if there are nested tables inside of it. Always test your pages by previewing them in browsers to be sure the page appears as you expect.*

4) Click inside the Point Arena row and position the pointer at the left end of the row, just on the table border. Click when the selection arrow appears; then change the background color to #6699CC.

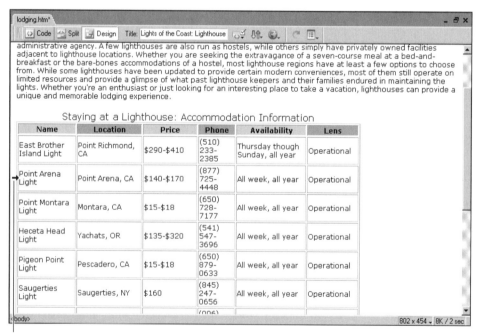

SELECTION ARROW

You may need to roll the pointer up and down the left border of the table to get the selection arrow to appear. As you place the cursor in position you all the cells in that row will become outlined in red. The selection arrow is a quick way to select a single row or column in a table. If you can't get the selection arrow or the red outlines to appear, try clicking the left border of the row. When you click the border, all cells in the table become selected and are displayed with black outlines.

5) Continue to change the color of other rows in the table to match the example.

The rows now alternate between white and blue.

NOTE *You can also quickly format tables with alternating colored rows automatically. Choose Commands > Format Table to open the Format Table dialog box, which allows you to select from a variety of preset formatting options as well as customize the appearance of your table through color, style, alignments, and alternate row options.*

6) Select the "Lens" column by clicking the green column width line that spans that column on the gray table width bar.

You have selected the entire column.

T I P *You can also select the Lens column by clicking the top cell of the column; then holding down the Shift key and clicking the bottom cell in that column.*

COLUMN WIDTH LINE   COLUMN MENU

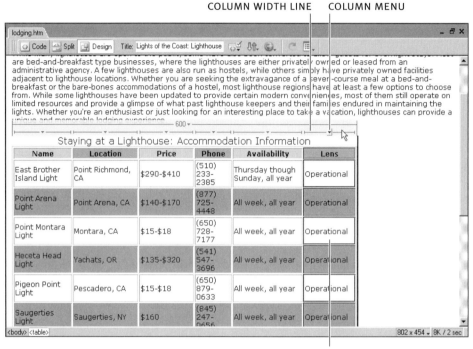

SELECTED COLUMN

The default setting for horizontal alignment does the same thing as the left setting—it aligns the contents of the selected cells to the left. The default setting for vertical alignment does the same thing as the middle setting—it aligns the contents of the selected cells to the middle. Because the top row is a header row, the contents of those cells are automatically centered.

9) In the Property inspector, change the horizontal alignment of the entire Lens column to Right.

The contents of all cells in the Lens column are now aligned to the right.

The lower half of the Property inspector contains the following cell attributes:

- **Merge:** Combines two or more selected cells into one cell.

- **Split:** Divides a single cell into multiple cells.

- **Horizontal:** Sets the horizontal alignment of the cell's contents to the browser default (browser defaults are usually left for regular cells and center for header cells) or to left, right, or center.

- **Vertical:** Sets the vertical alignment of the cell's contents to the browser's default (usually middle) or to top, middle, bottom, or baseline.

- **Width and Height:** Sets the width and height of selected cells in pixels. To use percentages, follow the value with a percent sign (%).

- **No wrap:** Prevents word wrapping; cells expand in width to accommodate all data. Normally, cells expand horizontally to accommodate the longest word and then expand vertically.

- **Header:** Formats the selected cell(s) as a table header. The contents of table header cells are bold and centered by default.

- **Background image (the top Bg option):** Sets the background image for the cells.

- **Background color (the bottom Bg option):** Sets the background color for the cells. Cell backgrounds appear inside the cells only—that is, the background does not flow over cell spacing or table borders. If your cell spacing and cell padding are not set to 0, gaps appear between the colored areas even if the border is set to 0. If you want to prevent these gaps, you should apply color to the entire table, or set cell spacing and cell padding to 0.

- **Border:** Sets the border color for the cells.

You may need to click the expander arrow on the right side of the Property inspector if you do not see these options. You will work with some of these options in the following exercises.

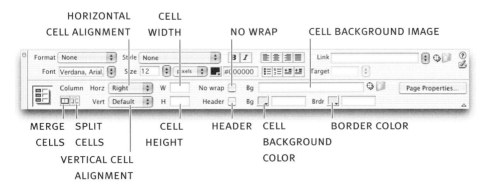

SORTING A TABLE

You can perform a simple table sort by sorting on the contents of a single column. You can also perform a more complicated sort by sorting on the contents of two columns. You can't sort tables that contain merged cells. The following exercise demonstrates sorting.

1) In the lodging.htm document, select the table and then choose Commands › Sort Table.

The Sort Table dialog box opens.

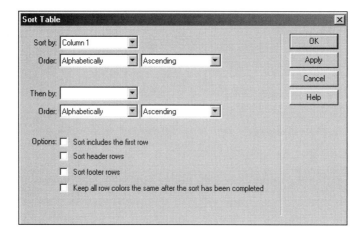

2) Set the following options.

Sort by: Select the column to sort. For this exercise, select Column 1 (default).

Order: Specify whether you want to sort the column alphabetically or numerically. For this exercise, select Alphabetically (default). This option is important when the contents of a column are numerical. An alphabetical sort applied to a list of one- and two-digit numbers results in an alphanumeric sort (such as 1, 10, 2, 20, 3, 30) rather than a straight numeric sort (such as 1, 2, 3, 10, 20, 30). Choose Ascending (A to Z or low to high) for the sort order (default).

Then by: For this exercise, leave it blank (default). Then By lets you choose to perform a secondary sort on a different column. The sort methods in the menu are the same as the methods that are available in Sort By.

Sort includes the first row: This option allows you to specify whether the first row is included in the sort. If the first row is a heading that shouldn't be moved (as it is in this exercise), leave this checkbox unchecked (default). For this exercise, leave this option unchecked.

Sort header rows: For this exercise, leave this option unchecked (default). The first row in the table contains the column headers; you don't want to sort them.

Sort footer rows: For this exercise, leave this option unchecked (default).

Keep all row colors the same after the sort has been completed: If you changed any attributes for a row, you can retain that attribute in the row by choosing this option. Suppose that you sort a table with a color in the first row. After sorting, the data in the first row moves to the second row. If this option is selected, the color moves with the data to the second row. If this option is not selected, the color remains in the first row. For this exercise, leave this option unchecked (default).

3) Click OK.

The table is now sorted alphabetically using the data in the first column, but the row headers remain in the first row. Save your document.

NOTE *When you apply the sort, portions of other rows may take on the background color of the alternating rows that you applied earlier due to a bug. You can remove the color by selecting the cells that should not use the background color, clicking the background color box on the Property inspector, and choosing default—default is the white square with the red diagonal line. Alternatively, you can select the hexadecimal color code in the text field, press Delete (Macintosh) or Backspace (Windows), and press Return (Macintosh) or Enter (Windows) to apply the change.*

MODIFYING A TABLE

After you create a table, you may find that it is too large or too small, or you may need to add columns and rows. You can adjust these table properties easily.

1) In the lodging.htm document, select the table and change the Width value on the Property inspector from 600 to 650. Press Return (Macintosh) or Enter (Windows) to apply the change.

You have enlarged the table.

NOTE *You can also adjust the size of the table by moving the pointer over the bottom or right edges of the table border. When the pointer changes to a two-headed arrow, drag the column border to adjust the table to the desired size. You can see the new width by selecting the table and looking at the number in the Width text field in the Property inspector. Use caution when dragging a border of a table to change its size. Whenever you drag table borders in this way, Dreamweaver automatically assigns and updates widths and/or heights. Sometimes, this may not be what you want. If you want to get rid of the widths or heights, click the Clear Column Widths and Clear Row Heights buttons in the Property inspector. You can also use the Clear All Heights and Clear All Widths commands in the table width menu accessible from the gray bar at the top of the table.*

2) Click in the right cell of the last row of the table (the lower right cell) and then press the Tab key.

If the pointer is in the last cell of a table, pressing the Tab key causes the insertion point to be placed in the leftmost cell of a new row.

> **TIP** *You can also add new rows and columns by choosing Modify > Table and selecting one of the following options: Insert Row (inserts one row above the current row); Insert Column (inserts one column to the left of the current column); Insert Rows or Columns (this option allows you to choose whether to insert rows or columns, specify the number of rows or columns that should be inserted, and to select where those rows or columns will appear.). You can also add new columns by clicking the green line spanning a column on the gray bar and choosing Insert Column Left or Insert Column Right.*

3) In the left cell of the row you just inserted, click and drag to the right to select all the cells in the row. Click the Merge Cells button in the Property inspector.

MERGE CELLS

The six cells now form one long cell that spans six columns. Any attributes of the first cell, such as color and alignment, are applied to the merged cell.

> **NOTE** *You can split cells in the same manner by clicking the Split Cell button in the Property inspector or by choosing Modify > Table > Split Cell. This method returns the number of cells to the original number if you merged them, or it can split a cell into any number of rows or columns.*

You can merge any number of cells in one column or any number of cells in one row. You can also merge cells in multiple rows and columns, but the cells to be merged must form a rectangle. You can't merge cells to create an "L" shape.

> **TIP** *To merge cells, you can also choose Modify > Table > Merge Cells. The keyboard shortcuts for merging rows are Option+Command+M (Macintosh) or Ctrl+Alt+M (Windows). Pressing just the M key also merges the selected cells.*

4) In the cell you have just merged, type © *2003, Lights of the Coast.*

Merging cells gives you a great deal of additional options for layout.

NOTE *If you need to delete a row, click the row and then choose Modify > Table > Delete Row. You can also Control-click (Macintosh) or right-click (Windows) on the table and choose Table > Delete Row from the context menu.*

5) With the insertion point in the last row of the table, choose Modify › Table › Insert Rows or Columns. In the Insert Rows or Columns dialog box that appears, choose Rows from the Insert options, type *1* in the Number of Rows text field, and choose Above the Selection in the Where options. Click OK.

The Insert Rows or Columns dialog box allows you to specify whether to insert before or after the current row. When you use this dialog box, you have control over where the new rows or columns are placed, and you can insert any number of rows or columns.

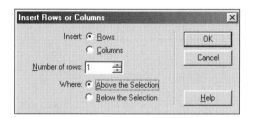

NOTE *If you choose Modify > Table > Insert Row, the new row is inserted above the current row by default. You can also Control-click (Macintosh) or right-click (Windows) the row above and choose Table > Insert Rows or Columns from the context menu.*

This new row you have inserted acts as a spacer between the copyright and the information about the lighthouses above it. Giving each section or block of information on your page a little space helps the viewer to differentiate between the text on the page—it is difficult to read information when there is a lot of text that all runs together.

EXPORTING A TABLE

If you need to extract information from a table to place in a database, a spreadsheet, or a word-processing or page-layout application, you can't just copy and paste the text. All you get is text with no row and column formatting. But you can export the table and save the file as a tab-delimited file that most word-processing and spreadsheet applications can read.

1) In the lodging.htm document, select the table.

You will export the selected table from Dreamweaver into a new file in the following steps.

2) Choose File > Export > Table.

The Export Table dialog box opens.

3) From the Delimiter menu, choose Tab (default).

Most word processing and spreadsheet applications can read both comma- and tab-delimited tables. When you choose File > Export > Table, Tab is selected by default. Your choices of delimiter values for the table data are Tab, Space, Comma, Semicolon, and Colon. If you are not sure which option to use, choose Tab.

4) From the Line Breaks menu, choose line breaks for the operating system you are using (default): Windows, Macintosh, or Unix.

Line breaks are the characters inserted at the end of each line. You worked with them in Lesson 2 when you imported text. When choosing which type of line breaks to use, select the operating system for which you are exporting the file. You may need to choose an operating system other than your own if the file will be used on a different platform.

5) Click Export. In the dialog box that opens, name the exported file `export_lodging.txt` and save it in the Lesson_05_Tables folder.

The entire table is exported to a new file with the name you chose. The file you created is an ASCII (American Standard Code for Information Interchange) formatted text file. In ASCII, numbers represent text characters. If you have Microsoft Excel or Microsoft Word, you can import the information into those programs using the delimited ASCII format. Check the documentation included with those programs for details on how to import such files.

You can save and close the lodging.htm document.

USING IMAGES IN TABLES

Tables are often used to construct the layout of a page with multiple images or to reassemble an image that has been sliced. An image may be sliced into several smaller images for it to be **optimized** for the Web (the process of optimizing includes decreasing the file size of the image while maintaining the highest possible image quality). The resulting pieces need to be aligned with each other using a table.

In this exercise, you create a table that will be used on pages throughout the "Lights of the Coast" project site.

1) Create a new HTML page, save it as lighthouse.htm and title it *Lights of the Coast*. This page will contain a number of tables.

2) Create a new table with the following settings: *5* **rows,** *3* **columns,** *617* **pixels wide,** *0* **Border thickness,** *0* **Cell padding, and** *0* **Cell spacing. Set the Header to None, leave the Caption text field blank, and type** *Lights of the Coast Content* **in the Summary text field.**

TIP *Each time you use the Table dialog box, Dreamweaver will automatically populate all options with the same values as you used for your last table.*

The table you create should look like the following example.

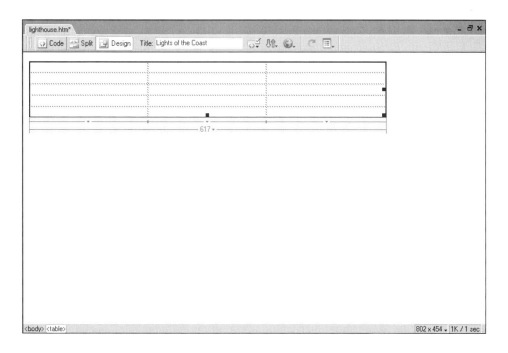

NOTE *Be sure to type the number 0 into the Border, Cell padding, and Cell spacing text fields. Leaving these fields blank will result in an actual value of 1 for both the Cell padding and Cell spacing.*

3) Select all five cells in the first column and merge them. In the second row, select and merge the two cells in the second and third columns. In the fourth row, select and merge the two cells in the second and third columns. In the fifth row, select and merge the two cells in the second and third columns.

Your table should now look like the following example.

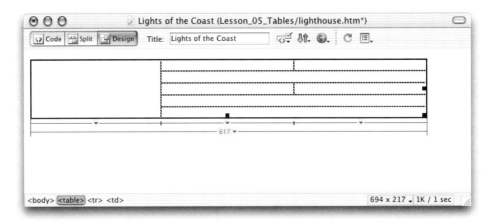

TIP *The structure of your table is represented by dotted lines because you defined the border as 0. With the cursor positioned over the green line that spans the with of the table in the gray Table Width bar, you can press Command (Macintosh) or Ctrl (Windows) to see the table structure displayed in a solid red line.*

4) Place the insertion point in the single cell of the first column and use the Vert menu on the Property inspector to change the vertical setting of the cell to "Top." Insert into the cell the nav_lighthouse.jpg from the Lesson_05_Tables/Images folder.

The image of the lighthouse you just inserted now stays at the top of this column, regardless of how tall the table eventually becomes.

NOTE *If a dialog box with image accessibility options opens after you select the image in the Select Image Source dialog box, you should go to Dreamweaver > Preferences (Macintosh) or Edit > Preferences (Windows) and select the accessibility category. Uncheck the Images box and click OK to turn the accessible images option off for this lesson.*

When you insert images into cells in Dreamweaver, the empty cells have a tendency to collapse and look as if they are no longer there. They are actually still there, but they have just been squished together. You can see this happen if you click outside of the table, or into another cell. You should not try to resize the cells at this point. When cells become squished together, you have several options for moving through the tables. Avoid dragging the borders of your table and its columns and rows in these cases—instead, navigate through tables using the arrow keys as well as the Expanded Tables mode, which you will learn to do in the following steps.

5) Click the Expanded button in the Layout category on the Insert bar.

EXPANDED TABLES MODE

TIP *You can also use the keyboard shortcut F6 to turn this mode on and off, or switch modes by choosing View > Table Mode and selecting the desired viewing mode from the submenu.*

An introductory dialog box, Getting Started in Expanded Tables Mode, appears. You can click OK to close the dialog box when you are done reading it.

A bar that reads "Expanded Tables Mode [exit]" appears across the top of the document window, just under the toolbar, to indicate that the Expanded Tables mode is active. You can return to Standard mode by either clicking the [exit] link on the bar or by clicking the Standard button in the Layout category on the Insert bar.

The Expanded Tables mode appears to enlarge your tables slightly and simultaneously gives the illusion of increasing the border, cell spacing, and cell padding. These appearance changes happen only in this mode—no actual changes are made to the size of your table or the properties of border, cell spacing, and cell padding. This mode does not represent how tables appear in browsers. Given the distortion that occurs when viewing your page in this mode, you should refrain from making any size changes to your tables in this mode. If possible, resize tables in Standard mode.

6) Select the lighthouse image that you inserted in step 4 and choose <empty> **from the Alt menu on the Property inspector.**
This image serves as a visual design element so alternative text is unnecessary. As mentioned in Lesson 3, avoid specifying alternative text for images that serve only layout or design purposes. Such images should use the <empty> option—do not leave the Alt text field blank.

167

7) Place the insertion point in the second column of the first row. Insert nav_titlebar.gif from the Images folder and with the image selected, type *Lights of the Coast* **into the Alt text field on the Property inspector.**

This image, now located in the center cell of the top row, is a logo header for the Lights of the Coast site. Using the alternative text to communicate the same message as is contained in the image is an important step.

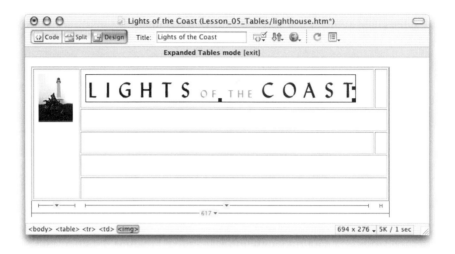

8) Click to place the insertion point in the cell that is located in the third row of the third column.

Because the Expanded Tables mode is active, you can easily click inside the cell.

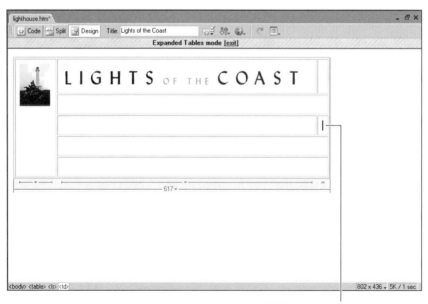

INSERTION POINT

If you were using Standard mode, you could still navigate through a collapsed table by using the arrow keys. To do so, you would select the title image "Lights of the Coast" and press the right arrow key once to move off the image. The insertion point would then be in the cell that contains the nav_titlebar.gif image, directly to the right of that image. At the right edge of the image, you would see a blinking cursor the same height as the image. You would then press the right arrow key once more to move into the next (third) column and then use the down arrow key once to move the insertion point into the third row. When columns collapse completely, it can be difficult to see the blinking cursor between the dotted lines that indicate the boundaries of the cells. Refrain from dragging the borders of the table and resizing it in order to see columns that have collapsed. Resizing your table changes its dimensions by adding height tags and width tags. The dimensions defined by those tags could create problems, such as causing the images to not line up flush with each other. If height or width tags are created, you can select the table and click the clear row heights and clear column widths buttons on the Property inspector. You may need to redefine the width of the table after clearing column widths. After the pointer is in the correct cell, typing a small amount of text causes the cell to expand. This expansion may help you see the columns more clearly. If you use this method, it is very important to be sure that you delete the text or replace it with the appropriate text or image(s). Extra characters can cause problems in some tables, particularly if you've calculated the table size solely for specific images.

9) Insert nav_rightspace.gif from the Images folder into the cell.

The nav_rightspace.gif image appears in the cell.

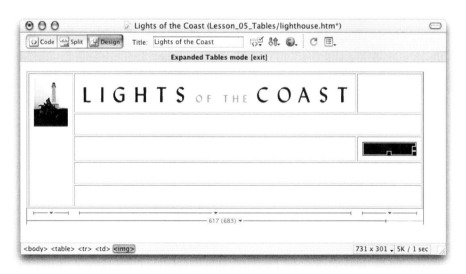

10) Click the Standard button in the Layout category on the Insert bar to switch back to Standard mode.

In Standard mode, you can see how the columns now align flush with the images. In the following exercises, using Standard mode allows you to see how the tables and images work together to create a seamless layout. You need to make sure that extra spaces don't get worked into the tables you create, which is difficult to watch for in Expanded mode because that viewing mode causes additional spacing.

11) Place the insertion point in the cell that is located in the second row—it spans the second and third columns of the table. Insert into the cell the nav_topline.gif from the Images folder. Place the insertion point in the cell that is located in the fourth row—it spans the second and third columns of the table. Insert into the cell the nav_botline2.gif from the Images folder. Click outside the table.

When you click outside the table, Dreamweaver causes the table to refresh, and the cell containing the nav_botline2.gif image now fits exactly around the edges of the image. This image and the nav_rightspace.gif image you inserted in the previous step are holding the spaces necessary to create the final look of this page. Tables often need images to force them to hold the dimensions you want. Without an image to hold that space, your columns may shift around as they did when you created the lighthouse lodging information table.

Your table now looks similar to the following example.

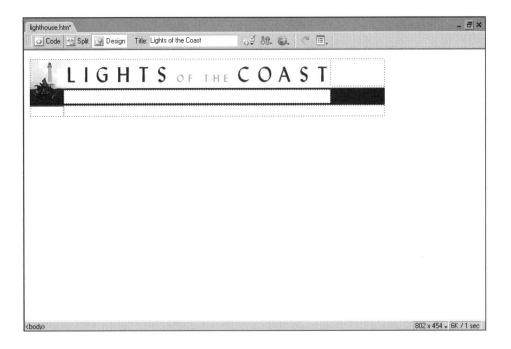

NESTING TABLES

A **nested** table is one that is placed within the cell of another table. Nested tables are used for a variety of purposes. In the earlier days of the Web, nesting tables was usually considered a bad practice because of the problems it caused (including sometimes crashing a viewer's browser). These days, however, browsers are capable of a great deal more. Nested tables are commonly used to create pages that otherwise have to use one incredibly complicated table or not be able to use the intended design at all. Nesting tables allows you to create more complex layouts and keep each of your tables as simple as possible. The more complex a single table is, the harder it is to create and the more likely it will be to break or have other viewing problems in browsers.

1) In the lighthouse.htm document, click outside the table and press Return (Macintosh) or Enter (Windows) several times. Create a new table with the following settings: *3* rows, *1* column, *93* pixels wide, *0* Border, *0* Cell padding, and *0* Cell spacing. Set the Header option to None, leave the Caption text field blank, and type *Basic navigation options* **in the Summary text field. Click OK.**

It is often easier to put together the table you plan to nest by creating it outside the larger table because you can clearly see the borders of the smaller table while you are inserting the necessary images and content, and you don't accidentally click in the larger table as you're trying to work with the smaller one.

2) Place the insertion point in the first row, and insert the nav_main.gif image into the cell. With the image selected, type *main* **into the Alt text field. Insert nav_introduction.gif into the second row, using** *introduction* **for the alternative text, and nav_credits.gif into the third row, using** *credits* **for the alt text.**

Your small table should now look like the following example.

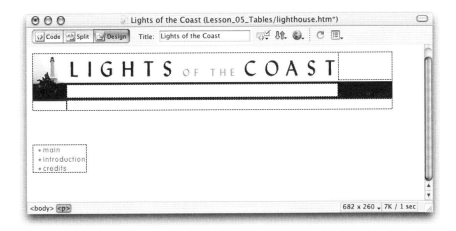

As you insert images, if your tables contain images that line up flush with one another as they do in this small table, you may not be able to see the dotted lines separating the individual cells.

NOTE *As you work with tables, keep in mind that the dotted lines, which Dreamweaver uses to indicate the cell and table borders, each take up one pixel of space. Those extra pixels of space created by the dotted lines do not exist when the document is seen in a browser. However, those pixels of space may cause tables viewed within Dreamweaver to look slightly larger than they really are. For example, you might have two tables in a document. The first table may have five columns and the second table may have only one column. The first table would appear in Dreamweaver to be four pixels wider than the first, even though if you were to view the page in a browser, both tables would be the same width. You can always turn off table borders by choosing View > Visual Aids > Table borders. On the other hand, table borders are generally very useful, and it can be very difficult to work with tables when you have them turned off.*

3) Select and copy the small table with the main, introduction, and credits images you just created. In the table at the top of the page, place the insertion point in the third column of the first row and use paste the table you copied into the cell.

The smaller table is now nested into the cell in the third column of the first row of the first table. In this exercise, you have nested a table to simplify the layout of the large table. You can now delete the original small table at the bottom of the page.

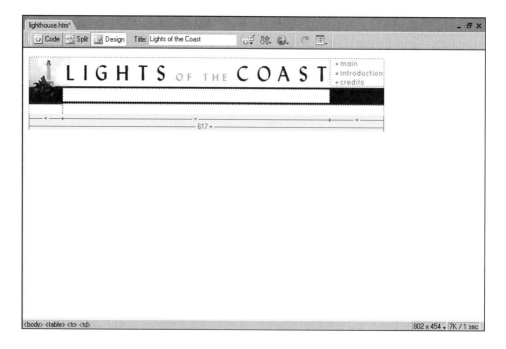

TIP *You can use Edit > Cut instead of Edit > Copy to copy and delete the small table at the same time.*

Try to avoid nesting tables more than five or six levels deep. Keep in mind that older browsers—especially older versions of Netscape—may have difficulty displaying too many levels of nested tables (sometimes due to the increased memory required to display those nested tables). To determine whether the nested tables you create will work correctly for your visitors, you need to test your pages in a variety of browsers on different platforms.

Don't get in the habit of creating extraneous nested tables. Nesting is a good technique that can be used to achieve cohesive, advanced layouts, but it should be done in a carefully considered and purposeful manner. If you find yourself nesting many levels of tables, you should probably rethink your layout. A simpler layout means that less code is created, making it more likely that the page will download quickly and there will be less potential for problems. If you end up with an improper display in a browser, multiple levels of nested tables can also make it more difficult to find the cause of those errors in the code.

4) Create a new table below the existing table with *1* **row,** *5* **columns,** *465* **pixels wide,** *0* **Border,** *0* **Cell padding, and** *0* **Cell spacing. Set the Header to None, leave the Caption text field blank, and type** *Main Navigation* **into the Summary text field. Click OK to insert the table.**

You are creating a second table to nest inside the larger table.

5) In the first column, insert nav_history.gif. Select the nav_history.gif image, and press the right arrow key twice to move off of the image and into the second column. In the second column, insert nav_technology.gif. Select the nav_technology.gif image, and press the right arrow key twice to move off of the image and into the third column. In the third column, insert nav_lights.gif. Select the nav_lights.gif image, and press the right arrow key twice to move off of the image and into the fourth column. In the fourth column, insert nav_resources.gif. Select the nav_resources.gif image, and press the right arrow key twice to move off of the image and into the fifth column. In the fifth column, insert nav_culture.gif. Give the images alt text of *history,* *technology,* *lights,* *resources,* **and** *culture,* **respectively.**

All images are located in the Images folder.

Your table should now look like the following example.

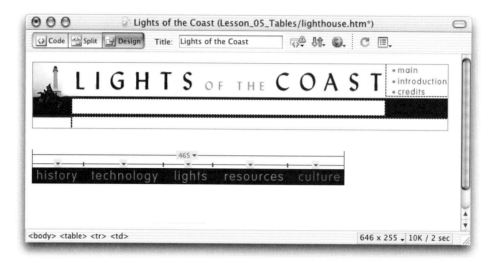

6) Copy the small table with the five images you just inserted. Place the insertion point in cell that is located in the second column of the third row of the table at the top of the page (the top of the currently empty rows) and paste the table into the cell.
The table is now nested into the cell in the second column of the second row of the first table. You can now delete the smaller table at the bottom of your document.

In this exercise you nested tables that have content of fixed widths—that content is the images you have placed in the table cells. In the last table you created, the combination of the widths of the five images equals the width you specified for that table. In a table such as this, if you were to replace one or more of those images with text typed directly into the cells (HTML text as opposed to a graphic), there would no longer be an object of a fixed width in those cells. You could define the widths of all five cells, but that often does not hold the cells to their defined dimensions. One technique to force cells to hold their dimensions is to create an additional row at the top of the table with spacer images in each cell. You would set the height of the spacer images in each cell to 1 pixel and set the width of each spacer image to the desired measurement. The combined widths of all five spacer images should equal the width of the table itself. Graphic programs such as Adobe's ImageReady and Macromedia's Fireworks often use spacer images in this manner when generating HTML for tables according to how an image has been sliced.

OUTLINING A TABLE

You can create borders for your tables by entering a number value into the border text field on the Property inspector as you did at the beginning of this lesson. However, table borders created using the border attribute display inconsistently in different browsers, particularly across different platforms. To get around this, you can nest tables to create a border or outline that is consistent and compatible with the various browsers and platforms. This technique also provides you with a greater degree of control over the appearance of the outline.

1) In the lighthouse.htm document, create a new table below the existing table with _1_ row and _1_ column. Make it _558_ pixels wide. The Border should be set to _0_, Cell padding should be set to _1_, and Cell spacing should be set to _0_. Leave the Header set to None, leave the Caption text field blank, and leave the Summary text field blank.

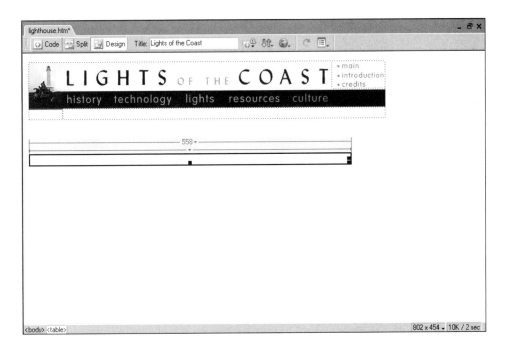

This is the first outer table. The cell padding defines the width of table outline that you are creating.

TIP *You can set a higher value for cell padding to increase the width of the table outline.*

2) Place the insertion point into the single cell. Use the Property inspector to set the background color of the cell to black (#000000).

The background color of this cell will be the color of the table outline.

3) With the insertion point still in the same cell, insert a table with the following settings: *1* **row,** *1* **column,** *100* **percent width, Border of** *0*, **Cell padding of** *6*, **and Cell spacing of** *0*. **Leave the Header set to None, leave the caption text field blank, and type** *Content* **into the Summary text field. Click OK.**

A table is now nested inside the first table. The nested table will expand to 100 percent of the available space for content in the cell—556 pixels. The first table is 558 pixels, but because it has a cell-padding value of 1, a single pixel space is created on all sides of the cell (top, bottom, left, and right). Therefore, the available space inside that cell is 2 pixels less that the total width of the table. The single pixel of space around the cell will create the outline effect.

NOTE *Although you could set the size of the inside table to a fixed width, using 100 percent will do the same thing while giving you the advantage of increased flexibility. For example, if you use a fixed width for the nested table and decide to change the size of the outside table, you also have to change the size of the nested table. However, if you use 100 percent for the width of the nested table, it is always displayed at the correct size—regardless of any changes you make to the outside table.*

4) Click to place the insertion point into the single cell of the nested table you just created. Use the Property inspector to set the background color of the cell to white (#FFFFFF).

The background of the nested table is now white, and you can see the outline effect created by the 1-pixel cell padding of the outer table.

5) Select and copy the outside table. Place the insertion point in the right cell of the bottom row of the table at the top of the page (the only remaining empty row), select Top from the Vert menu on the Property inspector, and paste the copied table into the cell.

Using the Tag Selector is a good way of selecting and navigating through nested tables. To select the outside table using the Tag Selector, click inside the white area of the nested table. Look to the tag selector and notice the <table> *tags. The rightmost* <table> *tag corresponds with the nested table. The* <table> *tag to the left corresponds with the outside table. Clicking a* <table> *tag selects the corresponding table.*

By selecting and copying the outside table, you copied everything within that table, which includes the nested table. The outlined table is now nested inside the first table and creates the effect of a page dropping down from the top bar. The outlined table expands downward as you insert content into it. At this point, you have three levels of nested tables.

The original outlined table at the bottom of the page is no longer necessary, so you should delete it.

Your page should now look similar to the following example.

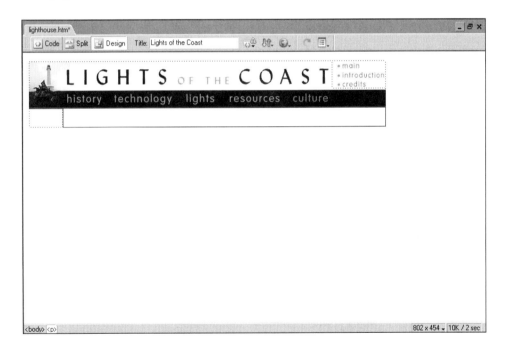

6) Choose Modify > Page Properties and click the Appearance category. Select bkg_inside_tan.gif for the background image, set all four margins (Left, Right, Top, and Bottom) to *0* pixels, and click OK. Save the file and preview it in the browser.
Inserting the background image shows you how the outlined table works with other elements on the page to create a unified look in the design. Setting the margins of the page to zero makes the table line up flush with the top and left sides of the browser,

177

as well as with the background image, which was created for a page with zero margins. As with the cell spacing and cell padding options, leaving the margin text fields blank is not the same as setting the margins to zero. Leaving the margins blank causes the page to use the browser defaults, which may vary from browser to browser.

Experiment with tables and layouts on your own pages to create effects that work with your designs.

DESIGNING FOR COMPUTER SCREENS

In the print world, a designer creates pages to be viewed in final form at a fixed size. The paper stock, printing quality, and size are all controlled. A Web designer, on the other hand, has to account for a greater number of possibilities. You have to consider not only the variety of browsers users might have, but also the size and resolution of their monitors. The number of screen types on which users can view Web pages has increased and will continue to do so. Users view Web pages on computers, TVs, cell phones, PDAs (such as the Palm), and more.

If you have only text on a page, the text reflows within the page based on the size of the browser window. As a Web designer, you then have no control over the look of the page. The user can maximize the window, making long, hard-to-read lines. If you want to control the flow of the text on the page, you can place your text within a table or use CSS to limit line length for text in a cell.

When you design a page with a fixed width, you may want to design to the lowest common denominator of monitor sizes that your audience will be using. If you think most of your users have 13-inch monitors, you should use that size. Remember that the browser takes up some room to the left and right of the screen, even if the user maximizes the window. There is no set rule for the amount of room a browser uses, so you should allow for the browser. For 13-inch monitors, for example, make the maximum page width 600 pixels (not accounting for space taken up by the browser and operating system). To determine the maximum page width, refer to the following chart.

RESOLUTION (IN PIXELS)	DEVICE
160×160	Palm-type device
240×320	Pocket PC
544×372	Web TV
640×240	Windows CE
640×480	13-inch monitor
800×600	15- to 17-inch monitor
1024×768	17- to 19-inch monitor
1200×1024	21-inch monitor

USING WINDOW SIZE TO CHECK LAYOUT

You can check your layout directly within Dreamweaver to determine what your page will look like on different-sized screens using the Window Size menu.

At the bottom of the lighthouse.htm document window, click the black arrow located to the right of the current window size display. Choose 760 × 420 (800 × 600 Maximized).

Windows Users: You must first click the Restore/Maximize button on the document window—not the Restore/Maximize button for the entire application. The document window will reduce to a floating window in the document space. You can only adjust the window size in this view. You can switch back to the tabbed interface after this exercise by clicking the document window Restore/Maximize button again.

The document window resets to 760 × 420. This size accounts for the space taken up by the browser and operating system on a screen at the 800 × 600 resolution.

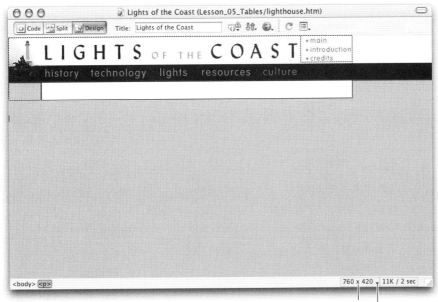

CURRENT WINDOW SIZE

WINDOW SIZE MENU

NOTE *You can also add your own size presets to the list by choosing Edit Sizes at the bottom of the menu.*

As you change the size of the Dreamweaver document window, you'll notice that the dimensions in the window size change to reflect the new size.

You can save and close the lighthouse.htm document.

CREATING A TABLE IN LAYOUT VIEW

Dreamweaver MX also provides a layout mode for creating tables. Layout mode works much like a page-layout program in which you can draw boxes on the page and then fill the boxes with text or graphics. You can resize the boxes and place the boxes anywhere on the page.

Some Dreamweaver features such as layers (covered in Lesson 16) do not function in Layout mode—you must use Standard mode when you need to use those features.

NOTE *In Layout mode, the exact numeric values of the widths and heights of the table and cells you create, as well as the placement of those cells, will be somewhat different from the examples shown here. Use the examples as guides for the general layout of your page.*

1) Create a new HTML document and save it as foghorns.htm in the Lesson_05_Tables folder. Title the document Lights of the Coast: Technology: Sound **and set the background color of the page to white.**

The page you are creating is a part of the Technology section of the "Lights of the Coast" project site. The page title you typed indicates this to the visitors of the site.

You will use the Layout mode to create a table in this document in the following steps.

2) Click the Layout button in the Layout category on the Insert bar.

LAYOUT MODE

You have switched to Layout mode, in which you can easily place elements on the page. You may see the info box titled "Getting Started in Layout Mode" which briefly describes the main tools: the layout cell and the layout table. You can click OK to close this dialog box.

NOTE *There is a checkbox for "Don't show me this message again." If you leave this box unchecked, the next time you restart Dreamweaver, you will see this dialog box again if you switch to Layout mode.*

180

A bar, with the text "Layout Mode [exit]" centered on it, appears just below the document window toolbar, appearing to be within the document itself. This bar is not visible in the browser because it is used only in Dreamweaver to indicate that you are working in Layout mode. As with Expanded mode, you can switch back to Standard mode by either clicking the Standard button in the Layout category on the Insert bar, or by clicking the [exit] link that appears on the bar across the top of the document while in Layout mode.

TIP *You can also choose View > Table Mode > Layout Mode or use the keyboard shortcut Command+F6 (Macintosh) or Ctrl+F6 (Windows) to switch to Layout mode.*

3) Click the Draw Layout Cell tool from the Layout Tools menu on the Insert bar.

After you select the Draw Layout Cell tool, the pointer changes to a plus sign (+) when you move it into the document window. The Tag Selector is replaced with a description of the tool you have selected.

A layout cell lets you draw a cell anywhere on the page. In Layout mode, you don't need to worry about the number or arrangement of rows and columns when creating your table—Dreamweaver automatically creates and manages the rows and columns when you designate the location of the cells on your page.

NOTE *You can't use the Layout Table tool to draw a table within the cell of another table in Layout mode. You must use Standard mode to nest tables.*

4) Place the pointer in the center of the page; then click and drag to draw the cell.

A layout table is drawn automatically to contain the cell. The layout table is drawn nearly as wide as the document window, although you can resize the table to any dimensions. The cell is outlined in blue to distinguish it from the table, which appears outlined in green. A solid blue line indicates that the insertion point is within the cell, whereas a dotted blue line indicates that the insertion point is not in the cell. All parts of the table other than the cell are shown in gray. The thin white lines indicate the rows and columns that Dreamweaver creates to construct the table when you draw layout cells. When you move the pointer over the border of the cell, it turns red to indicate which cell you are over.

By default, layout tables appear with a tab at the top. The tab makes it easier to identify the table. The tab causes the table to drop down slightly from the top of the page; this extra space does not exist in the browser. The table also appears with a bar at the bottom containing column widths and menus and the table width and menu. The bar, which serves the same purpose as the table header bar in Standard mode, may not be initially visible until you roll the pointer over the bottom boundary of the cell that you just created.

NOTE *To hide the tab and bar, choose View > Visual Aids > Table Widths. The rest of this lesson assumes that the default visual aids are active, and that you can see the tab and bar on the layout table.*

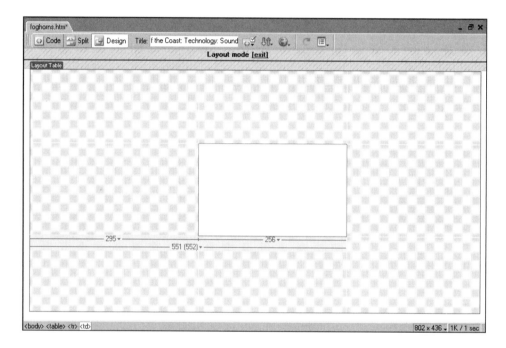

5) Insert the foghorn_title.gif graphic from the Lesson_05_Tables/Images folder into the layout cell you just drew.

TIP *From the Site portion of the Image Assets panel, you can just select and drag the graphic from the Assets panel into the cell on the page.*

You have inserted an image as you did in Lesson 3. The cell expands to fit the graphic if it was smaller than the size of the graphic. The new size is displayed in parentheses next to the original size of the column on the table widths bar.

NOTE *The table widths bar may disappear when you insert the image. To view it again, roll the pointer over the bottom edge of the cell.*

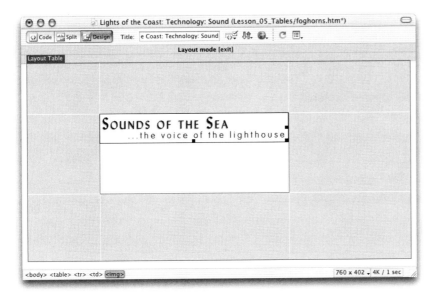

MODIFYING TABLE LAYOUT

As you design your pages in Layout mode, you will want to move, resize, or add new cells while adding content. A layout cell cannot overlap other cells and can't be moved outside the layout table.

1) In the foghorns.htm document, select the cell by moving the pointer over the border and clicking the border when it turns red.

The cell border turns blue and handles appear, which you can drag to resize the cell.

TIP *You can also Command-click (Macintosh) or Ctrl-click (Windows) within a cell to display the resize handles.*

2) If the cell is larger than the image, use the handles to drag the cell border to resize the cell, fitting it closely around the graphic. The cell should be the same size as the graphic.

TIP *Use the selection handle on the lower left corner of the cell to adjust the size if the table widths bar is obscuring the other selection handles on the bottom of the cell. Alternatively you can use the keyboard shortcut Command+Shift+I (Macintosh) or Ctrl+Shift+I (Windows) to hide all visual aids—turn the visual aids back on by repeating the command when you are done resizing the cell.*

183

In the Table tab, the size listed in the parentheses replaces the old size display. If the cell you initially created was smaller than the size of the graphic, the cell will have enlarged automatically to fit around the image exactly, and you don't need to resize it. If the cell you created was larger than the graphic, you must resize the cell to make sure that the borders of the layout cell line up flush with the edges of the image.

3) Click on the border of the cell (not on the resize handles) and drag the cell, moving it to the top and center of the page.

If you moved the cell to the right or left to center it, notice that the column numbers in the surrounding layout table change to display the new size.

4) Use the arrow keys to move the cell to the left.

The arrow keys move the cell 1 pixel at a time. Hold down the Shift key to move the cell 10 pixels at a time. Leave some space in the column between this cell and the side of the table. The column to the left of the cell containing the image should be 40 pixels wide.

5) Below the top cell, draw three more cells in a single column down the middle of the page, with a little space between them.

Your page should look similar to the example shown here. Don't be concerned about the sizes of the columns listed on the table width bar; they vary according to the exact placement of your layout cells.

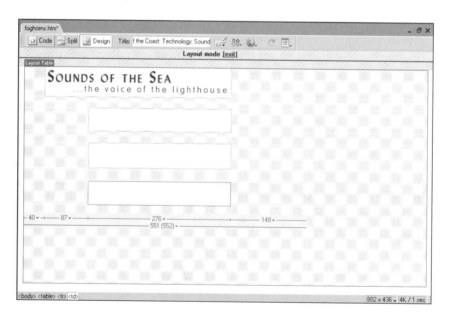

When you draw a cell on the page, white guides appear to help you place other cells that you want to align with the first cell. Use the horizontal guides to align the tops of the cells.

TIP *To draw multiple cells without clicking Draw Layout Cell more than once, hold down Command (Macintosh) or Ctrl (Windows) as you draw the first cell. You can continue to draw new cells until you release the modifier key.*

6) Of the three cells you just created, expand the topmost cell so it's as wide as the cell that contains the foghorn_title.gif graphic. Open foghorn.txt from the Lesson_05_Tables/Text folder. Copy the first paragraph and paste it into the first cell below the foghorn_title.gif graphic.

The cell expands if necessary to fit the content.

Macintosh Users: When you switch from the txt document back to the foghorns.htm document, Dreamweaver will rapidly switch back and forth between the two documents several times. Wait until it has stopped before trying to click in or paste the text into the foghorns.htm document. This is a bug and it will happen whenever you switch from the txt document to an HTML document that is in Layout mode.

7) Move both remaining cells to the far left, aligned with the left edges of the cells above. Draw one more cell to the right of those two cells. Copy the remaining text from the foghorn.txt file and paste it into the new cell.

NOTE *On both Macintosh and Windows, there is a bug that occurs if you have both a txt document (which opens in Code view) and an HTML document in Layout mode open at the same time. When you first opened the foghorn.txt document in the previous step, it appeared as normal; however, after you switch back to the foghorns.htm document to paste the text you've copied, the next time that you switch back to the foghorn.txt document you will see the layout bar across the top of the Code view document. The layout bar should not appear on a Code view document; this is a bug. You can click the [exit] link on the bar to make it disappear from the txt document.*

You will adjust the size of the new cell later in this lesson. Your page should look similar to the example shown here. Remember that the exact sizes of the columns are not important at this point.

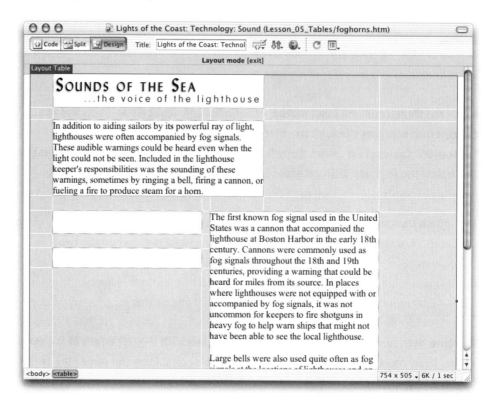

NOTE *If the lower left cell expands downward when you paste the text into the right cell, you can click the border of the empty left cell and use the handles to drag the bottom back upwards to its original size.*

8) Create a third cell below the two cells at the left. Insert fogsignal.jpg into the topmost of the three cells and insert foghorn.jpg into the bottom cell. Create a fourth cell below the cell containing the foghorn.jpg image, at the same width as the three cells above.

If the graphics are too large, the cell sizes enlarge horizontally or vertically as necessary to fit the graphics.

9) In the empty cell between the two foghorn images you inserted in the previous step, type the following caption: *Image above: Fog signal converted to diaphone at Point Montara, CA. Photograph post-1912, courtesy of Point Montara Light.* **Format the text as Verdana at 10 pixels.**

You will adjust the formatting of this cell in the following exercise.

10) In the empty cell below the foghorn.jpg image, type the following caption: *Image above: Compressor foghorns at Point Montara, CA. Photograph 1970, courtesy of Point Montara Light.* **Format the text for as Verdana at 10 pixels.**

Providing captions helps viewers understand the significance of each image.

11) Click the border of the cell to the right of the foghorn images that contains the two paragraphs of text to select it. Use one of the selection handles on the blue border to drag the left side of the cell to the left, toward the foghorn images, to enlarge the cell. Leave only a small space between it and the cells containing the foghorn images.

You want to enlarge the cell, not move it. Your page should now look similar to the example shown here.

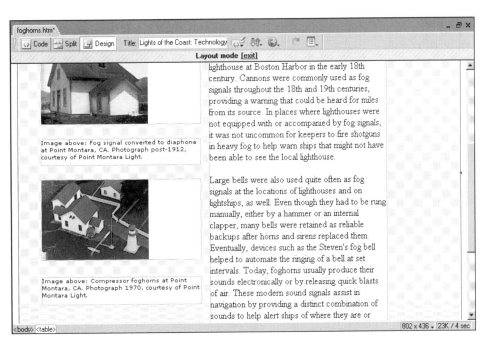

APPLYING CELL FORMATTING

As with Standard mode, you can change several table attributes, including cell color and alignment.

1) In the foghorns.htm document, select the cell in which you added the caption for the fogsignal.jpg image. Type the code #FFCC99 into the Bg color text field in the Property inspector. Set the background of the cell for the second caption to the same color.

The color of the cell changes to the color you selected. Be sure to select the cell so you can see the selection handles, as opposed to placing the insertion point inside the cell.

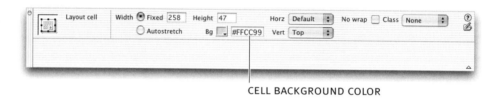

CELL BACKGROUND COLOR

NOTE *To change the background color of the entire table, select the table by clicking the green table border or any of the gray areas of the table. Click the Bg color box and choose a color for the table.*

2) Choose Center from the Horz menu in the Property inspector for the cells of both captions.

This step changes the alignment of the text in the cell to center.

3) Change the Vert setting to Middle for the cells of both captions.

This step centers the text vertically in the cell.

SPECIFYING LAYOUT WIDTH

In Layout mode, you can control the width of tables in two ways: by setting a fixed width, which is the default; or by using Autostretch, which causes the cells to change width depending on the width of the browser. In this exercise, you will control the width by applying Autostretch.

1) In the foghorns.htm document, select the top text cell just below the foghorn_title.gif graphic. Click the Autostretch option in the Width area on the Property inspector.

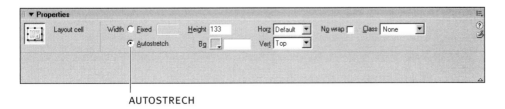

AUTOSTRECH

The Choose Spacer Image dialog box appears if a spacer image is not associated with your site.

If the dialog box appears, choose "Use an existing spacer image file," click OK, and locate spacer.gif in the Lesson_05_Tables/Images folder. The spacer file location is saved in your preferences. To change or remove the spacer image, choose Edit > Preferences and select the Layout Mode category and adjust the spacer image settings.

NOTE *The Choose Spacer Image dialog box includes an option to create a spacer-image file. If you are working on a site for which there is no existing spacer image, you should choose this option and click OK to navigate to the directory where you want Dreamweaver to save the spacer image. The Images folder is the best place.*

The Autostretch column is displayed in the table widths bar as a zigzagged line—you may have to scroll down to the bottom of the document to see it. Dreamweaver inserts spacer images to control the layout of the fixed-width columns when you select Autostretch. A spacer image controls the spacing in the layout but is not visible in the browser window.

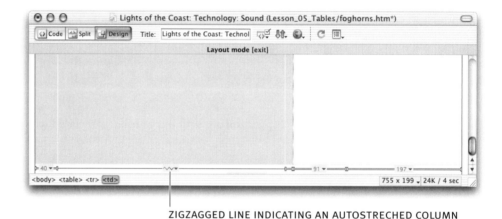

ZIGZAGGED LINE INDICATING AN AUTOSTRECHED COLUMN

TIP *You can also click a column's menu on the table width bar and choose Make Column Autostretch to apply the Autostretch option.*

2) Save and view the page in the browser; then change the width of the browser.
Notice that the column stretches as you change the width. When you select a column to Autostretch, you cause all cells in that column to Autostretch. Use the white guides on the page to determine whether another cell is within the column you've selected.

If you choose not to use spacer images, columns change size or even disappear if they do not hold content. You can insert and remove spacer images yourself or let Dreamweaver add them automatically when it creates an Autostretch column. To insert and remove these images yourself, choose one of the following options from the column-header menu:

• **Add Spacer Image:** The spacer image is inserted into the column. You do not see the spacer image, but the column might shift slightly.

- **Remove Spacer Image:** The spacer image is removed, and the column might shift.

- **Remove All Spacer Images:** Your whole layout might shift slightly—or dramatically, depending on your content. If you do not have content in some columns, they might disappear.

The column menus are contextual and change depending on which column you select. All three preceding options are not available in all columns.

You can close the foghorns.htm document.

USING A TRACING IMAGE

At times, you may be given pages that someone else has designed in a graphics program such as Macromedia FreeHand, Adobe Photoshop, or QuarkXPress, or you may have a screen shot of a page. If you can convert the page to a JPEG, GIF, or PNG graphic, you can import that image into Dreamweaver and use it as a guide, or **tracing image**, to re-create the HTML page.

The tracing image is visible only inside Dreamweaver. It is not embedded in the HTML code and is not displayed in the browser. The tracing image appears behind everything on your page in Dreamweaver. While you're using a tracing image, the background color or background image of your page is hidden, but that background color or image displays when you look at the page in a browser.

1) Create a new document and save it as lights.htm in the Lesson_05_Tables folder. Switch to Standard mode and title the page *Lights of the Coast: Lights*.

In this exercise, you'll insert a tracing image into this document.

2) Choose View > Tracing Image > Load.

The Select Image Source dialog box opens.

3) Choose the file table_trace.jpg, located in Lesson_05_Tables/Images; then click Open (Macintosh OS 9), Choose (Macintosh OS X), or OK (Windows).

The Page Properties dialog box opens.

4) Select the Tracing Image category. To see your image on the page, click Apply. Drag the Image Transparency slider to the left to lighten the image to 50 percent. Click Apply to see the change.

You want to be able to see the image but not be distracted by it.

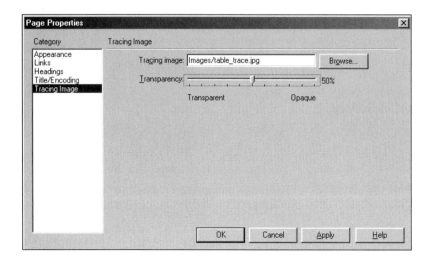

5) Click the Appearance category in the Page Properties dialog box and set the Left, Right, Top, and Bottom margins all to 0. Click OK to close the Page Properties dialog box.

Dreamweaver simulates the margin between the edge of the browser window and the items in the page. If you change this margin in the Page Properties dialog box, Dreamweaver uses the margin options you specify to place the tracing image. The default margin (used if the margin text field is left blank) may vary depending on the browser, but it is approximately 7 pixels.

NOTE *You can change the position of a tracing image by choosing View > Tracing Image > Adjust Position and specifying the x- and y-coordinate values. If you move the tracing image into the space reserved for the margin, as defined in the Page Properties dialog box, the coordinate values appear to be negative numbers. Choosing View > Tracing Image > Reset Position returns the tracing image to the top left corner of the document window with margin space (0 + margin, 0 + margin). Choosing View > Tracing Image > Align with Selection aligns the tracing image with the selected element. The top left corner of the tracing image is aligned with the top left corner of the selected element.*

192

6) Type *Creating the Lights-from bonfires to lenses* **at the top of the page.**

Notice how the text is displayed with the tracing image behind it. A tracing image can be your guide while you lay out a page. The use of a tracing image reinforces how it is helpful to have a clear and thought-out plan for the way your page will appear ahead of time.

You can save and close the lights.htm document.

WHAT YOU HAVE LEARNED

In this lesson, you have:

- Created a table (in Standard mode) (pages 144–145)
- Used attributes to make content within a table accessible to a wider audience, including those with disabilities (pages 146–150)
- Modified the table properties (including border, background, spacing, color, alignment, and size) (pages 146–150)
- Imported tabular data from an external document as a Dreamweaver table (pages 150–160)
- Sorted the information in a table (pages 160–161)
- Modified a table by adding and merging rows and columns to adjust the layout (pages 161–162)
- Exported a Dreamweaver table to an ASCII text file that other applications can read (pages 163–164)
- Created a table in which you inserted a variety of images (pages 165–170)
- Learned to nest tables by placing one table inside the cell of another table (pages 171–174)
- Used the technique of nesting tables to create an outline around a table (pages 175–178)
- Learned how the variety of screen sizes and screen resolutions can affect how you determine your page layout (pages 178–180)
- Used tables to lay out your pages (in Layout mode) (pages 180–191)
- Imported a tracing image that you used as a guide for your layout (pages 191–193)

developing style sheets

LESSON 6

Cascading Style Sheets (CSS) enable you to define how a variety of elements, such as text and images, display on your Web pages. The term "cascading" refers to the ordered sequence and precedence of styles. A style is a group of formatting attributes, identified by a single name, which tells the browser how to display an element. Styles in HTML documents give you a great deal of control over formatting. The advantage of using styles is that when you make a change to an attribute of the style, all the elements controlled by that style are automatically updated. You can make adjustments on a wide variety of settings from standard attributes—such as font, size, and color—to advanced attributes of text available only through CSS—such as the space between characters (tracking), and the space between lines (leading).

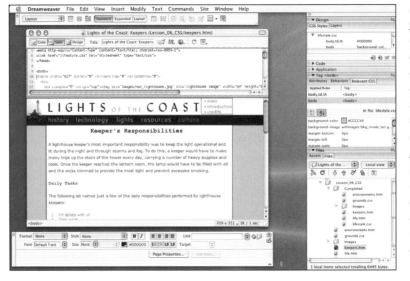

In this project, you will use CSS to apply a variety of format options to text using the three types of styles provided in Dreamweaver: HTML tag styles, custom styles, and CSS selector styles.

Using style sheets, you can, for example, create a paragraph with a half-inch margin, 20 points between the lines, and the text displayed in a 12-point font. This would not be possible without the use of CSS, which is supported by 4.0 or later browsers. Earlier browsers ignore CSS, although Internet Explorer 3.0 recognizes some style attributes. The best results are achieved with 5.0 and higher browsers, which support a wider range of features.

You can use an internal style—one that is stored inside the document—when you need to format a single page, or you can use an external style sheet—one that is stored outside of the Web page and linked to the current page—when you need to control several documents at once to keep the same style of text formatting on multiple pages. It is ideal to keep the treatment of text and layout consistent throughout your site because drastic changes in appearance might give viewers the impression that they have landed on another site.

Another advantage to using style sheets is the ability to keep the content of your Web pages separate from the formatting. Ultimately this means that you have more precise control over the appearance of your content, and inserting content into your Web site will become a quicker and less complicated process. Controlling the formatting of Web pages in style sheets allows you to create pages that are more compatible across different platforms and browsers.

To see examples of the finished pages for this lesson, open keepers.htm and life.htm from the Lesson_06_CSS/Completed folder.

WHAT YOU WILL LEARN

In this lesson, you will:

- Create an external style sheet
- Add styles to an existing style sheet
- Edit a style
- Create a custom style
- Link to an external style sheet
- Create an internal style
- Convert internal styles to external styles
- Use a style to create a page background
- Create a basic page layout

APPROXIMATE TIME

This lesson should take about two hours to complete.

LESSON FILES

Media Files:

Lesson_06_CSS/Images/ …(all files)

Starting Files:

*Lesson_02_Content/introduction.htm
    (or Lesson_02_Content/Completed/
    introduction.htm)*

Lesson_06_CSS/keepers.htm

Lesson_06_CSS/life.htm

Completed Project:

Lesson_06_CSS/Completed/environments.htm

Lesson_06_CSS/Completed/keepers.htm

Lesson_06_CSS/Completed/life.htm

Lesson_06_CSS/Completed/lifestyle.css

Lesson_06_CSS/Completed/grounds.css

UNDERSTANDING STYLES

At this point you've already used a number of CSS styles in previous lessons. Styles are an integrated part of Dreamweaver that define a wide variety of options and properties.

In Lesson 2 you began to format text with font face, size, and color attributes using the Property inspector. Dreamweaver defines such attributes through CSS styles. Each time you create a new combination of attributes in a page, Dreamweaver creates a new style, which is then listed in the Style menu on the Property inspector. In Lessons 1 through 5 you also worked with a variety of Page Properties including background color, background image, page margins, colors for the different states of links, and more; all of which are defined by CSS styles in Dreamweaver.

NOTE *You should be working in Standard mode throughout this exercise. If your document is displaying in Layout mode, switch to Standard mode by clicking the Standard Mode button in the Layout category of the Insert bar.*

1) Open introduction.htm from the Lesson_02_Content folder. Click the Split button on the document toolbar.

NOTE *If you do not have the introduction.htm file that you worked on in Lesson 2 you can open the introduction.htm file from the Completed folder in Lesson_02_Content.*

SPLIT VIEW SHOWS BOTH CODE AND DESIGN VIEWS

SHOW DESIGN VIEW   CODE VIEW

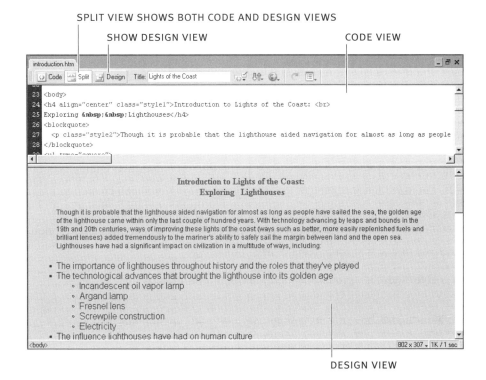

DESIGN VIEW

197

You now see a split view in the document window that shows both the Design view that you've been working with thus far in the lessons, and the corresponding code. You'll work more with this view in Lesson 14. By default the Code view is shown in the top portion of the document window, and the Design view is shown in the lower portion.

TIP *You can adjust the size of these views by placing the cursor over the bar that separates these two views. The pointer will turn into a double arrow and you can click and drag the bar as needed.*

2) In the Design view portion of the document window, select the word "Introduction" in the heading at the top of the page.

As you select the word "Introduction," the corresponding code in the Code view becomes highlighted. Notice the selected word in the Code view is preceded by <span class="style1">; span defines the selection of elements while class specifies which style is applied to the text enclosed by <span> (the opening tag) and </span> (the closing tag).

NOTE *The <span> tag is an inline element that defines items such as several words within a larger text block. It is similar to the <div> tag, which is a block-level element that defines entire blocks, similar to a paragraph.*

3) Scroll upward in the Code view until you see the following:

```
<style type="text/css">
<! --
body {
  background-color: #CCCC99;
}
```

CSS styles and attachments are placed between the <HEAD> and </HEAD> tags of the document. This code marks the beginning of a style sheet that contains all the information for the styles used in this page. It is known as an **internal style sheet** because it is embedded into the document. All styles that have been created in previous lessons using the Property inspector and the Page Properties dialog box have been internal styles. Dreamweaver MX 2004 automatically creates those styles whenever you define text formatting or page properties.

In CSS, a **style sheet** is a group of styles. A **style** (often referred to as a rule) is a set of properties that defines and controls the appearance of an element. In the code for introduction.htm, the style sheet is everything contained between <style

type="text/css"> (which defines the style sheet) and </style> (which ends the style sheet). The code Body { background-color: #CCCC99 } represents a single style (or rule).

Rules are comprised of selectors and declarations. A **selector** is the element that is being defined. A **declaration** is the combination of properties and their values. The **properties** are the attributes of that element that control the appearance and the **value** is the quantity or format that is specified. The structure of a style is selector { property: value } and property: value is the declaration.

For example, in the following style:

```
body { background-color: #CCCC99 }
```

the element being defined is the selector "body." The attribute of the background element that is being specified is the property of "background-color." The value that defines the color is #CCCC99.

You can close the introduction.htm document.

CREATING INTERNAL STYLES

Internal styles are used only in the current document. If you need to create style definitions for only one page in your site, you should use internal styles. If you want your site to have a cohesive design, you should use an external style sheet and link that style sheet to each document that you want to use that look.

TIP *Using external style sheets is recommended whenever possible. External styles are beneficial because they enable you to use styles in other documents. Additionally, because the formatting code for external styles is contained in a common external document, the pages that use that style sheet do not have to continually reload the formatting information; this causes less code to be used and therefore the pages download quicker. It also makes styles easier to update because they are all in one place. You learn to create external styles later in this lesson.*

You create several internal styles in this exercise.

1) Open the life.htm file from the Lesson_06_CSS folder.
This document contains paragraphs, headings, and an unordered list. It does not yet contain any styles, including those that are defined by the Page Properties and the Property inspector. Notice in the code that this document does not have a style sheet embedded in it at the top of the document like the introduction.htm file that you looked at in the previous exercise.

3) Set the following Page Properties: In the Appearance category, the Text Color should be #000000, the Background Color should be #CCCC99, the Background Image should be Images/bkg_inside_tan.gif, and all four margins should be set to 0. In the Links category, the Link color and Active Links should both be #660000, the Rollover Links should be #CC0000, and the Visited Links should be #333333.

Your document now contains an internal style sheet that specifies the various page properties that you set. Dreamweaver automatically created the style sheet when you defined the page properties. You can see the style sheet in the code, near the top of the document.

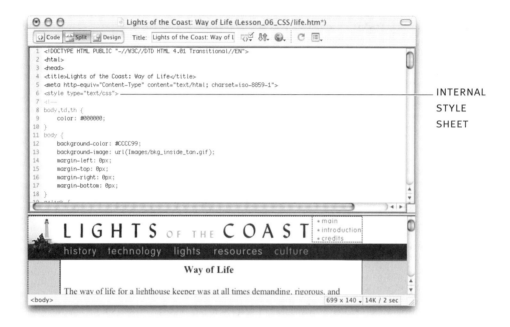

The CSS Styles panel, located on the Design panel group, now displays a list of the styles that were created when you defined the page properties.

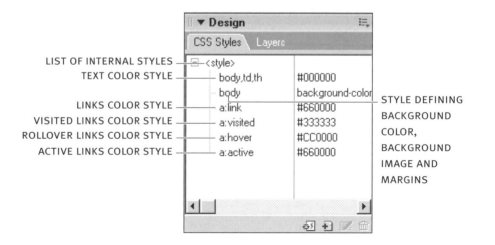

4) Click New CSS Style icon at the bottom of the CSS Styles panel.

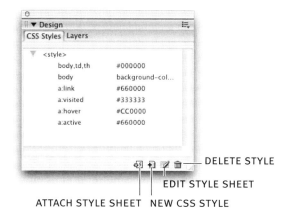

DELETE STYLE

EDIT STYLE SHEET

ATTACH STYLE SHEET   NEW CSS STYLE

The New CSS Style dialog box opens.

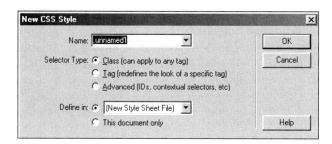

There are three different selector types (kinds of elements defined by styles) that you can use in Dreamweaver:

- **Class:** This type of selector allows you to create classes that are not tied to any particular elements. You can apply a single class to many different elements.
- **Tag:** This type of selector allows you to specify an HTML tag as the element that will be redefined by the style. The default appearance of the tag becomes modified by the style.

201

- **Advanced:** This type of selector allows you to create styles that are used for specific tag combinations (contextual selectors). This selector type also enables you to create IDs, which are similar to classes with one major exception: They can only be used once per page as a way of defining or uniquely identifying a particular element. Because of their unique nature, IDs are often used for scripting purposes and are indicated by a #.

5) Select Class from the Selector Type area of the New CSS Style dialog box.

The text field becomes a Name text field for creating a custom style.

If Class was not already selected, the default name .unnamed1 might not display in the text field when you switch the style type in the dialog box. If you were to cancel the new style and click the New CSS Style icon again, you would see the generic name .unnamed1 listed in the Name text field. Dreamweaver assigns generic names automatically in a numeric order: .unnamed1, .unnamed2, and so on. These names are not very descriptive and they can be especially unhelpful when you are creating multiple classes. It's best to get in the habit of giving your styles short names that are descriptive of their purposes.

6) Type *.boldstyle* **in the Name text field for the name of your class.**

A period before the name is required. If you delete the period, Dreamweaver automatically includes it at the beginning of the name, even if it isn't shown.

7) Select This document only in the Define in area and then click OK.

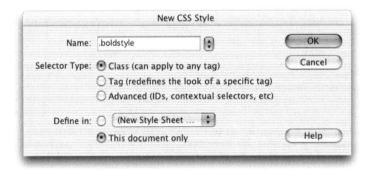

The document only option specifies that you are creating a new internal style. The CSS Style Definition for .boldstyle dialog box opens.

8) In the Type category of the CSS Style Definition dialog box, change the Weight option to bold, select normal from the Style menu, and type *#663300* **into the color text field. Leave all other options undefined and click OK.**

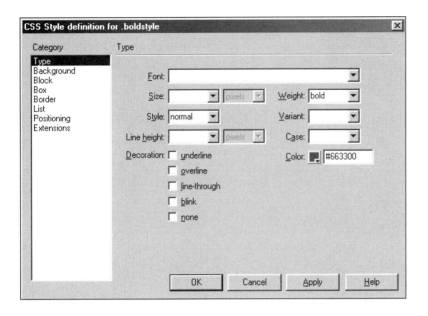

You see the class you just created displayed in the list of styles on the CSS Styles panel.

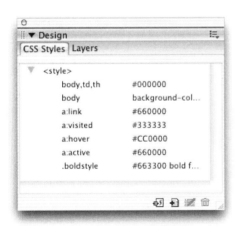

If you were to select the .boldstyle name in the CSS Styles panel, the Tag inspector would show Rule .boldstyle on the panel group title bar. You may need to expand the Tag inspector before the name changes to reflect the selection. The CSS properties tab, now the only tab available in the Tag inspector, contains the same categories that were available in the CSS Style Definition dialog box. If you expand the Font category, you can see the attributes of the .boldstyle class. The Tag inspector status

203

bar shows the name and location of the file in which the selected CSS Style is located. Enlarging the panel can help you see more of the path that describes the location of the file.

In the next steps, you'll apply the boldstyle class to certain items in the numbered list.

9) Select the word "Oil" in the numbered list near the top of the page. Choose boldstyle from the Style menu on the Property inspector to apply the style. Continue to apply the boldstyle to the terms in the numbered list "Paint," "Tools," "supplies," "Water," and "Coal."

The selected text changes to reflect the boldstyle class.

NOTE *If you want to remove the style formatting from text, place the insertion point within the text and choose None from the Style menu on the Property inspector. The style and its formatting are removed from the text, although the style will remain in the style sheet.*

10) Click the New CSS Style button on the CSS Styles panel. Set the Selector Type to Class, type *.highlight* **in the Name text field, and choose This document only in the Define in area. Click OK.**
The CSS Style Definition for .highlight dialog box appears.

204

Classes give you specific control over the formatting of your document. You can apply them the same way you apply styles in a word processor: by selecting the text and then applying the style. You can apply this style to text blocks or to individual words within blocks of text.

11) In the CSS Style Definition dialog box, choose Background from the Category list on the left.

The CSS Style Definition dialog box changes to display background options.

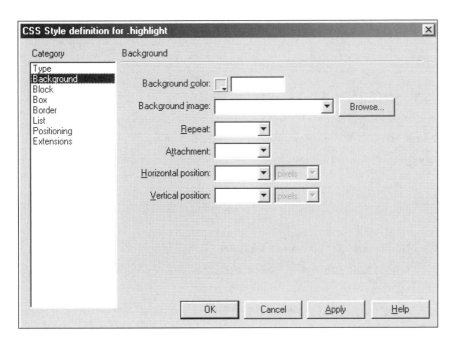

12) Set the Background Color to pale green (#CCFFFF) and click OK.

The highlight class you just created appears in the style list on the CSS Styles panel and is available in the Style menu on the Property inspector. There are now two classes in your internal style sheet: boldstyle and highlight.

13) Select the paragraph of text below the "Personal Resources" heading and apply the highlight style using the Style menu on the Property inspector.

The text appears to be highlighted with the pale green color. As with styles that are defined using the Property inspectors, classes display in the Style menu with visual representations.

You can save the life.htm file and leave it open for the next exercise.

CONVERTING INTERNAL STYLES TO EXTERNAL STYLES

Style sheets can be stored externally and linked to one or more documents. An **external style sheet** is a file that contains only CSS specifications. You can use external style sheets with multiple Web pages to ensure consistency from page to page.

If you have a document with internal styles and you decide you want to use those styles in other pages, you can easily export those styles to an external style sheet.

1) In the life.htm document, choose File › Export › CSS Styles.

The Export Styles As CSS File dialog box opens.

2) In the Save As text field, name your style sheet *lifestyle.css*. Save the file in the Lesson_06_CSS folder.

NOTE *You don't have to add the extension .css; it's appended to the document automatically upon saving if you don't include it.*

An external style sheet is created that contains the internal styles existing in the life.htm document[md]those that define the page properties as well as the boldstyle style and the highlight style.

NOTE *When you export styles, only internal styles are included in the new document. If there is an external style sheet attached to the document from which you are exporting internal styles, the styles in that external style sheet are not included in the new style sheet.*

If you want to use the external style sheet in the document from which you converted internal styles, you should remove the internal style sheet before linking the style sheet, which you will learn to do in the next exercise. Although Dreamweaver enables you to attach an external style sheet with styles that use the same names as those contained in an internal style sheet, you should delete the internal styles to avoid conflict, reduce the amount of code in your HTML document, and reduce the possibility of errors and confusion.

You can close the life.htm document.

LINKING TO AN EXISTING EXTERNAL STYLE SHEET

You now have an external style sheet with multiple style definitions. Because it is external, you can use this file with other documents by linking it to the Web pages that you want the style definitions to be applied to or made available to. You will need to manually apply any classes to paragraphs or selected text. Later in this lesson you learn to develop styles that redefine HTML tags as well as create contextual selectors—both style types will be applied automatically to all documents that have the style sheet attached.

NOTE *IDs, which can be created using the CSS Selector Styles type, are not automatically applied to documents when external style sheets are attached.*

1) Open the keepers.htm file from the Lesson_06_CSS folder.

This page has no internal or external styles.

In the following steps, you will link this document to the external style sheet that you created in the previous exercise from the internal styles in the life.html document. This will ensure that the text formatting is consistent between both pages.

NOTE *For the formatting to remain consistent as you continue to develop styles you would need to remove the internal style from the life.htm document and follow the steps in this exercise to attach the external style sheet. Using external style sheets will ensure that all documents linked to those style sheets will continually reflect any modifications to the styles those external style sheets contain. You can leave the life.htm document as is for this lesson.*

2) Click the Attach Style Sheet icon at the bottom of the CSS Styles panel.

ATTACH STYLE SHEET

The Attach External Style Sheet dialog box opens.

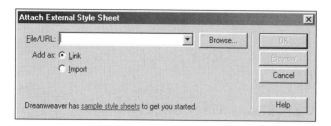

NOTE *Dreamweaver includes a number of predesigned CSS style sheets you can use in your own Web sites. To use one of these style sheets, click the sample style sheets link at the bottom of the Attach External Style Sheet dialog box. Select the style sheet you want to use from the Sample Style Sheets dialog box and click OK. You can use these style sheets as-is or use them as a starting point to develop your own. Clicking Cancel from the Sample Style Sheets dialog box returns you to the Attach External Style Sheet dialog box.*

If you are proficient in writing HTML and know how to write CSS, you can create a CSS page from scratch by choosing File > New and selecting the CSS document type from the Basic Page category on the General tab. A new document opens, in which Code view is the only available viewing mode.

For more information about CSS, choose O'REILLY CSS Reference from the Book menu on the Reference panel located in the Code panel group to learn more about CSS elements. Use the Style menu to choose CSS terms and read their descriptions. You'll work with the Reference panel more in Lesson 14. You can collapse the Code panel group to make more room for the other panels you'll use in this lesson. You might want to expand the Tag inspector panel group if it was closed to make room for the Reference panel.

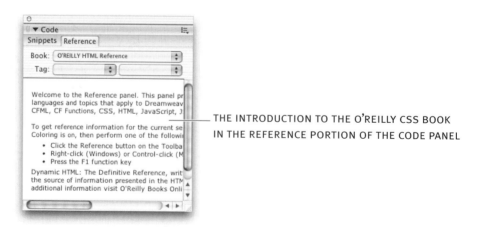

THE INTRODUCTION TO THE O'REILLY CSS BOOK
IN THE REFERENCE PORTION OF THE CODE PANEL

3) Click Browse and locate the lifestyle.css file that you created at the beginning of this lesson. Select the style sheet by clicking Choose (Macintosh) or OK (Windows) on the Select Style Sheet File dialog box. Verify that the Link option is selected from the Add As section of the Attach External Style Sheet dialog box and click OK.

The Link option was selected by default since is the first time that you are attaching a style sheet to the keepers.htm document. The Import option for attaching a style sheet does not work in Netscape Navigator 4.x; that browser ignores any style sheets that are attached using Import. When linking multiple style sheets, the Link option is usually used for the first style sheet, and Import is used for subsequent style sheets. If you already have an external style sheet linked to a document and you choose to add a link to a second style sheet, the Link option will be grayed-out and the Import option will be selected. Using the Link method for multiple style sheets can cause the browser to give the visitor a choice between the style sheets that will be used, which can be confusing to visitors and is usually not recommended or desired. Given the cascading nature of style sheets, when the first style sheet is linked and the second style sheet is imported, the second style sheet has priority and overrides any conflicting styles in the first sheet. Likewise, a third style sheet overrides any conflicts in the first and second sheets. The process of using multiple style sheets is known as cascading.

A technique often used in consideration of older browsers is to place all styles that are not compatible with those browsers into the second or other subsequent style sheets that use the Import option. That way older browsers use only the styles that they can recognize in the first style sheet; they are not affected by styles that may conflict or cause errors since they ignore style sheets linked with the Import option. Styles contained within subsequent style sheets can then override those created for older browsers in the first sheet.

The external style sheet lifestyle.css is now linked to the keepers.htm document. The page now reflects the formatting attributes that are specified in the external style sheet—at this point the background image and page margins are the most obvious of the styles that are defined in lifestyle.css.

CREATING EXTERNAL STYLES

Although you can easily change a variety of formatting attributes such as font face, size, and color in individual documents, external styles can expand your options and make it easy to apply those same styles to other documents within your site. Rather than recreating your styles in each page in which you want to use them, you can use an external style sheet to store all your styles, making those styles accessible to any document to which the style sheet is attached. This can speed up the formatting process greatly.

In this exercise, you create a new style in the lifestyle.css external style sheet by redefining an HTML tag. By redefining the Heading 3 (<h3>) HTML tag in this exercise, you tell the browser that any text using the <h3> tag should be displayed with the formatting you specify. This is useful because it allows you to alter the basic Heading 3 format so that all text that uses the Heading 3 format is formatted with the style attributes you specified.

1) Click the New CSS Style icon on the CSS Styles panel. In the Selector Type area, select Tag. Use the Tag menu to select h3.

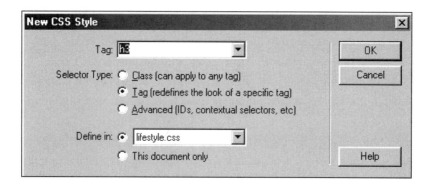

In this exercise, you are making a style for the format Heading 3. In HTML, the corresponding tag is <h3>. Tags are specified in the New CSS Style dialog box without the brackets that surround them in the code. The heading near the top of the document, Keeper's Responsibilities, is formatted as a Heading 3.

210

TIP *When you are creating a style that redefines an existing HTML tag, it is helpful to place the insertion point within text on the page that uses the same tag or select that tag in the Tag Selector before you create the style. Dreamweaver then automatically associates the HTML tag with the style that will be created as long as the Tag selector type is the default selection—the default selector type is whichever type was last used. If the Tag selector type is not the default, you can select it, click Cancel on the New CSS Style dialog box, and click New CSS Style again—Tag will be selected when the dialog box reopens. Selecting the tag prior to opening the New CSS Style dialog box can be helpful if you are not familiar with HTML. For example, you could click in the Keeper's Responsibilities heading and select the <h3> tag and then click the New CSS Style icon on the CSS Styles panel. If Tag is selected in the Selector Type area, the <h3> tag is displayed as h3 in the Tag text field.*

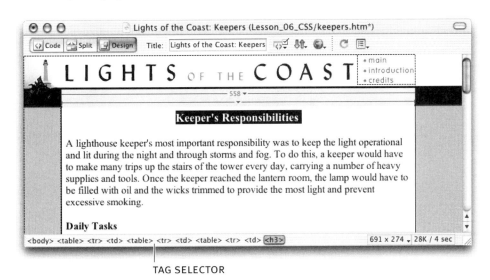

TAG SELECTOR

2) From the Define in area, select the menu option and choose lifestyle.css from the menu. Click OK.

TIP *Even if you select an option from the menu, you should still check to make sure the radio button for the menu option has been clicked.*

Because this is the only style sheet that is linked to the current document, (New Style Sheet File) and lifestyle.css are the only options in the menu. For documents that do not have any external style sheets attached, the only option in this menu would be (New Style Sheet File)

211

NOTE *You can create a new external style sheet while creating a new style by selecting (New Style Sheet File) in the menu option in the Define In area of the New CSS Style dialog box. When you create a new external style sheet for a style, the style sheet is automatically linked to the document for which it was created. You should save any such new external style sheets with the .css extension. To keep the file structure clean and organized, some sites keep all external styles sheets in a central location.*

The CSS Style Definition for h3 in lifestyle.css dialog box opens, which you use to define the formatting of Heading 3 tags.

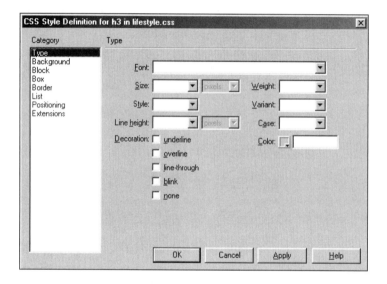

The CSS Style Definition dialog box always displays the selector of the style—the element that is being modified—and the name of the style sheet that it is being defined in. In this case, the selector is h3 and the style sheet is lifestyle.css.

3) In the Type category, select Courier New, Courier, mono from the Font menu. Select 18 from the first Size menu and change the measurement to points in the second Size menu. Select bold from the Weight menu and select the dark blue color #000033 in the Color area. Click OK.

TIP *To select the color, you can either type the hexidecimal color code into the color text field or you can click the color box—the color swatches will then appear and the pointer will become an eyedropper that you can use to select a color.*

When you click OK to close the CSS Style Definition dialog box, the lifestyle.css file automatically opens behind the keepers.htm document. CSS files are displayed in

Code View, which you will work with more in Lesson 14. If you make changes to the style sheet such as creating, editing or deleting styles, be sure to save the CSS document before closing it. If you close it without saving, you will lose any changes that you may have made. You may wish to periodically save your CSS document as well as your HTML document while you are working.

NOTE *You can use the Dreamweaver Preferences to adjust how you work with CSS. The CSS Styles category allows you to choose to open CSS files when they are modified—this option is on by default. You should leave this option selected for this lesson. Also included in this section of the Preferences are shorthand options that affect the way CSS is written by Dreamweaver.*

Redefined HTML tag styles are applied automatically throughout the document. The style you created is now reflected in the "Keeper's Responsibilities" heading. You can also see that the redefined HTML tag style is applied to currently active text (where the insertion point is located) by looking at the Relevant CSS tab in the Selection panel. The upper portion of the panel lists the rules (styles) that affect the selected object—in this case, the selected text. The attributes that are used in the selected rule (style) and their values are displayed in blue in the lower portion of the panel. You may have to scroll down to find the attributes that apply to the current selection. You can edit these elements directly through this panel by selecting and modifying a value, or adding a value to a previously undefined attribute.

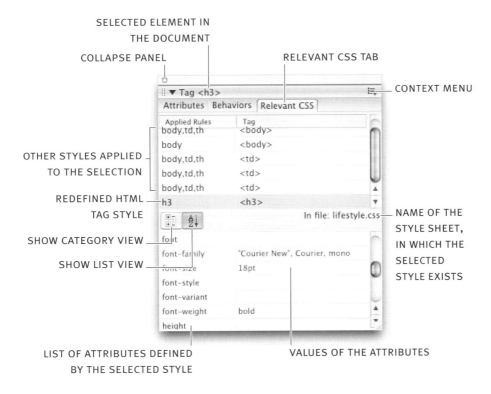

SELECTED ELEMENT IN THE DOCUMENT

COLLAPSE PANEL

RELEVANT CSS TAB

CONTEXT MENU

OTHER STYLES APPLIED TO THE SELECTION

REDEFINED HTML TAG STYLE

SHOW CATEGORY VIEW

SHOW LIST VIEW

NAME OF THE STYLE SHEET, IN WHICH THE SELECTED STYLE EXISTS

LIST OF ATTRIBUTES DEFINED BY THE SELECTED STYLE

VALUES OF THE ATTRIBUTES

4) Place the insertion point within the first paragraph below the "Keeper's Responsibilities" heading.

The Tag Selector at the lower left of the document window displays the HTML tag <p>, indicating that the insertion point is within the paragraph. The <p> tag defines a paragraph.

5) Click New CSS Style icon on the CSS Styles panel. By default, the Tag text field should display p, Tag should be selected in the Selector Type section, and the Define in section should show lifestyle.css selected in the menu. Make any changes necessary to match these values and then click OK.

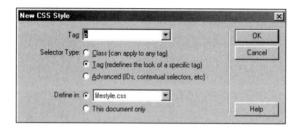

The new style you are creating will redefine the way text formatted with paragraph tags should appear—the selector is p and the style sheet is lifestyle.css.

6) In the Type category of the CSS Style Definition dialog box, select Verdana, Arial, Helvetica, Sans-serif from the Font menu. Select 12 from the Size menu and change the measurement to points in the second Size menu. Type *17* in the Line Height text field and change the measurement to points. Choose #333300 from the Color area and then click OK to close the dialog box and create the style.

TIP *You can click Apply to see your selections appear on the page while the dialog box is still open. If you want to make changes based on how the text appears, you can do so before closing the dialog box.*

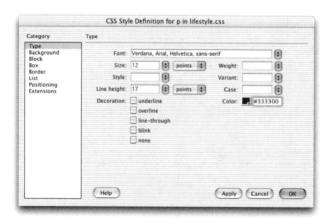

214

Any text that is contained within paragraph tags in the document will now appear with the formatting for the attributes that you defined in the external style sheet. The style sheet does not affect any text that has a different format applied to it, such as the subheading "Daily Tasks" or the numbered list.

NOTE *The most common units of measurement for defining text size in Web pages are pixels and points. Points are derived from print-based media and can be a good choice for pages that are intended for printing. Pixels on the other hand originate from digital media and describe a unit of measurement based on screen resolution. Consequently, pixels tend to translate more consistently from browser to browser and platform to platform than points. Small text that is readable on a Windows computer can be completely illegible on a Macintosh— a situation that occurs most often when developers use points to define text size.*

This discrepancy is the result of a fundamental difference in screen resolution. Macintosh screen resolution is 72 pixels-per-inch (ppi)—in the past this has been has been referred to as dots-per-inch (dpi)—whereas Windows screen resolution is 96 ppi. Because a point is $^{1}/_{72}$ of an inch, on a Macintosh it is the same as a pixel (an inch being 72 pixels). In Windows, a point is still $^{1}/_{72}$ of an inch; however, because an inch on a Windows computer is 96 pixels, a point is $^{1}/_{72}$ of 96—which comes out to roughly 1.3 pixels. Recent browsers are trying to overcome the difference by setting the default resolution for text in Macintosh browsers to 96 ppi.

There are several other measurement options available, including relative sizes that you learned about in Lesson 2 in comparison to absolute values, which require the selection of a unit of measurement. Inches, centimeters, and millimeters are the other print-based units available. Picas (one pica is 12 points), ems, exs and percent are other units of measurement. The percentage option relies on the size defined by the parent element or tag and therefore depends on inheriting a size attribute. You learn more about style precedence and inheritance later in this lesson.

While pixels or relative sizes, ems and percentages are recommended over points or other print-based units of measurement, the most important thing is to check your Web pages on different platforms and see how your text appears on both Macintosh and Windows computers.

7) Place the insertion point in the first line of the list that begins with "Fill lamps with oil." In the Tag Selector, click `<ol>`.

This procedure selects the list tag that controls the HTML formatting of the text. By selecting the `<ol>` tag (which applies to the entire list), you apply the formatting to both the list number and the list item at the same time. You also see the `<li>` tag (which applies only to an individual item in the list) in the Tag Selector.

8) Click New CSS Style on the CSS Styles panel. Verify that ol is displayed in the Tag text field, that Tag is selected in the Selector Type area, and that the style will be created in the lifestyle.css style sheet. Click OK to define the style in the CSS Style Definition dialog box. Set the font to Verdana, Arial, Helvetica, Sans-serif; set the size to 11 points; set the style to italic; and set the color to #666699. Click OK.

As you create styles, you see them listed in the CSS Styles panel. You may need to expand the list if it is collapsed in order to see the styles.

The ol style overrides the settings that you specified for the default body text color (black). You learn more about how to determine which styles are given priority later in this lesson.

9) In the document window, click in the heading "Daily Tasks," select the <h4> tag in the Tag Selector, and click New CSS Style on the CSS Styles panel. In the New CSS Style dialog box, verify that the Tag field displays h4, the Selector Type is Tag, and the style will be defined in lifestyle.css; then click OK. In the CSS Style Definition dialog box, set the font to Courier New, Courier, mono; set the size to 14 points; and set the color to #333366. Click OK.

This subheading is set to the Heading 4 format. You can see the <h4> tag displayed in the Tag Selector at the lower left of the document window, and you can also see Heading 4 displayed in the Format drop-down menu on the Property inspector.

216

At this point, your document should look similar to the example shown here.

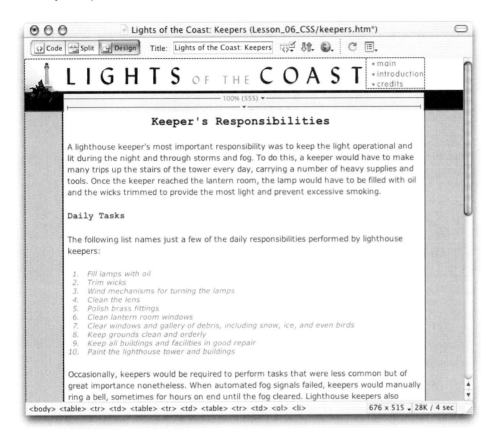

Leave the keepers.htm file open for the next exercise. Save both the keepers.html and lifestyle.css documents.

CREATING STYLES FOR TAG COMBINATIONS

The Advanced Selector Type enables you to create contextual selectors that are used to format combinations of tags—tags that appear within other tags. In this exercise, you specify a different format for text paragraphs with an alignment. Because you already created a style for the <p> tag, the paragraphs within the table currently reflect that formatting.

1) Place the cursor in the first paragraph located at the top of the document, just below the "Keeper's Responsibilities" heading.

The Tag Selector at the lower left of the document window shows the hierarchy of the code. The last two tags listed are <td><p>: table cell and paragraph, respectively. On the other hand, if you were to place the insertion point in the paragraph below the image further down on the page, the Tag Selector shows <div><p>: where div is an alignment (center) and p is the paragraph. Using CSS Selectors to specify tag combinations allows you to create a different style for the paragraph inside the table.

2) Click New CSS Style on the CSS Styles panel. Select Advanced in the Selector Type area and type *div p* in the Selector text field. Select lifestyle.css in the Define in area and click OK.

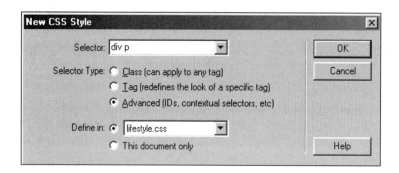

The div p typed in the Selector text field represents the alignment tag and the paragraph tag inside it. Whenever this specific combination of tags appears in a document linked to the lifestyle.css style sheet, the formatting you will choose in the following steps will be applied. By using div p, you specify that only paragraphs contained within a div, such as an alignment, will be affected.

NOTE *The Selector menu lists the four states applicable to links: a:link, a:visited, a:hover (not supported by all browsers), and a:active. This type of CSS Selector is known as a pseudoclass. Attributes of font-face, size, style, color, and underline can be set in the Page Properties dialog box in the Links category, which create internal styles for an individual document (covered in Lesson 4). If you want link styles to be contained in an external style sheet, you can export the internal styles or use the CSS Selector option, choose the desired state, and modify it accordingly.*

The CSS Style Definition dialog box opens.

3) Set the font to Geneva, Arial, Helvetica, sans-serif. Select 10 points for the size, type 14 into the line height text field and select points for the line height measurement. Select #000000 for the font color and click OK.

218

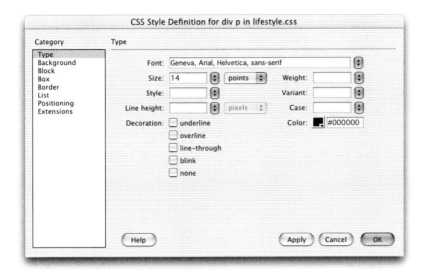

Your changes are reflected in the text that is centered below the image.

4) Save your changes to the keepers.htm and lifestyle.css documents and preview keepers.htm in a browser.

NOTE *Because your external styles sheet is not automatically saved, you must save it before previewing your page in the browser. If you do not save it before you preview, Dreamweaver will prompt you to do so.*

Because contextual selectors allow you to format tags that appear in sequence with other tags, the changes you made for the paragraph in the div do not affect the other paragraphs on the page.

EDITING AN EXISTING STYLE

One of the major advantages of using external style sheets is the ability to edit styles with ease and speed. Because changes are made only in the style sheets and not in the individual Web pages, you do not have to duplicate your modifications across a large number of documents. With external styles, formatting is not kept in the document (such as keepers.htm)—the only style information included is a reference that specifies which style should be used in the case of classes. Web pages tell the browser which external style sheets to use for instructions on how to display the formatting. The styles are applied to the elements by the browser at the time that a file is seen by a visitor. Any modifications are automatically reflected in every page that is attached to the edited style sheet at the time that it is viewed. Because formatting values are contained in the style sheet (lifestyle.css, for example), those values need to be modified in only that one location to affect all pages linked to the style sheet. This is useful because the appearance of an element such as text can be changed in several pages or even an entire site very quickly.

In this exercise, you edit a style in the lifestyle.css external style sheet.

1) Select p from the list of styles in the lifestyle.css on the CSS Styles panel.

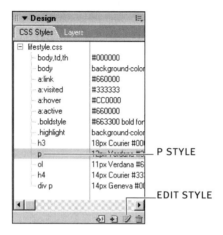

P STYLE

EDIT STYLE

The styles you create in the external style sheet lifestyle.css appear in the list on the CSS Styles panel.

When you select p from the CSS Styles panel, the CSS Properties tab becomes active on the Selection panel. The Selection panel indicates that the p style is currently selected and displays the attributes of that style in the CSS Styles appropriate group—Font is the group in this case. The group shows the style attributes, such as font family, font size, and color in this example.

SHOW LIST VIEW

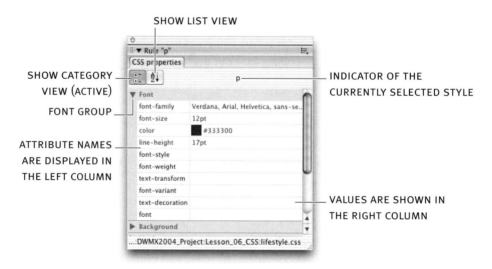

SHOW CATEGORY
VIEW (ACTIVE)

FONT GROUP

ATTRIBUTE NAMES
ARE DISPLAYED IN
THE LEFT COLUMN

INDICATOR OF THE
CURRENTLY SELECTED STYLE

VALUES ARE SHOWN IN
THE RIGHT COLUMN

TIP *You can make changes to the selected style using the list of attributes in CSS Properties section of the Selection panel group. Clicking the name of the attribute (in the left column) selects that attribute. Clicking the value (in the right column) allows you to change that value. For example, you can access a menu with the available font groups by clicking the name of the font, and you can access the color picker by clicking the color square.*

2) Click the Edit Style icon at the bottom of the CSS Styles panel.

The CSS Style Definition dialog box for the p element in the external lifestyle.css style sheet opens. This dialog box is the same as the CSS Style Definition dialog box you used in the previous exercise to choose formatting attributes for all text on the page that uses the <p> tag.

NOTE *If you click the Edit Style icon without first selecting the style you want to edit, Dreamweaver opens the Edit Style Sheet dialog box, in which you can select the style you want to edit. The Edit Style icon might be grayed-out if you do not have a style selected in the CSS Styles panel.*

3) In the CSS Style Definition dialog box, change the size from 12 points to 12 pixels by selecting pixels from the size measurement menu. Replace the value of 17 for the Line Height by typing *19* in the text field and change the Line Height measurement to pixels. Click OK.

Your changes are applied to the document. The font size may now appear slightly different on Windows computers (it should remain the same on the Macintosh), and the space between each line of text is greater. This style sheet is not yet used by any other documents; if other documents did use this style sheet, any text in those documents using the <p> tag would automatically be formatted according to the modifications you just made.

Save the lifestyle.css document. Leave both keepers.htm and lifestyle.css open.

WORKING WITH STYLE PRECEDENCE

When more than one style applies to the same element, the browser displays the attributes of each style in combination with the other styles—and those styles might conflict with each other. In case of such a conflict, the precedence of styles is determined by the cascading nature of CSS. Understanding how to manage and order your styles can help you to avoid unexpected results.

CSS is applied cumulatively, that is each style builds upon other styles if they apply to the same element, in an ordered sequence according to the following rules of origin, specificity and order.

ORIGIN

The **origin**, which is the source of a style, is evaluated first. The sequence of style origins is as follows, beginning with the lowest priority—what the browser uses first:

- Browser defaults (lowest priority)
- Styles created by the user
- Styles specified by the Web page (highest priority)

This means that browsers use their default formatting specifications, unless there is a style sheet that overrides those defaults. A user specified style sheet overrides browser defaults, while styles specified by the Web page override user specified styles.

1) Open the Internet Explorer browser. Macintosh users should choose Explorer › Preferences (Macintosh) and select the Web Content category from the Web Browser group in the scrolling list to the left. Windows users should choose Tools › Internet Options, select the General tab, and click the Accessibility button near the bottom of the dialog box.

TIP *If you do not have Explorer installed on your computer, you can use any Web browser to complete this step. The exact location and title of the section in which a user style sheet is specified may vary from browser to browser, and version to version. As a Web developer, it is recommended that you become familiar with a variety of browsers, so you may wish to repeat this step for other browsers. If you can't find the option for specifying a style sheet, try looking in the browser program's help or documentation.*

USER STYLE SHEET OPTION IN THE MACINTOSH INTERNET EXPLORER PREFERENCES

Visitors have the option to instruct browsers to apply style sheets of their choosing to the pages they visit. This option can provide greater accessibility by allowing users to adjust the appearance of Web pages through a style sheet that is optimized for their needs. This is an important option for users who may have visual disabilities. For instance, if a user has a hard time distinguishing small text against backgrounds that don't contrast well, that user may specify a style sheet with large text, and a color combination with a dramatic contrast such as black text on a white background. Although this option is available, the majority of your visitors will most likely have no style sheet specified so it is still important to consider the accessibility of your design when developing a site. Keep in mind the fact that some users may not know this option exists—don't rely on your visitors to make your site viewable. The more work they have to do to see your site, the less likely that they'll stick around to view the content. Design with the experiences of your audience in mind and aim to present sites as complete, seamless, and easy to use as possible for the best results (more visitors!).

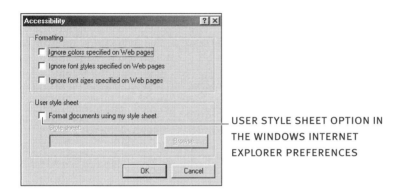

USER STYLE SHEET OPTION IN THE WINDOWS INTERNET EXPLORER PREFERENCES

If there are conflicting styles between a style sheet specified by the user and one specified by the Web page, the one specified by the Web page will be used. If a style sheet specified by a user defines the default font face as Verdana, and a style sheet specified by the Web page defines the default font color as green, the default text style will be both Verdana and green. This cumulative effect is known as **inheritance**.

NOTE *Styles can also be modified by the* **weight** *declaration, a method of establishing priority that is primarily intended to give the user an option for control over the style precedence. To increase the weight of a style,* !important *is included at the end of the style declaration, after the attribute values. Any style defined with* !important *in a style sheet specified by the user will override conflicting styles specified by the Web page—regardless of whether the styles defined by the Web page use the* !important *modifier. Older CSS standards allowed styles containing* !important *and originating from the Web page to override user specified styles containing* !important. *The change to give user specified styles containing the* !important *declaration priority is intended to give users control over styles—this can be important for visitors who need to view pages in certain ways. Use the modifier with discretion and consider whether it is truly necessary. A style using the* !important *modifier would appear:* body { color: #339900 !important }

You can close the browser Preferences (Macintosh) or Tools (Windows).

UNDERSTANDING SPECIFICITY

The precedence of style types depends on a system that determines which style is the most specific. Style **specificity** is based on values in the format of abc as follows:

- a is the number of IDs in the style
- b is the number of attributes that are defined by the style
- c is the number of element names in the selector.

Styles with higher specificity values are given priority over styles with lower values.

EXAMPLES OF HOW SPECIFICITY IS DETERMINED

SAMPLE STYLES	STYLE TYPE	A	B	C	SPECIFICITY (ABC) VALUE
p { color: #000000 }	Tag	0	1	1	11
This style specifies that all text contained within paragraph blocks will be black.					
td p { font-size: 22px }	Advanced (Contextual Selector)	0	1	2	12
This style specifies that all text contained within paragraph blocks that is also contained within a table cell will be 22 pixels.					
h5 { font-family: Verdana, Arial, Helvetica, sans-serif; font-size 18px }	Tag	0	2	1	21
This style specifies that all text formatted as a Heading 3 will be displayed in Verdana, Arial, Helvetica, sans-serif at a size of 18 pixels.					
.blue { font-style: normal; font-weight: bold; color: #0033CC }	Class	0	3	0	30
This style specifies that all text which the .boldstyle style is applied to will use the normal font style, be bold, and use a dark brown color (#663300)					
#left { font-size: 22px; color: #000000 }	Advanced (ID and Contextual Selector)	1	2	0	120
This style specifies that the text marked with the unique ID left will be 22 pixels and black.					

2) Switch to the lifestyle.css style sheet in Dreamweaver. Calculate the specificity values for the following styles: the h4 Tag, the highlight class, and the ol Tag.

After you have calculated the values, you can compare them with the values listed below the example of how your style sheet should appear and the example of how specificity determines the order of styles that follows.

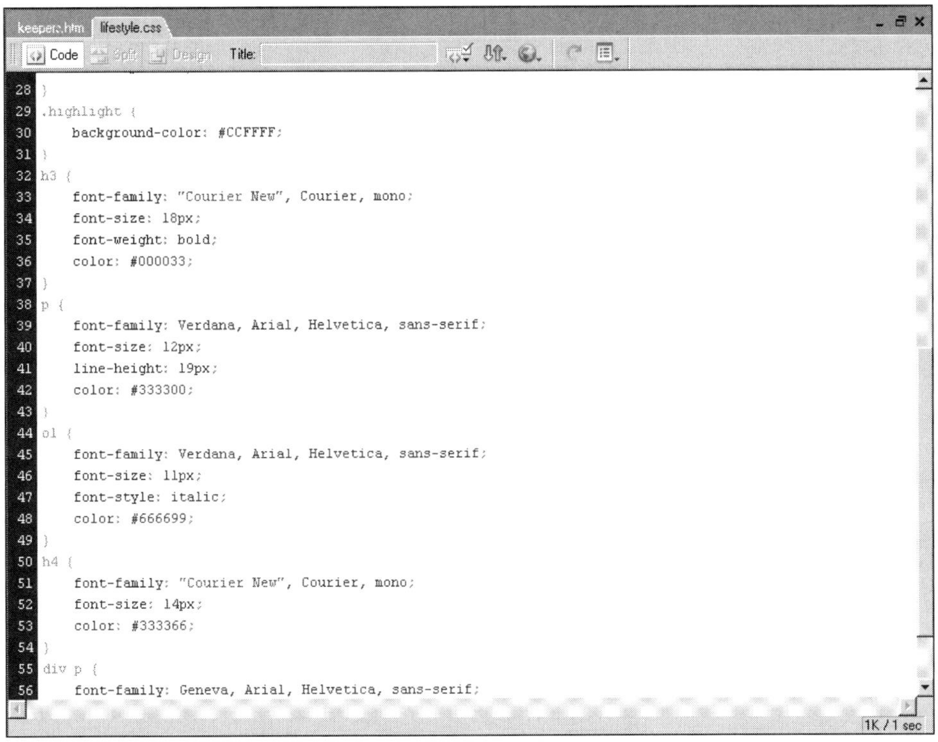

```
28  }
29  .highlight {
30      background-color: #CCFFFF;
31  }
32  h3 {
33      font-family: "Courier New", Courier, mono;
34      font-size: 18px;
35      font-weight: bold;
36      color: #000033;
37  }
38  p {
39      font-family: Verdana, Arial, Helvetica, sans-serif;
40      font-size: 12px;
41      line-height: 19px;
42      color: #333300;
43  }
44  ol {
45      font-family: Verdana, Arial, Helvetica, sans-serif;
46      font-size: 11px;
47      font-style: italic;
48      color: #666699;
49  }
50  h4 {
51      font-family: "Courier New", Courier, mono;
52      font-size: 14px;
53      color: #333366;
54  }
55  div p {
56      font-family: Geneva, Arial, Helvetica, sans-serif;
```

Here's an example of how specificity determines the order of styles: The Heading 3 tag redefinition style that you created earlier in this lesson overrides the color defined by the style that was created when you set the Text Color to black (#000000) in the Page Properties dialog box for the life.htm document. While the style that was created for text color was initially an internal style, it was exported along with the other internal styles from life.htm to create the external lifestyle.css style sheet. The h3 tag style has a higher specificity value (41) than the text color style (13). The text color style appears in the CSS document as: body, td, th { color: #000000 }

NOTE *Notice the commas separating the selectors in the style defining default text color shown above. The commas indicate that this style is not a Tag Combination similar to the one you created earlier for div p; instead this style defines a number of selectors as a group. It is more efficient to group selectors when their attributes will be identical, as opposed to creating three separate styles.*

In the lifestyle.css style sheet, the specificity values you calculated in this step should be:

- h4 (Tag): a = 0, b = 3, c = 1 (for a value of 31)

  There are no IDs (a) in this style; there are three attributes (b) of font-family, font-size, and color; and there is one selector (c), h4.

- highlight (Class): a = 0, b = 1, c = 0 (for a value of 10)

  There are no IDs (a) in this style; there is one attribute (b) of background-color; and there are no selectors (c).

- ol (Tag): a = 0, b = 4, c = 1 (for a value of 41)

  There are no IDs (a) in this style; there are four attributes (b) of font-family, font-size, font-style, and color; and there is one selector (c), ol.

NOTE *CSS specificity uses a large arbitrary number base to calculate the values of styles—it does not use base 10 because styles can potentially have more than 9 IDs, attributes, or elements. Suppose a style has no IDs, 14 attributes and 5 elements. In base 10 such as style would use a = 0, b = 14 and c = 5, so the value would be 145. In a numbering system with a large base, a = 0, b = E, and c = 5, so the value is E5. This is important because a style with one ID, one attribute and zero elements would have a value of 110 in both base 10 and a numbering system with a larger base. In base 10, the first style with a value of 145 would override the second style with a value of 110. However, in a numbering system with a larger base the second style with a value of 110 would override the first style with a value of E5, which is the correct order of specificity.*

Understanding Order

The **order** of styles, which concerns where styles are located, is as follows, beginning with the lowest:

- Brower defaults (the formatting that is farthest away from the text; lowest priority)
- External CSS Styles
- Internal CSS Styles
- Inline CSS Styles
- Local HTML formatting (the formatting that is closest to the text; highest priority—overrides any options set in the styles above if there are conflicts)

NOTE *An inline style is an instance of a style that is placed directly in the code. The use of inline styles is generally not recommended.* <H1 STYLE="color: #333333; font-family: Verdana, Arial, Helvetica, sans-serif"> *is an example of an inline style. Inline styles are defined within the content of the document and do not use any style sheet information at the top of the document—as internal styles do—or in a separate style sheet—as external styles do. Internal and external style sheets are significantly more powerful because inline styles merge content with formatting, and because they are single instances of a style definition that can't be used elsewhere.*

3) In the keepers.htm document, apply the highlight style to the word lamps in the first line of the numbered list.

The highlight style overrides the style that controls the formatting of the list.

The Relevant CSS portion of the Tag inspector will show you what styles are applied to the selected element. In this case, you can see that both the highlight style and the ol style are applied.

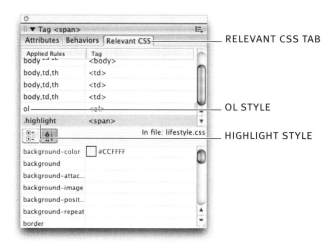

RELEVANT CSS TAB

OL STYLE

HIGHLIGHT STYLE

If there is more than one style applied by the author of the Web page (the origin) to the same text with conflicting attributes, priority is given to the specifications from the innermost style (the style closest to the text itself). The most recent styles are nested inside earlier styles. Because the last formatting attributes you apply are physically the closest tags to the text, they take precedence over earlier styles and control the final look of the text.

If your document uses an external style sheet, the styles in that sheet are applied across your document. Suppose, for example, that the external style sheet has definitions for Heading 3 and Heading 4, and that you also created an internal style within your document that redefines the Heading 3 tag. The internal style takes precedence if the attributes conflict with those in the external style. For example, if the internal style defines the H3 tag to be red and the external style defines the H3 to be blue and bold, the H3 tag will actually be red and bold. Only the attributes that conflict are affected.

Text formatting applied manually to ranges of text can also take precedence over other styles. In the example just presented, suppose that you used the Property inspector to apply a different color to one of the Heading 3 lines. Dreamweaver defines color and formatting selections from the Property inspector as internal custom styles. The Style menu on the Property inspector includes both internal and external styles.

Local HTML formatting overrides all styles. HTML formatting is no longer used by Dreamweaver to format text because the <font> tag is deprecated (marked for deletion) in HTML 4.0. The World Wide Web Consortium (W3C) has adopted CSS as the new standard. Although formatting with the <font> tag is still supported in manual coding through Dreamweaver as well as by browsers, taking advantage of the new standards enables you to design a more flexible and functional Web site.

N O T E *The World Wide Web Consortium (W3C) develops the Web standards that are implemented by browsers and other Internet devices.*

If you have attached a style sheet to a document and the browser does not display the formatting that you expect, check your style sheet and your document to see if you have other styles or local formatting that is overriding the styles you expect to see.

You can save and close both the keepers.htm and lifestyle.css documents.

SETTING BACKGROUNDS WITH CSS

The options for setting page backgrounds in standard HTML are limited: You can define a color and you can select a background image that tiles across the page. Although only those two basic background options exist in the Page Properties dialog box (which you began to use in Lessons 2 and 3, respectively), Dreamweaver MX 2004 uses CSS instead of HTML <body> tag attributes to set these background options. CSS also provides a number of additional settings that give you more control over the backgrounds of your pages.

You'll create a background for this document that looks similar to the one you used in Lesson 3 to create a black bar across a tan page, using a much smaller image with the additional CSS background options.

1) Create a new HTML document and save it as *environments.htm in the Lesson_06_CSS folder.* **Title the page** *Lights of the Coast: Lighthouse Environments.*

When you use the Page Properties dialog box to set that background image, as you did in Lesson 3, it tiles the image across the page, horizontally and vertically. This effect is sometimes used with small squares to repeat a pattern in the background. If you have a great deal of text that causes the page to scroll, the use of a background such as the bkg_inside_tan.gif image that you've used in previous lessons, eventually causes that black bar to repeat—how soon depends upon the height of the image. One technique that is used to prevent such a bar from repeating is to make the background image very tall. The drawback is an increased file size, which can sometimes be fairly significant.

2) Click the New CSS Style icon at the bottom of the CSS Styles panel.
The New CSS Style dialog box opens.

3) In the Selector Type area, choose Tag and select body from the menu of HTML tags. In the Define in area, select New Style Sheet from the menu and click OK. Save the file as *grounds.css* **in the Lesson_06_CSS folder.**

LIST OF HTML TAGS

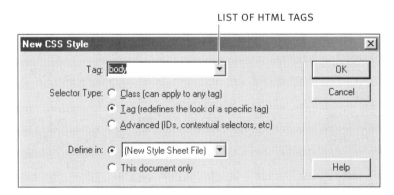

The CSS Style Definition dialog box appears for the body element.

4) Select Background from the list of categories. Type the hexadecimal code *#CCCC99* **into the Background Color text field. Click the Background Image Browse button and select wb_bar.gif from the Lesson_06_CSS/Images folder. In the CSS Style Definition dialog box, click the Repeat menu and choose repeat-x. Choose fixed from the Attachment menu, Left from the horizontal position menu, and Top from the Vertical Position menu. Click the Apply button to see the changes.**

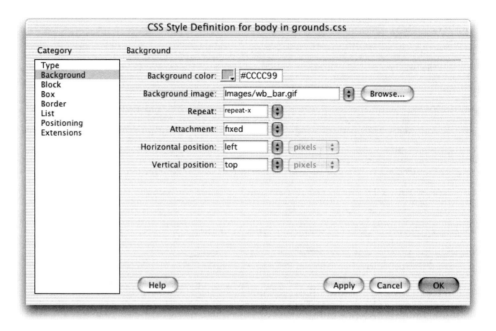

The **Background Color** option defines the color of the page.

The **Background Image** option allows you to specify an image to use in the background.

The **Repeat** option gives you four choices: repeat (tiles the image), repeat-x (tiles the image only on a single horizontal axis so the image repeats on one line across the page from left to right), repeat-y (tiles the image only on a single vertical axis so the image repeats on one line across the page from top to bottom), and no repeat (inserts only one instance of the image).

The **Horizontal Position** lets you define the location (or the starting position if the image repeats) of the image on the x (horizontal) axis. You can use one of the preset alignments (left, center, or right) or you can specify a numeric value and the measurement to be used. A measurement of 10 pixels, for example, positions the left side of the image 10 pixels from the left side of the browser.

230

The **Vertical Position** lets you define the location (or the starting position if the image repeats) of the image on the y (vertical) axis. You can use one of the preset alignments (top, center, or bottom) or you can specify a numeric value and the measurement to be used. A measurement of 10 pixels, for example, positions the top edge of the image 10 pixels from the top of the browser.

5) Click OK to close the dialog box. Save both the environments.htm and grounds.css files; then preview the environments.htm document in the browser.
By default the grounds.css opens automatically and appears behind the environments.htm file when you create the style.

TIP *Always remember to save your CSS file if you've made changes to it before previewing through the browser. If you don't Dreamweaver, will inform you that some files that are needed to preview the page haven't been saved and gives you the option to save them.*

In this exercise, you defined the background properties of the document through an external style sheet. When you specify background colors and images in the Page Properties dialog box however, Dreamweaver automatically defines them through internal styles. If after defining the external style, you decide to edit the background color or image via Page Properties, the internal style that Dreamweaver creates takes precedence and overrides the external style. You can switch back to the external style by changing the background color to default and removing the background image specification in the Page Properties dialog box.

You've now created a background that looks exactly like the one that was used in life.htm and keepers.htm, however with this new background the white and black bars will never repeat, regardless of how long the page becomes. In addition, whereas the original bkg_inside_tan.gif was 618 bytes and 33 × 2500 pixels, the wb_bar.gif is only 174 bytes and 33 × 80 pixels. Both images are relatively small in file size, but any savings will contribute to a smaller page, and a quicker download for your visitors.

You can apply this same background style to any page by linking the grounds.css style sheet to the desired document. Any existing internal styles that define background attributes override the corresponding portion of the style in the grounds.css style sheet for that document.

NOTE *CSS specifications are not all supported by every browser. Make sure you preview your pages in both Netscape Navigator and Internet Explorer to check whether the attribute you select is supported. The newest versions have the most support for CSS.*

CREATING A BASIC CSS LAYOUT

CSS is a great way to control the layout and appearance of your Web site. CSS can be used in combination with or as an alternative to creating layouts with tables. Although many sites are migrating toward the use of CSS instead of tables, CSS functionality is best achieved with recent browsers (5.0 and up) that can support the widest range of features. CSS does not yet provide as complete control as can be achieved through the combination of tables and CSS. Part of the issue is a result of problems with browser compatibility. Many browsers do not yet support the full range of CSS specifications. Although 4.0 browsers support CSS, that support is limited. As a result, layouts created using CSS may not work as expected for a fairly large number of users. Tables offer a layout method that is currently more compatible with a larger number of browsers; however, there are drawbacks to using tables. Tables, particularly complicated ones, can cause your page to load slowly. They are require a great deal more code, and often necessitate the use of spacer gifs to force the table to hold its position. One of the primary drawbacks is the combination of content with formatting and appearance. The benefits of CSS include the ease and speed with which a CSS-based site can be updated, a consistent appearance, less code, and faster download time. With CSS, content is separated from the design and attributes that define appearance. The advantages to using CSS for layout also include increased accessibility, flexibility, and efficiency. The important things to consider when deciding what layout tools to use in a Web page are what works best for the particular layout that you are trying to achieve, and what the majority of your visitors will be able to access.

In this exercise, you will create a basic single column for the text on the environment.htm document, similar to the outlined table that you created in Lesson 5.

1) In the environment.htm document, click the New CSS Style icon on the CSS Styles panel. Choose Class and type _column_ in the Name text field. Select the grounds.css style sheet from the Define in menu and click OK.

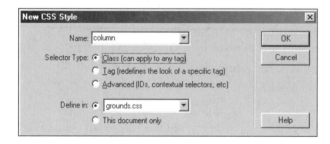

You're beginning to set up the class that will be used to define the look of a simple column for this page.

2) Select Background from the list of categories. Choose white (#FFFFFF) from the Background Color picker.

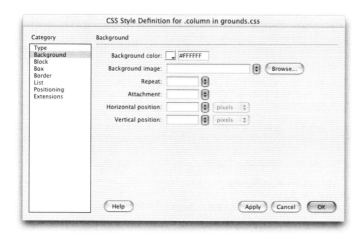

The options in the Background category allow you to specify attributes such as color and background image, as you did in the previous exercise. This time however, instead of applying a background to the entire page, you are applying it only to a specific class; a class that you can then apply multiple elements if you choose. In this step, you defined the background color of the column that will appear on top of the tan page background.

3) Select Box from the list of categories. Type *600* **in the Width text field and verify that the pixels option is selected in the measurement menu. In the Padding section, type** *8* **in the Top text field. The Same for all box should be checked and pixels should be selected in the measurement menu (these are the default settings). In the Margin section, uncheck the Same for all box and type** *50* **in the Top text field. Leave the remaining margins (right, bottom, and left) undefined.**

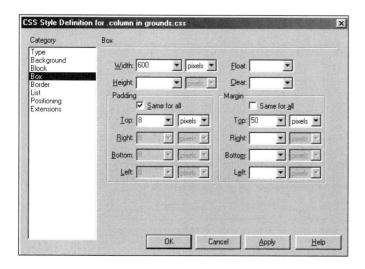

233

The Box category provides a number of options to control the container you are creating. In this case, you have defined the width of the column you will create as 600 pixels. The padding works the same as cell padding within a table—it creates the specified amount of space between the edge of the box and the content it contains. The margin defines the space that will exist between the edges of the browser and the edges of the column as well as the space that would exist between the column and any additional elements that might be created outside of the column.

4) Select Border from the list of categories. Select Solid from the Top menu in the Style section. In the Width section uncheck the Same for all box, Type _1_ in the Top, Right, and Left in the text fields and type _3_ in the Bottom text field, then verify that the pixels option is selected in the measurement menu. Select black (#000000) from the Top color picker in the Color section and leave the Same for sll box checked. Click OK to close the CSS Style Definition dialog box.

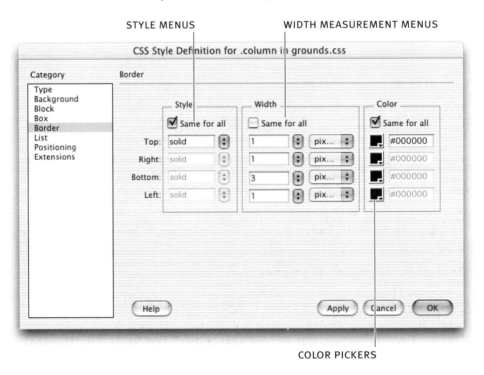

The border options allow you to define how the column appears. By giving it a solid, black border, you are creating a column with an effect similar to the one achieved by outlining a table in Lesson 5. With CSS however, you have far more control over the outline—the bottom side of the column will display with a thicker border than the other sides.

NOTE *There are a total of eight categories available for style definition. You've used four: Type, Background, Box, and Border. The other four categories are as follows:*

- **Block**: *Provides additional text spacing and positioning options.*

- **List**: *Provides options to control the formatting of ordered and unordered lists.*

- **Positioning**: *Provides options to control where elements are located. Dreamweaver considers any element with positioning options defined to be a Layer. (Layers are covered in Lesson 16.) You can integrate CSS and Layers for more complex layouts.*

- **Extensions**: *Provides additional options, some of which are not widely supported.*

5) Select the Insert Div Tag option from the Layout category on the Insert bar.

TOP LEFT

The Insert Div Tag dialog box opens.

6) Select column from the Class menu. Leave the ID text field blank and the Insert menu on the default selection of At insertion point. Click OK.

CLASS MENU

The div requires a class, which you learned to create through the first four steps of this exercise.

At this point, you have a white box with a black outline in your document. Dreamweaver automatically places text inside of the box that reads: Content for class "column" Goes Here.

7) Roll the pointer over the black border of the box. When the line turns red, indicating that you can select the div, click the border.

The div is selected as you can see by the bold <div.column#content> in the Tag Selector.

8) Save both the environments.htm and grounds.css documents.

You now have a column in which you can place content. Because this layout is created with an external style sheet, you can easily apply to many other documents for a consistent appearance. You can use techniques like this to create more complex layouts without using tables.

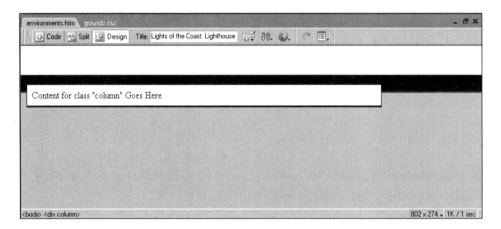

You can close the environments.htm file.

NOTE *You can also experiment with several of the CSS based layouts that are provided for your use as samples within Dreamweaver. To do so, open the New Document dialog box and choose the Page Designs (CSS) category in the General portion of the dialog box. Choose a style sheet such as Halo Left Nav from the Page Designs list. Click Create on the New Document dialog box.*

Halo is a new look—an interface design created by Macromedia for a number of MX Elements that are made available for a number of products in Studio MX 2004 (including Dreamweaver). You've already used the Image Viewer Flash element in Lesson 3, which also uses the Halo appearance. You can read more about Halo and MX Elements at: www.macromedia.com/software/mx2004/halo.

Dreamweaver will create the new style sheet. You will be prompted to create an HTML file as well as to copy the files that are necessary (if any) to your site. Clicking the folder icon will allow you to choose the location in which these files will be placed as well as allow you to create a new folder for the files. During the process of copying the necessary files to your site, you may see preliminary content appear in the HTML document—it will refresh after the files have been copied. The Halo Left Nav style sheet will create a page that looks similar to the following example. You can preview it in the browser to see how it will look.

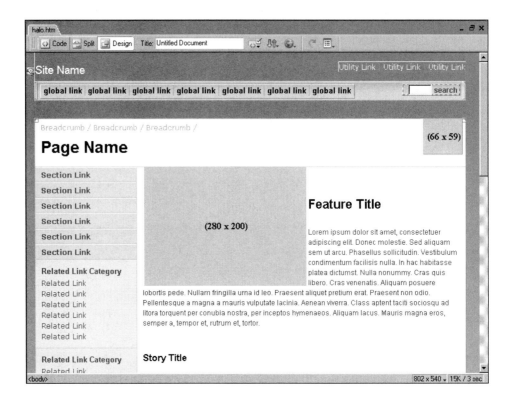

WHAT YOU HAVE LEARNED

In this lesson, you have:

- Created an internal style to use the same text formatting quickly and easily (pages 199–204)

- Created a class that can be applied to different kinds of text formats (pages 205–206)

- Converted internal styles to external styles so they can be used by other documents (pages 206–207)

- Linked to an external style sheet from another document to use the same text formatting (pages 207–209)

- Created external styles specifying text formatting that can be used to maintain consistency in the look of text throughout a Web site (pages 210–217)

- Added multiple styles to an existing style sheet by redefining HTML tags (pages 217–219)

- Edited a style in the external style sheet to affect all documents linked to it (pages 219–228)

- Set a background with a small image that tiles in a single horizontal line over a background color (pages 228–231)

- Created a basic single column layout using a div and CSS class (pages 232–238)

using library items

LESSON 7

There are many items and groups of items that you may need to create and repeat on multiple pages throughout your Web site. These items may include, but are not limited to, navigation, copyright information, headers, and footers. Dreamweaver lets you store these often-used portions of content as **library items**. Creating library items for these elements allows you to quickly and easily insert the same content into many documents. If you need to change information, such as copyright dates that may appear on a large number of pages throughout your site, library items make it possible for you to edit the content and update all documents that reference it with a single command. Without a library item, you have to open each page and modify the information individually. On a small site, doing this might not be difficult; however, on a very large site, it can be time-consuming and can greatly increase the probability of errors.

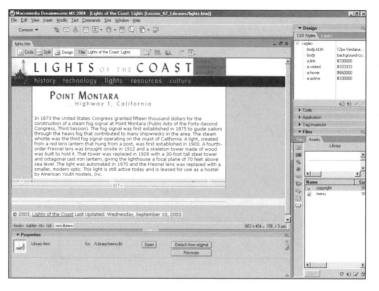

In this project, you will add a library item to a page. After you modify the library item, you will use the update feature to quickly and efficiently make the same changes to all pages containing that item on the site.

Library items provide a way for you to maintain consistency and automate the process of updating your site. Library items enable you to repeat certain elements on pages that can still have different layouts. Effective use of library items can be a timesaver, not only in the development stage of your Web site, but also in ongoing maintenance tasks.

To see examples of the finished pages for this chapter, open culture.htm, lights.htm, and technology.htm from the Lesson_07_Libraries/Completed folder.

WHAT YOU WILL LEARN

In this lesson, you will:

- Learn when and why to use library items
- Create and insert a library item
- Re-create a library item
- Edit an existing library item
- Update all references to a library item
- Detach a library item

APPROXIMATE TIME

This lesson should take about one hour to complete.

LESSON FILES

Media Files:

Lesson_07_Libraries/Images/…(all files)

Starting Files:

Lesson_07_Libraries/culture.htm
Lesson_07_Libraries/lights.htm
Lesson_07_Libraries/technology.htm

Completed Project:

Lesson_07_Libraries/Completed/culture.htm
Lesson_07_Libraries/Completed/lights.htm
Lesson_07_Libraries/Completed/technology.htm

NOTE *Library items contained within documents in the completed folders have been named with the _completed suffix to differentiate them from the library items that you create in this lesson. The original library items are not included—if you want to see them, follow the steps in the section "Re-creating a Library Item."*

CREATING A LIBRARY ITEM

A library item is a portion of content that can be reused on multiple pages. It is separated from the pages in your site and kept in a file located in the Library. The library item consists of the code for specific content—it is not an HTML page in and of itself. You can create a library item by selecting one or more elements in a document and adding them to the Library. When you do this, Dreamweaver converts the selection into non-editable content that is linked to the corresponding library item. The following exercise demonstrates this process.

1) Open culture.htm from the Lesson_07_Libraries folder.

Library items can only include content that appears between the `<BODY>` and `</BODY>` tags. They can include any document elements such as text, tables, forms, images, Java applets, plug-ins, or ActiveX elements.

2) Select the copyright text, the Lights of the Coast text with email link, the modification date, and the horizontal rule.

TIP *Be sure to select the non-breaking space that is just before the copyright character. Because this document has margins of 0 defined, this space is necessary to provide a buffer between the edge of the browser window and the copyright text, which is outside the table. (Non-breaking spaces were covered in Lesson 2.)*

The text and horizontal rule are highlighted.

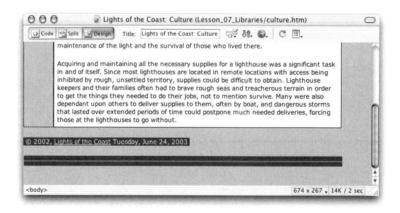

To create a library item out of multiple elements, those elements must form a contiguous selection in the document. If you need noncontiguous items to function as a library item does, you need to create multiple library items.

The copyright text, email address, and modification date are standard information that might be used at the bottom of all pages within a Web site. Libraries can be very useful for this type of information.

TIP *A library item containing relative paths (such as links to pages or images) can be placed in any level of your site's directory structure—it doesn't have to reside on the same level as the original library item. Dreamweaver automatically calculates the correct paths to any elements that the library item may contain. Document-relative and site root-relative paths were covered in Lessons 3 and 4.*

3) Click the Assets tab in the Files panel group and click the Library button on the lower left of the Assets panel to open the Library.

NOTE *Because of a bug in the Macintosh version of Dreamweaver, the Files panel group may be renamed Assets. Details can be found in the Defining a Local Site exercise in Lesson 1.*

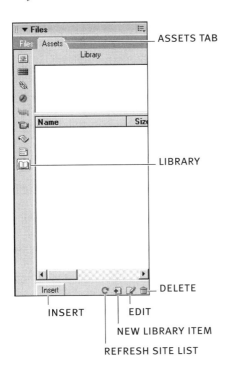

— ASSETS TAB

— LIBRARY

— DELETE

INSERT
EDIT
NEW LIBRARY ITEM
REFRESH SITE LIST

The Library category of the Assets panel opens, in which you will manage all of your library items.

4) Click the New Library Item button at the bottom of the Library category of the Assets panel.

243

TIP *You can also choose Modify > Library > Add Object to Library or drag the selected objects from the document window to the lower half of the Library panel in order to create a new library item.*

An alert box appears to inform you that the selection may not look the same in other documents because style specifications are not included in library items. The references to styles (for example, **<SPAN CLASS="green"> green text </SPAN>**) are preserved, but the style does not take effect when the library item is inserted in a document unless the style sheet containing that style is linked to the document. The Library panel offers a visual reminder of this (in addition to a warning message) by displaying the text as it would appear if the style sheet were omitted. The best way to make sure that style sheet information is included is to use external style sheets and remember to link them to all documents that need to make use of their styles. CSS was covered in Lesson 6. Click OK to close the alert box.

A new library icon appears in the Library category of the Assets panel alongside a text field highlighting the generic name Untitled.

NOTE *On the Macintosh, the library item will not be displayed in the preview area until you click the library item icon in the Assets panel list.*

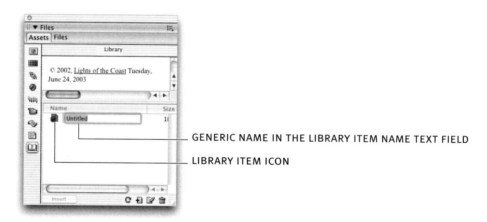

GENERIC NAME IN THE LIBRARY ITEM NAME TEXT FIELD

LIBRARY ITEM ICON

NOTE *When you create a library item, Dreamweaver creates a folder named Library at the top level of your local root folder and stores every library item that you create in that location. The Library folder must remain in its original location at the root level of your site in order for the library feature to function. This Library folder and the library files it contains are only stored locally; they do not need to be uploaded to a server unless you want to share them with other members of your Web team. Dreamweaver saves each library item with the .lbi file extension.*

5) Type *copyright* **as the name for the new library item and then press Return (Macintosh) or Enter (Windows).**

The library item is now known as copyright in the Library panel. Giving your library items descriptive names will help you to manage them throughout your site. The names are for your reference only and will not be displayed to the user in a browser window.

You should name your library items immediately after creating them. Although you can rename library items, any instances of a library item in documents may not be updated with the new name, due to a bug.

A preview of the library item, created from the elements you selected in step 2, appears at the top of the panel. You might need to click the library item icon to refresh the preview in order to see the elements.

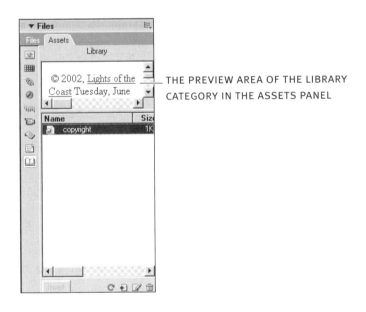

THE PREVIEW AREA OF THE LIBRARY CATEGORY IN THE ASSETS PANEL

When you deselect the text in the culture.htm document window, it displays with a pale yellow background. The yellow background is a Dreamweaver visual aid indicating that the group of elements is linked to a library item and is not directly editable—the yellow background does not display in the browser. This block of text is now considered one item, so clicking any part of it selects the entire library item. You can save and close the culture.htm document.

PLACING A LIBRARY ITEM ON A PAGE

Placing a library item in a document inserts the contents of the library item file and creates a reference to that library item. When you insert a library item, the actual HTML is inserted, which means that the content always appears—even if the library item is not available in the Library folder. Dreamweaver inserts comments in the code around the item to show the name of the library file and the reference to the original item. The comments and reference are not visible in the browser window. The reference to the external library item file is what makes it possible to update the content on an entire site all at once simply by changing the library item.

1) Open lights.htm and place the insertion point on a blank line at the bottom of the document.

In the following steps, you will place the library item you created in the previous exercise into this document.

NOTE *If the Library panel is not visible, choose Window > Assets and click the Library button in the Assets panel. The Assets panel is located in the Files panel group.*

2) Select the copyright library item in the Library category of the Assets panel and click the Insert button in the lower left corner of the panel to insert the item into the document.

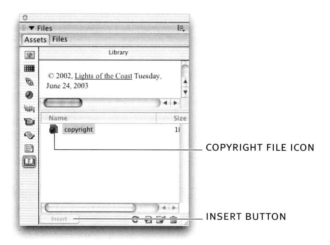

COPYRIGHT FILE ICON

INSERT BUTTON

TIP *Alternatively, you can drag the copyright file icon from the Library panel to the location where you want it to appear in the document window.*

The text and rule are added to the document. The copyright library item is shown with a yellow background. Although library items are highlighted with yellow by default, the color can be changed or turned off completely in the Preferences dialog box. This item cannot be modified directly on the page. You will modify library items in the next exercise.

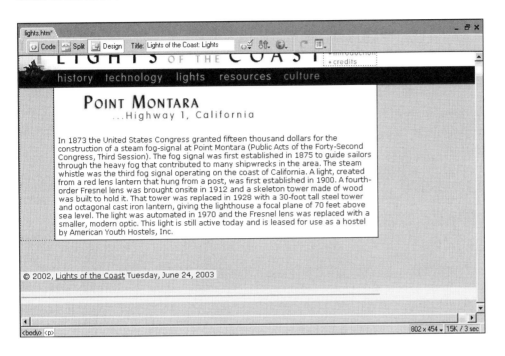

You can use the Property inspector to see the name of the source file and to perform maintenance functions for the library item that is selected in the document window. The Property inspector has several options:

- **Src:** Displays the filename and location of the source file for the library item. You can open the library item for editing with the Open option. You must save the file to keep the changes you make.

- **Detach from original:** Breaks the link between the selected library item and its source file. The content of the library item becomes editable, but it can no longer be updated by the library update functions.

- **Recreate:** Overwrites the original library item with the current selection. Use this option to create library items again if the library file isn't present, the item's name has been changed, or the item has been edited.

3) Open technology.htm and place the insertion point on a blank line at the bottom of the document.

You will place a detached copy of the library item with copyright information on this page so it is editable in the document.

4) Hold down Option (Macintosh) or Ctrl (Windows) and drag the copyright file icon from the Library panel to the bottom of the document.

The library content is copied into the document but is not linked to the library, so there is no yellow highlighting. The elements can be modified directly on the page because they are not connected to a library item. Because these elements are detached, they are not updated if any changes are made to the original library item.

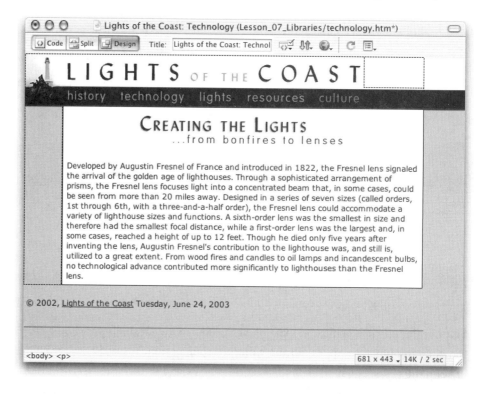

You can save and close the technology.htm document. Save the lights.htm document, but leave it open for the next exercise.

248

RE-CREATING A LIBRARY ITEM

If a library item is accidentally deleted from the Library category of the Assets panel and you still have a page showing the library item, you can re-create it.

1) In the lights.htm document, select the navigational library item at the top right of the page by clicking once on the introduction image, located just to the right of the Lights of the Coast title graphic.

This is a library item that is not available in your Library folder. It is a simple table with three images, like other tables you created in Lesson 5. When you clicked the introduction image, the entire library item became selected and grayed-out to show that it can't be edited within the document. You can also tell that it is a library item by looking at the Tag Selector, which displays <mm:libitem>. Although this element was marked as a library item in the document window, it does not appear in the Library category of the Assets panel because the original item is not contained in your site.

You can't see any of the yellow highlights on this library item because there is no space between the images in the table. The highlight that indicates a library item shows up around the items contained in a library item—it does not display over the top of an image.

2) Click Recreate on the Property inspector.

RECREATE BUTTON

The library item file is re-created with the item name used on this page; it now shows up titled as "menu" in the Library category of the Assets panel.

TIP *You can also right-click (Macintosh and Windows) or Control-click (Macintosh single button mice) to open a context menu that contains the Recreate option and other choices related to the selected library item.*

Save and close the lights.htm document.

MODIFYING A LIBRARY ITEM

When you edit a library item, you need to edit the item's source file in the Library folder. A source file can be either the original library item, or one that was re-created using the techniques from the previous exercise. Editing a library item changes the library item only. When you finish editing, Dreamweaver prompts you to update all the pages in the site that use the item, letting you choose whether or not to make these changes throughout the entire site. Dreamweaver accomplishes the update by searching for comments that reference the library file you just edited and then replacing the old HTML code with your new HTML code. If you remove the library comments from the code, the contents are no longer associated with the library item and can no longer be changed by updating the library item.

NOTE *Any modifications to the library item must be made to the source file that is located in the Library folder. If you want to edit the content directly in a document, you must first break the link to the library item. To do this, use the Detach from original button on the Property inspector or hold down Ctrl (Windows) or Option (Macintosh) when inserting the item.*

1) Double-click the copyright file icon on the Library category of the Assets panel.

NOTE *If the Library category of the Assets panel is not open, choose Window > Assets and click the Library icon on the Assets panel.*

250

Dreamweaver opens the copyright library item for editing. When library items are inserted on a page, they take on the properties of that document; text and link colors change according to the default colors set for the document (unless you have specified the styles in the library item).

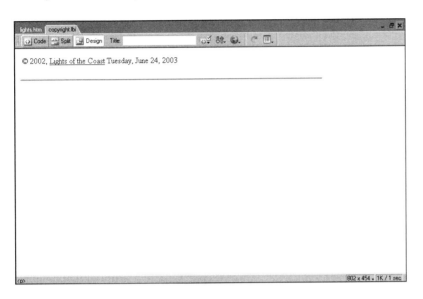

TIP *Alternatively, you can select copyright on the Library panel and then click Edit on the panel. You can also select the library item on a page and click Open in the Property inspector.*

2) In the document window of the copyright library item, copyright.lbi, select the horizontal rule and move it in front of the space at the beginning of the copyright line in order to move it above the copyright line. Change the height of the horizontal rule from undefined to a value of 1. Save the document.

TIP *The horizontal line will not go all the way to the edge of the document window in the library item source file because it is displayed as if the document had margins. As you drag the horizontal rule in front of the copyright symbol, you will see the insertion point. Watch for the small amount of space that indicates the non-breaking space as you move it slightly from left to right. You can also drag the horizontal rule just above the copyright information.*

The Update Library Items dialog box opens with a list of all the files in your site that use the copyright library item.

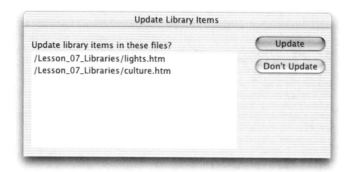

3) Click Update to update all the documents in your site that use the copyright library item.

The Update Pages dialog box shows which pages have been updated with your changes.

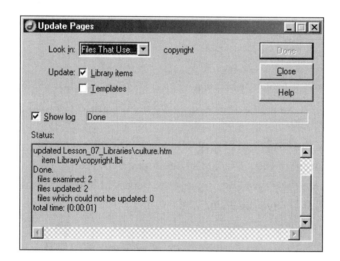

NOTE *If you have a large site, you might prefer to wait to update your site with all your changes at once. In that case, click the Don't Update button when you save the library item.*

4) Click Close to close the Update Pages dialog box.

The horizontal rule should be in its new location in both culture.htm and lights.htm.

UPDATING LIBRARY REFERENCES

If you choose not to update your pages at the time you edit a library item, but decide to do so later, Dreamweaver lets you do all the updating with a single command. For instance, you may want to wait to update pages at a later time if your Web team members have pages checked out that contain library items.

NOTE *If you are using Check In and Check Out, a site maintenance feature covered in Lesson 12, and you want to make updates to pages using a library item, Dreamweaver asks you if you want to check out the pages containing that library item. You must say yes to allow Dreamweaver to check out the file if you want it to be updated.*

1) In the copyright.lbi file, change the copyright date to 2003, type *Last Updated:* **in front of the last saved date and save the document. Click Don't Update in the Update Library Items dialog box.**

Neither culture.htm nor lights.htm shows the new copyright date yet.

2) From the menu bar, choose Modify > Library > Update Pages.
The Update Pages dialog box opens.

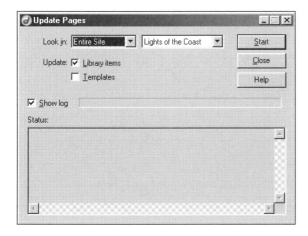

253

3) In the Look in menu, verify that Entire Site is chosen.

The menu to the right displays the current site, Lights of the Coast. You're choosing to update all files that use library items. Using these options, all library item references throughout the site will be updated—for all library items, not just copyright.lbi. You can choose to update references to a single library item by choosing Files That Use from the Look in menu, and selecting the desired library item from the menu to the right.

4) In the Update check boxes, verify that the Library items box is checked and the Templates box is unchecked. Check the Show log box and click Start.

The Update Pages dialog box shows which files were updated.

NOTE *For this exercise, the Update Pages dialog box shows that several files were not updated—these files are the final examples in the Completed folder.*

5) Click Close to close the dialog box.

The new copyright date appears in both culture.htm and lights.htm. You can close the copyright library item document.

NOTE *Similar functionality can be acheived through the use of Server Side Includes (SSI). In order to include SSI on your pages however, your server must be configured to support SSI.*

WHAT YOU HAVE LEARNED

In this lesson, you have:

- Learned how to use library items for elements that need to be repeated on many pages within a site (pages 241–245)

- Created a library item using the Library category of the Assets panel, inserted it on a page with a link to the library item, and inserted it on another page without a link to the library item (pages 245–249)

- Used the Property inspector to re-create a library item that was missing from the Library panel (pages 249–250)

- Edited an existing library item from the Library panel and applied the changes to all pages in the site that used that item (pages 250–252)

- Updated all references to a library item (pages 253–254)

using templates

LESSON 8

A template is a document you can use as the base for creating other documents. Each document based on a template uses the same layout and structure as the template. Creating a template involves designating the areas that need to be editable in documents that are based on the template; all other portions of a template are locked and controlled by the parent template. Templates are similar to Library items in that they provide a quick way to update structure and content across many pages.

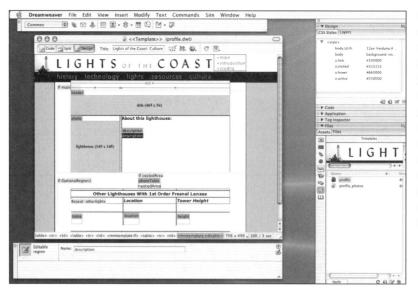

In this lesson, you will create a template from an existing page, build other pages using that template, and modify the pages by editing the template.

Whether you have a large Web site with many sections or a number of pages that all use a common design, you can create a template to speed up the production process. By using a template, you can change or update the look of your site, changing multiple pages within a few minutes. Templates are useful when you have a team working together to build an area of the site. The Web designer can create a template, inserting placeholders for the parts of the page that can be edited. The overall design of the page remains locked. Team members can build and edit pages based on a template using either Dreamweaver or Macromedia's Contribute, a program geared towards non-technical users such as content editors who may have little or no experience creating Web sites.

The advantages of templates are best seen in two situations: when you have a section or set of pages that need to use an identical design and layout or when a designer creates the look of the pages but content editors add the content to the pages. If you simply want pages with the same headers and footers but different layouts in-between, use libraries (covered in Lesson 7). But if you want to use the same design on several pages, use templates. Libraries allow you to have certain elements or groups of elements repeated throughout your site, giving you more control over the layouts of the individual pages, whereas templates enable you to make use of the same layout and design. For example, say you have an online catalog of your products and you want all the pages to look the same except for the product picture, description, and price. If you create a template, you can have your team build the pages, either with Dreamweaver or Macromedia's Contribute, and each page will look the same.

To see examples of the finished pages for this chapter, open pt_arena.htm, pt_cabrillo.htm, pt_reyes.htm, and pt_reyes_photos.htm from the Lesson_08_Templates/Completed folder.

WHAT YOU WILL LEARN

In this lesson, you will:

- Create a template

- Add editable regions to the template

- Remove editable regions from the template

- Create optional regions

- Insert repeating regions

- Change the template highlight colors

- Build multiple pages based on the template

- Update a site by changing the template

- Define editable tag attributes

- Create a nested template

APPROXIMATE TIME

This lesson should take about two hours to complete.

LESSON FILES

Media Files:

Lesson_08_Templates/Images/…(all files)

Starting Files:

Lesson_08_Templates/profile.htm
Lesson_08_Templates/images_table.htm
Lesson_08_Templates/lights.htm

Completed Project:

Lesson_08_Templates/Completed…(all files)

NOTE *The templates used to create the files in the Completed folder are profile_photos_completed.dwt. These two files are located in the Completed/Template_Files folder, so that they will not conflict or be confused with the template files you will be creating in this lesson. In an actual site, the correct location for these files would be the Templates folder that is created by Dreamweaver as you work through this lesson. If you need to use the templates for the completed files, you should move them into the Templates folder.*

CREATING TEMPLATES

A template defines the layout and design of the subsequent pages you will create from it. In this lesson, the template you will create provides the navigation, the site identity, and the look and feel of the profiles section in the "Lights of the Coast" project site.

When creating a template, your first step usually includes the development of the page design—which has already been done for you in this project. The profile.htm document has the structure, layout, and navigation—it contains everything except for the contents that will be defined in pages based on the template you create from this page.

In this lesson, you'll create a series of Web pages from a common template, each profiling a different lighthouse. You'll begin the process in this exercise by using an existing page to create the template and then create other pages from that template in subsequent exercises.

1) Open profile.htm from the Lesson_08_Templates folder.

In this document, the materials that would be placed in the content areas and that are intended to change from page to page are represented by placeholder images and descriptive placeholder text. You learned to create placeholder images in Lesson 3. You'll use an extension to create large blocks of placeholder text in Lesson 17.

2) Choose File › Save As Template.

The Save As Template dialog box opens. You can select the site in which you want to save the template. For this project, you should save it within the "Lights of the Coast" site.

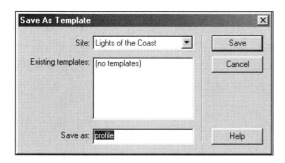

Dreamweaver automatically names the template "profile"—the name of your file. For this exercise, use this automatic name. It accurately describes the purpose of the template.

TIP *If you want to change the name of the template, type the new name in the Save as text field. The template name is for reference by you and your team only—it will not be known to the visitors of your site. Try to use names for your templates that are as descriptive as possible.*

This page has now been saved as a template, and you can use it to build other pages later in this lesson.

3) Click Save to close the dialog box. Click Yes when Dreamweaver displays an alert box that asks "Update Links?"

Updating the links will allow Dreamweaver to keep the paths to links and images correct.

Your template has been added to your site and saved in the Templates folder with an extension of .dwt. Dreamweaver automatically adds the Templates folder if one doesn't already exist. You may need to click the Refresh button on the Files panel to see the Templates folder. Leave this file open to use in the next exercise.

The file you are working with is now profile.dwt, and the top of the document window displays <<Template>> (profile.dwt).

4) Click the Assets tab in the Files panel group and select the Templates category.

TIP *Because you have a template open, profile.dwt, the Assets panel may open the Templates category automatically.*

The Assets panel is now open to the Templates category. The template you just created appears in the list, and any future templates you create in this site will also appear here. When a template is selected in the list, a portion of that document will appear in the preview area at the top of the panel.

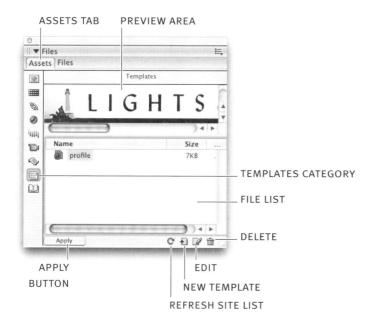

ASSETS TAB   PREVIEW AREA

TEMPLATES CATEGORY

FILE LIST

DELETE

APPLY BUTTON

EDIT

NEW TEMPLATE

REFRESH SITE LIST

NOTE *Instead of saving a page as a template from one that was already created, as you just did, you can also create a new blank template by clicking the New Template icon at the bottom of the Templates Assets panel. A new untitled template is added to the list of templates in the panel. While that template is still selected, enter a name for the template. Alternatively, you can create a template from scratch by choosing Template page from the Category list in the General portion of the New Document dialog box. The Templates tab of the New Document dialog box is for creating pages based on already existing templates—it does not allow you to create new templates.*

ADDING EDITABLE AREAS TO A TEMPLATE

The second step in creating a template is to define the areas of the page that should be editable in documents that are based on the template. (Editable areas are the portions of the document that can be modified in pages that are based on the template.)

As a rule, all areas of a template are initially locked. If you want to change information on pages that use the template, you need to create the editable areas or regions. In many Web sites, these regions are often content areas. Everything in the template that is not explicitly defined as editable is locked in pages that are based on the template. You can make changes to both the editable and locked areas while editing the original template, but on a page built from a template, you can make changes only in the editable regions.

1) In profile.dwt, select the placeholder image called "title" (located in the top row of the table for the profiles content). Use the Tag Selector at the bottom of the document window to select the cell that contains the image by clicking the `<td>` **tag just to the left of the** `<img#title>` **tag.**

The `<img#title>` tag is the corresponding code for the title placeholder image. The `<td>` tag is the corresponding code for the cell that contains that image.

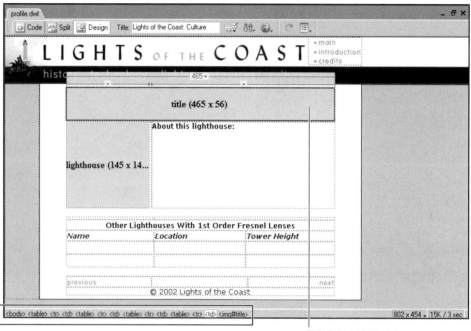

TITLE PLACEHOLDER IMAGE

TAG SELECTOR   `<TD>` TAG   `<IMG#TITLE>` TAG

This section of the page needs to be editable so you can change the content in subsequent pages.

NOTE *If the file <<Template>> (profile.dwt) is not already open, you can open it from the Templates category of the Assets panel. The template you just created in the previous exercise—profile.dwt—appears in the list as "profile." In the Assets panel, double-click the name of the template to open it. Alternatively, you can select the name in the Assets panel list and click Edit at the bottom of the panel.*

2) From the Templates menu in the Common category of the Insert bar, click the Editable Region icon.

262

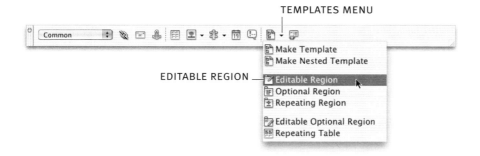

The New Editable Region dialog box opens. The Name text field will initially contain a generic name that is generated by Dreamweaver—the number at the end of the name is automatically incremented and may vary from the one shown in the example below.

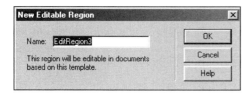

3) Type *header* in the Name text field and click OK.

Don't use any special characters (quotation marks, brackets, and so on) for region names. Make each name unique—you can't use the same region name more than once in the same template.

In the document window the editable area appears outlined in blue with a tab at the top displaying the name of the region. The extra space that appears between the top border of the table and the placeholder image is due to the editable region tab. No extra space is actually inserted.

If you don't see the region names and outlines, choose View > Visual Aids > Invisible Elements.

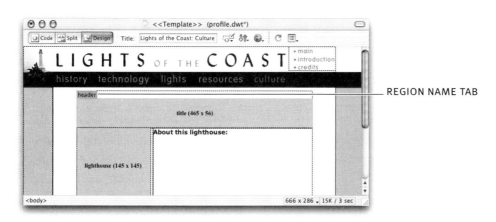

REGION NAME TAB

263

NOTE *Multiple table cells can't be designated as a single editable region. If you need multiple cells to be editable, you must either make the entire table editable or break it up into several editable regions. If you try to select multiple cells within a table and make them editable, the whole table becomes an editable region.*

4) Click inside the cell containing the text "About this lighthouse:" located below the header cell you just defined as editable. Position the insertion point after the colon (:) and press Return to create a new paragraph—don't select the cell. Click the Editable Region button in the Templates menu on the Insert bar, name the region *description***, and click OK.**

A new editable region is created inside the cell. You'll see the same blue outline with a tab at the top displaying the name of the editable region, and the word "description" is placed inside the editable area. Later, when you apply this template to a document, you will select the text inside this area and replace it with text, images, or other content.

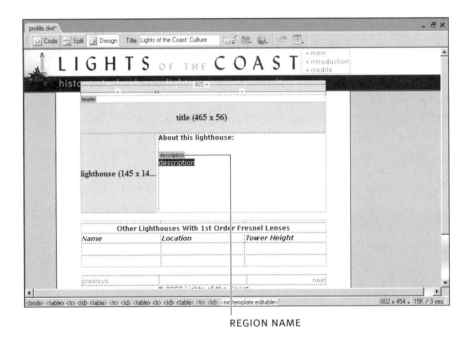

REGION NAME

NOTE *With this method, anything in the cell before or after selection in the blue outline is uneditable in documents based on the template.*

5) Use the Tag Selector, as you did with the cell for the title placeholder, to select the cell that contains the lighthouse image placeholder. Click the Editable Region button in the Templates menu on the Insert bar, name the region *photo***, and click OK.**

The names of all editable regions that you create are listed at the bottom of the Modify > Templates menu. A checkmark appears next to an editable region in this

264

list if one is selected, if the insertion point is in that region, or if an item in that region is selected.

6) Select the Next button in the table at the bottom of the page and make it an editable region named *next*. **Do the same for the Previous button, naming the region** *previous*; **and for the cell with the copyright information, naming the region** *copyright*.

Anything that has to change in documents based on the template, including links, needs to be in an editable region.

When creating links in your original template file, use the folder icon to browse for the link or use the Point-to-File link creator. Both are located on the Property inspector. Don't type the link directly into the link field on the Property inspector; this procedure can cause the links in your template to not work properly. Because templates are saved in the Templates folder, the pathnames might be different from what you expect. Dreamweaver can automatically generate the correct path when you direct it to the linked file using either of the two suggested methods.

7) Save your file.

The region names appear on tabs above all the outlined areas to help you identify which areas you designated as editable.

265

NOTE *Many of the tools and features available for creating and editing your original templates will only be available in the Design view, which you have been working in. Some template controls are not available if you are in Code view, which you will work with in Lesson 14. If you are working in Code view and find yourself unable to perform certain template operations, switch to Design view.*

Leave this file open to use in the next exercise.

REMOVING EDITABLE REGIONS

You have designated certain areas of the template as "editable." You can also lock them again. Elements in locked areas can't be changed on a page that was created from the template. Any elements located in locked areas must be edited on the original template file.

1) In the profile.dwt document, click the tab for the region copyright in the document window to select it.

The Tag Selector at the bottom of the document window displays the template markup <mmtemplate:editable>. Dreamweaver displays the tag in bold on the Tag Selector to indicated that it is selected.

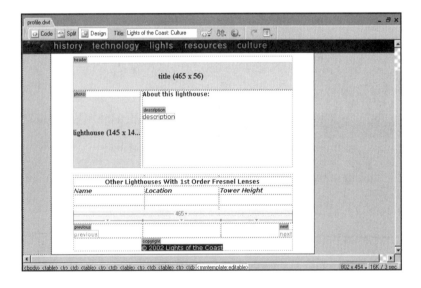

NOTE *If the template file that you want to edit is not open, you can double-click the name of the desired template in the Templates category of the Assets panel to open it. You can use the Assets panel to move, rename, and delete template files. Use caution when deleting template files because they cannot be re-created as easily as library items can.*

2) Choose Modify > Templates > Remove Template Markup.

266

The outline designating the copyright cell as editable disappears, and that portion of the template is now locked and can no longer be changed in files that are based on this template.

NOTE *If you remove an editable region from a template that has already had subsequent pages built from it, any of those pages that you modified previously in the editable region are changed when you update the pages after saving the template (you will learn how to update pages later in this lesson). Any modifications to the region are deleted on those pages because the area of the previously editable region changes to reflect the area as it appears in the template. You have the option of selecting a region in which the content that is located in the area being removed will be placed.*

CREATING OPTIONAL CONTENT

The optional content feature allows you to define whether the content is hidden or displayed in the pages based on the template. It enables you to set conditional or specific values for displaying content. You control these values through template parameters and conditional expressions.

You can create an optional content region to use certain elements in some template based pages but not others. The capability to allow specific elements to be included on an individual basis gives your template a great deal of flexibility. Some pages, for example, may need illustrations and descriptions. You can create a table that controls the layout for such illustrations and descriptions and then define it as an optional content region. Documents based on the template will then have the capability to insert those regions or leave them out.

1) In the profile.dwt document, select the table containing "Other Lighthouses With 1st Order Fresnel Lenses" and the line of blank space above it by clicking just to the right of the table and dragging upward and just to the right of the table above.
The table looks grayed-out to indicate that it has been selected, although the line break element before it does not appear grayed-out. This table will be optional on pages that use the profile template.

TIP *You can check to see that the line of blank space is selected by looking at the code, in which you should see the table selected, as well as the <br> tag immediately above it. The <br> tag is located between the table containing "Other Lighthouses With 1ˢᵗ Order Fresnel Lenses" and the table directly above it which contains the header, photo, and description regions.*

2) Click the Optional Region button in the Templates menu on the Insert bar.

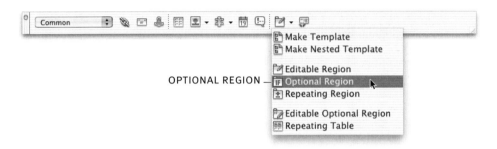

The New Optional Region dialog box opens with the Basic tab active.

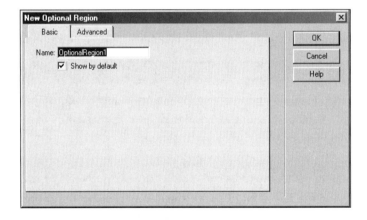

3) In the Basic tab of the New Optional Region dialog box, uncheck the Show by default box. Click OK to close the dialog box.

When creating your own Web site, if the content you define as optional will be used on the majority of your pages, you should leave this box checked. In this lesson, however, only one of the pages will use this content, so it is easier when creating subsequent pages if this content is hidden by default.

In this example, you are using the default name for the optional region.

NOTE *If you already created an optional content region elsewhere on the page, the Advanced tab of the Optional Content dialog box lets you link that existing optional content region with the new one that you are creating. The Advanced tab also lets you create Template Expressions.*

After you click OK, a blue outline surrounds the table and shows a blank line of space between the top of the table and the outline. A tab with the name of the region appears at the upper left corner of this outline. The bottom of the table lines up flush with the bottom of the outline, indicating there is no space after the table included in the region.

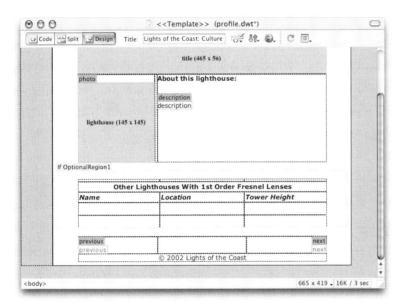

An optional region is not editable. You must define the area of the optional region that should be editable. This allows you to define only a portion of the area as editable, which you will do later in this lesson.

INSERTING REPEATING REGIONS

A **repeating region** is an area on the page that needs to be duplicated one or more times. Repeating regions can be particularly useful when you need to have multiple entries, possibly a varying number, placed on pages built from your templates. For example, if a template is created for food recipes and each page based on the template covers a different recipe, the list of ingredients varies on each page. If the list items are defined as repeating regions, you can then add as many of those regions as necessary to each individual page. Repeating regions allow you to have specific control over the appearance of multiple entries. In this exercise, the table listing other lighthouses will use repeating regions.

269

1) In the profile.dwt document, select the two empty rows at the bottom of the table for "Other Lighthouses With 1st Order Fresnel Lenses."

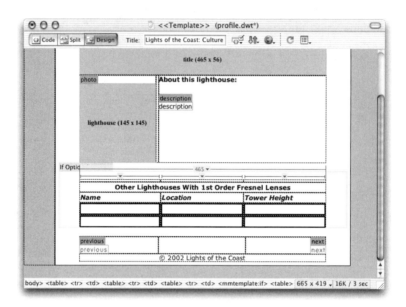

Outlines appear around the cells to indicate that they are selected.

2) Click the Repeating Region button in the Templates menu on the Insert bar.

The New Repeating Region dialog box opens.

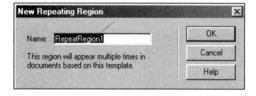

3) Name the region *otherlights* **and click OK.**

The rows you selected become outlined in a light blue color, and a tab at the top of the outline displays the name "otherlights." The highlight color for repeating regions is the same as the highlight color for optional regions and is lighter than the color for editable regions.

270

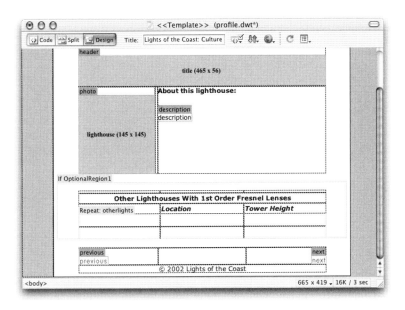

When developing your own Web sites, you might want to change the color of the highlighted regions if they don't show up against the colors used in your page. Choose Dreamweaver > Preferences (Macintosh) or Edit > Preferences (Windows) and select the Highlighting category. Click the Editable regions color box and select a highlight color or enter the hexadecimal value directly into the text field. Do the same as needed for the other highlight colors. The editable region color appears in the template itself and in documents based on the template; the locked region color appears only in documents based on the template. The default colors are blue (#66CCCC) for editable regions and pale yellow (#FFFFCC) for locked regions. You can click the Show boxes to enable or disable the display of these colors in the Document window. These highlight colors show in the document window only if the option to view invisible elements is enabled. If invisible elements such as the highlighting on template regions do not appear in the document window, choose View > Visual Aids > Invisible Elements and check that the Show boxes are checked for the template visual aid elements in the Highlighting category in the preferences. If template-based pages are being built by a number of people on your team, you should keep in mind that other team members may be using the default color settings.

4) Select the first cell in the bottom row, in the same column as the word "Name," in the empty row that you just made a repeating region. Click the Editable Region button in the Templates menu on the Insert bar and type *name* **for the region name.**

The otherlights repeating region tab might block the contents of the cells behind it, including in this case, the word Name.

To make changes within a repeating region in any subsequent documents that are based on your profile template, the repeating region must contain as many editable regions as necessary. Repeating regions are locked by default; you must define which areas inside of the repeating region need to be made editable.

5) Repeat step 4 for the next two cells in the bottom row, naming them *location* **and** *height*. **Save the file.**

Your document should look like the example shown here.

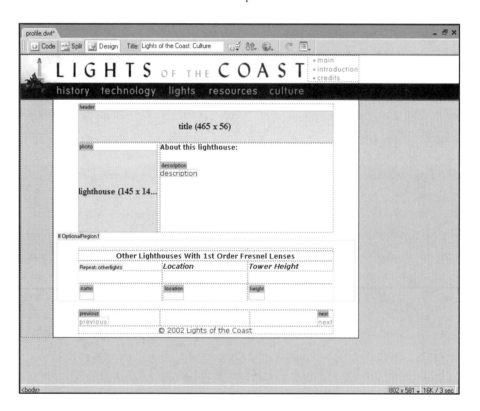

You should save and close the profile.dwt file.

BUILDING PAGES BASED ON A TEMPLATE

The next step in creating a site that makes use of templates is to create the actual pages that are based on your original template.

In this exercise, you will create new pages that use the profile template you created in the previous exercises of this lesson. These pages will inherit the contents of that original template. The only portions of the page you can change in these new pages are those parts you defined as editable in the template.

The graphics you need for building the pages are located in the Lesson_08_Templates/Images folder.

1) Choose File › New and select the Templates tab in the New Document dialog box.
The New Document dialog box opens. In the Templates portion of the box, a list of the sites you defined and a list of all the templates you created for the chosen site appears.

SITE LIST   TEMPLATES LIST   TEMPLATES TAB

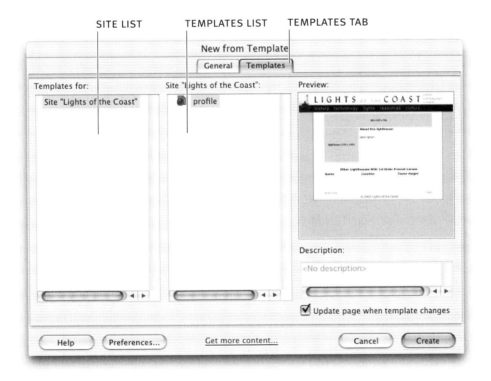

2) Choose profile from the list of templates for the "Lights of the Coast" site, leave the Update page when Template changes box checked, and then click Create.

273

A new page is created from the template. Although this document displays the inherited content, it still needs to be saved.

3) Save the file as pt_arena.htm in the Lesson_08_Templates folder. Change the title of the page to *Lights of the Coast: Lights: Point Arena.*

In the new page, you see the highlight color of the locked regions (the default color is pale yellow) outlining the page. You also see the template name on a tab of the same color at the upper right corner of the document window.

The pointer changes to a circle with a line through it when you roll over it or try to click any of the locked regions, which indicates that those areas are not editable.

4) Replace the title placeholder in the header region by double-clicking the placeholder image and then choosing the pt_arena_header.gif image from the Images folder in Lesson_08_Templates. Replace the lighthouse placeholder in the photo region with the pt_arena_img.jpg image and give it a 1-pixel border.

The placeholder images are now replaced with real content in this template-based document.

5) Open the pt_arena.txt file from Lesson_08_Templates/Text. Select and copy all the text and paste it within the description region of your pt_arena.htm file, replacing the text "description."

The text appears within an outlined border. The border color is the color of the editable regions. A tab at the upper left corner of the region displays the name of the region. When the region name is displayed within the cell as it is here, you should delete the title before placing text or images so that the title of the editable region does not remain on the page.

NOTE *Sometimes, formatting text causes the table to expand. If you change to a style that uses smaller sized text, you won't be able to get the table to shrink back to the proper size by clicking outside the table, as you would do in a regular document. Because this document is based on a template, you have to close and reopen the file for tables to adjust to the proper size in regard to their contents. You won't be able to change the size of the text in this document, unless you create a new style, because the internal style sheet that defines the text is not editable.*

Your page should now look like the following figure.

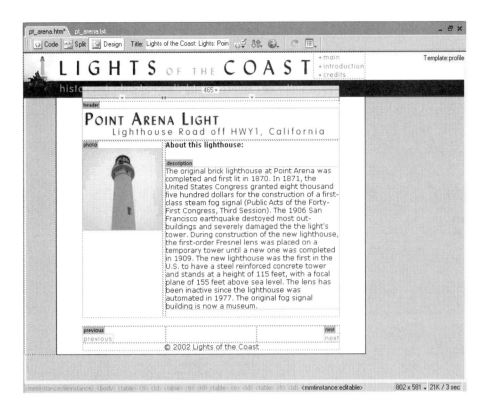

You can save and close the pt_arena.htm file.

7) Repeat steps 1 through 6 to create pt_cabrillo.htm and pt_reyes.htm in the Lesson_08_Templates folder. Use the text from the pt_cabrillo.txt and pt_reyes.txt files in the Text folder and the images from the Images folder.

NOTE *Clicking the More option in the Create New column on the Start Page is a quick way to open the New Document dialog box.*

The Point Cabrillo images are pt_cabrillo_header.gif and pt_cabrillo_img.jpg. The title for the Point Cabrillo document should be Lights of the Coast: Lights: Point Cabrillo.

The Point Reyes images are pt_reyes_header.gif and pt_reyes_img.jpg. The title for the Point Reyes document should be Lights of the Coast: Lights: Point Reyes.

You have now created three pages from the profile template. You can close the pt_cabrillo.htm file. Leave the pt_reyes.htm file open for the next exercise.

CONTROLLING OPTIONAL CONTENT

When you created the profile template at the beginning of this lesson, you defined the table for a list of other lighthouses, with 1st Order Fresnel lenses as an optional region that is hidden by default on pages based on that template. When you create and edit new pages using a template, you can show or hide any optional content areas that were created in the original template. In this exercise, you will prepare to develop the optional content for the Point Reyes Lighthouse profile by displaying the region.

1) In the pt_reyes.htm document, choose Modify > Template Properties.

TIP *The Template Properties option is located near the top of the Modify menu, next to the Page Properties option.*

The Template Properties dialog box opens.

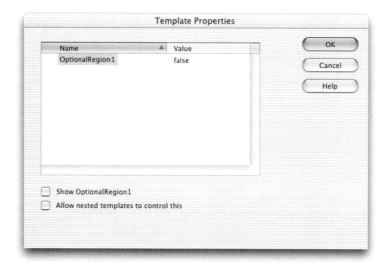

2) Select OptionalRegion1 from the list of names and check the Show OptionalRegion1 checkbox.

After you select the region, options become available beneath the list boxes.

The value listed for OptionalRegion1 in the list of values changes from false (hidden) to true (shown).

3) Click OK to close the Template Properties dialog box.

You return to your document, and the table you created in the optional region on the profile template is now displayed in the pt_reyes.htm document. Keep this file open for the next exercise.

276

ADDING REPEATING ENTRIES

The table for "Other Lighthouses With 1st Order Fresnel Lenses" that is now displayed in the pt_reyes.htm document contains the repeating region you created earlier in the profile template. In this exercise, you will use the repeating region to insert entries for five lighthouses.

1) In the "name" editable region in the pt_reyes.htm document located on the now visible optional region, type *Robben Island Lighthouse*; **type** *Table Bay, South Africa* **in the "location" editable region; and type** *59 feet* **in the "height" editable region.**

The editable regions you placed in each cell allow you to enter content into the repeating regions.

TIP *You can use the Tab key to jump from one region to another in this row, just like you would in a table to move from cell to cell. You can't, however, use the Tab key to create a new row. To insert a new row you must follow the next step.*

2) On the Repeat: otherlights tab, click the plus sign (+) button.

A duplicate of the repeating region is added below the row in which you typed the information for the Robben Island Lighthouse. Because both the spacer row and the row for the information were selected when you defined the repeating region, the spacer row is included. When you created the repeating region in the template, if you had selected only the last row for the information, there would be no spacer row.

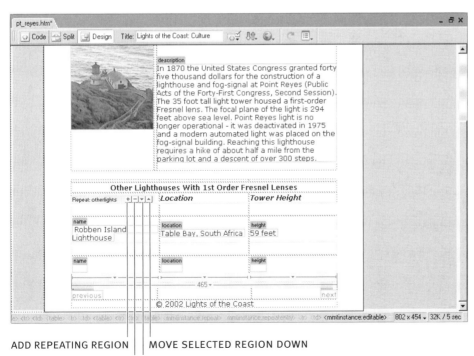

ADD REPEATING REGION | | MOVE SELECTED REGION DOWN
DELETE REPEATING REGION | MOVE SELECTED REGION UP

The four buttons on the repeating region tab allow you to add, delete, and change the order of the entries in this region.

3) Use the lighthouse information that follows to add four more entries to the table.

You need to add a new repeating region as described in step 2 for each of the four entries.

NAME	LOCATION	TOWER HEIGHT
Inubo-Saki Lighthouse	Cape Inubo, Japan	103 feet
South Stack Lighthouse	Holyhead Island, UK	197 feet
Jupiter Inlet Lighthouse	Jupiter, Florida	105 feet
St. Bees Lighthouse	St. Bees Head, UK	56 feet

You now have five entries of lighthouse information in this table.

4) Place the insertion point in the cell for the Inubo-Saki Lighthouse. Use the up arrow button on the repeating region tab to move this entry up to the top of the list.

The arrow buttons allow you to move the entries up or down in the region.

5) Use the up and down arrow buttons on the repeating region tab to adjust the remaining entries in the table so the names appear in alphabetical order. Save the file.

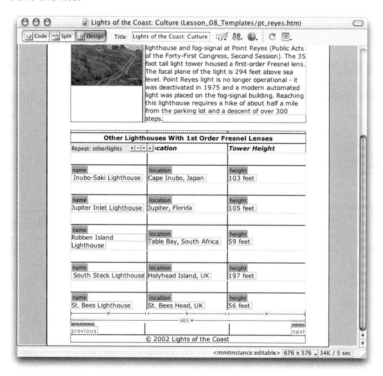

You can save and close the pt_reyes.htm file.

MODIFYING A TEMPLATE

The use of a template makes it very easy to build multiple pages using the design of your original template. The person creating the page can just add the content that changes from page to page, but can't make changes to any of the locked areas.

The real time savings comes when you need to make changes to all the pages that were built using the template. Without a template, you'd have to edit each page. With the use of a template, you simply edit the original template file to update all the pages built with the template.

1) In the Templates category of the Assets panel, double-click the profile template.

The original template you created earlier in this lesson opens.

2) Select the Lights navigation button, located on the black bar near the top of the page. Click the folder icon next to the Link text box in the Property inspector and browse to find the lights.htm file in the Lesson_08_Templates folder.

The Lights navigation button is now linked to the lights.htm file.

3) Change the copyright date at the bottom of the page to *2003*. **Save the template.**

Because you made changes to the template, the Update Template Files dialog box opens, displaying a list of all the files that were built from this template.

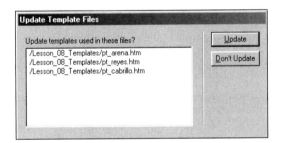

4) Click Update to modify all the pages with the changes you just made. Close the log of updates that appears.

TIP *When creating your own Web sites, you can choose Don't Update if you want. You can later update the pages by choosing Modify > Templates > Update Pages.*

The pt_arena.htm, pt_cabrillo.htm, and pt_reyes.htm documents that you created earlier from the template are all updated with the new link and date. The ability to update all pages associated with a template can be very useful. If you have a navigation section of the template with graphics for links (like the Lights of the Coast pages you're working with), you can set those graphics and their links in the template. If the links change, you simply change the template, and all pages designed with the template are updated.

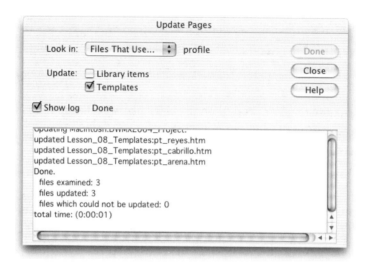

NOTE *You can detach a page from a template by choosing Modify > Templates > Detach from Template. A detached page is completely editable, but it no longer updates if the template changes. You can also uncheck the Update Page When Template Changes checkbox on the New Document dialog box to create a copy of the page, completely independent from the template. This procedure creates a page that functions much like stationery and does not have any template markup. Pages created in this manner don't update if the template changes.*

5) Open the pt_arena.htm file and preview it in the browser.

The link to the Lights page should work on this page, as well as on the other two pages you built from the template: pt_cabrillo.htmland pt_reyes.htm.

NOTE *If you want to create content that is controlled by CSS (covered in Lesson 6) you can use an external style sheet to make it possible to update the style sheet without having to update the template.*

CREATING EDITABLE TAG ATTRIBUTES

Editable tag attributes allow you to define tags that can be changed in the subsequent documents based on the original template.

1) In the profile template, profile.dwt, select the table in the optical region and set the background color of the table to #FFFFFF (white) by using the Bg color text field on the Property inspector.

The document window outlines the table to show that it is selected.

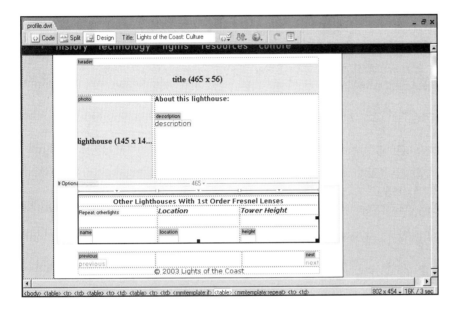

2) Choose Modify > Templates > Make Attribute Editable.

The Editable Tag Attributes dialog box opens.

3) In the Editable Tag Attributes dialog box, select BGCOLOR from the Attribute menu.

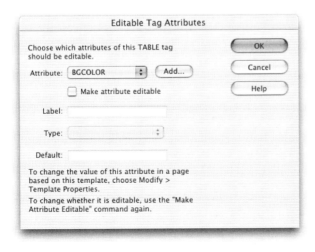

The BGCOLOR attribute appears in this menu only because a background color was defined for the table. For an attribute to appear, you must set that attribute initially. The other attributes listed are WIDTH, BORDER, CELLPADDING, and CELLSPACING—all properties of the table that were defined.

NOTE *If you want to define an attribute as editable and it is not listed in the Attribute drop-down menu, you can click Add and enter the name of the attribute you want to add. Attribute names must be typed in uppercase. If you define the attribute first, as you did in this exercise, the Label, Type, and Default settings are set automatically. Adding an attribute yourself requires you to be familiar with HTML tags and their attributes. You can use the Reference panel to learn more about tags and their attributes. For example, if you select TD in the Tag menu on the Reference panel, you can learn about that tag's attributes by clicking the Description menu and selecting one of the tag attributes, such as bgcolor. You'll learn more about HTML and the Reference panel in Lesson 4.*

4) Click the Make attribute editable checkbox. Leave the Label, Type, and Default settings as they are and click OK. Save the profile template, click Update, close the Update Pages dialog box, and close the template file profile.dwt.
When you click the Make attribute editable checkbox, the value of the attribute is inserted into the Default text field as it is defined in the template.

The Editable Tag Attributes dialog box closes. The background color of the table is now an editable tag attribute. The profile.dwt template might not display as expected if you preview it in the browser after making the bgcolor attribute editable. For Dreamweaver to create the necessary template markup that allows it to control all documents based on the template, the code displayed in the Bg text field is @@bgcolor@@. This kind of markup is necessary for the template to function, and it doesn't cause viewing irregularities in the final documents that are based on the template.

NOTE *To relock a tag that has previously been defined as editable, you must select the tag and choose Modify > Templates > Make Attribute Editable. Select the attribute you want to lock from the Attribute drop-down menu and uncheck the Make attribute editable checkbox.*

MODIFYING AN EDITABLE TAG ATTRIBUTE

The ability to create editable tag attributes makes the possibilities for creating templates much greater. You can potentially make a wide variety of tag attributes editable, which gives you a great deal of control over the individual documents created from your original template. Attributes such as background color, alignment, and size can increase the usefulness and flexibility of your template-based documents.

282

1) Open the pt_reyes.htm document and choose Modify > Template Properties.

The Template Properties dialog box opens, and the bgcolor tag attribute that you made editable in the previous exercise now appears in the Name list. You can see in the Value column that the default setting for this attribute is #FFFFFF.

2) Select the bgcolor attribute.

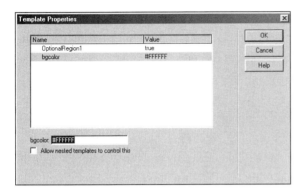

Options for editing the tag appear below the list. In this case, you are provided with a text field in which you can change the color.

3) Replace #FFFFFF in the bgcolor text field with *#CCCCCC* **and then click OK to close the dialog box.**

The color of the optional table is now changed to light gray.

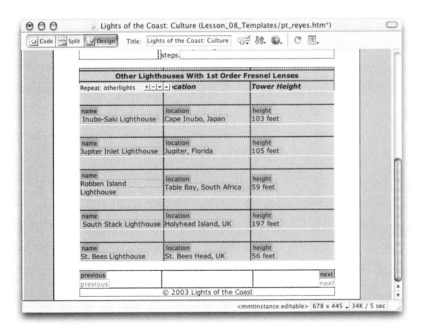

You can save and close the pt_reyes.htm file.

TIP *Knowing HTML helps you to make the most of editable tag attributes. If you don't know HTML, using the Reference panel helps you understand the different tags and the functions of their attributes. Defining the attribute before you choose to make it editable also helps. If you do know HTML, you can make use of a very powerful template feature.*

CREATING NESTED TEMPLATES

A **nested template** is one that inherits a master layout from a base template. You can create a base template with the main content that should appear on all pages and then use a nested template to create specific content or a layout style for a certain section in your site. If you have an additional section—in which you want to use a different layout while keeping the main site components such as main navigation, footer, and header—you can create another nested template that is also based on your main template. Nested templates are most useful for creating a series of page styles with variations in their layout and design that derive their common content from a main template. You'll need to make some modifications to the profile template in the following steps before you can create the nested template.

1) Open the profiles template, profile.dwt, from the Assets panel. Select the first table that contains the header, photo, and description regions. Click the Optional Region on the Templates tab of the Insert bar. Title the region *mainTable* **and click OK.**

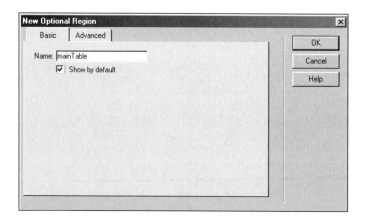

You left the Show by default option checked because most documents that you'll want to create based on the profile template need that table.

You have made this table an optional region, so you can discard it when you create a nested template.

2) Place the insertion point to the right of the main table you just made an optional region. Select the <mmtemplate:if> tag in the Tag Selector and press the right arrow key once. Press Return (Macintosh) or Enter (Windows) to create a blank paragraph below the optional main table. Click the Optional Region button in the Templates menu on the Insert bar. Title the region *nestedArea*, uncheck the Show by Default checkbox, and click OK. Double-click the words nestedArea inside the if nestedArea region to select the text nestedArea; then click the Editable Region button in the Templates menu on the Insert bar. Title the region *photoTable* and click OK.

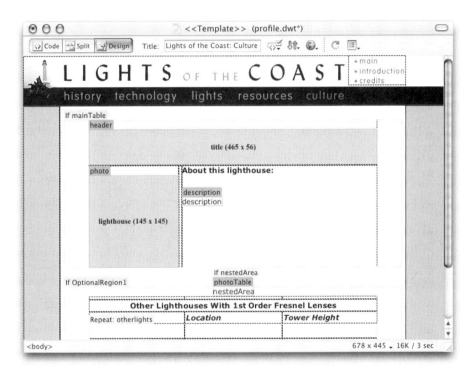

This empty, editable optional region allows you to place content in this space in your nested template without affecting the layout of the pages that are based on the original profile template.

3) Save the profile.dwt document and click Update to update all pages that use the profile template. Close the Update Pages dialog box and the profile.dwt document.
Now that you have modified the original profile template, you are ready to create the nested template in the remaining steps.

4) Choose File > New. From the Templates tab, locate the profile template and click Create.
A new page using the profile template is created. You'll use the profile template as your base template in this exercise.

5) Choose File > Save As Template, name the nested template you are creating
profile_photos, **and click Save.**

By saving the document you created from the original template as a template itself, you create a nested template. Now that you have created the nested template, you can edit it. Dreamweaver automatically adds the extension .dwt so you don't have to specify it yourself.

6) Choose Modify > Template Properties. Select nestedArea from the list and check the Show nestedArea checkbox below the list. Select mainTable from the list and uncheck the Show mainTable checkbox below the list. Click OK to close the dialog box.

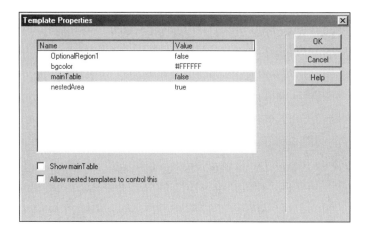

The mainTable region is hidden, and the nestedArea now appears on the page. Most of the page is locked, as it was defined in the original template. You now need to create editable regions in the nested template.

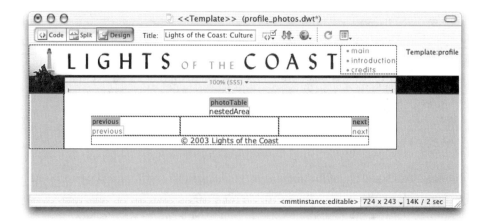

7) Open images_table.htm from the Lesson_08_Templates folder. Select and copy the table on the page. In the profile_photos.dwt document, replace the text nestedArea that appears in the photoTable region with the copied table. Close the images_table.htm document.

You will use this new template to create a page with photographs of the Point Reyes Lighthouse. This page needs to have many of the same elements as the other documents in the Lighthouse Profiles section, yet it also needs to have a substantially different layout due to the type of materials that will be contained on the page.

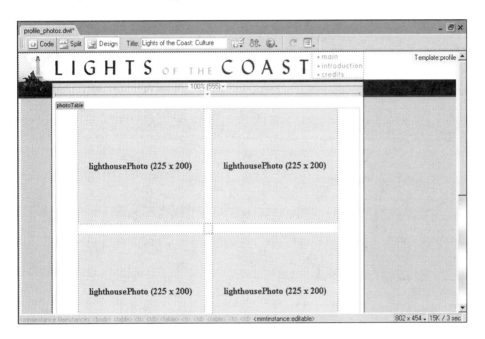

8) Select each of the placeholder images and make them individual editable regions.

The table on this page uses a layout specifically designed to display additional photographs of the lighthouses. You can use region names of photo1, photo2, and so on.

As you create the new regions, notice that the photoTable region containing them turns orange, indicating that it is part of the nested template and is not editable in the pages based off this template.

9) Save and close the profile_photos.dwt template document. Choose File > New and select the Templates tab. Choose profile_photos and click Create. Save the new document as `pt_reyes_photos.htm`.

You have now created a document based on a nested template that is controlled by the base profile template you created at the beginning of this lesson.

10) Place the following photos in the pt_reyes_photos.htm document: pt_reyes1.jpg, pt_reyes2.jpg, pt_reyes3.jpg, pt_reyes4.jpg, pt_reyes5.jpg, and pt_reyes6.jpg. Give each image a 1-pixel border.

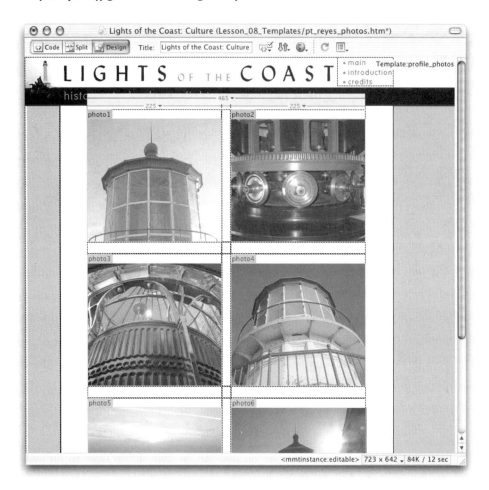

You can save and close the pt_reyes_photos.htm document.

WHAT YOU HAVE LEARNED

In this lesson, you have:

- Created a template from an existing page by saving the page as a template (pages 259–261)

- Added editable areas to the template to allow changes to be made on pages built from that template (pages 261–266)

- Removed editable areas from the template to prevent changes from being made on pages built from that template (pages 266–267)

- Created optional content areas that can be shown or hidden in subsequent pages (pages 267–276)

- Inserted repeating regions that allow pages based on the template to have as many or as few entries as needed (pages 269–272)

- Changed the template highlight colors for both editable and locked regions (pages 270–272)

- Built multiple pages based on the template to create pages with the same layout (pages 277–278)

- Made changes to the template and updated multiple pages within the site to reflect those changes (pages 278–280)

- Created and used editable tag attributes for more control over specific elements (pages 281–284)

- Nested a template to create a variation on the main layout that is still controlled by the original template (pages 284–288)

creating frames

LESSON 9

A standard HTML page consists of one region that encompasses the entire browser window. Frames split the browser window into two or more panes; each pane contains independent HTML content. Each of these independent regions is a subset of the larger browser window that contains them. Frames are commonly used to define navigation and content areas for a page. Typically, the navigation area remains constant, and the content area changes each time a navigation link is clicked. This use of frames can be extremely helpful to a user for navigation through a site. Using frames can also make

In this lesson, you'll create and change the properties of framesets and frames, resize frames, and use links to control their contents.

a site easier to modify because there is only one navigation page to update. On the other hand, frames can degrade a Web site if they are poorly implemented: They might be confusing and disorienting to users if they do not provide a clear site structure, they might make it difficult for users to bookmark or find their way back to a previous page, or they might make the content difficult to view if they are not properly sized and formatted.

When a user views a Web page that was created with two frames, the browser is actually using three separate files to display the page: the frameset file and the two files containing the content that appears inside each of the two frames. A frameset is an HTML file that is invisible to the user and defines the structure of a Web page with frames. A frameset stores information about the size and location of each frame, along with the names of the files that supply the content for each of the frames. Each frame is a separate HTML file. Frames have borders that can be turned off so the frames are not readily apparent to the user, or they can be turned on to clearly split the window into different panes. Other options include scroll bars and the possibility of allowing the user to resize the frames by dragging the borders.

In this lesson, you'll work with frames to create a Web page with a navigation area and a content area. You'll develop a set of pages that all appear in the content frame when the user selects a link from the navigation frame, and you'll learn how to target links to different frames. You'll also learn how to include content for browsers that do not support frames.

To see an example of the finished page for this chapter, open locations.htm from the Lesson_09_Frames/Completed folder.

WHAT YOU WILL LEARN

In this lesson, you will:

- Create a frameset
- Save a frameset
- Create frames and nested frames
- Resize frames
- Change frameset and frame properties
- Create documents within frames
- Target frame content
- Create NoFrames content

APPROXIMATE TIME

This lesson should take about one hour to complete.

LESSON FILES

Media Files:

Lesson_09_Frames/Images/…(all files)

Starting Files:

Lesson_09_Frames/Text/…(all files)
Lesson_09_Frames/copyright.htm

Completed Project:

Lesson_09_Frames/Completed/about.htm
Lesson_09_Frames/Completed/construction.htm
Lesson_09_Frames/Completed/local_history.htm
Lesson_09_Frames/Completed/locations.htm
Lesson_09_Frames/Completed/relocation.htm
Lesson_09_Frames/Completed/title_bar.htm

CREATING A FRAMESET

A frameset defines the overall look of a page that uses frames—the number of frame areas on the page, the size of each frame, and the border attributes. A frameset itself does not contain any content; it specifies what HTML document will be used in each frame. The frameset document is the file that you link to when calling up a frames-based Web page. In this lesson, you create a Web page consisting of three frames. The left frame holds navigation elements that remain constant; the right frame displays pages with content relative to the links clicked in the navigation frame; and the top frame contains the title of the site.

There are two ways to create a frameset in Dreamweaver: You can manually insert the frames or you can choose from several predefined framesets. If you choose a predefined frameset, the frameset and frames are automatically set up for you. This process is a quick way to create a layout using frames because most of the work is done for you. You just need to name the individual pages.

In this exercise, you use a predefined frameset to make a Web page that uses frames.

1) Choose File > New and select Framesets from the Category list in the General portion of the New Document dialog box.

TIP *You can also access the Framesets portion of the New Document dialog box by clicking Framesets in the "Create from Samples" list on the Start Page.*

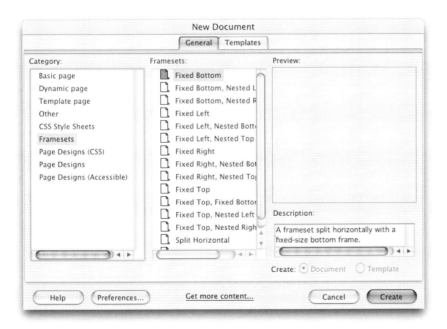

The New Document dialog box contains a variety of presets that you can use when creating a new frameset. As you browse the Framesets list, samples showing the basic frame structure are displayed in the preview area at the right, along with a description.

NOTE *You can also create a frameset from a standard HTML document by selecting the Layout menu on the Insert bar and choosing a frameset preset from the Frames menu.*

THE FRAMES MENU IN THE LAYOUT
CATEGORY OF THE INSERT BAR

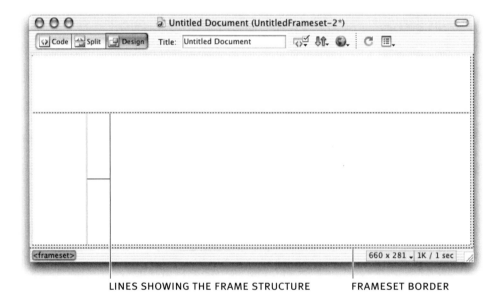

2) Select Fixed Top, Nested Left from the Framesets list and click Create.

A frameset can be made of either rows or columns, but not both. Framesets can be nested to create a layout like the one you chose with multiple rows and multiple columns.

A dotted border appears around the page edges in the document window, and lines in the document window show the frame structure.

LINES SHOWING THE FRAME STRUCTURE   FRAMESET BORDER

294

The page is divided into three frames: a short frame on the top and a taller frame on the bottom that contains a nested frameset. (This second frameset is called a **nested frameset** because it is inside another frame.) The single bottom frame is divided into two frames: a narrow frame on the left and a wider frame on the right. Several of Dreamweaver's predefined framesets use nested framesets. You can use combinations of these predefined framesets to come up with any frame layout you want. Thin gray lines mark the divisions between frames.

NOTE *To insert frames manually, open a new HTML document and choose View > Visual Aids > Frame Borders to turn on the dotted frame border around the page edges of the document window. Click the border and drag it into the document window. The document becomes split horizontally (if you drag from the top or bottom of the border) or vertically (if you drag from the left or right sides of the border). If you drag the border from the corner, the document becomes divided into four frames. You can also choose Modify > Frameset > Split Frame Left, Right, Up, or Down. If you selected the wrong frames configuration or need to reduce the number of frames in your frameset, you can remove the extra frames by dragging the border of the unwanted frame to the edge of the page or atop another frame. The extra frame disappears.*

Leave this file open to use in the next exercise.

SAVING A FRAMESET

When you have the number of frames you want, you need to save the frameset. The frameset file is the file that you reference when linking to this Web page. The frameset, as well as the files for each frame, needs to be saved before you can preview the page in a browser. If you attempt to preview the page in the browser prior to saving, Dreamweaver displays a message stating that the frameset and frame files all need to be saved to preview. You can save each file individually or you can save all open files at once. In this exercise, you save only the frameset.

1) In the document window, verify that the frameset is selected by checking the Tag Selector, which should display `<frameset>` **in bold.**

When you create a frameset, it is automatically selected. Clicking anywhere in the document window deselects the frameset because you would be clicking inside a frame. Clicking inside a frame is similar to clicking inside a table cell; placing the insertion point inside a cell will make that cell active, but will not give you access to the same properties that you would be able to edit if the entire table itself were selected. Likewise, to modify a frameset, you must select the frameset itself.

THE DOTTED BORDER OF THE FRAMESET

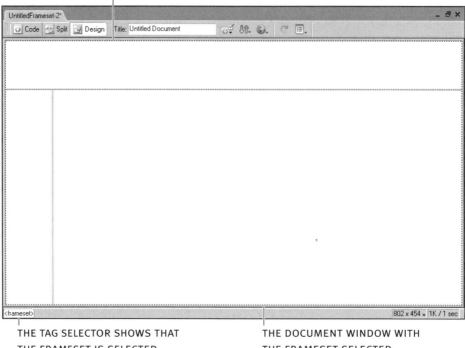

THE TAG SELECTOR SHOWS THAT
THE FRAMESET IS SELECTED

THE DOCUMENT WINDOW WITH
THE FRAMESET SELECTED

If the frameset is not selected, you can select it by clicking the border around the edges of the document window. You can also select the frameset by choosing Window > Frames and then clicking the outermost border enclosing the frames in the Frames panel. The Frames panel shows you a simplified version of the structure of frames in the document.

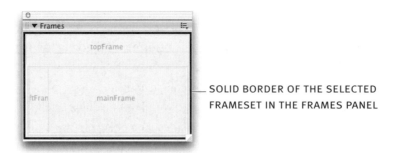

SOLID BORDER OF THE SELECTED
FRAMESET IN THE FRAMES PANEL

When the frameset is selected, the document window is outlined by a dotted line and the Tag Selector at the bottom of the window displays <frameset>. The document's title bar shows "Untitled Document (UntitledFrameset-1)," and the Property inspector shows the frameset properties. The number (-1, -2, and so on) of your untitled document might vary depending on how many new documents you created since you opened Dreamweaver.

NOTE *If the frameset is not selected, an individual frame is selected instead and the frames border around the document window is a solid black line. If a nested frameset is selected, the border of the frame that contains it is surrounded with a dotted line.*

In the Frames panel, a selected frameset is displayed with a thick border around the perimeter of the panel and the frames are displayed with a grayed-out border.

2) Choose File > Save Frameset As and save the file as *locations.htm* **in the Lesson_09_Frames folder.**

The document's title bar shows that the location of the file and the filename is Lesson_09_Frames/locations.htm.

NOTE *For Windows users the document tabs will display only the name of the file. The Dreamweaver program title bar will display the location and name of the selected file.*

3) With the frameset still selected, type *Lights of the Coast: Locations* **for the page title.**

If you don't have the frameset selected when you title the page, you might be titling one of the pages that correspond with an individual frame—not the actual frameset file. Refer to the Frames panel to check what is selected; it helps to ensure that you are working within the frame or frameset that you intend to edit.

Leave the locations.htm file open to use in the next exercise.

RESIZING FRAMES IN A FRAMESET

You can use the Property inspector to specify the size of your frames, or you can simply drag the borders in the document window to perform the same task. In addition to specifying a size in the Property inspector, you can also determine how browsers allocate space to frames when there is not enough room to display all frames at full size.

1) In the document window, verify that the frameset is selected by positioning the pointer over the horizontal border between the top and bottom frames. When the pointer changes to a double arrow, click the border once to select the frameset.

DOUBLE ARROW   HORIZONTAL BORDER OF THE MAIN FRAMESET

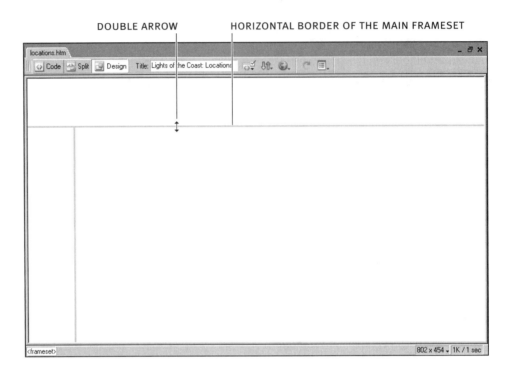

The main frameset is selected, and the Property inspector shows the frameset properties. The Property inspector changes depending on whether you selected a frameset or a frame. To change the size of the frames, you need to make sure that you selected the frameset.

THE PROPERTY INSPECTOR SHOWING FRAMESET
PROPERTIES FOR THE MAIN FRAMESET   TOP ROW SELECTED

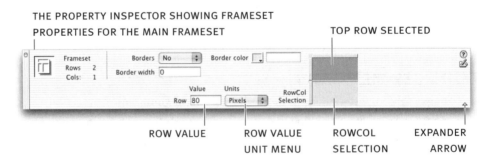

ROW VALUE   ROW VALUE   ROWCOL   EXPANDER
                UNIT MENU   SELECTION   ARROW

NOTE *Click the expander arrow on the Property inspector to view all Frameset properties if they are not already visible.*

298

2) Drag the border between the top and bottom frames until the top frame is 50 pixels high.

Use the Row Value in the Property inspector to check the height, or type **50** in the Row Value text field when the top row is selected in the RowCol Selection area to get the exact height. Make sure that Pixels is selected from the Units menu. The top row in the RowCol Selection should be dark to indicate it is active.

3) With the frameset still selected, click the bottom row in the RowCol Selection area on the Property inspector to select the bottom row within the frameset. Next to the Row Value text field, verify that Relative is selected from the Units menu.

When you use the RowCol Selection on the Property inspector to select a row or column, you are selecting that row or column within the frameset, which enables you to modify the properties of the frameset as they apply to that specific row or column. You are not selecting a frame.

Setting the value of the bottom row to Relative allows the bottom row to expand or contract depending on how large the user's browser is and how much space is left after the top row is allocated the 50 pixels that were assigned to it. By default, Dreamweaver automatically places a 1 in the Row Value text field.

NOTE *If you view the HTML code for the frameset size, you see* frameset rows="50,*". *The 1 in the Row Value text field, in conjunction with the Relative unit chosen from the menu, is the same as the asterisk (*) in the code; it represents a size that is relative or proportional to the other rows in the frameset.*

4) In the Frames panel, click the nested frameset, represented by the thick inner border around the two columns in the bottom row, to select it. In the visual representation of the frame on the Property inspector, click the left column in the RowCol Selection area to select the left column.

In your document, the outer frameset is made up of rows, whereas the nested frameset is composed of columns.

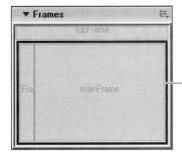

THE NESTED FRAMESET SELECTED IN THE FRAMES PANEL

The left column in the Property inspector darkens to indicate it has been selected.

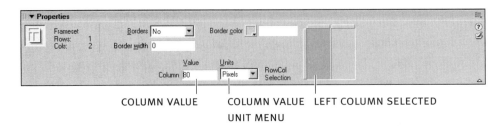

COLUMN VALUE   COLUMN VALUE LEFT COLUMN SELECTED
UNIT MENU

5) In the Column Value text field of the Property inspector, type _150_ and press Return (Macintosh) or Enter (Windows). Verify that Pixels is selected from the Units menu.

The left column's width is adjusted to 150 pixels.

When you are deciding how to resize the column, keep these units of measurement in mind:

- **Pixels:** This option sets the absolute size of the selected column or row to the number of pixels that you enter. It is the best option for any frame that needs to have a set size. If other columns or rows are defined by a different unit, those other columns or rows are allocated space only after rows or columns specified in pixels are their full size.

- **Percent:** This option specifies a percentage that the current column or row should take up in its frameset. Columns or rows specified with units set to Percent are allocated space after columns or rows with units set to Pixels and before columns or rows with units set to Relative.

- **Relative:** This option specifies that the current column or row is allocated space using the current proportions relative to the other columns and rows. Columns or rows with units set to Relative are allocated space after columns or rows with units set to Pixels and Percent, but they take up all remaining space. If you set the bottom or the right frame to relative, the frame size changes to fill the remaining width or height of the browser window.

6) In the Property inspector, click the right column in the RowCol Selection area to select the right column of the nested frameset. Next to the Column Value text field, verify that Relative is selected from the Units menu.

This procedure enables the right column to expand or contract, depending on how large the user's browser is and how much space remains after the left column is allocated the 150 pixels assigned to it.

300

7) Save the frameset by choosing File > Save Frameset.

If this command is not available, first select the outer frameset by clicking the border between the top and bottom frames.

TIP *If you have the frameset selected, Command+S (Macintosh) or Ctrl+S (Windows) saves the frameset only.*

Leave the locations.htm file open to use in the next exercise.

SPECIFYING FRAME PROPERTIES

When you create a frameset, get in the habit of naming each frame. The name you assign to a frame is not the filename of the document that corresponds with the frame. A frame name serves to identify the framed area of the document for your reference. Naming your frames is important when you create links to display pages within a framed area. In the previous exercise, you used the predefined top and left framesets. Each frame in the frameset was already given a default name. In this exercise, you change the name to reflect the future content of the frame.

1) Select the top frame by clicking the top frame in the Frames panel.

TIP *If the Frames panel is not open, choose Window > Frames.*

Selecting the top frame in the Frames panel is not the same as placing the insertion point inside the top frame by clicking in the document window. Selecting the frame makes the properties for that frame available to you in the Property inspector. Clicking in the frame in the document window makes the standard text properties appear for that frame's document. If the insertion point is in the top frame, it is the active frame; however, you can't make changes to the frame properties. To affect the properties of the frame itself, it needs to be selected.

TIP *You can also Shift+Option-click (Macintosh) or Alt-click (Windows) in the top frame in the document window to select the frame.*

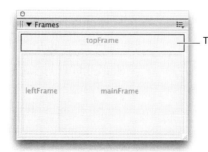 TOP FRAME SELECTED IN THE FRAMES PANEL

The Frames panel shows a thin black border around the top frame with the name "topFrame" shown in the center. The Property inspector displays frame properties for topFrame.

2) In the Frame name text field on the Property inspector, type _title_ to replace the default name topFrame. Press Return (Macintosh) or Enter (Windows) to apply the name change.

SCROLL MENU   OPTION TO ALLOW USERS TO RESIZE A FRAME

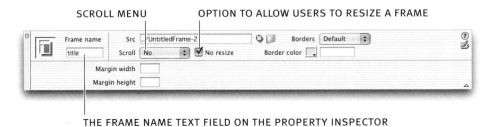

THE FRAME NAME TEXT FIELD ON THE PROPERTY INSPECTOR

The Frames panel displays the word "title" in the top frame. You can always refer to the Frames panel for the name of a particular frame. Frame names are often used to target links to load in specific frames. You learned about targeting links in Lesson 4.

NOTE *When naming frames, don't use spaces, hyphens, periods, or special characters in the frame name; and don't begin the name with an underscore. Using any of these characters can cause problems with code or scripting.*

3) Verify that No is selected in the Scroll menu and that the No resize box is checked on the Property inspector.

The scroll option, which defines when scroll bars appear, applies to both vertical and horizontal scroll bars. The Auto setting displays scroll bars whenever there is not enough room in the frame to display the content of the page. The Default option is the browser default setting, which is usually Auto. Be careful how you set this option: if it is set to No and the frame is not large enough to display all the contents, the user cannot scroll to see the rest of the content; if it is set to Yes and the contents fit within the frame, scroll bars that are grayed out still take up space on the page, even though it isn't possible to scroll.

No resize locks the size of the frame when viewed in the browser. If this option is unchecked, users can drag the frame borders in their browser window. Regardless of whether this option is checked or unchecked, it does not affect your ability to resize frames within Dreamweaver.

Don't forget that visitors to your Web site have a wide range of monitor sizes and resolutions. With frames, it is particularly important when designing sites on large, high-resolution screens to account for smaller screens. Frames-based pages might encounter problems on screens that are larger or smaller than those that they were designed for. Small screens, for instance, might cause your pages to suffer problems such as too much scrolling, which can make it extremely difficult for users. By testing your pages in a variety of environments, you can be sure to accommodate the widest possible range of sizes and resolutions. Be aware that such size issues can also lead to printing problems. You might want to provide alternatives, such as printer-friendly pages, if you use frames in your site.

NOTE *Printer-friendly pages are 530 pixels wide (printable width) and use a bare minimum of graphics. Navigation should also be minimal, such as text links at the bottom of the page. A background color of white and the use of black text is best for readability against the white background of paper. Serif fonts are good choices for pages intended primarily for printing; likewise, keep your text at a size that can be read easily, such as 12 points or larger.*

4) Select the lower left frame and name it *nav*. Scroll should be set to No, and the No resize box should be checked.

On the Property inspector, notice that the Borders menu has Default selected. The predefined framesets that you used to create the page layout are automatically set to have no frame borders. When the Default setting is selected for the Borders option of an individual frame, that frame uses the setting of the parent frameset. If another setting (Yes or No) is selected, the frame overrides the setting of the parent frameset.

The Frames panel displays the name "nav" in the lower left frame.

5) Select the lower right frame and name it *content*. Scroll should be set to Auto and the No resize box should be checked.

On the Property inspector, notice that the text fields for Margin width and Margin height are blank. This is the default for the predefined framesets you used to lay out your page. Margin width sets the left and right margins of the frame in pixels. Margin height sets the top and bottom margins of the frame in pixels. Leaving them blank uses the browser default, which might vary in size depending on the browser version and type.

The Frames panel displays the name "content" in the lower right frame.

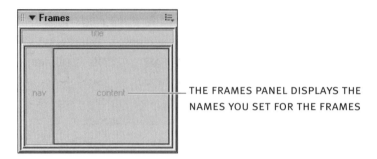

THE FRAMES PANEL DISPLAYS THE
NAMES YOU SET FOR THE FRAMES

6) Choose File > Save Frameset.

When you change Frame properties, you are actually modifying the frameset, locations.htm. Frame and frameset properties are both defined within the frameset.

Leave the locations.htm file open to use in the next exercise.

CREATING AND EDITING FRAMES CONTENT

Remember that the content of a frame resides in a separate HTML page—not in the frameset. You can create the individual frame pages separately or within the constraints of a frame. Using the frameset to help you design the pages to be contained in each frame is always a good idea. That way, you don't create a page that's too wide or too narrow for the frame. Your users will find the pages difficult to view if they have to scroll in multiple directions to see all the content.

In this exercise, you will add content to each page in the frameset.

1) Place the insertion point in the title frame (the top frame) in the document window.

The document title bar (Macintosh) or the Dreamweaver program title bar (Windows) changes to show that this is an untitled and unsaved document.

2) Choose File > Save Frame. Save the file as title_bar.htm in the Lesson_09_Frames folder and title it *Lights of the Coast: Locations: Title.* **Use the Appearance category in the Page Properties to set the background color to white and all four margins (top, bottom, left, and right) to a value of 0.**

The document title bar (Macintosh) or the Dreamweaver program title bar (Windows) changes to reflect the title and filename for the document in this frame. Visitors are not likely to see the title of this page because the browser uses the title of the frameset in the browser window. Still, it is good practice to always title your documents so that if the page is opened in a window by itself for any reason, it has a title.

3) Insert the lights_title.gif from the Lesson_09_Frames/Images folder into the title frame, center it, and type *Lights of the Coast* **into the Alt text field on the Property inspector. Save the frame.**

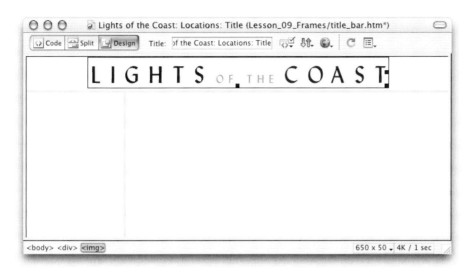

As you edit your pages, remember to save often. When you use the Save keyboard shortcut Command+S (Macintosh) or Ctrl+S (Windows), you save only the file that corresponds with currently selected frame, or the frameset if it is selected. The Save command does not save each document; you must save them individually or use the File > Save All option. If you want to save the file displayed in another frame, just click inside that frame in the document window and then save. You can refer to the Frames panel to check which frame is selected when you are saving. The names of all frames displayed in the Frames panel are grayed- out except for the name of the frame in which the insertion point is located.

4) Place the insertion point in the content frame (the lower right frame). Save the file as about.htm in the Lesson_09_Frames folder and title it *Lights of the Coast: Locations: About.* **Use the Page Properties to set the background of the document to white and the text to black. Use the Links category of the Page Properties to set the link color to #660000, rollover link color to #CC0000, the visited link color to #333333, and the active link color to #660000.**

The document title bar (Macintish) or the Dreamweaver program title bar (Windows) changes to reflect the title and filename for the document in this frame.

5) In the about.htm document, insert a table with the following attributes: 2 rows, 1 column, 95 percent, a Border of 0, Cell Padding of 3, Cell Spacing of 3, no Header, no Caption and the text *Learning about the roles of lighthouses throughout history* **for the Summary. Place the about_header.gif in the first row and give it the following alternative text:** *About the Lights.* **Open Lesson_09_Frames/Text/about.txt, copy the text and paste it into the second row. Format this text as Verdana at 12 pixels.**

This is the content page that corresponds with the About link that you will create in the navigation frame later in this lesson.

6) With the insertion point in the second row of the table, press Tab to create a third row. Place the about_lights.jpg image from the Lesson_09_Frames/Images folder in the new row. Center the image; give it a 1-pixel border and a V space of 5; and use *Lighthouse photograph* **for the alternative text. Save the file.**

Your content frame should now look like the example shown here.

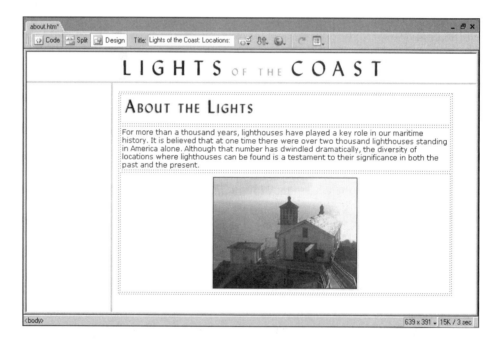

7) Place the insertion point in the nav frame (the lower left frame). Save the file as nav.htm in the Lesson_09_Frames folder and title it *Lights of the Coast: Locations: Nav.* **Use the Page Properties to set the background of the document to white, the text to black, and all margins to 2. Set the link color to #660000, rollover link color to #CC0000, the visited link color to #333333, and the active link color to #660000.**

This frame will contain the navigation for your pages.

8) In the nav.htm document, insert a table with the following attributes: 5 rows, 1 column, 147 pixels, a Border of 0, Cell Padding of 3, Cell Spacing of 1, no Header, no Caption, and the text *navigation* for the Summary. Place about.gif in the first row with *About* for the alternative text. Place the local.gif in the second row with *Local* for the alternative text. Place the construction.gif in the second row with *Construction* for the alternative text. Place the relocation.gif in the second row with *Relocation* for the alternative text.

Your nav frame should now look like the example shown here. The last row of the table will be used for a link to copyright information.

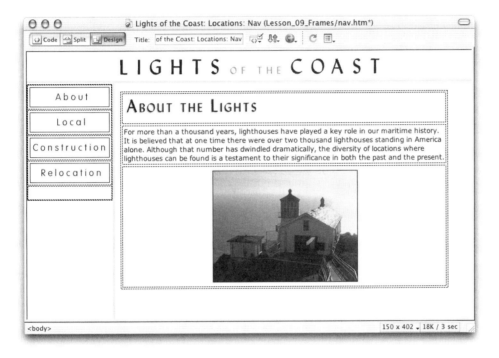

NOTE *You can use an interactive element called a **navigation bar** in frame-based pages to create a way for visitors to get visual feedback while exploring pages. While you can create a navigation bar yourself, Dreamweaver provides a tool that you can use to create one. A navigation bar is a set of images that are linked to a variety of pages. Navigation bars use JavaScript (covered in Lesson 11), allowing you to add up to four states based on user interaction for each image. The first state of an image occurs when the page loads; the second state of an image is displayed when the user rolls over the image. When the user clicks the image, the third state is shown. The fourth state of an image is used when the visitor rolls over an image after that image is clicked. The navigation bar is effective for giving visitors responses to their actions so that they understand what pages they are looking at based on the state displayed by the navigation images.*

CREATING OTHER CONTENT DOCUMENTS

You now need to create additional documents that will also appear in the content frame.

1) Create a new HTML document from the Basic Page category of the New Document dialog box. Save the file as local_history.htm in the Lesson_09_Frames folder and title it *Lights of the Coast: Locations: Local History*. **Use the Page Properties to set the background to white and the text to black. Set the link color to #660000, the rollover link color to #CC0000, the visited link color to #333333, and the active link color to #660000.**

The document title bar changes to reflect the title and filename for the document.

2) In the local_history.htm document, insert a table with the following attributes: 2 rows, 1 column, 95 percent, a Border of 0, Cell Padding of 3, Cell Spacing of 3, no Header, no Caption, and the text *Exploring the locations where lighthouses are built* **for the Summary. In the first row, place the location_header.gif image with the alternative text** *Determining the Location – choosing where to build lighthouses*. **Copy the text from Lesson_09_Frames/Text/local_history.txt and place it in the second row. Format this text as Verdana at 12 pixels and save the page.**

This is the content page that will correspond with a Local History link; you will create a link to this page from the nav frame later in this lesson.

3) Repeat steps 1 and 2 to create construction.htm in the Lesson_09_Frames folder. Title it *Lights of the Coast: Locations: Construction* **and use** *Understanding the construction and preservation of lighthouses* **for the table summary. Use construct_header.gif for the graphic header with** *Preserving the Lights – –years of reconstruction* **for the alternative text. Use construction.txt for the text in the second row.**

This is the content page that will correspond with a Construction link you will create in the nav frame later in this lesson.

4) Repeat steps 1 and 2 to create relocation.htm in the Lesson_09_Frames folder. Title it *Lights of the Coast: Locations: Relocation* **and use** *Replacing and relocating lighthouses* **for the table summary. Use relocate_header.gif for the graphic header with** *Relocating the Lights – moving from their original location* **for the alternative text. Use relocation.txt for the text in the second row.**

This is the content page that will correspond with a Relocation link you will create in the nav frame later in this lesson.

You can close local_history.htm, construction.htm, and relocation.htm. Leave the locations.htm file open to use in the next exercise.

OPENING AN EXISTING PAGE IN A FRAME

You already started several content pages, so now you need to make sure they fit in the content frame. You can open those files directly in the frame to check or edit them.

1) In the locations.htm document window, click inside the content frame.

This is the frame in which you want the about, local_history, construction, and relocation pages to appear.

2) Choose File › Open in Frame. Choose local_history.htm from the dialog box.

The page is loaded into the content frame and is available for editing.

3) Place the local_history.jpg image from the Lesson_09_Frames/Images folder on a new paragraph line between the first two paragraphs; then center the image and use *Lighthouse photograph* **for its alternative text. Give the image a 1-pixel border and save the file.**

Depending on the size of the text and of the window in which your frameset is displayed, the content on this page might require scrolling. With the frame properties set to auto scroll, the browser will use scroll bars only if they are needed.

4) Open construction.htm in the content frame. Place and center the construction.jpg image on a new paragraph line between the first two paragraphs, and use *Lighthouse photograph* **for its alternative text. Give the image a 1-pixel border and save the file.**

Take care when saving your frames, and exercise caution when using the Save All Frames command in the File menu. This command saves all open pages contained in your frames and the frameset. The files that initially appear within each frame are defined in the frameset. If you choose File > Save All Frames while you are editing other pages within the frames (by using File > Open in Frame), you redefine the frameset.

5) Open relocation.htm in the content frame. Place and center the relocation.jpg image on a new paragraph line between the first two paragraphs and use *Lighthouse photograph* **for its alternative text. Give the image a 1-pixel border and save the file.**

Your page should now look like the following example. You can preview the page in the browser to see how it looks. All pages need to be saved before you can preview frames in the browser. Dreamweaver will warn you and ask if you want to save the pages if any unsaved changes have been made.

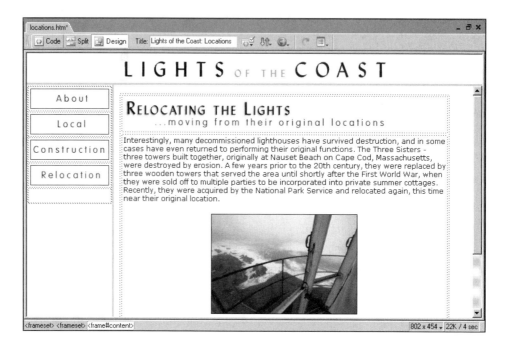

CHECKING FRAME CONTENT

As you create and edit pages within frames, it can be easy to accidentally place the wrong content in a frame. You can use the Property inspector to ensure that the correct pages are loaded into each of the frames for the initial view of your Web page.

1) Select the title frame by clicking the top frame in the Frames panel. In the Src text field on the Property inspector, make sure that title_bar.htm is selected. If it isn't, click the folder icon to find and select it.

The Property inspector shows Frame properties for the title frame.

SOURCE FOR THE FILE THAT APPEARS IN THE SELECTED FRAME

2) Select the nav frame by clicking the lower left frame in the Frames panel. In the Src text field on the Property inspector, make sure that nav.htm is selected. If it isn't, click the folder icon to find and select it.

The Property inspector shows Frame properties for the nav frame.

3) Select the content frame by clicking the lower right frame in the Frames panel. Next to the Src text field on the Property inspector, click the folder icon to find and select about.htm. Save the frameset.

The relocation.htm was selected because it was the last document that you worked with in this frame. If you open a page within a frame to edit it, saving the frameset causes that file to become the default page for that frame when the frameset document loads. The about.htm file is the document you want to appear at first in the content frame of the final frameset.

The Property inspector shows frame properties for the content frame.

You can open Web pages from a variety of sources in a frame by typing the URL of the desired page in the Src text field on the Property inspector. The page you call up does not have to reside on the same server as the frameset. The capability to open pages from other servers can be a drawback where the ethical use of content is concerned. Some frames-based pages are used to open content developed by others, without their permission. Be sure to respect the copyright of content that is not your own and avoid giving visitors the impression that materials are from your Web site if they aren't.

NOTE *If you are concerned about your pages being called up in someone else's frame, there is something you can do about it. You might be able to determine whether this is a problem by reviewing your site logs; check with your system administrator or Web host for more information. You can also create a JavaScript that opens your page in its own window if it is called from a frame.*

CONTROLLING FRAME CONTENT WITH LINKS

After you have created the content document pages, you need to link the navigation elements to those pages that should display in the content area of your Web page. To get the content to appear in its proper location, you need to target the link to the desired frame.

1) Select the about.gif image and link it to about.htm. In the Property inspector, press Return (Macintosh) or Enter (Windows) to apply the link, and select content from the Target drop-down menu while the image is still selected.

By default, links are targeted to the frame or window in which they are located. However, these images should link to documents that open in the content frame, not the nav frame.

LINK TEXT FIELD   TARGET MENU

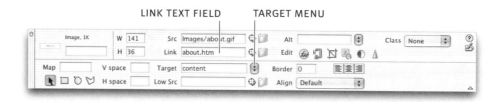

Each time you create a new frame, the name of that frame is automatically added to the Target menu. Clear, concise, and descriptive names serve you best. Although Dreamweaver's default frame names give you an idea of the frame location, those generic names can still be difficult and confusing to sort out when you try to make a document open in a certain frame.

NOTE *If you are working on a document that will be loaded in a frame and you are not working on it inside the frameset, as you are in this lesson, you don't have the option in the Target menu to select the names of any frames. Dreamweaver displays only the names of frames that are available in the current document in the target menu. In these cases, you need to type the exact name of the frame in which you want the page to open into the target text field.*

2) Repeat step 1 to link local.gif to local_history.htm, construction.gif to construction.htm, and relocation.gif to relocation.htm. Each of these links should be targeted to the content frame.

There are other options available in the Target menu.

_blank loads the linked document in a new, unnamed browser window.

_parent loads the linked document in the parent frameset of the frame that contains the link. If the frame containing the link is not nested, the linked document loads into the full browser window.

312

_self loads the linked document in the same frame or window as the link. This target is implied, so you usually don't have to specify it.

_top loads the linked document in the full browser window, thereby removing all frames.

3) Type *Copyright* **in the fifth row of the navigation table, center it, and format it as Verdana at 10 pixels. Select "Copyright" and create a link to copyright.htm by typing copyright.htm in the link text field on the Property inspector and select content from the Target menu.**

The Copyright document is now placed in the content frame (the lower right frame) when the Copyright link is clicked in the browser.

4) Save the file and preview it in the browser.

When previewing your frames pages in the browser, you might get a dialog box informing you that all the frames need to be saved. Click OK to save all frames and the frameset.

When you click the Copyright link, the copyright.htm document displays in the content frame.

TIP *If your pages don't appear in the frames you expect them to, check to see that you have selected the correct frame from the Target drop-down menu in the Property inspector for each link.*

The links should open all the pages in the content frame—if not, you need to correct the target using the Target menu for any links that do not open in that frame.

CREATING NOFRAMES CONTENT

In Dreamweaver, you can create content that is ignored by frames-capable browsers, and is displayed in older and text-based browsers or in other browsers that do not support frames. This information, called NoFrames content, is also used by search engine spiders, screen readers, and portable Internet devices that do not support frames. The NoFrames content you create is placed in the frameset file. When a browser that doesn't support frames loads the frameset file, the browser displays only the NoFrames content.

1) In the locations.htm document, select the frameset.

The locations.htm document is the page the browser loads initially, so the NoFrames content is specified here.

2) Choose Modify > Frameset > Edit NoFrames Content.

TIP *If the Frameset option in the Modify menu is grayed-out, you might have a frame selected.*

The document window changes to display the NoFrames page, and the words "NoFrames Content" appear at the top. This is still the locations.htm document; you are just seeing a different view of the page's content.

NOFRAMES CONTENT VIEW

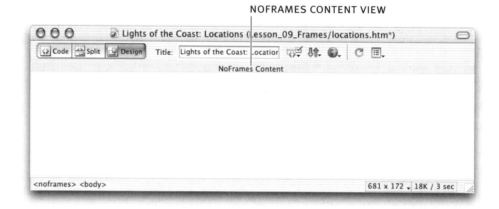

3) Open the about.txt document; then select and copy all the text. Create the NoFrames content in the document window by pasting in the text you copied from the about.txt text file.

Alternative content can contain elements from a standard html page. It will be enclosed between the <noframes> and </noframes> tags. Only browsers that do not support frames see this content. The content should be relatively simple—browsers that do not support frames are likely to not support JavaScript, image maps, and other types of complex elements. Some Web sites use NoFrames content to provide simple alternative pages or to direct users to a text-based version of the Web site, whereas other sites use NoFrames content to display a message to users that the site is available only to frames-capable browsers.

4) Choose Modify > Frameset > Edit NoFrames Content. Choose File > Save All and close all of your documents.

The document window changes to hide the NoFrames content and returns to the normal view of the frameset document.

NOTE *When you finish editing the NoFrames content, you might be inclined to close the window because you can't see the original document. If you do, you close the frameset and all the frame pages. You then have to open them up again if you want to continue editing them.*

WHAT YOU HAVE LEARNED

In this lesson, you have:

- Created a frameset to define the layout of frames within your document (pages 293–295)
- Saved a frameset and learned how to save other frames individually, as well as how to save them all at once (pages 295–297)
- Created frames and nested frames to modify the layout of your page using predefined framesets (pages 299–301)
- Resized frames by changing the dimensions in the Property inspector (pages 297–301)
- Changed frameset and frame properties using the Frames panel and the Property inspector (pages 301–304)
- Created documents within frames by inserting elements directly into the frames and by opening existing documents in the frames (pages 308–310)
- Targeted frame content into other frames to control where the pages appear (pages 310–313)
- Created NoFrames content for browsers that are unable to display frames (pages 313–315)

creating forms

LESSON 10

You may need to collect information from the visitors to your Web site. The types of information that may need to be gathered can include feedback about the site, user registration, responses to polls, and buying products (e-commerce). From gathering different types of information to creating an opportunity for visitors to interact with your site, forms provide the necessary user interface that enables you to obtain data. Forms allow you to ask visitors for specific information or to give them an opportunity to send feedback, questions, or requests to you. Visitor registrations and product orders often require the functionality of forms. Forms are often used in conjunction

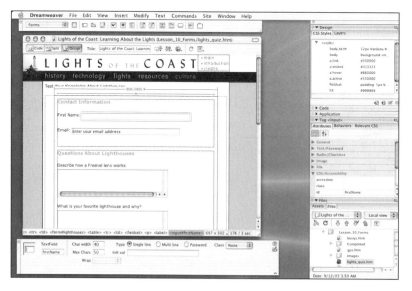

In this project, you will build a form with various text fields, checkboxes, radio buttons, submit and reset buttons, and a menu.

with databases and can enable visitors to perform searches and post information to be included in a database. A form contains fields in which users enter information. These fields can be text fields, radio buttons, checkboxes, menus, or lists, to name a few.

Form data is usually sent to a database on a server, to an email address, or to an application that will process it. The processing of forms can be done through dynamic pages (which use languages such as PHP, JSP, ColdFusion, and more to access dynamic content sources such as databases) or CGI (Common Gateway Interface) scripts. CGI is a standard protocol that acts as the communication link between the data from the form and the server. In this lesson, you will be creating the form that a visitor will see. Because you will not be working with dynamic pages or CGI scripts, you do not need access to a server to complete this lesson.

To see an example of the finished page for this lesson, open lights_quiz.htm from the Lesson_10_Forms/Completed folder.

WHAT YOU WILL LEARN

In this lesson, you will:

- Create a form on a Web page
- Divide form content into groups
- Create accessible forms
- Add single-line text fields
- Add a multi-line text field
- Add checkboxes
- Add radio buttons
- Add list/menu items
- Add hidden fields
- Add buttons
- Format a form using CSS
- Create a jump menu
- Test a form

APPROXIMATE TIME

This lesson should take about one hour to complete.

LESSON FILES

Media Files:

Lesson_10_Forms/Images/…(all files)

Starting Files:

Lesson_10_Forms/buoys.htm

Lesson_10_Forms/gps.htm

Lesson_10_Forms/lights_quiz.htm

Lesson_10_Forms/radar.htm

Lesson_10_Forms/related_navigation.htm

Lesson_10_Forms/sonar.htm

Completed Project:

Lesson_10_Forms/buoys.htm

Lesson_10_Forms/gps.htm

Lesson_10_Forms/lights_quiz.htm

Lesson_10_Forms/radar.htm

Lesson_10_Forms/related_navigation.htm

Lesson_10_Forms/sonar.htm

BUILDING YOUR FORM

Before you add elements such as individual fields and buttons to a page, the form that contains those elements must be created. Forms act as the containers for fields, buttons, menus, and other objects that visitors can use to enter or select information; forms also specify what happens with the data when it is submitted. In this exercise, you will create the form area.

1) Open the lights_quiz.htm document from the Lesson_10_Forms folder. Position the insertion point in the blank paragraph below the text "Test your knowledge about lighthouses." Click the Form button in the Forms category of the Insert bar.

TIP *You can also insert a form by choosing Insert > Form > Form.*

FORM

FORMS CATEGORY

The area occupied by the form is identified visually by red dotted lines in the document window; that area is defined by the <form> and </form> tags in the code. These red lines are invisible elements that are displayed only in Dreamweaver; when you view the page within a browser, there is nothing to mark the form area. These red lines are not draggable—the size of the form area depends on what you place inside the form and it expands horizontally to the full extent available and vertically as much as necessary to accommodate the contents. The form you placed on the page extends to occupy the entire width of the cell.

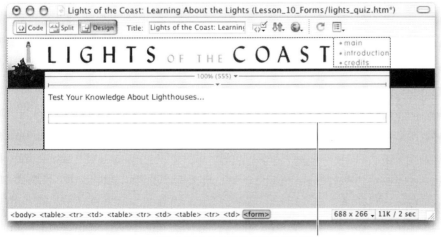

RED DOTTED LINES INDICATE THE
AREA OCCUPIED BY THE FORM

319

If invisible elements are not turned on, a message box appears, letting you know that you won't be able to see the form. Click OK to close the message box and then choose View > Visual Aids > Invisible Elements so you can see the red dotted boundary of the form. If invisible elements are turned on, you do not see the warning message. The Form delimiter box must also be checked in the Invisible Elements category of the Dreamweaver preferences— it is checked by default.

You can place multiple forms on one page. However, it is not possible to nest a form inside of another form in HTML. Because of this restriction, Dreamweaver prevents forms from becoming accidentally nested by disabling the insertion of one form into another form. The option to insert a form will not be grayed-out, but no form is inserted if you attempt to place one form inside of another. If form tags have been inserted manually within a form, Dreamweaver highlights the tags that are incorrect to bring the error to your attention.

2) Select the form by clicking the red dotted line.

TIP *You can also use the Tag Selector to select the form if the insertion point is inside the form.*

The Property inspector changes to display form properties.

NOTE *If the Property inspector is not visible, choose Window > Properties.*

FORM PROPERTIES ON THE PROPERTY INSPECTOR

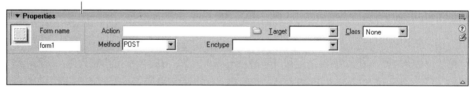

3) Replace the default name form1 in the Form name text field on the Property inspector by typing `lighthouses`.

Dreamweaver generates generic names for forms. The names automatically increment numerically each time you create a form: form1, form2, and so on. All form names must be unique and use no special characters. Form names are important identifiers, particularly if you have more than one form on a page or if you are using a database for information that is collected or requested via the form. Form names are also used to control forms through the use of scripting languages such as JavaScript.

4) Place the insertion point into the form and choose Insert > Table. Set the table to 3 rows and 1 column. The table width should be 90 percent. Set the border to 0, cell padding to 0, and cell spacing to 10. Choose None for the Header, leave the Accessibility options blank, and click OK.

The table improves the layout of the form. Using tables makes it easy to align text or images with the form fields to label them.

5) Select the table and choose Center from the Align menu on the Property inspector.

You can place a table inside a form or you can place a form in a table, but the table in question must completely contain or be contained by the form.

GROUPING FORM CONTENT

Before you start to put your form together, you should take the time to develop a thorough outline of the contents. After you have an outline of the information that you will be requesting from visitors, you can divide that information into logical groups based on similarity of content. The form that you are creating in this lesson can be split up into three sections: Contact Information; Questions About Lighthouses; and Send Your Answers. After you determine the sections into which your form will be divided, you are ready to use **fieldsets** to create those sections within the form itself. Fieldsets are form elements that are used to create individual sections of content within a form. Grouping the contents of your form into smaller, self-contained sections makes it easier for visitors to understand and complete the form. It offers a way for them to immediately grasp the overall structure of the form.

1) Place the insertion point in the first row of the table you created in the previous exercise. In the Forms category of the Insert bar, click the Fieldset button.

FIELDSET

The Fieldset dialog box opens.

2) In the Label text field type *Contact Information* **and click OK. Click back in the document window to refresh the view.**

When you click the Fieldset button, Dreamweaver will swtich to Split view (showing both Code and Design views.) After you click OK on the Fieldset dialog box, the Property inspector will inform you that changes have been made to the code. You can leave the document window in Split view because you will create more Fieldsets in the following steps. Clicking back in the document window will refresh the view— you do not have to press the Refresh button or F5 as instructed by the Property inspector. You won't see the Fieldset appear until you click in the document window and the view refreshes.

A fieldset expands to occupy the full amount of space that is available to it. The top cell of the table you created in the previous exercise serves to establish the boundaries of the fieldset and control the layout. Similar to forms, fieldsets can be placed within a table, or you can place a table in a fieldset, but the table must completely contain or be contained by the fieldset.

3) Place the insertion point in the second row and click the Fieldset button on the Insert bar. In the Label text field, type *Questions About Lighthouses* **and click OK. Click back in the document window to refresh the view.**

The label that you specify for a fieldset is also known as a **legend**. It serves as a caption for the section; a way to identify the contents. When creating legends for fieldsets in your own forms, be as clear as possible. These labels should accurately reflect what their fieldsets contain.

4) Place the insertion point in the third row and click the Fieldset button on the Insert bar. In the Label text field, type *Send Your Answers* **and click OK. Click back in the document window to refresh the view.**

Fieldsets indicate their group by placing an outline around all the form objects that it contains. You won't see the outlines of fieldsets until you preview your page in the browser.

12) Save the file and preview it in the browser.

Leave this file open for the next exercise.

ADDING SINGLE-LINE TEXT FIELDS

Text fields are for gathering information that the user can type in. Single-line text fields are used for short concise answers such a word or phrase. Typical single-line text fields collect names, portions of addresses, and email information from users. Single-line text fields are also used for basic searches, in which the visitor types words describing the desired information into the field.

You must place all form fields and buttons within the red dotted lines; otherwise, they are not a part of the form. If you try to insert form fields outside the red lines, Dreamweaver displays an alert box with Yes or No options, asking whether you want to add a form tag. If you choose No, the field or buttons will not function as a part of any form.

1) Choose Dreamweaver › Preferences (Macintosh) or Edit › Preferences (Windows). Select the Accessibility category and check the Form Objects box; then click OK.

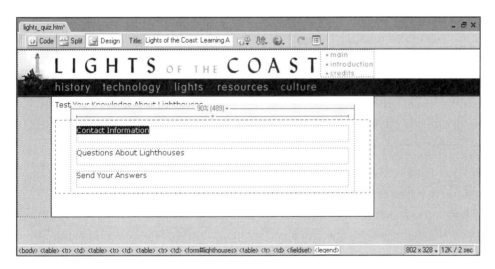

Creating accessible forms from the beginning helps to reach a wider audience. It is important to include accessible attributes to enable users who may need to use assistive technology such as screen readers. If your forms do not include these attributes, it may be difficult for some people to fill out the form.

2) In the lights_quiz.htm document, place the insertion point in the text Contact Information. Use the Tag Selector to select the ‹legend› tag, press the right arrow key once and press Return (Macintosh) or Enter (Windows).

TAG SELECTOR   ‹LEGEND› TAG

Form objects must be inserted in the fieldset, but not inside the legend. If you were to place the insertion point at the end of the legend and press Return, a second set of legend tags would be created. There should not be a second set of legend tags.

When you create a paragraph return after the legend, there will appear to be some space above and below the blinking cursor. When you are inserting form objects into a fieldset, it may be difficult to tell where the fieldset ends because there is no visual indication of the fieldset boundaries. For example, clicking at the very bottom of the first row actually puts the insertion point inside the first cell but outside of the first fieldset. This empty paragraph line will appear in each of the cells—do not use it to insert form objects in this lesson. Using Split view as you insert objects may help you to determine whether the insertion point is in the correct place.

3) In the Forms category on the Insert bar, click the Text Field button.

TEXT FIELD

TIP *You can also choose Insert > Form > Text Field.*

The Input Tag Accessibility Attributes dialog box opens.

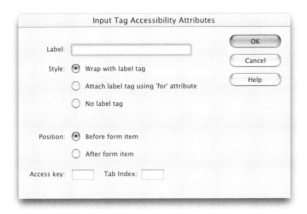

4) Type *First Name:* **in the Label text field.**

Labels provide clear information that specifies the purpose for all your form objects (text fields, checkboxes, and so on.) so your visitors know what information they are supposed to enter into those fields. Without being identified with labels, forms can be very confusing. Labels are included in both the document window as a visual description of the text field and as an attribute within the HTML code that identifies the corresponding text field. Use concise and descriptive labels whenever possible.

5) In the Style section, select Wrap with label tag. In the Position section, select Before form item. Leave the Access key and Tab index text fields blank.

The **Wrap with label tag** option surrounds form objects with a label tag. With this option, the form object should always remain next to the text label in the document window. If the form object is moved, this option prevents it from being separated from the label tag—not using this option can cause a great deal of confusion for viewers using screen readers because the label will no longer be associated with a form object that has been moved. A text field created using this method appears in the code as <label>First and Last Name<input type="text" name="textfield"></label>

The **Attach label tag using 'for'** attribute option creates a stand-alone label that is identified with the corresponding text field through an id. Using this option allows you to separate the form object from the text that labels it in the document window, which you may need to do for layout purposes. This method is more flexible because it continues to function properly regardless of whether the form object is separated from the corresponding text. If you are not sure which Style method to use, select this one. A text field created using this method appears in the code as <label for="textfield">First and Last Name</label><input type="text" name="textfield" id="textfield">

The No label tag bypasses the label option. If you use this option, you can add labels later using the Label button in the Forms category on the Insert bar.

There are two additional accessibility attributes that are available:

- **Access Key:** The Access key text field allows you to create a keyboard shortcut for the form object by specifying a character that visitors can use in combination with the Option (Macintosh) or Alt (Windows) modifier keys. Although visitors can use the Tab key to jump from one form object to the next, access keys can provide a much quicker way to jump immediately to any form object on the page. When creating access keys, take particular care to not use characters that may conflict with standard keyboard shortcuts. If you use access keys, it is a good idea to let your visitors know—provide instructions at the top of the form or in a pop-up window (which you will learn to create in Lesson 11) and indicate the keyboard shortcut next to its corresponding text field. Keyboard shortcut indicators should be as clear and unobtrusive as possible. On the Macintosh keyboard, shortcuts are listed next to menu items with a visual icon representing the modifier key. In Windows, however, the appropriate character is underlined to indicate the shortcut. Whichever method you decide to use, be consistent and clear—and let your visitors know by mentioning it in the instructions or help information.

- **Tab Index:** Many Web users use the Tab key when filling out forms; the Tab key provides a way to move through a form quickly by switching the focus from one form object or link to another. The order in which the Tab key changes the focus depends upon the order in which the object and links occur in the code. Although the default order in which the focus changes is usually what you expect, it is possible that the visual layout of a form may be presented so that the perceived order is different from the actual order of those objects in the code. In such cases, using the Tab Index field to specify the focus order by assigning numbers to form objects may help visitors to move through the form. Alternatively, you may want to apply the Tab Index only to fields that are required. When specifying a Tab Index, you need to start with 1, followed by 2, and so on. Do not skip any numbers.

If you do not use the accessibility feature when inserting form objects, you will not be prompted to specify a label. Although you can type a label for the form object in the document window, that text will not be contained in <label> and </label> tags unless you add those tags to the code manually or use the Label button in the Forms category on the Insert bar.

6) Click OK to insert the text field.

The single-line text field is placed in the form along with the text label; both are automatically selected.

7) Click in the document window just to the right of the text field to deselect it and the label. Click the text field to select only the text field; then replace textfield in the TextField name text field on the Property inspector by typing *firstName***.**

TEXT FIELD PROPERTIES ON THE PROPERTY INSPECTOR

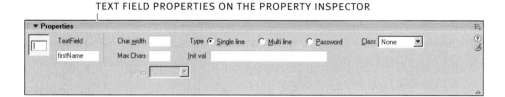

TIP *Names are required for all fields. Dreamweaver assigns generic names automatically in a numeric order: textfield, textfield2, and so on. When the form is submitted, the name of the text field identifies the information that was entered into the field. In this case, "firstName" signifies that the information entered into this field is the visitor's first name.*

Do not use any spaces or special characters in the name, and remember that names are case-sensitive when used with scripts such as CGI scripts or JavaScripts.

It is important to remember to name all of your fields with short, descriptive names. Suppose that you have two text fields on a page with labels next to them, prompting the user to enter a home phone number into one field and a work phone number into the other. If those fields are named textfield and textfield2, their names will not give you any indication about which number is the home number and which is the work number. On the other hand, by giving the fields more descriptive names, such as worknumber and homenumber, you can avoid confusion over the identity of the information. Visitors will not see or be affected by field names—naming the fields is for the benefit of you and your Web team.

8) With the text field form object still selected, click in the Char Width text field on the Property inspector and type *40***. Press Return (Macintosh) or Enter (Windows).**
Char Width, or character width, is the number of visible characters that will display in the text field. The width of the text field increases the available space so that it can show approximately 40 characters. The initial width of the text field is approximately 24 characters. The actual dimensions of the text field vary from browsers to browser, based on the text size used for that text field, which may be defined through CSS or left to browser defaults. The height of the text field is also dependent upon the text size.

NOTE *You can apply a CSS style to a text field by selecting the desired style from the Class menu on the Property inspector when the text field is selected.*

327

9) With the text field form object still selected, click in the Max Chars text field on the Property inspector and type *50*. Press Return (Macintosh) or Enter (Windows).

Max Chars, or maximum characters, limits the total number of characters a user can enter. Initially, this text field is blank and the number of characters a user can enter is unlimited.

If the Max Chars value is larger than Char Width, users can continue to type, and the text will scroll to the left within the field as the user types beyond the visible area. The scrollable area ends at the Max Char value.

NOTE *If your form sends information to a database, you need to make sure that the value for maximum characters matches the maximum set for the corresponding field in the database.*

10) Place the insertion point to the right of the First Name text field in the document window. Select the `<label>` tag in the Tag Selector, press the right arrow key once and then press Return (Macintosh) or Enter (Windows). Click the Text Field button on the Insert bar and type *Email:* in the label text field on the Input Tag Accessibility Attributes dialog box. Verify that Wrap with label tag is selected in the Style section and that Before form item is selected in the Position section, leave the other fields blank, and click OK. Select the text field and use the Property inspector to set the name of the field to *email*, the Char Width to *40* and the Max Char to *70*. Press Return (Macintosh) or Enter (Windows), or click in the document window to apply the change.

This field accepts the user's email address.

It is important to create a new paragraph that exists outside the <label> tags that wrap around the previous form object; otherwise, the new form object can become nested within the previous object's label tags, or the tags might overlap or cause other difficulties. You can avoid this by selecting the <label> tags in the Tag Selector and using the arrow keys to move just outside those tags, as you have done in this step. It may help to use Split view while you are inserting these objects.

TIP *Be careful when setting the Max Char for fields that accept information such as email addresses and URLs. Users can't enter a complete URL or any other information if that information is longer than the Max Char value because they can't type past the limit you set.*

11) With the email field still selected, type *Enter your email address* in the Init Val text field on the Property inspector.

The Init Val, or initial value, enables you to set text that will appear in the text field when the visitor loads the page. Init Val can help give the user an example of the kind of information that is being requested of them. Visitors can replace the initial value text with text of their own. Initial values are useful for prompting users to enter information or displaying example text. Although the user can change the text, use this option with caution. Users who want to get through the form quickly may accidentally skip a field that already has text in it, perhaps thinking they have already filled it out. Initial values may be a disadvantage if a visitor skips over the field because it looks as if it has already been filled out.

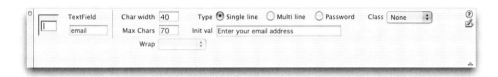

12) Save the file and preview it in the browser.

Leave this file open for the next exercise.

NOTE *A regular text field displays the information in the browser as you type it in. A password text field looks the same as any other text field, but the text displayed onscreen is hidden by bullets or asterisks as you type. The password option only hides the text in the field from someone looking over your shoulder as you type—it does not encrypt or secure your data. To encrypt data, you must have secure server software running on the Web server—talk to your Web administrator for detailed information on securing data using SSL (Secure Sockets Layer). To create a password field, insert a standard single-line text field and select Password for the Type option on the Property inspector. This option causes asterisks or bullets to appear when a user enters data in this field. Password text fields can be only single-line text fields. The Max Chars value for passwords should be set at the limit for passwords on your server.*

ADDING MULTI-LINE TEXT FIELDS

You can use **multi-line text fields** to collect larger amounts of information from a user by providing a text area with multiple lines in which the visitor can type. Typical multi-line text fields collect comments and feedback from visitors. In this exercise, you will place a multi-line text field in the table inside the form.

1) In the lights_quiz.htm document, place the insertion point inside the Questions About Lighthouses text in the legend for the second fieldset. Use the Tag Selector to select the <legend> tag, press the right arrow key once and then press Return (Macintosh) or Enter (Windows).

The insertion point is now where it should be: outside of the legend tags, but inside the fieldset.

2) In the Forms category on the Insert bar, click the Textarea button.

TEXT AREA

> **TIP** *You can also insert a multi-line text field by choosing Insert > Form > Textarea.*

The Input Tag Accessibility Attributes dialog box opens. In Dreamweaver a multi-line text field is known as a textarea.

3) In the Label text field, type *Describe how a Fresnel lens works.* **Wrap with label tag should be selected in the Style section and Before form item should be selected in the position section. Leave the remaining fields blank and click OK.**
The multi-line text field and its corresponding label text appear in the document window.

4) Place a line break between the label text and the multi-line text field. Select the multi-line text field.

> **TIP** *To place a line break directly between the label and the text field, select the text field and press the left arrow key once. Then insert the line break.*

The Property inspector shows Text Field properties because the multi-line text field is selected.

MULTI-LINE TEXT FIELD PROPERTIES ON THE PROPERTY INSPECTOR

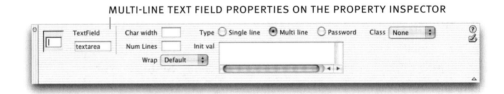

> **TIP** *You can convert a single-line text field to a multi-line text area by selecting the text field and choosing Multi line in the Type option on the Property inspector.*

5) In the Name text field on the Property inspector, replace textarea with *fresnel***. In the Char Width text field, type** *40***.**

When you use multi-line text fields, you see an additional option on the Property inspector. The Wrap menu is available only for multi-line text fields. It is grayed-out for both single-line and password text fields. Wrap specifies how text that is typed into a multi-line field is displayed if there is more text than will fit in the visible area. Leave the Wrap option set to Default for this exercise.

The Wrap options, which are described as follows, are Default, Off, Virtual, and Physical:

- **Default** uses the browser default. This option is selected automatically when you select Multi line for the Type option.

- **Off** stops text from wrapping to the next line. Text continues on one line until the Return or Enter key is pressed. The text scrolls to the left as the visitor types beyond the limit of the visible area.

- **Virtual** wraps text to the next line, but wrap is not applied to the data when it is submitted.

- **Physical** wraps text to the next line, and wrap is applied to the data when it is submitted.

6) Type *4* **in the Num Lines text field on the Property inspector.**

This option dictates how many lines appear in the scrollable area. It does not limit the number of lines users can enter. The text will scroll upward as the user types beyond the number that is set to display.

7) Place the insertion point to the right of the multi-line text field and select the `<label>` **tag in the Tag selector. Press the right arrow key once and press Return (Macintosh) or Enter (Windows). Repeat steps 2 through 6 to create a second text area. Use** *What is your favorite lighthouse and why?* **for the label; the other accessibility attributes should be the same as those in step 3. Name the field** *favorite* **and apply the same attributes that you set for the previous multi-line text area in steps 5 and 6.**

Your document should now look similar to the example shown here.

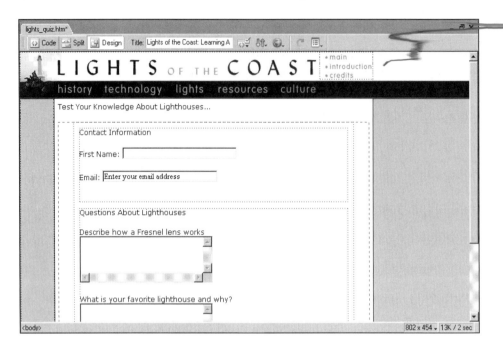

Save the lights_quiz.htm document and leave it open for the next exercise.

ADDING CHECKBOXES

Checkboxes allow users to choose one or more options in a group of related items. Checkboxes are typically used when you want the user to choose as many of the listed options as desired. If you want your user to choose only one selection, you should use a radio button as demonstrated in the exercise that follows this one. In this exercise, you will insert a group of checkboxes.

1) Place the insertion point to the right of the last multi-line text field you inserted, select the `<label>` **tag in the Tag selector, press the right arrow key once, and press Return (Macintosh) or Enter (Windows). Type** *Which of these fuel sources have been used in lighthouses?* **Add a line break after the text by pressing Shift+Return (Macintosh) or Shift+Enter (Windows); then type** *(check all that apply),* **followed by another line break.**

Recall from Lesson 2 that a line break moves the insertion point to the next line without inserting a blank line, as a regular paragraph return would do.

2) In the Forms category on the Insert bar, click the Checkbox button.

CHECKBOX

TIP *You can also choose Insert > Form > Check Box.*

The Input Tag Accessibility Attributes dialog box opens.

3) In the Label text field, type *Sperm whale oil*. **Select Wrap with label tag in the Style section and select After form item in the position section. Leave the other fields blank and click OK.**
A checkbox is inserted into the form, along with the corresponding label text.

4) Select only the checkbox. In the CheckBox name text field on the Property inspector, replace "checkbox" with *sources*. **In the Checked Value text field, type** *whale*.

TIP *If both the label and checkbox are selected, the Property inspector does not display the CheckBox properties.*

CHECKBOX PROPERTIES ON THE PROPERTY INSPECTOR

If a visitor checks the Sperm whale oil checkbox, the *whale* value indicates that the corresponding checkbox has been selected and the *sources* value identifies the group of checkboxes. You can designate a number of checkboxes as a group by giving them all the same names—be sure, however, to give them individual, clear and accurate values.

5) Place a line break after the space that exists after the Sperm Whale Oil label. Repeat steps 2 through 5 to add checkboxes using *Hydrogen*, *Kerosene*, **and** *Solar Power* **for the labels. Each checkbox and its corresponding label should be on their own lines. In the CheckBox name text field on the Property inspector, replace "checkbox" each time with** *sources*. **Type** *hydrogen*, *kerosene*, **and** *solar*, **in each Checked Value text field, respectively.**

333

Placing the insertion point after the space that exists after the labels is important because the insertion point will be placed outside of the label tag that surrounds the checkbox and text. You can verify this by looking at the Tag Selector. If you see <p><label> at the right end of the tag hierarchy, the insertion point is still between the label tags, and you need to move it. If you see only the <p> tag, you are ready to insert the line break in preparation for the next checkbox.

The last tag in the hierarchy of code for the position of the insertion point is displayed at the right end of the Tag Selector. The Tag Selector hierarchy always begins with <body>, however, you may not see the <body> tag at the left (beginning) of the Tag Selector if the hierarchy of tags is too long to be fully displayed. Tags in the Tag Selector will begin to disappear on the left in order to make room for the more recent tags. Expanding the document window will give the Tag Selector more room if you want to see the other tags.

As you continue to insert form objects, the table expands downward to accommodate its content. As this happens, the red dotted line of the form may appear to overlap the table and not be pushed down along with the bottom of the table. If this happens, click outside the table in the document window to cause Dreamweaver to refresh the view.

6) Place a paragraph return after the space that exists after the Solar Power label. Type *Which of the following have contributed to making lighthouses not as vital as they once were?* **and then insert a line break. Repeat steps 2 through 5 to add checkboxes using** *Radar, Global positioning systems, Navigational buoys,* **and** *All of the above* **for the labels. In the CheckBox name text field on the Property inspector, replace "checkbox" each time with** *obsolete.* **Type** *radar, global, buoys,* **and** *all* **in each Checked Value text field, respectively.**

Your document should now look similar to the example shown here.

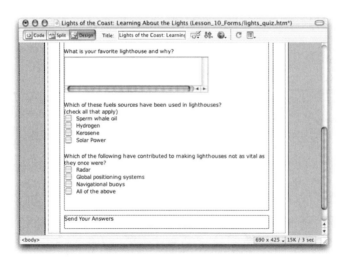

Save the lights_quiz.htm document and leave it open for the next exercise.

ADDING RADIO BUTTONS

Radio buttons are a group of options. Selecting one option automatically deselects all other options. Typical uses for radio buttons are credit card selections, yes/no answers, and other kinds of multiple choices where you want the visitor to select only one item. In this exercise, you will insert a group of radio buttons into the table.

1) Place a paragraph return after the space that exists after the All of the above label. Type *Who invented the Fresnel lens?*, **followed by a line break.**

In the next step, you will place the radio buttons on the new line below this text.

2) In the Forms category of the Insert bar, click the Radio Group button.

TIP *You can also choose Insert > Form > Radio Group.*

RADIO GROUP

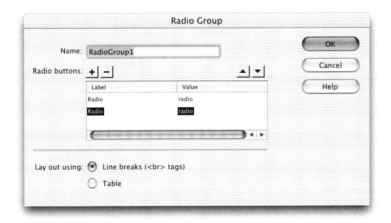

The Radio Group dialog box appears.

3) In the radio group dialog box, type *whoInvented* **in the Name text field.**

When using radio buttons, you must use the same name for each radio button in the same group. Radio buttons are meant to allow only one selection.

NOTE *If you insert radio buttons one by one (either by using the Radio Button button on the Insert bar or by using the Insert > Form > Radio Button menu option), you can make those buttons all part of the same group by giving them the same name. Using the same name for multiple radio buttons indicates that those buttons are part of the same group. If the names are not the same, the radio buttons will be treated as different groups and negate the purpose of using radio buttons. You can also insert a single radio button, but keep in mind that once your visitor clicks the button, the only way for that visitor to deselect the button will be to reset the form, which will also clear any information the visitor has typed or selected in other form objects.*

Also keep in mind that the names of form objects are case-sensitive when used with CGI and JavaScripts, so "whoInvented" is not the same as "whoinvented."

4) Click the first instance of "Radio" in the Radio Buttons list area and replace that text with *Fresnel August*. **Use the same name in the corresponding Value text field. Click the second instance of "Radio" and replace it with** *Argand Fresnel*. **Use the same name in the corresponding Value text field.**

By default, every Radio Group has at least two radio buttons. You can add more as needed. Clicking an instance in the Label or Value lists highlights the text and allows you to change it.

5) Click the plus (+) button and replace the new instance of "Radio" with *Augustin Fresnel*. **Use the same name in the corresponding Value text field. Add one more entry to the list:** *August Argand*. **Use the same name in the corresponding Value text field.**

You can add or delete entries by using the plus (+) and minus (–) buttons. You can also adjust the order of entries by selecting them and using the arrow buttons to move them up or down in the list.

When a form is submitted, the values are sent to the script that processes the form on the server. It is important to be sure you give each radio button a different value so you know which option the user chose.

6) Leave the line breaks option selected in the Lay Out Using area and click OK to close the Radio Group dialog box. Delete the last break that occurs just beneath the last radio button.

The line breaks option places the radio buttons in your document with each entry on a separate line. The table option inserts a table with each entry in a separate row.

Label tags are automatically created using the values you entered. Because the text labels that are visible in the document window should always be next to their corresponding radio buttons, the label tags surround those buttons in the same manner that the Wrap with label tag option inserts a label tag for text fields.

7) Preview the page in the browser and test the radio buttons by clicking each one.
When you click one to select it, the other one should deselect. You must preview the file in the browser to see the effect; form objects do not appear selected or checked in the Dreamweaver document window.

Save lights_quiz.htm document and leave it open for the next exercise.

ADDING LIST AND MENU ITEMS

You can create a scrolling list or menu from which visitors can make selections. A **scrolling list** gives you the option to allow users to make multiple contiguous or noncontiguous selections. A menu restricts users to one selection. In both types, items chosen by the user are highlighted.

1) Place a new paragraph return after the space that exists after the August Argand radio button label. Click the List/Menu button in the Forms category of the Insert bar.

TIP *You can also choose Insert > Form > List/Menu.*

LIST/MENU

The Input Tag Accessibility Attributes dialog box opens.

NOTE *As explained in the Adding Single-Line Text Fields exercise earlier in this lesson, do not use the blank paragraph line at the bottom of the cell. You need to create a new paragraph by clicking to the right of the space after the August Argand label and pressing Return (Macintosh) or Enter (Windows).*

2) Type *Unique markings are painted on lighthouses to:* **in the Label text field. Wrap with label tag should be selected in the Style section, and Before form item should be selected in the position section. Leave the remaining fields blank and click OK.**
A small menu and the corresponding label are inserted into the form. Dreamweaver inserts a drop-down menu by default.

3) Insert a line break between the label text and the menu. Select only the menu to display the properties in the Property inspector.

The Property inspector displays List/Menu properties.

LIST/MENU PROPERTIES ON THE PROPERTY INSPECTOR

4) On the Property inspector, select List for the Type option and change Height to *4*. **Check the Allow multiple check box for the Selections option.**

You changed the format to a scrolling list. You must change the height to a value that is greater than 1 for the form object to change from a menu to a list.

The list format has an additional option that is not available for menus: You can choose to allow or not allow multiple selections by checking or unchecking the Allow multiple box for the Selections option. This option is unchecked by default. If you check the selections box, users can make multiple noncontiguous selections by using Command-click on the Macintosh and Ctrl-click on Windows. Users may make contiguous selections by using Shift-click on both Macintosh and Windows. If you decide to allow multiple selections, it is a good idea to inform your visitors that they can make multiple selections (and to tell them how to do so). Many users may not know these commands. It is always best to provide your visitors with all the information and tools they need to interact with your site.

You can also set a height for the scrolling list by typing in the Height text field the number of lines you want to be visible. Be sure to enter a line height value of more than 1; otherwise, the scrolling list displays as a menu.

5) In the List/Menu name text field on the Property inspector, replace select with *markings*; **then click the List Values button.**

The List Values dialog box opens. This dialog box is the same for both List and Menu entries.

6) In the Item Label field, type *scare away birds* **and then press Tab. In the Value field, type** *scarebirds*.

The longest item in the list values box determines the width of the list/menu. You can't resize a list or menu by dragging it or specifying dimensions.

7) Press Tab or click the plus sign (+) in the upper-left area of the dialog box to add another option to the menu.

Use the minus sign (–) to delete items from the List Values box.

8) Repeat steps 7 and 8, adding *hide them in the fog,* *make them look different,* *make them beautiful,* *make them visible,* **and** *camouflage them* **to the list. Change the Value field to match the name of each region using** *fog,* *different,* *beautiful,* *visible,* **and** *camouflage,* **respectively.**

Use the arrows above the Value field if you want to reorder the list.

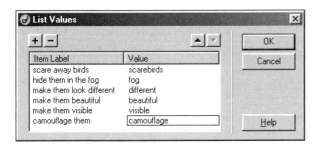

9) Click OK to close the dialog box.

The list shows the items you just added.

An additional option on the Property inspector for list/menu items is the Initially selected box. You can choose to have any one of the items in the list be selected when the page loads. This option might not be desirable for scrolling lists, but it is helpful to have a sample choice or instruction such as "Choose one…" appear on the first line for menu items.

NOTE *If you choose an item to select initially, there is no way to deselect it. To deselect it, you would have to open the List Values dialog box, delete the item that was selected, and add it to the list again.*

10) Insert a line break after the list and type *(select the most appropriate options—make multiple selections with Command-Click on the Macintosh and Ctrl-Click on Windows).*

It is good to always give instructions for selecting items in case a visitor doesn't know how to make multiple selections. It can save your users a lot of frustration, making it more likely that they will finish filling out your form!

ADDING BUTTONS

Forms often have two buttons: one to send the form data (Submit) and one to clear the form (Reset). The Submit button tells the browser to send the data. The Reset button clears all the information from the fields on the page.

NOTE *A form created for a basic search function usually has only one Submit button, which is often labeled Search or Go.*

1) Place the insertion point in the text Send Your Answers in the third fieldset. Use the Tag Selector to select the `<legend>` tag, press the right arrow key once, and press Return (Macintosh) or Enter (Windows). Click the Button button in the Forms category on the Insert bar.

TIP *You can also choose Insert > Form > Button.*

BUTTON

The Input Tag Accessibility Attributes dialog box opens.

2) Leave the Label text field blank and select No label tag in the Style area. Leave the Position options as they are and leave the remaining fields blank. Click OK.

A Submit button is placed in the form, and the Property inspector displays Button properties. The accessibility attributes are unnecessary because the label is on the button itself. Because a Submit button is the default, you do not need to change any of the options for this button.

3) Position the insertion point to the right of the Submit button. Click the Button button on the Insert bar and repeat step 2 to set the accessibility attributes to the same value that was used for the Submit button.

A second Submit button is placed in the form. The only difference is the name—this button is called submit2 because no two buttons can have the same name. The only form objects that can have the same name are radio buttons that are in the same group and checkboxes that are in the same group. The button you are working with in this exercise is different because it cannot be grouped with other buttons and it will have its own action assigned to it in the next step.

4) With the second Submit button selected, choose Reset form from the Action options on the Property inspector.

The text in the Label text field automatically changes to Reset. The action of this button causes all text fields, checkboxes and radio buttons to clear and revert to their original state (when the page was first loaded in the browser).

The third Action option is None. Unlike Submit and Reset, the None button option has no action attached to it. It can be used in conjunction with a script to perform another task. A JavaScript routine, for example, can be used to perform calculations such as totals or interest and return the end value to the user.

5) In the Label text field, replace Reset by typing *Clear Form*. **In the Button Name text field, change the default name to** *reset*.

It is a good idea to name your buttons clearly, with consideration for your users' expectations. Submit and Reset are standard form-button labels that people understand because of their widespread use. Take care with the placement of the Reset button and make the label obvious so that visitors do not accidentally click it when they are trying to submit the form.

NOTE *You can use images in place of the standard buttons by using the image field button on the Property inspector to insert an image as a form element and then inserting the appropriate value, such as value="Submit", into the code. You might want to use images to customize the appearance of buttons. It is important to make sure that any images you use in this manner are obviously meant to be buttons.*

CREATING HIDDEN FIELDS

Sometimes, you may need to include information with your form that shouldn't be displayed to the visitor or left to the visitor to fill in. In these kinds of circumstances, you can use **hidden fields**, which do not display in the browser. Hidden fields are often used with server-side scripting when specific information is required for processing the form: for gathering the name, order number, or other relevant information about a product that is being purchased; to provide an email address and a subject header if the form will be sent to email; for including the URL of a page to which you want to redirect visitors after they have filled out your form; for passing information from one form to another; or for requiring certain fields to be completed by the visitor. In such cases, server-side scripting is required to process the hidden fields. JavaScript can

341

also be combined with hidden fields (in what is known as **client-side scripting**) for situations in which server-side scripting is not needed or available. In client-side scripting, the visitor's browser (the client) processes the scripts. You'll learn more about JavaScript in Lesson 11.

If no scripting is used in connection with the hidden field when the form is submitted for processing, the hidden fields embedded in the form are included just like values from other form objects.

1) Place the insertion point along the very bottom of the second row of the table.

The insertion point is now in the cell above the one that contains the Send Your Answers fieldset. You can place hidden fields at any point in the document.

Now that the insertion point is in the line at the bottom of the second cell, it is no longer inside of the fieldset labeled Questions About Lighthouses. This is OK in this case because the hidden field that you will insert in the following steps will not be visible to the Visitor; the placement is not important.

2) On the Forms category on the Insert bar, click the Hidden Field button.

HIDDEN FIELD

A hidden field is inserted into the document. The hidden field icon is a visual aid for invisible elements similar to named anchor icons—it is not displayed in the browser.

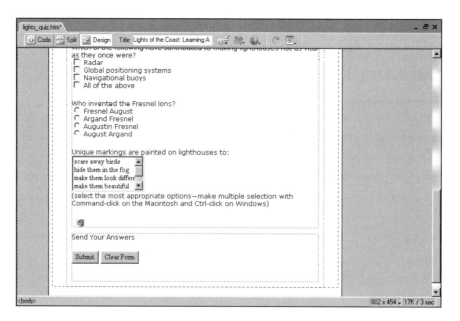

3) With the hidden field selected, replace the default name of hiddenfield by typing *examTitle* **into the HiddenField text field. Type** *Testing Lighthouse Knowledge* **into the Value text field on the Property inspector.**

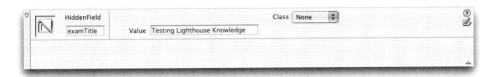

In this case, you are including the title of this form as a predefined value for the hidden field. Information that always remains the same can be passed to dynamic pages and CGI scripts through these kinds of hidden fields. Hidden fields using values that are set in this manner are not encrypted or secure—they can easily be seen in the document source code through the browser. Do not place any information that is sensitive (such as passwords) into these kinds of hidden fields. Secure hidden fields can be created when dynamically generating the value of the field through the use of dynamic pages or CGI scripts.

The name and value of hidden fields are usually dependent upon the script that is being used to process them. For example, some scripts that send the data to an email address may use *recipient* as the name of the hidden field and the email address to which the data should be sent as the value. This name and value pair does not function unless you have the script that processes the recipient field on your server.

NOTE *File fields are another field type that you can use in forms. A file field makes it possible for you to let visitors send files to you via your form. This capability can be useful when you need to receive documents relating to the data collected in the form. For example, a file field might be made available on a job application for which you want the visitor to submit a resume. File fields rely on the server to process the data received by the form and upload or otherwise direct the file to an appropriate location.*

FORMATTING FORMS

You can use CSS styles (covered in Lesson 6) to make forms more consistent with the look and feel of your site.

1) Place the insertion point in the legend Contact Information in the first fieldset. In the Tag Selector, select the <fieldset> **tag. Click the New CSS Style button on the CSS Styles panel. For the Selector Type, choose Tag. Use the menu to the right of the Tag text field to select fieldset if it is not already displayed in the text field. In the Define In section, choose This document only and then click OK.**

You can create a style for the fieldset to control the look of the outlines surrounding individual sections of the form.

2) Select Box from the category list. In the Padding section, type 5 into the Top text field and leave the Same for all box checked.

The padding gives the form objects some space so that they are not right up against the fieldset outline.

3) Select Border from the category list. In the Style section, select solid from the Top menu and leave the Same for all box checked. In the Width section, type 1 into the Top text field, make sure pixels is selected, and leave the Same for all box checked. In the Color section, type #CCCC99 into the Top text field and leave the Same for all box checked. Click OK.

NOTE *If clicking the Border category doesn not switch the CSS Style definition dialog box to the Border category, click the OK button to create the style then select the fieldset style in the CSS Styles panel and click the Edit Style button on the bottom of the panel. The fieldset style will be contained in the <style> list on the CSS Styles panel, which contains all the internal styles used in the lights_quiz.htm document. The active category of the CSS Styles definition dialog box is indicated by the highlight on the category name in the Category list and by the name of the category that appears above all of the category options. Because of a bug that happens mostly on Windows, when you are trying to switch to a different category the name will highlight but the options and the category name above them will not change. After creating the syle and clicking the Edit Style button, you can continue to develop the style as directed in the previous step.*

The border creates the effect for the outline.

NOTE *You will not be able to see the effects of the CSS style on the fieldset in the document window because Dreamweaver does not display fieldsets. You will need to preview the page in a browser to see the effect.*

4) Click the New CSS Style button on the CSS Styles panel. For the Selector Type, choose Tag. Use the menu to the right of the Tag text field to select h5 and choose This document only in the Define in area. In the Type category, set the color to #999999. Click OK.

You can also just place the insertion pont within the text and choose H5 from the Format menu on the Property inspector instead of selecting it because headings are applied to entire text blocks.

This style will be used for the legends that designate the different sections of the form.

5) Select the legend text Contact Information. On the Property inspector, change the format to Heading 5. Style the legends for the other two fieldsets in the same way.
Save the file and preview it in the browser. Your form now matches the feel of the rest of the colors and style.

PROCESSING FORMS

Whether your form is intended to submit information to or retrieve information from a database, perform a search function, or otherwise process data, you need to define what will happen with that data and how it will be handled to make your form functional. This definition is done through Action and Method options in the Property inspector while the form is selected.

You can use Dreamweaver to develop dynamic Web pages and applications that can be used to process forms and make use of databases. Creating and working with a dynamic, database-enabled Web site requires a connection to a server. The type of server and its configuration determine which scripting language (such as PHP, ASP, JSP and ColdFusion) can be used. Because creating a site that makes use of dynamic pages and databases is beyond the scope of this book and because you may not have access to a server with the dynamic pages or CGI scripts needed to process forms while you complete this lesson, the following information is presented as reference material only. Talk to your ISP (Internet Service Provider) or Web administrator to get the information you need to set the Action and Method options to work with the scripts used on your server.

Action tells the browser what to do with the form data. It specifies the path or URL to the location and the name of a server-side application (usually a CGI script or a dynamic page) that processes the information when the user clicks the Submit button. CGI scripts are located on the Web server that processes the data sent by a form.

Method defines how the form data is handled: GET, POST, or Default. Data sent by a form is a continuous string of text from the information typed by the user. GET appends form contents to the URL specified in the Action text field; that information is therefore visible in the browser's address bar. GET is not a secure method of transferring data, so it should not be used for sensitive information such as credit card information or Social Security numbers. The GET method can send only a limited amount of information because restrictions are often imposed on the lengths of URLs by browsers and servers. This limitation can vary, so the GET method is also not a good choice for forms in which the visitor may have entered a lot of information—long forms lose any information exceeding the size or length restriction. The POST method, on the other hand, is capable of sending far more information and is more reliable and secure. It is the most common method used in scripts to send form data. POST uses an HTTP request to send the form value in the body of a message. Default uses the browser's default method, which is usually GET.

TESTING YOUR FORMS

It is possible to send a form to an email address if you don't have a CGI script running on your server through the use of a mailto (an email link, covered in Lesson 4) for the form action, which should be used only to test your forms. This method has a number of flaws, including errors that occur as a result of the browser not being configured to send mail or not being able to connect with an email program, and the absolute lack of security. You should always use dynamic pages or CGI scripts for processing forms.

NOTE *Although the mailto action gives you a way to initially test your form, it is not a substitute for testing your form with the corresponding server scripts. You should always be sure to thoroughly test pages in a live environment to be sure that your scripts are working as expected before making them available to visitors.*

1) In the lights_quiz.htm document, select the form by clicking `<form#lighthouse>` **on the Tag Selector. In the Action field of the form on the Property inspector, type** `mailto:` **followed by your email address, with no spaces after the colon.**

You should remember to include the colon and no spaces. This is the same way you inserted manual email links in Lesson 4.

2) Choose POST from the Method drop-down menu and type `text/plain` **into the Enctype text field.**

You have set the encode type to plain text; otherwise, the text sent will be encoded into an almost unreadable form.

The enctype defines how the data in the form is encoded. The text/plain value formats the information with each form element on a separate line. Using this value makes it easier to read the results in an email. If you don't define an enctype value, browsers use a default value that formats the data. Because the default is the one that should be used in most circumstances, you will usually not need to specify an enctype. This example is an exception because you are sending the data in an email to test the form.

TIP *To add a subject line to your form, change the Action to this:* ***mailto:YourEmailAddress? Subject=Title for Subject goes here.*** *The* ?Subject= *defines the text that follows as the subject. You can uses spaces in the subject, but do not use any other special characters such as quote marks, apostrophes, periods, or slashes (other than the* ?Subject= *that separates the email and the subject) because they will interfere with the HTML code. This may not work with every browser and should not be used in any way other than the testing of your form.*

Remember that the mailto action does not work reliably in all browsers. Use it only for testing. If your browser is not configured to send email, you can't test the form in this manner.

3) Save the file and test it in the browser.

The form results should be sent to the email address you specified.

4) Use the Tag Selector to select the `<form#lighthouse>` tag. Delete the text in the Action text field and change the Method to GET. Save the file and test it in the browser.

This is another way to test your forms. Instead of the results being sent via email, the browser will remain on the page with the form and the results of the form are appended to the URL in the Address field on your browser window.

You can close this file.

347

CREATING JUMP MENUS

A **jump menu** is a menu that contains links to other pages in your site or to other Web sites. Similar to regular links, the jump menu can link to any type of file, including graphics or PDF files. The jump menu provides an easy-to-use interface for linking to pages in your site, if you don't make the list too long.

A jump menu, which is embedded in a form, looks like a menu list in the browser. It does not need an action or method, as described in the previous section, because the jump menu doesn't cause data to be sent, received, or processed.

1) Open the related_navigation.htm file from the Lesson_10_Forms folder. Place the insertion point at the end of the line of text "Learn more about navigation:". Click the Jump Menu icon from the Forms category in the Insert bar.

TIP *Alternatively, you can choose Insert > Form > Jump Menu.*

JUMP MENU

The Jump Menu dialog box opens. By default, there is one item listed in the menu: unnamed1. Dreamweaver assigns generic names automatically in numerical order: unnamed1, unnamed2, and so on.

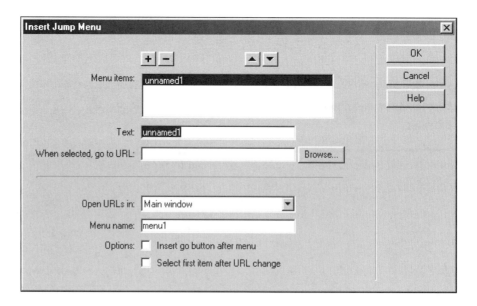

2) In the Text text field of the Jump Menu dialog box, type *Pick One*. **Type** # **in the When selected, go to URL text field.**

The first item in the menu list appears in the first line of the menu. Because the user sees this item initially in the menu list, the first line should be a short description of the list or a short instruction to let the user know that this is a jump menu.

3) In the Options area, choose Select first item after URL change.

This selection forces the menu list to display the first menu item in the list when the user returns to this page; otherwise, the list displays the most recent option chosen.

NOTE *The Open URLs in menu can be used to target links to specific frames, as you did in Lesson 9. For this exercise, you should leave the default Main Window selected.*

4) Click the plus sign (+) button to add a new menu item. Type *Radar* **in the Text field, press Tab, and type** *radar.htm* **in the When selected, go to URL text field. Repeat this step, entering** *Sonar*, *sonar.htm*; *GPS*, *gps.htm*; **and** *Buoys*, *buoys.htm*. **Click OK after you finish.**

When these items are selected in the browser window, they link to their appropriate pages. A link is activated when the user selects the corresponding item.

NOTE *If you want to add a Go button to your list, select the Insert go button after menu checkbox.*

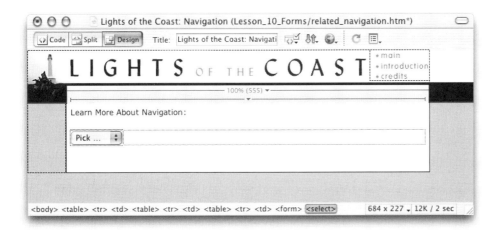

Dreamweaver automatically inserts the required form when you insert the jump menu, as you can see by the dotted red lines. Because the insertion point was at the end of the line of text, the jump menu is created just below the text. If you want the prompt text "Learn more about navigation" to appear on the same line as the jump menu, you need to move that text into the form. Using tables, as you did with the lights_quiz.htm file, gives you more control over the layout of your forms.

TIP *Use the up and down arrow icons to adjust the order of the items in the menu.*

When you click OK, the inserted menu may appear to be very short. You'll preview the page in the browser to see how it will really look to a visitor.

5) Save the file and preview it in the browser.

After you create the jump menu, you can make changes by using the Property inspector. The Property inspector gives you limited editing capability, allowing you to change the text the user sees and change the order in which the text appears in the list.

NOTE *For more extensive editing control, JavaScript can be incorporated with jump menus.*

WHAT YOU HAVE LEARNED

In this lesson, you have:

- Created a form on a Web page to place form fields into, enabling visitors to send information to you (pages 319–321)

- Divided the form contents into groups and used fieldsets to contain their form objects (pages 321–322)

- Used accessible attributes to create a form that can be used by a wide audience (pages 323–329)

- Added single-line text fields using options including width and maximum number of characters (pages 323–329)

- Added a multi-line text field and set options for the number of lines, maximum characters, and wrap method (pages 329–332)

- Added checkboxes to allow users to select multiple choices (pages 332–334)

- Added radio buttons to limit users to a single choice (pages 335–337)

- Added list boxes and menus with multiple items and specified an item to be selected initially (pages 337–339)

- Added buttons for Submit and Reset for users to send or clear the form (pages 340–342)

- Inserted a hidden field to include information in the form that is not visible to visitors (pages 342–343)

- Formatted the form using CSS (pages 343–345)

- Tested a form with a mailto action to be sure it is functioning correctly (pages 346–347)

- Created a jump menu that allows users to navigate through the site (pages 348–350)

adding user interactivity

LESSON 11

Interactivity and user feedback are important components of Web sites that, when integrated effectively, can bring about a variety of benefits. These benefits include helping your visitors better understand the content and purpose of your site, assisting users to more easily and directly navigate your pages, and providing visitors with a more enjoyable and productive user experience.

There are many ways to bring interactivity to a Web site. Dynamic and database-driven pages, Flash, and QTVR (Quick Time Virtual Reality—movies which support 360° panoramas and interactive components) are a few examples of the many tools that can be used to create interactive pages. One of the most common and effective tools for creating interactive Web sites is JavaScript, which is used primarily for client-side scripting; that is, the scripts are included on the Web pages and processed by the browser. Other scripts, including those used by JSP (Java Server Page) are server-side scripts; they are processed by the server and delivered to the user.

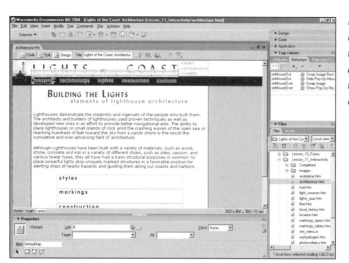

In this project, you will create rollovers with images that are already on the page and learn how to make more than one image on the page change at the same time.

Dreamweaver simplifies the process of using standard JavaScript functions by providing behaviors—prewritten JavaScript code routines that you can easily incorporate into your Web site. A behavior combines a user event (such as moving the pointer over a graphic button in the browser) with an action or series of actions that take place as result of that event. You can use behaviors to add interactivity to your pages, enabling your users to receive feedback based on their actions, and to change or otherwise control the information they see. In this lesson, you will use Dreamweaver behaviors to create rollovers, new browser windows, and menus. Dreamweaver includes a number of predefined behaviors; you can extend Dreamweaver by obtaining additional behaviors or, if you are proficient with JavaScript, you can create your own behaviors. (Extending Dreamweaver is covered in Lesson 17.)

To see examples of the finished pages: open Lesson_11_Interactivity/Completed/local_history.htm for the basic rollover; open Lesson_11_Interactivity/Completed/architecture.htm for the multiple rollovers, Popup message, status-bar message and Pop-Up menu; open Lesson_11_Interactivity/Completed/markings_tables.htm for the browser redirect; and open Lesson_11_Interactivity/Completed/light_sources.htm for the new browser window.

WHAT YOU WILL LEARN

In this lesson, you will:

- Create rollovers
- Add user interactivity to your pages by using behaviors
- Add multiple behaviors to one user action
- Add behaviors to image maps
- Create a status bar message
- Redirect users based on the version of their browser
- Open a new browser window
- Create a pop-up menu

APPROXIMATE TIME

This lesson should take about two hours to complete.

LESSON FILES

Media Files:
Lesson_11_Interactivity/Images/…(all files)

Starting Files:
Lesson_11_Interactivity/…(all files)

Completed Project:
Lesson_11_Interactivity/Completed/…(all files)

353

INSERTING A ROLLOVER IMAGE

One of the most common uses of JavaScript on Web pages is to create a **rollover**—an image that changes when the user moves the pointer over it. Rollovers combine the use of two images within the same space. When a visitor first arrives at a page that uses rollovers, those image combinations are displayed in their original states. As the pointer moves over the rollover image, a new image is swapped into its place. The new image is sometimes referred to as the "on" or "over" state of an image. As the user rolls the pointer off of the image, it can either swap back to the original image or remain changed. A rollover is a basic application of interactivity—it gives the user a response to the act of moving the pointer over the image. This response is often a visual effect to the existing image, such as lighting up a button, highlighting a tab, or changing the apparent depth to make a navigational element appear active. The rollover response can also incorporate additional information into the new image such as a description or explanation of content.

Web site interactivity primarily concerns the user experience; it's what occurs between the visitor and the Web site. Interaction requires an action and a response—it's a two-way communication process. Incorporating interactivity into your pages—designating the response that your site gives to visitor's actions—can bring more complexity and depth to the experience of visiting your site. Web sites that encourage action or participation are likely to be more successful, functional, and memorable—to have a greater impact upon the visitor—than those in which the user is stuck in a passive situation.

You can create rollovers in Dreamweaver without ever looking at the HTML or JavaScript code. A rollover is a simple behavior that is included in the Common category of the Insert bar. When you use this method, Dreamweaver creates the behavior behind the scenes.

1) Open local_history.htm from the Lesson_11_Interactivity folder. Click in the document window to place the insertion point at the top of the page. From the Common category of the Insert bar, select the Rollover Image button from the Images menu.

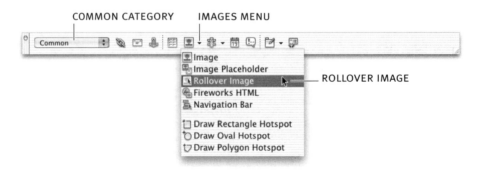

The Insert Rollover Image dialog box opens.

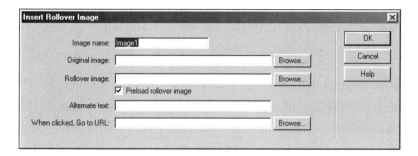

Dreamweaver steps you through the process of creating rollovers in this dialog box. If you haven't already placed the images that you want to create rollovers from on the page, you might prefer this method because it enables you to insert an image and define it as a rollover at the same time. In the next exercise, you will create rollovers for images that have already been placed on the page.

TIP *Alternatively, you can choose Insert > Interactive Images > Rollover Image to insert a rollover image using the same dialog box.*

2) In the Image name text field, type *local* for the image name.

This field enables you to name the image. If you don't name your rollover images, Dreamweaver assigns generic names automatically in a numeric order: Image1, Image2, etc. When creating your Web pages, it is more helpful if you make it a standard practice to give all rollovers specific and meaningful names that clearly indicate what they are for. When naming your images, don't use spaces or any special characters, and do not begin the name with a number; any of these actions can cause problems with scripting and your rollovers may not function properly as a result.

3) Click the Browse button next to the Original image text field and select the local_off.gif in the Lesson_11_Interactivity/Images folder.

This image appears on the page before the user rolls over it.

4) Click the Browse button next to the Rollover image text field and select the rollover image local_on.gif in the Lesson_11_Interactivity/Images folder.

When this page is viewed in a browser, the visitor initially sees the local_off.gif image. The local_on.gif image replaces the local_off.gif image when the user rolls over local_off.gif in the browser window.

TIP *When making rollover graphics, create both the original image and the image that will swap at the same dimensions. If both images are not the same size, the second rollover image is resized to the size of the first image. Resizing distorts the second image because that image has only the space held by the first image available to it.*

5) Type *Locations* **in the Alternate text text field. Click the Browse button next to the When clicked, Go to URL text field and find the file location.htm in the Lesson_11_Interactivity folder. Leave the Preload rollover image box checked and then click OK.**

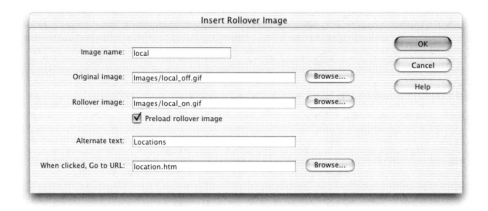

The Preload rollover image option is checked by default and it is highly recommended. This setting causes the secondary image to load when the document loads into the visitor's browser. If this setting is not checked, the image does not load until the visitor rolls over the primary image and the browser requests that rollover image from the server. Loading the image along with the rest of the page makes the rollovers happen more quickly, eliminating any lag caused by the download occurring at the time the user rolls over the image.

The rollover now links to the file you chose. The file you chose in the When clicked, Go to URL text field now appears in the Link text field on the Property inspector when the image is selected.

If you leave the text field blank, Dreamweaver places a number sign (#), otherwise known as a **null link**, in the Link text field of the Property inspector. The number sign tells the browser to display the pointing hand when the user rolls over the graphic. The number sign also causes the browser to stay on the same page if the rollover is clicked in the browser. You can replace the number sign with a link value to go to a different page or URL, but do not leave the Link text field in the Property inspector empty because doing so removes the JavaScript that creates the rollover.

356

When the rollover image is selected, the resulting behavior appears in the Behaviors panel, which you'll use in the next exercise.

6) Save your file and test it in the browser.

You can close this file.

> **TIP** *When creating your graphics, make the file sizes as small as possible. Remember that with rollovers, you are displaying not one but two images for the same button. The file size of a rollover like the one you inserted in this exercise is increased because there are two images to download. The amount of increase depends upon the size of the images.*

ADDING BEHAVIORS

This exercise demonstrates the process of creating rollovers from graphics that have already been placed on the page. The result is the same as the last exercise—an image swaps to show a different image when the user rolls over it. In this exercise, however, you are using a different method to insert rollovers: You will insert the behavior for the rollover using the Behaviors panel. When you are creating your own Web pages, you should use this method if you have already placed your original images on a page. If the original images are not yet on the page, you can use the method from the previous exercise to set both the original image and the rollover image in one step.

1) Open the architecture.htm from the Lesson_11_Interactivity folder.

The file contains a number of tables and graphics that have already been placed for you, using the techniques you have learned in Lessons 3 and 5.

2) Name the three images in the nested table near the bottom of the page using the image name text field in the Property inspector. The image names should be as follows: styles_off.gif should be named *styles*, markings_off.gif should be named *markings*, and construction_off.gif should be named *construction*.

IMAGE NAME TEXT FIELD

Naming the images to match their content or their function is a good method. This naming practice helps to clearly indicate which images are associated with the chosen names.

3) Select the Styles image. Open the Tag inspector and click the Behaviors tab.

The Behaviors panel opens.

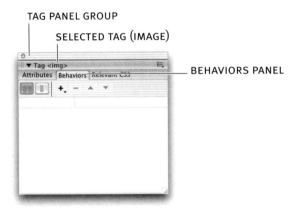

TIP *You can also choose Window > Behaviors to open the Behaviors panel.*

4) Click the plus sign (+) button on the Behaviors panel and choose Swap Image from the Actions menu.

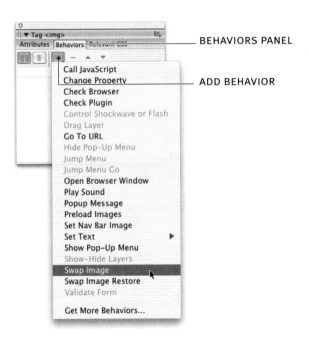

The Swap Image dialog box opens. The Swap Image behavior is what creates the rollover effect you used in the previous exercise: it swaps a new image in to replace the original image that the visitor rolled over. The behavior is a combination of an action and an event.

358

An **action** is what happens as a result of user interaction. When you select an action, Dreamweaver adds that action to the list in the Behaviors panel. The Actions menu displays or disables actions depending on which element you selected in the document window. The action is this case is the swapping of one image for another.

Dreamweaver also adds an appropriate event (or events) for that action automatically. The **event** is what causes the action to occur. An event could be the user rolling over an image or clicking a button, for example. In this case, the event is onMouseOver, which is the Dreamweaver default for rollovers. You will learn to select specific events later in this lesson.

THE IMAGE NAMED STYLES IS SELECTED

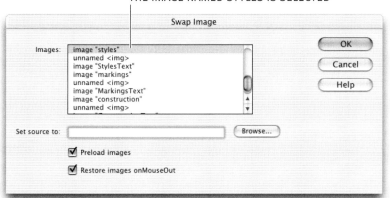

5) In the Images list, make sure that the styles image is selected.

The image is listed as "styles," which is the name that you defined (in step 2 of this exercise) for the image that you selected and added an action to through the Behaviors panel (in step 4 of this exercise). By selecting the styles image in the image list in the Swap Image dialog box, you designate that when a user rolls over that image, it is replaced with a rollover image. You will choose the rollover image in the next step.

NOTE *If you were to choose a different image from this list, the selected image would be replaced with the rollover image when the user rolls over the styles image because the styles image is the one to which the behavior is applied—you will do that in the next exercise.*

Keep in mind that if you don't name your images, they all appear with the name, "unnamed <img>" in this dialog box. You can see a number of instances of "unnamed <img>" in this dialog box because you named only three images. This is why it is so important to name your images properly; it is very hard to work with behaviors if the images are not clearly and logically named. In a list full of unnamed images, it can be difficult to distinguish which images you are working with.

359

6) Click the Browse button next to the Set source to text field and find the styles_on.gif image in the Images folder. Click Choose (Macintosh) or OK (Windows) to select the image for use as the rollover image.

Set source to defines what the rollover image will be. Setting the source is the same as choosing the rollover in the previous exercise. Generally, the original appearance of an image is known as the "off" state, and the instance of the rollover when the user moves the pointer over the image and the image changes is known as the "on" state. Images used for the "on" states often look as if a button has been pressed or a word has been highlighted to indicate to the visitor that the object is an active or linked element.

All the rollover graphics you will use for this exercise are in the Images folder, and the names of the rollover-image files have the suffix _on. Developing a logical and ordered naming system for your images, such as history.gif for the original image and history_on.gif or history_over.gif for the rollover image, will help you keep graphics organized and will make it easier to find the appropriate image.

After choosing the image, you are returned to the Swap Image dialog box. An asterisk appears at the right end of the image name in the Images list to indicate that an alternative image has been assigned to it for the rollover.

7) Make sure that the Preload images and Restore images onMouseOut **checkboxes are checked; then click OK.**

As with the rollovers you inserted in the previous exercise, the Preload images option is checked by default. This option causes the images to be loaded at the time the page is called up by the browser instead of waiting to load until the browser needs to display the image.

The Restore image's onMouseOut option is also checked by default and is recommended. This option makes your swapped images revert to the original images when the user rolls off them.

NOTE *Restore images onMouseOut is done by Swap Image Restore, which is available as a separate action in the Behaviors panel.*

Both portions of the behavior are now listed in the Behaviors panel: The onMouseOver event causes the Swap Image action and the onMouseOut event causes the Swap Image Restore action. The combination of these actions and events creates the rollover effect—the image swaps when the visitor moves the pointer over the image and it swaps back when the visitor moves the pointer off the image.

8) Repeat steps 3 through 7 for the Markings and Construction buttons, using markings_on.gif and construction_on.gif for the rollover images that you define in the Set source to text field.

If you ever need to delete a behavior, you can select the object in the document window that contains the behavior, select the action in the Behaviors panel that you want to delete and then click the minus sign (–) button at the top of the Behaviors panel. You can also delete a behavior by selecting it and then pressing Delete (Macintosh) or Backspace (Windows).

NOTE *When you delete the link or null link that is contained in the link text field on the Property inspector for an image that is associated with a rollover, the behavior is removed. Sometimes when behaviors are removed, everything on the page becomes selected; simply click in the document window to deselect the contents.*

When one of the images to which you have applied the Swamp Image behavior is selected, the Link text field on the Property inspector displays javascript:; because the page to which that image will link has not yet been defined. The javascript:; (the default for manually applied behaviors if no link is specified) and # (the default for the Insert Rollover option if no link is specified) both serve the same purpose: they are null links that cause the visitor to remain on the current page. However, the # character also refers to named anchors and causes the page to refresh jumping the user back up to the top of the page. Do not delete this placeholder link; it is necessary for the rollovers to function because there is no link defined yet. A link is required because this behavior needs to be applied to an <a> (anchor) tag.

9) Save your file and test the rollovers in your browser.

Notice the images change when you roll over them.

SWAPPING MULTIPLE IMAGES WITH ONE EVENT

You can create more complex interactions with visitors by applying multiple actions to a single event. For example, you can have several images swap from their original images to their rollover images at the same time as a result of the same event. This technique might be used to cause two images to swap out, each from their original image to the rollover image, when the user rolls over one button.

In this exercise, you will apply a behavior to the Styles graphic, which causes the spacer image that exists below it to swap to an image with the Styles caption as the user rolls over the Styles button. At the same time, the Styles button changes from its original image to the rollover you defined in the previous exercise. For the additional rollover to occur using the same event, you will edit the existing Swap Image action and define the additional image swap in this exercise.

1) In the architecture.htm document, select the Styles image and then double-click the existing Swap Image action in the Behaviors panel.

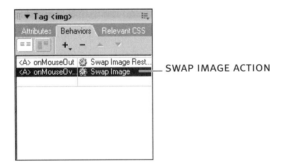

SWAP IMAGE ACTION

Make sure that you double-click the Swap Image action, not the Swap Image Restore action.

The Swap Image dialog box opens.

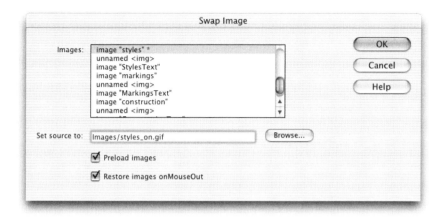

2) In the Swap Image dialog box, select the image named StylesText. Click the Browse button to the right of the Set source to text field and choose the styles_text_on.gif image from the Lesson_11_Interactivity/Images folder.

The StylesText image, which is the blank image underneath the styles graphic, has already been named for you. In this step, you are selecting that blank image in the Swap Image dialog box so you can replace it with the styles caption image that will display more information to the viewer.

Look at the Images list in the Swap Image dialog box. Images with an asterisk at the end of the name have been assigned a rollover image. The styles image, for example, has an asterisk next to it because you defined a rollover for that image in the last exercise. Now the StylesText image also has an asterisk next to it because you have assigned a rollover for that image in this step. Checking this list is a quick way to verify which images will swap from their original images to rollover images.

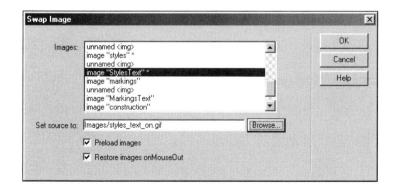

3) Click OK to close the Swap Image dialog box. Then repeat the same process of steps 1 and 2 for the remaining images in the table Markings and Construction.

The blank images are already named for you: MarkingsTextOff and ConstructionTextOff. The images to swap are indicated by the _on suffix and are located in the Images folder. Swapping multiple images can be useful for giving the user additional information, but keep in mind that too many extra image swaps on one action can slow a browser down.

4) Save your file again and test it in the browser.

When you move your pointer over each button, the button image should change, and the corresponding description text image should also change. When you move away from the button, both the button and the description text graphic should return to the original images.

ADDING BEHAVIORS TO IMAGE MAPS

Moving the pointer over any portion of a standard rollover image calls up the JavaScript script and causes the image swap to happen. There may be times, however, when you want the rollover to occur only when the user rolls over a certain part of the image. In such cases, you can use image maps to define those hotspot areas.

1) In architecture.htm, use the image name text field on the Property inspector to name all the navigational images that are located in a row near the top of the page: nav_history.gif should be named *history*, nav_technology.gif should be named *technology*, nav_lights.gif should be named *lights*, nav_resources.gif should be named *resources*, and nav_culture.gif should be named *culture*.

TIP *If the table widths bar obscures the navigational image, click outside of the table.*

If you were to create standard rollovers for these navigational images, the areas between each of the words would cause the swap image to occur. By using image maps to define the hotspots on the images, you can control when the rollover happens.

2) Select the nav_history.gif image and use the Rectangular Hotspot tool on the Property inspector to draw an image map closely around the word history.

IMAGE NAME

RECTANGULAR HOTSPOT TOOL

364

The image map makes only the word history on the nav_history.gif image clickable.

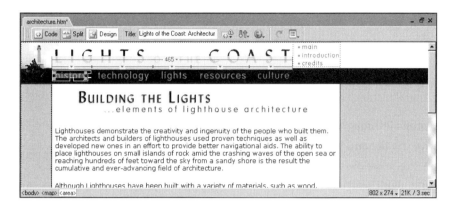

3) Click the plus sign (+) button on the Behaviors panel and choose Swap Image from the Actions menu.

You are applying a swap image behavior to an image map. The behavior does not apply to any area of the image surrounding the image map.

TIP *Because you just created the image map, it is automatically selected. If you are not applying the behavior directly after creating the image map, you should choose the pointer tool on the Property inspector and click the image map to select it.*

4) In the Images list, make sure that the history image is selected. Click the Browse button next to the Set source to text field and find nav_history_on.gif in the Images folder. Click Choose (Macintosh) or OK (Windows) to pick the image and return to the Swap Image dialog box.

You have now selected the image that will replace the nav_history.gif image when you roll over the hotspot in a browser. The entire image will be replaced, even if the clickable area is only on a certain portion of the original image.

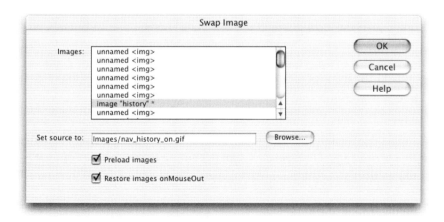

365

5) Make sure that the Preload Images and Restore images onMouseOut checkboxes are checked; then click OK.

The dialog box closes, and you return to the document window. Whenever the image map on the nav_history.gif image is selected, you can see the Swap Image listed in the Behaviors panel. If you have the image selected but do not have the image map selected, you do not see the swap image listed in the Behaviors panel.

6) Repeat steps 2 through 5 for the technology, lights, resources, and culture images. Save the file and test your work in the browser.

The images to use for the swaps are indicated by the _on suffix. Using image maps in combination with behaviors can give you a significant amount of additional control over your images, actions, and events.

Your document should now display the image maps fitting closely around each of the navigation words, as the following example shows.

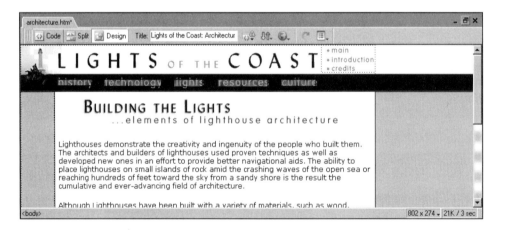

EDITING ACTIONS AND EVENTS

You can edit the actions and events that combine to make behaviors in several ways: You can change the event to which an action corresponds, you can attach several actions to a single event, and you can change the order in which those actions occur. For example, in the previous exercise, Swap Image was the action and OnMouseOver was the event that corresponded to the rollover behavior. In this exercise, you will add an action for a pop-up message and select a corresponding event.

1) In the architecture.htm document, select the Markings image in the nested table near the bottom of the page. Click the plus sign (+) button in the Behaviors panel and choose Popup Message from the Actions menu.

The Popup Message dialog box opens, displaying a text field in which you can type your message.

2) Type *How unique markings differentiate lighthouses* **and click OK.**

The Popup Message action and the corresponding event appear in the Behaviors panel.

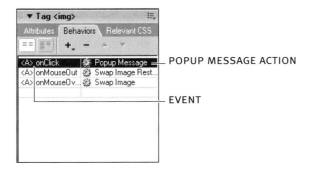

3) Click the event in the Behaviors panel. From the menu that appears to the right of the current event, select the <A> onMouseOut **event.**

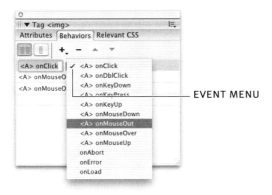

The events that are available in this menu might differ depending on the action and the browser type you choose. The Events menu appears only when you select an event in the Behaviors panel.

NOTE *You can choose what browser type to display events for by making a choice from the Show Events For portion of the Add Behavior menu. You can choose to show events for a specific browser version, such as IE 6.0, or for all browsers of a specified version number, such as 4.0 and later browsers. After you select a browser type, you can select an event in the Behaviors panel to make the Events menu available. The Events menu then lists only those events that are available for the browser type that you chose.*

The Events menu is divided into two types of events: those that require the <A> (anchor) tag to function and those that do not. The events that require the <A> (anchor) tag are shown at the top of the menu, preceded by the <A> indicator. If you insert a rollover image (either by choosing Insert > Interactive Images > Rollover Image or by choosing Insert Rollover Image from the Insert bar), as you did in the first exercise of this lesson, Dreamweaver adds the anchor for you by inserting a number sign (#) into the Link text field of the Property inspector. If you use the technique presented in the second exercise and apply a behavior to an image that is already on the page, Dreamweaver adds the anchor for you by inserting javascript:; into the Link text field of the Property inspector. If you need to apply a behavior to another element, such as text, you need to add a null link using a number sign (#) or a working link in the link text field on the Property inspector yourself. At the bottom of the Events menu, Dreamweaver displays events such as onLoad that are used without the <A> (anchor) tag.

4) Click the up arrow button in the Behaviors panel to move the Popup Message behavior to the top of the list.

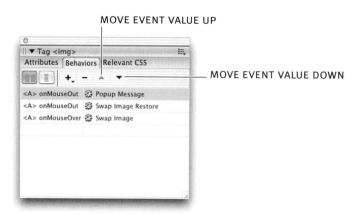

MOVE EVENT VALUE UP

MOVE EVENT VALUE DOWN

The browser performs the actions in the order in which they appear in the Behaviors panel list. The up arrow moves the action up in the list; the down arrow moves the action down in the list. Use these buttons to change the order in which actions are executed by the browser.

5) Save and preview the page in the browser.

Use care when adding the Popup Message behavior to your pages. Similar to pop-up windows, which you will learn to create later in this lesson, pop-up messages can quickly annoy your visitors when overused.

Leave this file open to use in the next exercise.

CREATING A STATUS BAR MESSAGE

A status bar message can give users extra information about where links will lead them. This message, which appears in the status bar at the bottom of the browser window, replaces the default display of the URL or path to the linked page.

1) In the architecture.htm document, select the Styles image. Click the plus sign (+) button in the Behaviors panel and choose Set Text > Set Text of Status Bar from the Add Behavior menu of actions.

The Set Text of Status Bar dialog box opens, displaying a text field in which you can type your message.

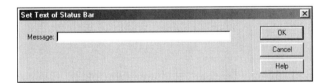

2) Type *Architectural styles used in lighthouses* **and click OK.**

If you use status bar messages, a concise description of the linked material helps users navigate your pages.

The Set Text of Status Bar action now appears in the Behaviors panel.

3) Save the file and test it in the browser.

When you move your pointer over the Styles button, you see the message you created displayed in the status bar at the bottom of the browser window. You can leave the architecture.htm file open; you will use it again later in this lesson.

CHECKING THE BROWSER

Not all browsers support a wide range of JavaScript events and other advanced features—some, particularly 3.0 and 4.0 browsers, have very limited support. With the Check Browser action, you can detect which browsers are being used by the visitors to your Web site and redirect users to another page if you want to provide advanced features that won't display correctly in other browsers. For example, if your page contains layers (covered in Lesson 16), you could create a page without the layers and redirect users with 4.0 browsers to the page that uses layers. Users with older browsers or with JavaScript turned off would remain on the page that doesn't use layers.

This exercise uses a page built with tables and a similar page built with layers. You will add a Check Browser behavior and redirect the users with 4.0 browsers to the page that uses layers.

If you do use this feature, it can be good to keep the page that contains the Check Browser behavior very small so that it loads and redirects the visitor quickly. If it is too large, it may take a considerable amount of time to load, causing visitors to have to wait not only for that page to load but also for the one to which they are redirected to load.

1) Open the markings_tables.htm file in the Lesson_11_Interactivity folder.

This file was created with tables and thus displays properly in most browsers. This page was created using the techniques you have learned up to this point.

2) Select the <body> tag by clicking <body> in the Tag Selector (in the lower left corner of the document window).

The action is attached to the <body> tag to redirect a user when the page loads. You should see <body> displayed in the title bar of the Behaviors panel, indicating that the <body> tag is selected. All the content in the document appears selected.

3) Click the plus sign (+) button in the Behaviors panel and choose Check Browser from the Add Behavior menu of actions.

The Check Browser dialog box opens.

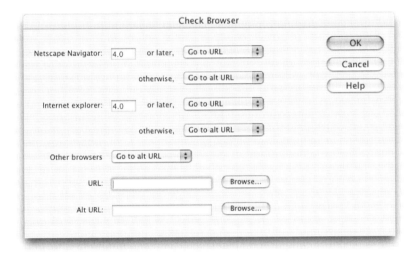

4) For both Netscape 4.0 and Explorer 4.0 or later, choose Go to URL from the appropriate menu. For both Netscape and Explorer Otherwise, choose Stay on This Page. For Other Browsers, choose Stay on This Page.

When you use the Check Browser behavior, if you tried to use this behavior to redirect users with older browsers to another page, it would not work for anyone who uses a browser that does not support JavaScript or who simply turned off JavaScript.

5) Click the Browse button next to the URL text field and locate the markings_layers.htm file in the Lesson_11_Interactivity folder.

The markings_layers.htm file is the page to which users of the latest browsers will be redirected—it was created using layers, which you will learn about in Lesson 16.

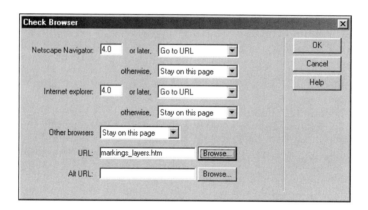

6) Click OK to insert the JavaScript into your page.

The onLoad event appears with the corresponding Check Browser action in the Behaviors panel.

7) Save the file and test the page in your browser.

If you do not have a 4.0 or later browser, you remain on the static page.

If you have a 4.0 or later browser, you may briefly see the markings_tables.htm page before the browser redirects you to the page with layers, marking_layers.htm. To avoid this, you can create a very basic page that contains the Check Browser behavior along with only the same background color or image as the final page and redirect all browser versions: older browsers to a page that can be displayed correctly and newer browsers to a different page with more advanced features.

You can close this file.

OPENING A NEW BROWSER WINDOW

This exercise will demonstrate how to open a new browser window when the page loads, which can be used for displaying an advertisement, definition terms, or a wide variety of other information. You could open a browser window by using the _blank target along with a standard link, but you wouldn't have any control over the attributes of that new window. On the other hand, the Open Browser window lets you control the size along with a number of attributes of the new browser window, such as scroll bars and menu bars.

TIP *Although the Open Browser Window option is easy to add, think it through before using it on a Web page. Make sure that the extra window is necessary. Users are often irritated with new windows that continually pop up as they browse the Web. Moderation is important— whether you are creating new browser windows or using other behaviors, be sure to consider the amount of feedback or interactive options you are offering the visitor, and strike a balance between too little (which doesn't provide enough information) and too much (which can often be overbearing). Understanding your visitors' prior experiences with Web sites and other media helps you tailor the experience they will have while viewing and interacting with your site.*

1) Open the light_sources.htm file in the Lesson_11_Interactivity folder. Select the bolded word "lime" near the end of the first paragraph and place a null link (#) into the Link text field on the Property inspector.

You need to use a null link for two reasons: The behavior that you will use to open a new browser window requires the <a> (anchor) tag to be applied—the text must have a link of some type to attach a behavior to it. Also, the light_sources.htm page should remain in the original browser window when the new window is opened. The null link enables you to attach the Open Browser Window behavior while remaining on the same page in the original window.

2) Place the insertion point in the word "lime" and click the plus sign (+) button in the Behaviors panel to add a new behavior and then select Open Browser Window in the list.

The Open Browser Window dialog box opens. You placed the insertion point in the word "lime" because it needs to be deselected for the Open Browser Window option to be available to you in the menu.

3) Click the Browse button and locate the lime.htm file.

This file is the page that will load in the new window.

4) Type 350 for the window width and 100 for the window height; then click OK.

The width and height are chosen based on the size of the content in the new window. If you are simply displaying a banner ad, you should set the size of the new window to the width and height of that ad image. If the content has more elements, you should adjust the size of the window accordingly. You can also set a number of window attributes as needed. The additional attributes for new windows are as follows:

- **Navigation toolbar:** The row of browser buttons that includes Back, Forward, Home, and Reload. Leave this box unchecked for this exercise.

- **Location toolbar:** The row of browser options that includes the location field. Leave this box unchecked for this exercise.

- **Status bar:** The area at the bottom of the browser window in which messages (such as the load time remaining and the URLs associated with links) appear. Leave this box unchecked for this exercise.

- **Menu bar:** The area of the browser window (Windows) or desktop (Macintosh) in which menus such as File, Edit, View, Go, and Help appear. You should set this option if you want users to be able to navigate from the new window. If you do not set this option, users can only close or minimize the window (Windows) or close the window or quit the application (Macintosh) from the new window. Leave this box unchecked for this exercise.

- **Scrollbars as Needed:** Specifies that scroll bars should appear if the content extends beyond the visible area. Scroll bars do not appear if you do not set this option. If the Resize Handles option is also turned off, users have no way of seeing content that extends beyond the original size of the window. If this is the case, you need to make sure that the window is sized appropriately for the content of the page. If the window is too small or too large and has no scroll bars, it will be very frustrating for users. Leave this box unchecked for this exercise.

- **Resize handles:** Specifies that users should be able to resize the window, either by dragging the lower right corner of the window or by clicking the Maximize button (Windows) or size box (Macintosh) in the upper right corner. If you do not set this option, the resize controls are unavailable and the user cannot drag the lower right corner of the window. Leave this box unchecked for this exercise.

- **Window name:** The name of the new window. You should name the new window if you want to target it with links or control it with JavaScript. Leave this text field blank for this exercise.

The Open Browser Window action and the onClick event are now displayed in the Behaviors panel.

5) Repeat steps 1 through 4 for the rest of the bolded terms on the page.

The pages to use for the remaining terms are oxyhydrogen.htm, fuel.htm, acetylene.htm, and photovoltaics.htm.

6) Save your file and test your page in the browser.

A new window opens with definitions for terms that appear in the light_sources.htm document when you follow the link applied to the term.

CREATING A POP-UP MENU

You can integrate JavaScript Pop-Up menus with your navigation to give your visitors a list of choices and quick access to various sections of the site. Dreamweaver's Pop-Up Menu script works in both Netscape (versions 4 and up) and Explorer (versions 4 and up).

1) In the architecture.htm document, click the image map on the history image that you created earlier in this lesson to select the image map.

You can verify that the image map has been selected by looking for the blue selection handles that appear around the defined area of the image map. When it is selected, you should see two actions listed in the Behaviors panel from when you created a rollover for this image earlier in this lesson.

2) Click the plus sign (+) button in the Behaviors panel and choose Show Pop-Up Menu from the Actions menu.

The Show Pop-Up Menu dialog box appears with the Contents tab active. You will use this portion of the dialog box to define the choices you want to present your visitor with.

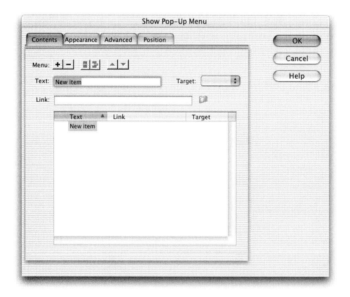

3) In the Text text field, replace the default text "New Item" by typing *Location***. Click the folder icon next to the Link text field, browse for location.htm, and select it.**

The Location item is added to the list of menu items. For this item, you are selecting the location.htm document that you created at the beginning of this lesson.

4) Click the Menu plus sign (+) button to add a new item. Replace the default text "New Item" by typing *Light Sources*. **Click the folder icon next to the Link text field, browse for light_sources.htm, and select it. Add a third item to the list, name it** *Local History*, **and link it to local_history.htm. Add a fourth item to the list, name it** *Markings*, **and link it to markings_layers.htm.**

The names of menu items and the corresponding pages to which they link can be edited by selecting an item in the list and using the Text and Link text fields to make changes.

TIP *Shorter and more concise menu options help to keep your design clean and easy to use.*

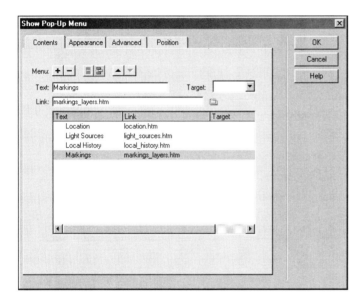

TIP *To delete an item, select it in the list of menu items and click the Menu minus sign (–) button.*

5) Select Light Sources in the list of menu items. Click the Move item up arrow button to move the Light Sources item to the top of the list. Select Location in the list and click the Move item down arrow button to move it to the bottom of the list.

The order of menu items can be rearranged easily with the Menu arrow buttons.

NOTE *You can create subcategories of menu items by selecting the item you want to make a subcategory and clicking the indent item button. Use the Outdent Item button to move an item to a higher category level.*

6) Click the Appearance tab on the Show Pop-Up Menu dialog box. Select Vertical menu from the orientation menu. Select the Verdana font set from the Font menu and enter *10* in the Size text field. There should be no bold or italic styling, and the alignment should be left.

You may need to click back onto the Font menu for the preview area to refresh and show your menu at the size you chose. The preview will also refresh when you specify the colors in the next step.

Here, you are matching the text options for the Pop-Up menu to the styles used in the "Lights of the Coast" project site.

NOTE *If you have fewer than four choices in your menu list, Dreamweaver repeats the last entry until there are four choices in the preview shown in this dialog box—this is for display purposes only and won't happen in your document.*

7) Use the color boxes to set the following: Up state Text #CCCCCC (gray), Up state Cell #000000 (black), Over state Text #FFCC66 (pale orange), Over state Cell #000000 (black).

These options enable you to set the look of the pop-up menu to match the style of the navigational images as closely as possible. You can see how the menu will look in the preview area of the Show Pop Up Menu dialog box. The second menu option appears with the Over State colors applied to it; the other menu options appear with the Up State colors. The preview is approximate; it may not appear in a browser exactly as you see it here.

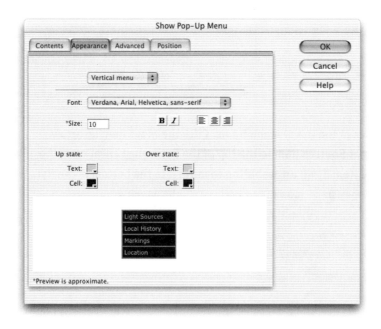

8) Click the Advanced tab on the Show Pop-Up Menu dialog box. Verify that the default settings are as follows: Cell width and Cell height menu choices should be set to Automatic, the Cell padding to 3, the Cell spacing to 0, the Text indent to 0, and the Menu delay to 1000. Make any changes necessary to match the settings listed here. In the Pop-Up borders section, check the Show borders box and set the border width to 0. Set the Border color to #666666 (gray), the Shadow color to #333333 (dark gray), and the Highlight color to #FFFFFF (white).

The menu delay controls how long it takes for the menu to disappear after the visitor rolls off of it.

Leaving the box for Show Borders checked while setting the border to a size of 0 turns off the outside borders but leaves thin lines separating the individual menu items from each other. You may not see the lines in the previous area, but you should see them when you preview your page at the end of this exercise.

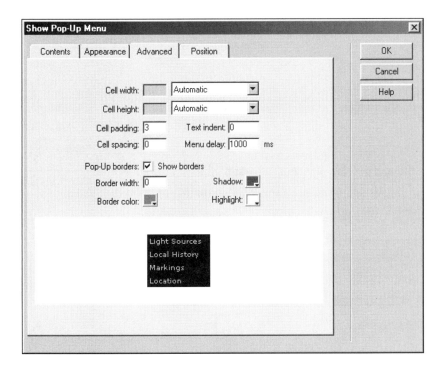

9) Click the Position tab on the Show Pop-Up Menu dialog box. Click the second Menu Position button from the left. Type an X value of *5* and a Y value of *26*. Make sure that the Hide Menu on MouseOut Event box is checked. Click OK.

In addition to the X and Y axis, you can use the four general placement buttons on this portion of the Show Pop-Up Menu dialog box to position your menu on the page.

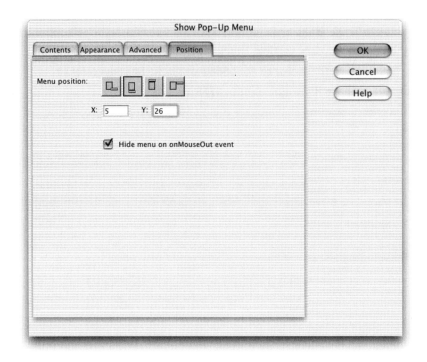

10) Save the file and preview it in your browser.

The Show Pop-Up Menu behavior is now listed in the Behaviors panel. It is split into two portions: Show Pop-Up Menu and Hide Pop-Up Menu.

To insert the pop-up menu, Dreamweaver creates an external JavaScript file with the .js extension. Usually named mm_menu.js, this file is necessary for the pop-up menu to function. It is, however, a fairly large file (in this case, the single menu is approximately 30KB), so you need to judge whether the addition of scripts like this one are of a size that your visitors can download quickly and easily.

Test your menus as much as is possible. When you roll over the history navigation image, you see the pop-up menu that you created in this exercise appear below the word "history." The settings that you applied for appearance and position make the menu look integrated with the rest of the navigation. The menu should appear in your browser similar to the following example.

NOTE *With this version of the Show Pop-Up Menu behavior, there are some discrepancies between how the menus appear in various browsers on the Macintosh versus Windows. You need to adjust the positioning of the menu.*

You can close the architecture.htm file.

VALIDATING FORMS

Whether accidentally or intentionally, users sometimes enter the wrong information or skip a field entirely. Instead of waiting until the form is sent, you can check data as the user enters it or just before the form has been sent to the server. The Validate Form behavior checks the contents of text fields in a form to ensure that the user has entered the proper information. Forms were covered in Lesson 10.

In this exercise, you will add a behavior that checks the information typed into a form to be sure that all required text fields have been filled out and that the information is the right type of data.

1) Open the lights_quiz.htm document and select the email field. Click the plus (+) button on the Behaviors panel and choose Validate Form from the Add Behavior menu.

The Validate Form dialog box opens with a list of the form objects in the document; the first object in the Named fields list is selected by default, which in this case is the FirstName text field. The list also specifies which form the objects are contained in, which is helpful if you have more than one form on a page.

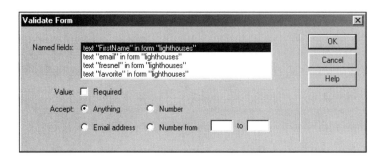

Checkboxes, radio buttons, and list/menu objects can't be validated with the Validate Form behavior.

2) Select the email field from the Named Fields list on the dialog box. In the Value section, check the Required box.

Checking the Required box specifies that it is necessary for the email field to contain data. The Validate Form action is added to the Behaviors panel with the onBlur event. An error message is displayed if the user tabs to the next field without filling in this one. The onBlur event is activated when the user leaves the text field. In this example, if the user tabs to the next field in the form, leaving the email text field blank, an error message is displayed. If the user clicks into specific fields (not tabbing through the form), this initial validation check is ignored.

3) Choose Email Address from the Accept area and click OK.

This option checks whether or not the text field contains an @ symbol. It checks only whether @ was included—it can't check that an email address actually exists or functions.

The Number option specifies that the field should contain only numbers. The Number from option specifies that the field should contain a number that is within the given range of numbers, which is particularly useful for years.

Although it may seem like a good idea to validate each field as the user moves along through the form, use this technique with care—it may annoy your visitors. Many people skip certain questions and come back to them later, after filling out the rest of the form. Applying the validate behavior to the Submit button, as you will do in the following steps, is a good alternative.

NOTE *Forms can also be validated using server-side scripts.*

The Validate Form behavior is displayed in the list of behaviors attached to the selected object (the email text field in this case) in the Behaviors panel. The events that are available for form objects are different from those available when you apply behaviors to the <a> (anchor) tag. The event for the Validate Form action is onBlur, which occurs when the form object that is currently active or in focus loses the focus. An object loses focus any time a user moves to a different object, which results in another drawback to applying the Validate Form behavior directly to any given form object. It the visitor never clicks or tabs to the form object that you have applied the Validate Form behavior to, the object never receives focus—the object is validated only if it first receives focus. Because users may simply click to the next section to bypass a number of fields, they may skip the required field entirely. Applying the behavior to the Submit button instead, as you will do in the next step, solves this problem.

4) Select the Submit button in the document window. Click the plus sign (+) button on the Behaviors panel and choose Validate Form from the Add Behavior menu.
The Validate Form dialog box opens.

5) Verify that the FirstName text field is selected in the Named Fields list and check the Required box in the Value section. In the Accept area, verify that Anything is selected and then click OK.

Anything specifies that the field is required, but that it does not need to have a certain type of data. Now when the user clicks the Submit button, the checks will be made.

NOTE *If you set an initial value for a text field, validating that field is not useful (particularly if you select the Anything option) because there is already text in the field.*

The Validate Form action is added to the Behaviors panel with the onClick event.

6) Save the file and test it in your browser.

Click in the email field and then press Tab without entering any data. You see an error message generated by the Validate Form behavior. You may not want to rely on the individual field check to validate a form because if you click to place the insertion point in another field, you do not see an error message—it only works if the user moves into the required field. If the visitor does not use the Tab key and never places the insertion point into the required field, the error message does not display.

NOTE *To add the email field to the checks that occur when the Submit button is clicked, open the Validate Form dialog box again by double-clicking the Validate Form action in the Behaviors panel. Select the email field and the desired option. Click OK when you are done.*

You can close the lights_quiz.htm file.

WHAT YOU HAVE LEARNED

In this lesson, you have:

- Created basic rollovers (pages 354–357)

- Learned how to edit the behaviors by choosing different events and adding actions while creating a pop-up message (pages 356–366)

- Learned how to make multiple images on the page change when the user rolls over one by adding multiple behaviors to one user action (pages 361–364)

- Created a JavaScript pop-up menu with multiple menu items (pages 364–366)

- Created a status bar message to give your viewers more information about a link when they roll over it (pages 369–370)

- Used the Check Browser behavior to redirect users to different pages based on the browser version they are using (pages 370–373)

- Used a behavior to make a new browser window open when the page loads (pages 373–375)

- Learned to make portions of a form required by using a behavior to validate certain fields (pages 381–384)

managing
your site

LESSON 12

Developing a Web site generally begins with the planning phase during which you conceive of the idea for a site, develop the site file and navigational structures, gather content, and design the look and feel of the site. These steps of preparation usually occur before you start working in Dreamweaver—for the project site you are working with throughout this book, Lights of the Coast, these steps were already done for you, as described in Lesson 1. The planning phase is followed by the production phase,

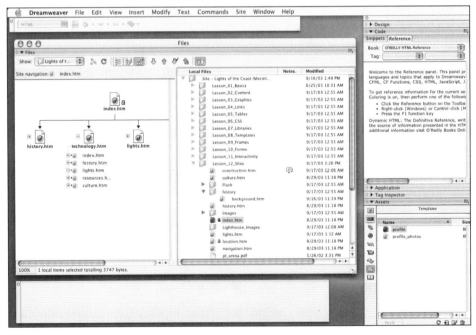

In this lesson, you'll work with the Files panel to manage files and connect to a remote site.

during which you use Dreamweaver to build and test the actual pages of a site, as you learned to do over the course of Lessons 2 through 11.

The work that is put into a Web site does not end when you complete the production phase. After production, the Web site needs to be made available to the audience— this is done through a procedure known as *launching*, in which the site is announced and promoted after being uploaded to a server. In addition, many Web sites need to constantly evolve, right along with the changing needs and desires of their audiences, to remain effective and continue to draw new and repeat visitors. The ongoing process of making changes, updating and adding new content, and constantly optimizing a Web site is known as *site maintenance*. The transition from the production phase to the maintenance phase of a Web site involves setting the site up on a server, thoroughly testing the site, going through the process of launching the site, and preparing for ongoing management and maintenance.

Site management, which is a vital part of Web development, is important to the continued use of a site. Dreamweaver provides extensive management tools that enable you to easily update and control your Web site, maintaining site files that are located in the local root folder as well as on the remote server. Dreamweaver uses site definitions to keep track of your files, allowing updates to be made automatically when you use site tools to perform maintenance tasks including moving, adding, and deleting files and folders. Managing the workflow of a team can be done through a variety of tools that are geared toward coordinating teamwork and collaborative efforts. Through Dreamweaver, you can manage multiple Web sites, import and export site settings, and even perform quick transfers by creating connections to servers without having to go through the process of setting up a site.

NOTE *There may be an overlap between the planning, production, and maintenance phases; and the specifics of what is done in each phase may vary from site to site. For example, testing should occur regularly before and after the launch—basic testing by previewing pages in the browser was covered in Lesson 1; more in-depth testing is covered in Lesson 13.*

WHAT YOU WILL LEARN

In this lesson, you will:

- Learn about the purposes and uses of the Files panel

- Perform site-management functions within the Files panel

- Customize the Files panel

- Create a site map and use it to manage your files

- Understand the difference between a local site and a remote site

- Set up a connection to a remote site

- Copy files to and from a remote site

APPROXIMATE TIME

This lesson should take about one hour to complete.

LESSON FILES

Media Files:

Lesson_12_Sites/Images/...(all files)

Starting Files:

Lesson_12_Sites/...(all files)

USING THE FILES PANEL

The Files panel, which displays the file and folder structure of your site, can be viewed either as a docked panel or in an expanded mode as a larger window. You can use the Files panel, in either the collapsed or expanded views, to perform a wide variety of maintenance tasks such as adding, deleting, renaming, and moving files and folders. Doing all file maintenance within a Dreamweaver site ensures that the paths to links, images, and other elements are automatically updated if necessary—Dreamweaver tracks your changes and updates your files based on any changes that you make within a defined site. Conversely, if you make file or folder changes in the Finder (Macintosh), in My Computer (Windows), or in Windows Explorer File Manager (Windows), Dreamweaver doesn't recognize the changes and cannot keep the paths correct.

1) Open the Files panel group and select the Files tab.

Macintosh Users: As described in Lesson 1, in the Macintosh version of Dreamweaver the Files panel group will be renamed Assets after you expand the Files panel in step 2 of this exercise. Although you can change the name back by clicking the context menu in the upper right corner of the Files (or Assets) panel group and choosing Rename Panel Group, this solution will not permanently change the name— the name will change back to Assets the next time you expand the Files panel.

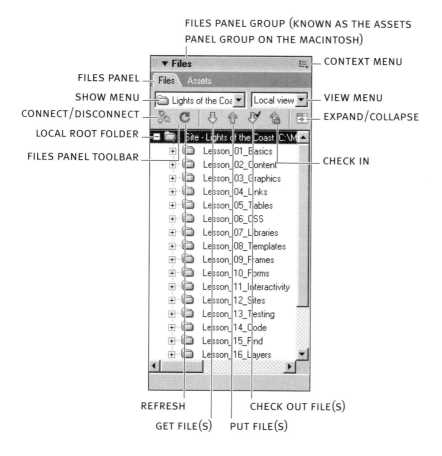

FILES PANEL GROUP (KNOWN AS THE ASSETS PANEL GROUP ON THE MACINTOSH)

CONTEXT MENU

FILES PANEL

SHOW MENU

VIEW MENU

CONNECT/DISCONNECT

EXPAND/COLLAPSE

LOCAL ROOT FOLDER

FILES PANEL TOOLBAR

CHECK IN

REFRESH

CHECK OUT FILE(S)

GET FILE(S)   PUT FILE(S)

389

By default, the Files panel is initially accessible through the collapsed view in which the panel is docked with the Assets panel in the Files panel group, and only the local files are visible. The Files panel contains a site toolbar as well as extensive context menu options with functions specifically for site maintenance. The Show menu allows you to switch to any site that you have defined or to your computer. The View menu at the top of the panel allows you to switch between the Local View, Remote View, Testing Server, and Map View options.

2) Verify that the site Lights of the Coast is selected in the Site menu and click the Expand button on the Files panel toolbar.

Macintosh Users: You should close the Start page, if it is open, by clicking the Close Window button in the upper left corner of the window. You'll be working with the Files panel for the majority of this lesson and the Start page may obscure the expanded Files panel at times.

Windows users do not need to close the Start page because the expanded Files panel expands to fill the space occupied by the Dreamweaver application.

After you click the Expand button, the Files panel opens into its own expanded window, as shown in the following figure. You'll be using the expanded Files panel throughout this lesson.

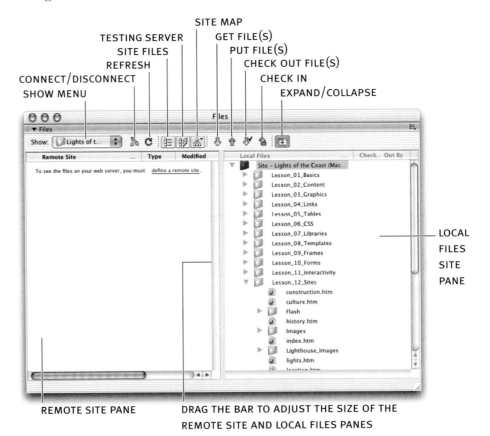

Your local files appear in the right pane of the Files panel (the Local Files pane). Any time the Files panel is expanded, you can collapse it back to the Files panel group (now called Assets on the Macintosh) by clicking the Expand/ Collapse button again. The local files consist of everything within the root folder, DWMX_Project, which you defined in Lesson 1. In this window, that root folder is listed by the name you gave to the site in Lesson 1: Lights of the Coast.

At this point, you see help text displayed in the left pane of the Files panel window (the remote pane). This help text lets you know that to see the files that exist on your Web server listed in this pane, you need to define a remote site. You can adjust the size of the panes by dragging the bar that separates them.

NOTE *You will define a remote site later in this lesson. Clicking "define a remote site" opens the Site Definition dialog box to the Remote Info category of the Advanced tab. When you connect to the remote site, the remote files appear in the left pane.*

The main Files panel tools are located on the toolbar:

- The Show menu lists all the sites that you have defined and gives you access to other files on your computer and quick connections to remote sites. To open a particular site, simply select the desired site from the menu. For this exercise, you should have Lights of the Coast selected.

- Connect/Disconnect connects to or disconnects from the remote site. Because you have not yet defined a remote site, clicking this button opens the Site Definition dialog box. By default, Dreamweaver disconnects a remote FTP site if it has been idle for more than 30 minutes.

TIP *If you need to change the time limit, you should choose Edit > Preferences (while the Files panel is in the collapsed view), select the Site category, and change the number listed in the Minutes Idle text field for FTP Connection.*

- Refresh does what you would expect: it refreshes the local and remote directory lists. Any changes that were made to the file lists will be shown after a refresh. If you made changes to your site outside of Dreamweaver, in the Finder (Macintosh) or Windows Explorer (Windows), you may need to refresh your Local Files in order to see the changes.

- The set of three buttons gives you four different view options: Site Files, Testing Server, Map Only, and Map and Files. The active view is highlighted, and the default is Site Files.

- Get File(s) copies the selected file(s) from the remote site to your local folder, overwriting any existing local copies. This option is not functional at this time because a remote site has not been defined.

- Put File(s) copies the selected file(s) from the local folder to the remote site, overwriting any existing remote copies. This option is not functional at this time because a remote site has not been defined.

- Check Out File(s) copies the selected file(s) from the remote server to your local folder, overwriting any existing copies. The file is then marked as "checked out" on the server. The Check In/Check Out feature is a great tool for collaborating on a Web site. If a file is checked out, Dreamweaver prevents anyone else from editing that file. This option is not functional at this time because a remote site has not been defined and the Check In/Check Out option has not yet been enabled for the Lights of the Coast project site.

- Check In copies the selected file(s) from your local folder to the remote server, overwriting any existing remote copies. The file that exists on the remote server is then available for editing by others. The copy of the file that exists in your local folder (usually on your computer) becomes read-only and is not editable unless you check it out. This option is not functional at this time because a remote site has not been defined and the Check In/Check Out option has not yet been enabled for the Lights of the Coast project site.

- The menu options File, Edit, View, and Site are located in the context menu in the upper right corner of the expanded Files panel (Macintosh) or across the upper left of the expanded Files panel (Windows). The context menu is also available on the upper right of the Files (Assets on Macintosh) panel group, providing access to the menus when the Files panel is collapsed for both Macintosh and Windows.

ACCESSING FILES OUTSIDE A DREAMWEAVER SITE ON YOUR COMPUTER

The Files panel can be used to access and work with files that may be located outside of your site's root folder. At times, you may need to access files such as source files for graphics or page layouts that are not usually included in root folders.

1) Select Computer (Macintosh) or Desktop (Windows) from the Show menu on the Files panel.

Arrows (Macintosh) or plus/minus icons (Windows) allow you to expand or collapse the various drives and folders that may be accessible through your computer.

VIEWING FILES THROUGH THE
COMPUTER ON THE MACINTOSH

VIEWING FILES THROUGH THE
DESKTOP ON WINDOWS

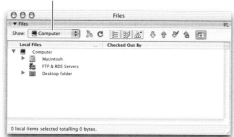

2) Click the arrow next to the Computer icon (Macintosh) or plus sign next to the Desktop icon (Windows) to browse your drives and files.

Any folder that is designated as the root folder for a Dreamweaver defined site will be green. All other folders will be blue (Macintosh) or yellow (Windows).

Dragging and dropping files between Site folders and your Computer or Desktop creates copies of the files in the new location. If you drag and drop files inside of a Site folder, those files are moved to the new location.

NOTE *If you need to drag and drop files to or from a Site folder and the Computer (Macintosh) or Desktop (Windows), you must do so within the Dreamweaver Files panel or in the Finder (Macintosh), in My Computer (Windows), or in Windows Explorer File Manager (Windows). You cannot drag items out of the Files panel into folders in the Finder (Macintosh), in My Computer (Windows), or in Windows Explorer File Manager (Windows), or vice-versa.*

You can open files in other programs by double-clicking them. Dreamweaver uses the program that it associates with the file you chose to open it.

NOTE *You can change the associated programs by choosing Edit > Preferences and selecting File Types/Editors from the category list. Select, add, or delete file extensions in the extensions list; use the editors list to define which programs to use when opening files with the selected extensions.*

ADDING NEW FOLDERS AND FILES TO A SITE

You can create new folders and pages in your site directly from the Files panel, which enables you to quickly set up a site's file and folder structure. You can immediately create pages that act as placeholders and add the content at a later time.

1) Select the Lights of the Coast site in the Show menu, make sure Local view is selected in the View menu on the Files panel, and open the Lesson_12_Sites folder by clicking the arrow (Macintosh) or plus icon (Windows). Right-click or Control-click (Macintosh single-button mouse) the Lesson_12_Sites folder.

TIP *You may want to collapse other lesson folders if any are open to give yourself more room in the Files panel and make it quicker to scroll through the contents of the site.*

A context menu opens, displaying a variety of options. The options available through this menu vary, depending upon what is selected. The context menu is a quick way to access many of Dreamweaver's functions and can help speed up your production.

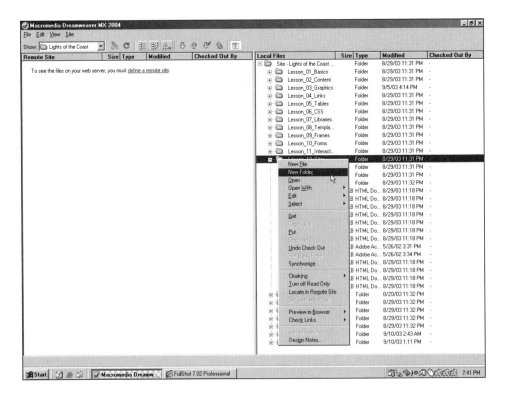

2) Choose New Folder from the context menu.

A new untitled folder is added within the Lesson_12_Sites folder. Because you just created the folder, the name is highlighted and displayed with a heavy line around the text field to indicate that you can name the folder.

3) Type *history* and press Return (Macintosh) or Enter (Windows) to name the new folder.

The new folder displays the name you have just given it.

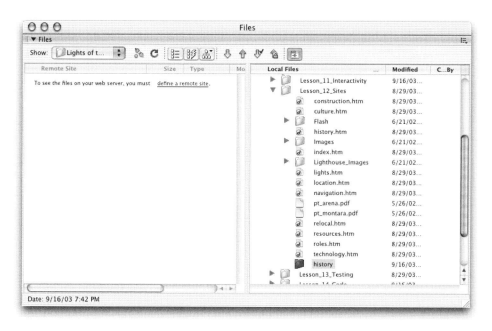

TIP *Clicking elsewhere in the Files panel causes the name to become deselected. If that happens and you still need to name the folder, you need to click the name of the folder, pause, and then click it again. Selecting the title allows you to edit it. Don't double-click; it will open the folder.*

4) Right-click or Control-click (Macintosh single-button mouse) the history folder you just created inside the Lesson_12_Sites folder in the Files panel.

You are clicking next to the folder in which you want a new folder or file to appear.

The context menu opens.

5) Choose New File from the context menu.

A new unnamed document is created in the history folder. The name field is highlighted, indicating that you need to type a name for this document.

TIP *You may need to expand the folder and click the new document filename to make it editable.*

6) Type *background.htm* and press Return (Macintosh) or Enter (Windows) to name the new file.

Don't forget to include the .htm extension for the filename. All documents that you create in a site must have the appropriate extension for their document type.

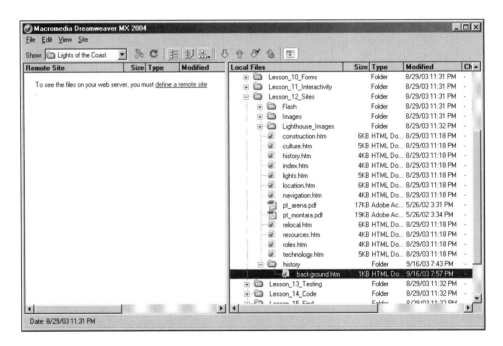

TIP *If your filenames are too long for the Local Files column, they appear to be cut off, which is just a result of the limited space for display in the Files panel. You can see the full filename by pausing the pointer over the file and waiting for the name to pop up, or by adjusting the positions of the columns. Click and drag the vertical lines separating the column titles to adjust them.*

CREATING A SITE MAP

A **site map** gives you a visual representation of a selected portion of your site. It does not display all the pages in your site; rather, it starts with a page that has been defined as the home page and shows you all pages that the home page links to. It continues down the hierarchy of links until it reaches a dead-end page—one with no links. If you have "orphaned" pages that cannot be reached through direct paths from the home page, they do not display in the site map.

1) In the Files panel, select the index.htm file that is located inside the Lesson_12_Sites folder. Click the context menu on the Files panel (Macintosh). Choose Site > Set as Home Page.

You will not see the result of this command until you create the site map. Now that you have defined the home page, you can create the site map. A home page must be created to give the site map a starting point.

TIP *Alternatively, you can right-click or Control-click (Macintosh single-button mouse) the file and choose Set As Home Page from the context menu in order designated the selected the file as the home page of the current site.*

The files used in this exercise have been created for you using the techniques you have learned so far in this book.

NOTE *Home pages are often named index followed by the appropriate extension. Index files and their extensions were covered in Lesson 4.*

2) Click the Site Map button on the toolbar and choose Map Only from the menu that appears.

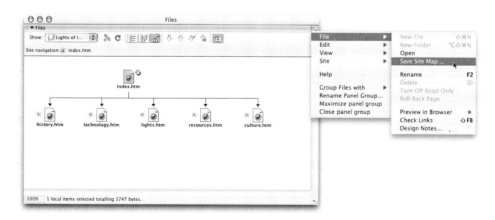

NOTE *Any time you resize the Files panel, the view will revert to Map and Files. You will have to reselect Map Only in that case.*

The site map is a graphical representation of your site; the home page is displayed at the top level of the site map. A link from one page to another is indicated by a line that is drawn from the file containing the link to every page that it links to. Arrowheads at the ends of this line point to each linked page. Pages that contain links are displayed with a plus or minus sign just to the left of the file. Clicking the plus sign displays a list of the linked pages, each with its own plus signs. Broken links (those that don't work) are displayed in red type. External links, such as email links and URLs, are blue and are indicated with a small globe.

TIP *You can adjust the Map view by choosing View > Layout from the context menu (Macintosh) or by choosing View > Layout (Windows). The Site Definition dialog box opens, displaying the Site Map Layout options. By default, Dreamweaver displays the site map horizontally. If the home page has many links, there might not be enough room on the site map to show all the pages. You can change the number of columns and the column width to make the site map fit a single page for easier viewing. You can also switch the layout to a vertical format, which is used in the collapsed view of the Files panel.*

3) Click the Context menu (Macintosh). Choose File > Save Site Map.

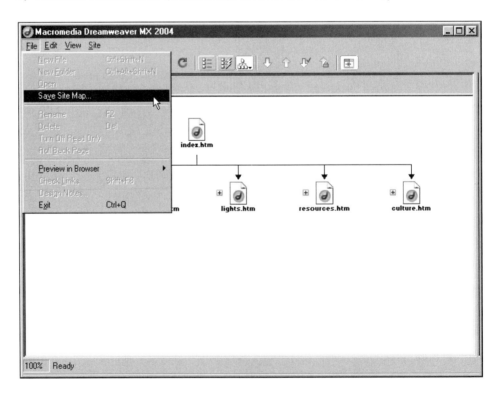

The Save Site Map dialog box opens so you can save the site map as a graphic. At times, you may need to share the site map with people outside Dreamweaver. The option to save the site map as a graphic makes it easier to show that site map to others. On Macintosh computers, you can choose whether to save the graphic in PICT or JPEG format. On Windows computers, you can choose to save the site-map graphic in either BMP or PNG format.

TIP *If you are using the Map and Files view, you cannot access the site map functions if the Local Files pane is active. If Save Site Map is grayed-out, go back to the Files panel and click the empty white space of the site-map pane to make sure it is active. Then go back and choose the Save Site Map command again.*

4) In the File name text box, type *lighthouse_site.jpg* **(Macintosh) or** *lighthouse_site.bmp* **(Windows). Save the file into the Lesson_12_Sites folder.**
The site map is saved as a graphic that can be printed or viewed in an image editor.

VIEWING A SUBSET OF THE ENTIRE SITE

As your site becomes larger and more complex, the site map might become too big to see in the Files panel. You can refine the view to show just a selected page and its links.

1) In the Files panel, select the history.htm page in the site map.
Viewing history.htm as a subset lets you focus on any pages that can be accessed with history.htm as the starting point, which can be helpful if you have a large site.

2) Click the context menu in the upper right corner of the Files panel (Macintosh). Choose View > View as Root.

TIP *Alternatively, you can set the View as Root option by right-clicking or Control-clicking (Macintosh single-button mouse) the file to access the context menu from which you can choose the View As Root option.*

The site map changes to show the history.htm page as the root (the top level) and its links (the second level). Below the site toolbar is a gray bar displaying the hierarchy of the site, beginning with the file you set as the home page and ending with the file that you chose to view as the root of the site. For this exercise, you should see index.htm > history.htm. You may see a red arrow just after the index.htm file on this bar if there is not enough room to display the full file path.

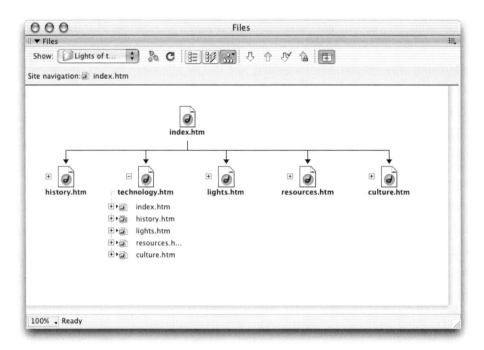

NOTE *This structural site navigation works the same way as breadcrumb navigation, which is used on many sites. **Breadcrumbs** show the visitor the hierarchical path from the main page of the site to the page they are on. They usually appear near the top of the page. Each part of the site listed in the breadcrumb path is normally linked to that section. For example, the breadcrumb navigation for the roles.htm page would be* Main > History > Roles. *In this example, the text "Main" would be linked to the index.htm page, and "History" would be linked to the history.htm page. "Roles" is not linked—it is at the end of the breadcrumbs, which indicates to the visitor that the page being viewed is the Roles page.*

3) Click the Dreamweaver file icon to the left of index.htm on the Site Navigation bar, the home page for the Lights of the Coast site.

The site root is returned to your home page.

WORKING WITH LINKS IN SITE MAP VIEW

You can control what files display in the site map by choosing to hide individual linked files. Files are hidden only in the Map view—they are still visible in the Local Files list. You can also make changes to the files by adding or deleting links.

1) Click the plus sign to the left of technology.htm in the site map.

The list of files that technology.htm links to are displayed.

2) Click the history.htm file icon in the list of links in technology.htm to select the link to the history.htm file.

The file is selected in the Map view.

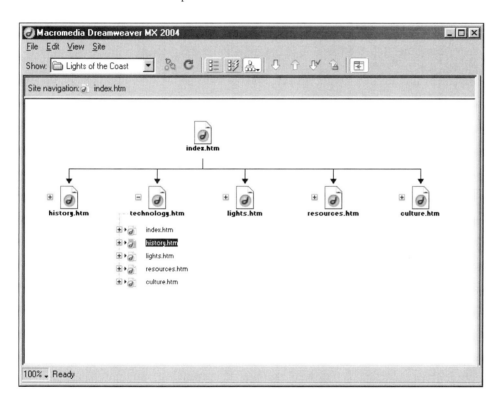

3) Click the context menu (Macintosh). Choose View > Show/Hide Link.

The history.htm file disappears from the list.

4) Click the context menu (Macintosh). Choose View > Show Files Marked As Hidden.

This option lets you temporarily view all files marked as hidden. The history.htm filename is italicized to indicate that it is a hidden link.

5) Select the italicized history.htm. Click the context menu (Macintosh). Choose View > Show/Hide Link.

The history file is no longer marked as hidden and appears as normal—not italicized—in the site map.

6) Select the Map and Files view from the Site Map menu and select the background.htm file from the file list. Click the context menu (Macintosh). Choose Site > Set as Home Page.

You created the background.htm file in the Lesson_12_Sites/history folder earlier in this lesson.

7) Select the background.htm file in the Map View pane, click the Point to File icon and drag the point to file icon to history.htm in the Lesson_12_Sites folder in the Local Files pane. Release the mouse button when the history.htm file becomes highlighted.

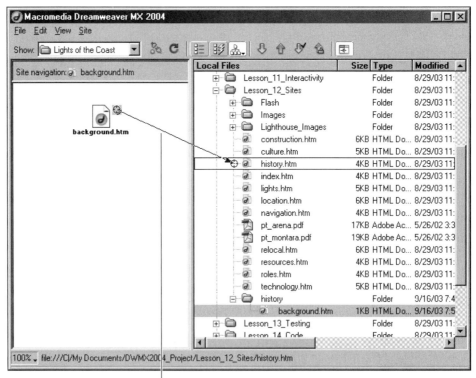

USING THE POINT TO FILE TOOL IN THE FILES PANEL

As you drag, the pointer becomes an arrow and a Point to File icon. A blue line is drawn as you drag from the background.htm file to the history.htm file. When you release the pointer, history.htm shows up in the Site Map view. The link to history.htm has been inserted into the background.htm document. If you open background.htm you will see the link.

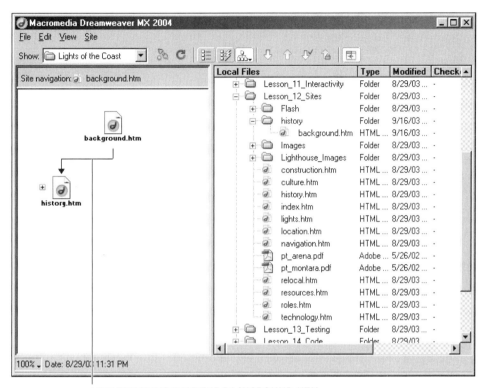

LINE INDICATES THAT THE BACKGROUND.HTM
FILE CONTAINS A LINK TO THE HISTORY.HTM FILE

TIP *You can also add, remove, and change links from the Site > Site Map View submenu.*

8) In the Local Files pane of the File panel, select the index.htm file in the Lesson_12_Sites folder. Click the context menu (Macintosh). Choose Site › Site Map View › Set as Home Page.

The index.htm file is now defined as the home page again.

MODIFYING PAGES FROM THE FILES PANEL

As you view pages in the site map and move the pointer over the pages, you'll see information about each page in the status area (the bottom bar) of the Files panel.

1) Switch to the Map Only view and place the pointer over the filename technology.htm.

The status bar at the bottom of the Files panel shows the title and size of the document as well as the date it was created. Make sure that you roll over the filename, not the file icon. The information doesn't appear in the status bar unless the pointer hovers over the name of the file. You can see by the information that appears on the status bar that the technology.htm document is untitled.

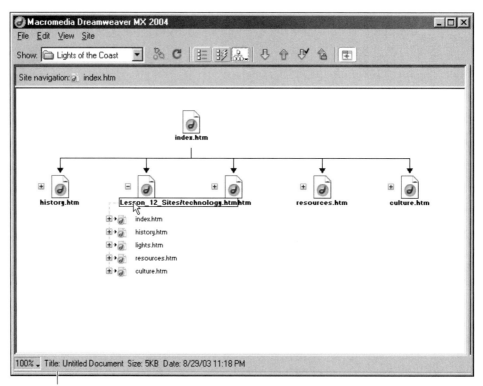

THE STATUS BAR CONTAINS INFORMATION ABOUT THE ACTIVE FILE

If you forgot to title a page or want to change a title, you can do so in the Files panel.

2) Click the context menu (Macintosh). Choose View > Show Page Titles to see page titles instead of filenames in the site map.

The list is regenerated to display the files by title.

3) Locate the page titled "Untitled Document" and click the title once to select it. Pause and then click the title again.

A rectangle is placed around the title to indicate that it can be edited. Don't double-click; you don't want to open the file. You just need to select the title so you can edit it.

4) Type *Lights of the Coast: Technology* **as the new title and press Return (Macintosh) or Enter (Windows).**

The site map shows the new title.

NOTE *You can open a page for editing from the Files panel by double-clicking the file in either the site-map pane or the Local Folder pane.*

5) Click the context menu (Macintosh). Choose View > Show Page Titles to switch the view from titles back to filenames.

The checkmark next to Show Page Titles will be removed and the files switch back to displaying their filenames.

6) Click the Site Files button on the Files panel toolbar to switch to the list of files and then select the relocal.htm file.

TIP *You may want to shrink the left pane (the remote view area) by dragging the bar between the two panes to the left. This procedure will give you more room to work with in the Local Files pane, making it easier to see the files.*

When you need to change the name of one of your files, you should change the name in the Files panel to preserve the link information maintained by Dreamweaver. If you change the filename outside Dreamweaver—for either an HTML file or a graphics file—Dreamweaver has no way to track your changes. If you make the change within the Files panel, Dreamweaver updates all pages that link to the file or contain the graphic.

7) With relocal.htm selected, and click the filename to make it editable. Change the filename to *relocation.htm* **and press Return (Macintosh) or Enter (Windows).**

The relocal.htm filename becomes highlighted at the first click, and a rectangle appears around the filename, indicating that it can be edited at the second click.

The Update Files dialog box opens, listing all the files affected by this name change.

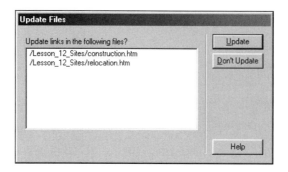

8) Click Update to update the files with the new filename.

The site map and files list now show the new filename.

NOTE *Dreamweaver makes the filename change within each file in the list that references the changed file. If a file in the list is open, Dreamweaver makes the change but does not save or close the file.*

9) In Files panel, open the Lighthouse_Images folder in Lesson_12_Sites.

Only one image, lightshine.jpg, is in the folder. If a file or folder is not in its proper place, you can move the file or folder to its correct location. Making this change in the Files panel ensures that all the link information remains correct and intact.

10) Drag the lightshine.jpg image's icon to the Images folder in the Lesson_12_Sites folder, which is located above the Lighthouse_Images folder.

Any files that use this image will be affected by the move; you need to fix the path to the image. The Update Files dialog box opens, asking whether affected files should be updated.

406

11) Click Update to keep the link to this graphic correct.

The graphic moves to the Images folder. Any references to it in the HTML files are still working. If you were to move the file outside of Dreamweaver, the paths would not update and this image would appear to be "broken." This means that when displayed in the document window or browser, a generic image icon would appear in its place, indicating that the file could not be found at the location specified in the HTML.

NOTE *Dreamweaver allows you to customize the Files panel by reordering, showing, hiding, or adding columns. To make changes to the columns in the Files panel, choose Site > Manage Sites to open the Site Definition dialog box and then select the File View Columns list. You can use the up or down arrow buttons to change the order of the columns. The Options Show check box controls which columns are displayed in the Files panel. You can also add or delete columns, and associate them with Design Notes. You will learn more about Design Notes later in this lesson. The rest of the book assumes that you are using the default arrangement of columns in the Files panel and have made no changes. You can use the scroll bar at the bottom of the Local Files pane to see all the columns.*

CONNECTING TO A REMOTE SITE

In Lesson 1, you created a local site—that is, a folder on your hard drive to store all the folders and files needed for your site. Throughout Lessons 2 through 11, you developed pages in the local site. When you create your own sites, however, you need to copy your local files to a remote site after you have completed the production phase of creating your site for visitors to see the Web pages. Typically, the remote site is on a server specified by your host, Web administrator, or client, but it can also be on a local network.

TIP *It is a good idea to transfer your site to a live server—ideally the one on which the site will actually reside—and test that site to be sure that everything works as expected. Because you are transferring the site to a different location, there is always the possibility that something may not work as it did in the previous location. It is best to determine whether any such problems exist and fix the situation before launching the site—making it available to the public or other intended audience. Testing is covered in Lesson 13.*

1) Choose Site › Manage Sites.

TIP *Windows users can also use the Site menu located on the expanded view of the Files panel.*

The Manage Sites dialog box opens.

2) Select the project site, Lights of the Coast, and click the Edit button. The Advanced Tab should be active by default; if not, click the Advanced Tab.

The Site Definition for Lights of the Coast dialog box opens.

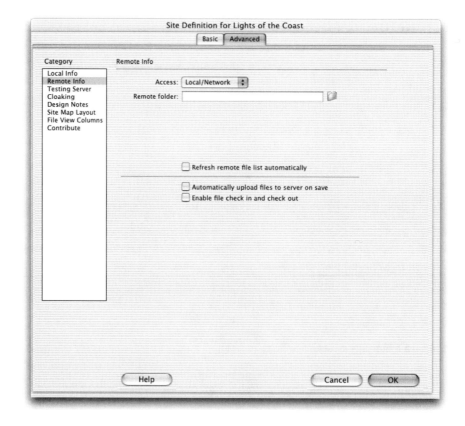

408

3) Choose Remote Info from the Category list on the left side of the dialog box.

The Remote Info section of the Define Sites dialog box is where you enter information to tell Dreamweaver which remote site to connect to and the attributes of that remote site.

The current selection is None, as you specified when the Lights of the Coast site was first set up in Lesson 1.

4) From the Access menu, choose Local/Network.

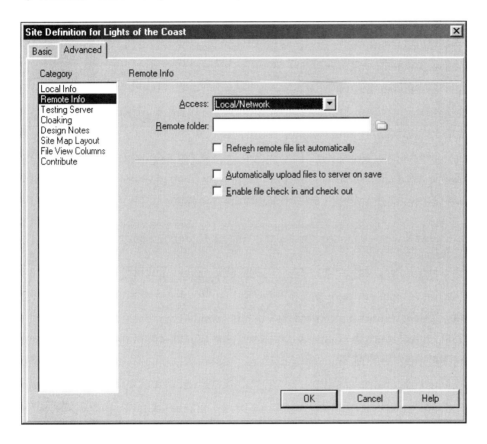

In the following steps, you will create a folder to simulate a remote FTP (File Transfer Protocol) site. This procedure enables you to experiment with the Get and Put functions, as well as additional site-management functions, without the need to have access to a remote server. In many cases, the Local/Network option is used when you have access to another computer on a network that will house the remote folder. In this instance, it will be on your own computer.

NOTE *FTP access is a common method of getting files from or putting files on a remote site. Because you may not have access to a remote FTP site while you complete this lesson, the following information is presented as reference material only. Consult your network administrator or host to set these options correctly. The following list of options is available by choosing FTP from the Access menu in the Remote Info portion of the Site Definition dialog box.*

- **FTP host:** *The host name of your Web server (such as macromedia.com).*

- **Host directory:** *The directory on the remote site in which documents visible to the public are stored (also known as the* **site root***).*

- **Login and Password:** *Your login name and password on the server. If you deselect the Save check box, you'll be prompted for a password each time you connect to the remote site.*

- **Use passive FTP:** *Used when you have a firewall between your computer and the server. This option is unchecked by default.*

- **Use firewall:** *Used if you are connecting to the remote server from behind a firewall. This option is unchecked by default. The Firewall settings are located in the Dreamweaver Preferences, which you can access quickly by clicking the Firewall Settings button.*

- **Use Secure FTP (SFTP):** *Used when you have an SFTP server, which uses encryption to create secure connections. This option is unchecked by default.*

5) Click the folder icon to the right of the Remote Folder text box to specify the remote folder.

The Choose remote folder for site Lights of the Coast dialog box opens.

6) Choose a location on your hard disk that is outside your root folder, DWMX_Project. Click the New Folder button, type LightsRemote **for the folder name, and select it.**

The remote folder must be outside your local root folder.

Macintosh users: Select the LightsRemote folder and click Choose.

Windows users: Select the LightsRemote folder and click Open; then click Select to use the LightsRemote folder as your remote folder.

This folder will act as a stand-in for a remote server.

7) Leave the three checkboxes for additional site options unchecked, click OK to save your site information, and click Done to close the Manage Sites dialog box.

You can always edit your site information later by choosing Site > Manage Sites to open the Manage Sites dialog box and then selecting the site you want change. For this exercise, you left the Refresh File List Automatically box checked and the Check In/Out options unchecked.

8) Click the Refresh button on the Files panel.

The Files panel now displays the empty remote folder in the Remote Site pane of the Files panel. The path from your hard disk to the folder is displayed next to the folder icon. You can roll over the folder name to see the full path.

In this situation, you defined a local folder, so the Connect icon button at the top of the Files panel is not active because you are already connected. The Connect button logs you on to a specified remote server when you are not automatically connected, such as when you use the FTP option.

UPLOADING FILES

After you have a remote site defined, you need to upload any existing files to that location. You can upload an entire site all at once—doing so replaces any and all files that already exist on the server—or you can upload only those files that are new or changed.

1) In the Local Files pane of the Files panel, select the top-level folder Site—Lights of the Coast and click the Put button on the Files panel toolbar.

TIP *The Put button is the blue arrow that points towards the top of the Files panel. The Get button is the green arrow that points towards the bottom of the Files panel.*

When Dreamweaver displays a message asking if you are sure that you want to put the entire site, click OK.

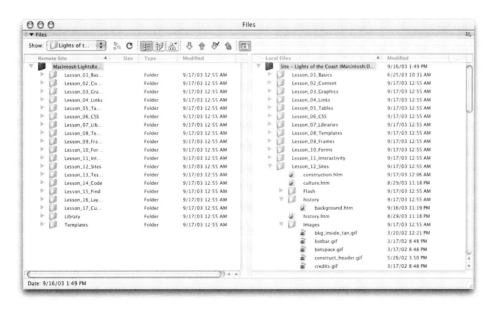

The entire site is copied to the remote folder. You can upload folders and their contents or single files by selecting the item(s) and clicking the Put button. Use Shift-click to select multiple contiguous items (those that are right next to each other), or use Command-click (Macintosh) or Ctrl-click (Windows) to select multiple noncontiguous items (those that are separated by other items).

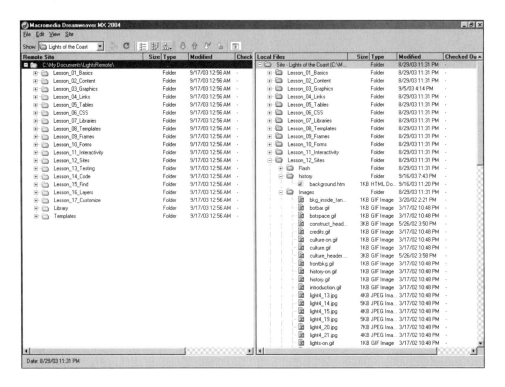

2) In the Local Files pane, find and double-click the lights.htm file in the Lesson_12_Sites folder to open it. Click the image of the lighthouse around which the text wraps, click the Reset Image to Original Size button on the Property inspector, and type *Point Montara* **in the Alt text field. Save and close the file.**

TIP *The Reset Image to Original Size button is just to the right of the image width and height text fields. You used this button in Lesson 3 when you worked with images.*

This file now has a newer modification date than the lights.htm that exists in the remote folder.

Windows Users: When you open the lights.htm file, the Files panel will automatically collapse back into the Site panel in the Files panel group. Open the Files panel to the expanded version by clicking the Expand button on the Files panel when you are done working with the lights.htm document.

Macintosh Users: If the Start page opens when you close the lights.htm files, you can close it so that it does not get in the way of the Files panel.

3) Select the top-level folder Site—Lights of the Coast. Click the context menu (Macintosh). Choose Edit > Select Newer Local.

Dreamweaver compares the modification dates of all local files with the corresponding file information in the remote site and selects only the newest local files. On the Macintosh, Dreamweaver will go through a process of opening and closing the folders in your site as it examines the modification dates. On both Macintosh and Windows, wait until Dreamweaver has completed this process—it may take several minutes to sort through all the files.

When Dreamweaver is done, the lights.htm file in the Lesson_12_Sites folder should be selected.

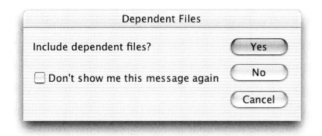

NOTE *There are two additional options that you can use when selecting site files that have been recently created or modified. Select Newer Remote will select the files on the remote site that are newer than the corresponding files in your local folder. Select Recently Modified will compare and select new or changed files in both locations.*

4) Click the Put File(s) button on the Files panel toolbar.

The Dependent Files dialog box may open. Your choices are Yes, No, and Cancel:

- Yes sends any images on the selected pages, along with the HTML pages themselves, to the server.

- No sends only the HTML pages. If you changed only the HTML page, and the images are already on the server, you have no reason to send the images again, so you should click No. If you have modified an image or added an image to the page, you should click Yes.

- Cancel prevents the transfer from occurring and closes the dialog box.

NOTE *The Dependent Files dialog box also contains the Don't Ask Me Again check box. If this option has been checked previously, you will not see the Dependent Files dialog box. If you don't see the Dependent Files dialog box, but want to have the choice, choose Dreamweaver > Preferences (Macintosh) or Edit > Preferences (Windows). Select the Site category and check the two Dependent Files boxes for the options to Prompt on Get/Check Out and Prompt on Put/Check In.*

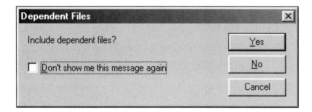

5) Click No if you see the Dependent Files dialog box.

You haven't modified any of the dependent files in this exercise, so it is not necessary to replace them in the LightsRemote remote folder.

NOTE *When you reset the size of the image in step 2, the image was reset to the actual dimensions of the image. Only the HTML size attributes in the lights.htm document were changed. The image source file itself, lightshine.jpg, did not change.*

The selected file is uploaded (copied) to the remote site.

When the upload has finished, you will see a list of files in the remote-site pane that mirrors the list in the Local Folder pane.

NOTE *Another way to upload or download only files that have been created or changed is to synchronize your local and remote sites. Synchronizing ensures that you maintain a parallel file and folder structure between the local folder and remote site—that the files in one location are duplicates of the corresponding files in the other location.*

To synchronize your site, Dreamweaver compares the modification dates of existing files on both the local or remote site. Synchronizing enables you to update only the files that have been created or changed. To synchronize a site, choose Site > Synchronize from context menu on the Files panel (Macintosh) or choose Site > Synchronize in the expanded Files panel (Windows). You can choose how to synchronize by selecting a direction from the Direction menu. Put newer files to remote uploads files only if Dreamweaver finds any files in your local folder that are newer than those on the remote site. Get newer files from remote downloads files only if Dreamweaver finds any files on the remote site that are newer than those contained in your local folder. Get and Put newer files transfers files in both directions. To start the process, click the Preview button. Dreamweaver scans the files located in both the local and remote folders and compares the modification dates. After Dreamweaver is done scanning the local and remote folders, it opens a list of the files that it determines are necessary to transfer. This dialog box lists the action (Put or Get), the filename, and the status. For each file, you have the option to uncheck the action box, which causes Dreamweaver to skip the transfer of that file. The number of files to be updated is listed at the bottom of this dialog box.

Use the synchronize function cautiously if you are using Check In/Out because synchronizing Gets and Puts files—even if you are using Check In/Out. It does not check files in or out; it merely replaces them. You'll learn more about Check In/Out in the later in this lesson. When the transfer is done, the list of site files informs you how many files were updated. You can click Save Log to create a log of the file transfer if you need to keep track of when files were transferred.

CLOAKING FILES AND FOLDERS

While you are developing your Web site, you may want to prevent certain files from being uploaded or downloaded. For example, if you have a large number of Flash and QuickTime movies embedded in your pages, you may not want to replace those Flash and QuickTime files in your local folder or on the remote server every time you get or put files—but you may want other dependent files to be automatically uploaded. You might also have source files for graphics in your local folder—source files are typically not uploaded to remote servers because they are not necessary for visitors to view the Web pages and they can take up a great deal of space.

You can **cloak** folders or file types to exclude them from site transfer functions including Synchronize, Get and Put, and Check In/Out. Cloaked folders and file types are also excluded from site wide operations such as select newer local and newer remote, checking links, search/replace, reports, and library/template updating. Cloaked folder and file types do not appear in the Assets or Files panels.

NOTE *Cloaking, like many Dreamweaver Site functions, is not recognized by other FTP programs. The data needed by Dreamweaver to maintain information on the folders you will cloak in this exercise will be contained in the Library folder. This folder takes up very little space and should not be deleted from either the local or remote locations.*

1) In the Local Files pane of the Files panel, select the Flash folder that is located in the Lesson_12_Sites folder.

This folder contains a Flash file, LenseDemoY.swf.

You cannot cloak individual files; you must cloak either entire folders or all files of a certain file type.

TIP *A good way to organize your site is to keep all your media files together in the same folder. For instance, if your site has a large number of PDF (Portable Document Format) files, creating a folder solely for PDF files will help keep your site organized and make it easier to maintain.*

2) Click the context menu and choose Site > Cloaking > Cloak (Macintosh) or right-click and choose Cloaking > Cloak (Windows).

NOTE *Cloaking should be turned on by default, but if the Cloak option is grayed-out, you should click the context menu and choose Site > Cloaking > Enable Cloaking (Macintosh) or choose Site > Cloaking > Enable Cloaking (Windows). Macintosh users can also Control-click to access the context menu and cloak settings.*

The Flash folder icon is now displayed with a diagonal red line across it in both the Local Files and Remote Site panes of the Files panel. The diagonal red line indicates that the file has been cloaked and will be excluded from site operations. If you open the folder, you will see that the LenseDemoY.swf file also has a diagonal red line through its file icon.

TIP *You can uncloak the folder to include it in site operations by right-clicking or Control-clicking (Macintosh single button mice) the folder and choosing Cloaking > Uncloak.*

3) Right-click or Control-click (Macintosh single button mice) the Flash folder and choose Cloaking > Settings.

The Advanced tab of Site Definition dialog box will open with the Cloaking category selected.

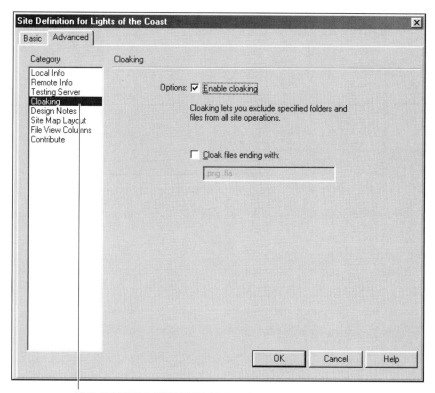

THE CLOAKING CATEGORY OF THE SITE DEFINITION DIALOG BOX

4) Check the Cloak files ending with check box. Click in the text field at the end of the list of default file extensions already in the text field. Press the spacebar and type *.pdf* **into the text field.**

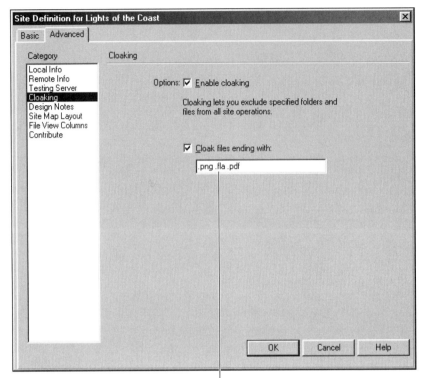

EXTENSIONS FOR CLOAKED FILES
ARE SEPARATED BY A SPACE

You can insert additional file extensions into the text field to cloak more than one kind of file. In order to cloak multiple file types, the extensions must be separated by a space, as demonstrated by the default .png .fla extensions that were originally listed in the text field. Fireworks source files use the .png extension; Flash source files use the .fla extension. You can also insert extensions for other common source files, such as the .psd Adobe Photoshop file extension.

5) Click OK to close the Site Definition dialog box and click OK when Dreamweaver tells you that the cache will be re-created. Click the Refresh button on the Files panel when the process is complete.

All PDF files contained in the Lights of the Coast project site are now cloaked. There are two PDF files in the Lesson_12_Sites folder that are now displayed with diagonal red lines through their file icons: pt_montara.pdf and pt_arena.pdf. All PDF files are now excluded from site operations.

6) Right-click or Control-click (Macintosh single button mice) and choose Cloaking › Enable Cloaking.

The checkmark is removed from the Enable Cloaking option to indicate that Cloaking is now disabled for the "Lights of the Coast" project site. This is an easy way to temporarily remove cloaking from your site's folders and files. If you choose Site > Cloaking > Enable Cloaking again, cloaking will become enabled again, and all previously cloaked folders and files will be recloaked. Cloaking is enabled on all sites by default. You must have cloaking enabled in order to cloak folders and file types.

CHECKING IN AND CHECKING OUT

If you are working on a team, the Check In/Out options can make collaborating on a Web site much easier. When this feature is activated, if a team member checks out a file for editing, Dreamweaver locks the checked-out file on the remote server so that no one else on the team is able to edit the file until it is checked back in. As long as the entire team is using Dreamweaver and all team members enable Check In/Out, use the Files panel and are connected to the remote server, the Check In/Out feature lets your group know when someone else is working on a specific file, preventing accidental overwriting of material or duplicate efforts.

1) Choose Site › Manage Sites.

The Manage Sites dialog box opens.

2) Choose the Lights of the Coast project site in the list and click the Edit button.

The Site Definition for Lights of the Coast dialog box opens.

3) Choose Remote Info in the Category list in the Advanced portion of the dialog box.

The remote-site information is displayed.

4) In the Check In/Out area, check the Enable file check in and check out box.

One additional check box and two additional text boxes appear. Files become checked out automatically as you open them if Check out files when opening is checked. You must be connected to the remote site for this feature to function properly; if you are not connected, Dreamweaver connects to the remote site automatically.

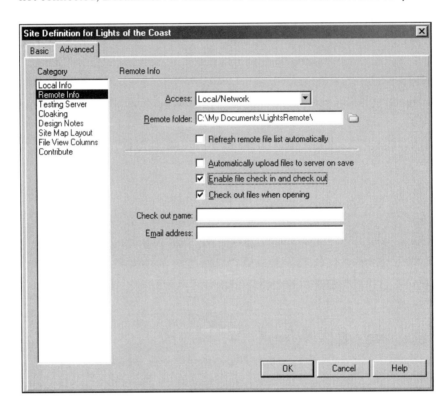

The additional text boxes are Check Out Name and Email Address.

5) Type a check-out name and your email address in the appropriate text fields. Click OK in the Site Definition dialog box and Done in the Manage Sites dialog box.

Your check out name is only for group reference; it can be your full name or simply a username. This name will display in the Checked out by column of the Files panel when you check out a file. Your email address is available to allow team members to contact you with questions.

6) In the Files list view of the Files panel, select the index.htm page in the Lesson_12_Sites Folder and click the Check In button at the top of the window. Do the same for the location.htm page. Click No if asked whether you want to include dependent files.

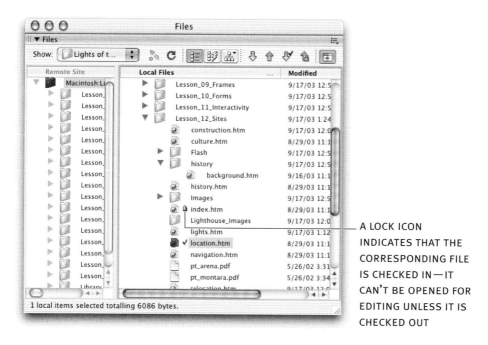

A LOCK ICON INDICATES THAT THE CORRESPONDING FILE IS CHECKED IN—IT CAN'T BE OPENED FOR EDITING UNLESS IT IS CHECKED OUT

Dreamweaver uploads the selected files to the remote folder. In the Local Folder pane of the Files panel, the files are marked with a small lock icon to let you know the files have been checked in and will need to be checked out for you to edit them locally.

When you work with a group of people and use the Check In/Out feature, it is important for everyone to use the Check In and Check Out File(s) icons instead of the Get File(s) and Put File(s) icons to upload and download files.

If you already have a local copy of your remote site, you must check in each local file for the Check In/Out feature to work properly. When you enable Check In/Out, keep in mind that your files are not automatically checked into the remote server. The check and lock icons indicate the status of a file. A check indicates that a file is checked out; a lock indicates that a file is checked in. If a file has neither a check nor a lock, it has no Check In/Out status. Such an unmarked file is available to open or edit. If you are working with team members and using Check In/Out, it is a good idea to check out and check in your entire site once you enable Check In/Out so that no unmarked files are opened and edited accidentally.

7) In the Files panel, select the location.htm page in the Lesson_12_Sites Folder. Click the Check Out File(s) button at the top of the panel. Click No if asked whether you want to include dependent files.

To ensure that you will be working with the most recent version, the file is downloaded to your local site. The file is marked in both the local and remote panes with a small green checkmark next to the file icon, indicating the file has been checked-out by you. The Checked out by columns in both the local and remote panes show your check out name in the form of a clickable link to your email address. Files checked out by other members of your team are displayed with a red checkmark, indicating that you cannot check those files out until they have been checked back in.

If you attempt to open a file that someone else has checked out, Dreamweaver informs you that the file is already checked out and gives you several options. You can cancel opening the file, open the file to view it, or override the checkout.

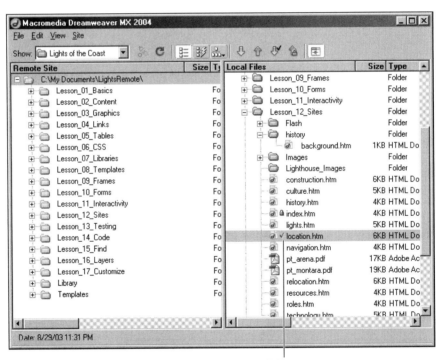

A CHECK ICON INDICATES THAT THE
CORRESPONDING FILE IS CHECKED OUT—IT CAN'T
BE OPENED FOR EDITING BY OTHER TEAM MEMBERS
UNLESS THE PERSON WHO HAS IT CHECKED OUT
CHECKS IT BACK INTO THE REMOTE SITE

For the Check In/Out feature to work properly, everyone on your team should be using Dreamweaver. Other FTP programs don't recognize the Check In/Out feature. Other programs will be able to overwrite files, negating the purpose of checking files in and out. When you use the Check In/Out feature, FTP programs can see the files that Dreamweaver creates: For each file that is checked out, an LCK file is created on the server, letting Dreamweaver know that the file is checked out. For this exercise, you may be able to see the locations.html.lck file in the Finder (Macintosh) or Windows Explorer (Windows). Don't delete these files! They are required for the functionality of the Check In/Out feature and take up very little space.

8) In the Files panel, select the location.htm page in the local panel. Click the Check In button at the top of the window. Click No if asked whether you want to include dependent files.

This file is now checked in and cannot be edited until it is checked out again. You can leave the Check In/Out feature enabled—it is necessary for an exercise later in this lesson.

TIP *If Check In/Out is disabled and you want to unlock files, you can click the context menu on the Files (or Assets) panel group and choose File > Turn Off Read Only. You can also access this option by right-clicking or Control-clicking (Macintosh single button mouse) the file and choosing Unlock.*

USING DESIGN NOTES

Design notes are useful for keeping track of information related to your files. These notes are for your information only; they are hidden text files that cannot be accessed or displayed in browsers by the users of your site. You can share information with your co-workers easily by uploading design notes to the remote server. These notes can be used with all files in your site.

1) Choose Site > Manage Sites. Select the Lights of the Coast site and click Edit. Select the File View Columns category and select the Notes item in the list of File View Columns. Check the Show box in the options section. Click OK to apply the changes to the Site and click Done on the Manage Sites dialog box.

The Notes column must be enabled for you to see the design note that you will create in the Files panel.

2) In the Files panel, select the construction.htm file. Click the context menu on the Files panel and choose File > Design Notes (Macintosh) or right-click the construction.htm file and choose Design Notes.

TIP *You can also attach a design note from the Files panel by double-clicking the Notes column for the selected file or by choosing the option from the context menu, which you can access by right-clicking or Control-clicking (Macintosh single button mouse) the file.*

The Design Notes dialog box appears. You can use the method used in this step to attach a design note to a file when it is selected in the Files panel or when the file is open in the document window. The Basic Info tab displays information about the file to which the note will be attached and the path of that file in the site. You can change the status of the file by making a choice from the Status menu.

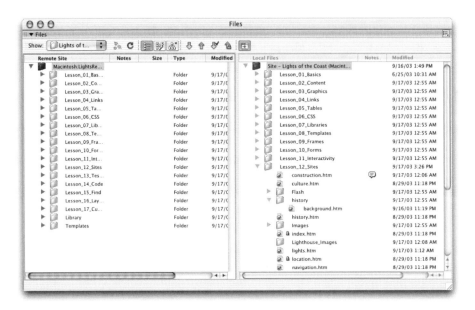

NOTE *The Design Notes category in the Site Definition dialog box allows you to turn design notes on or off. By default, both the Maintain Design Notes and the Upload Design Notes for sharing boxes are checked. Dreamweaver automatically uploads or downloads the design notes for any file you get, put, check in, or check out from the remote server when the Upload Design Notes for sharing check box is checked.*

3) Click the Date icon above the right corner of the Notes text box. Select revision1 from the Status menu and check the Show when file is opened box. Click OK.

The date is inserted into the first line of the Notes text box. Use this area to enter any important information about your files.

The Show when file is opened box at the bottom of this window allows you have this note displayed when the file is opened—a good way to be sure your team members take notice of your notes.

The Design Notes dialog box closes, and the note is attached to the construction.htm file with the information you added.

4) Click the Expand/Collapse button on the Files panel to expand the panel.

The Design Notes icon is displayed as a yellow text bubble in the Notes column, located to the right of the filename, indicating that a note is attached to the file.

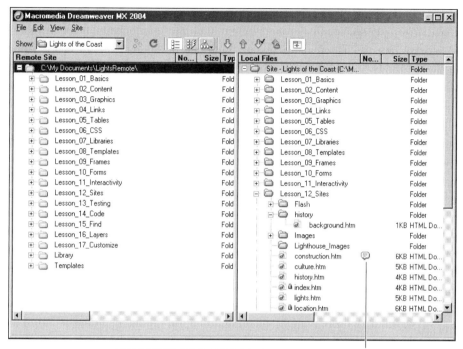

THE DESIGN NOTE ICON INDICATES THAT THERE IS
A NOTE ATTACHED TO THE CORRESPONDING FILE

TIP *To edit the note, double-click the Design Notes icon (the yellow bubble) to reopen the Design Notes dialog box.*

EXPORTING SITE DEFINITIONS

The Site Export function allows you to select a site from your list of sites and move it to another computer. This function is useful for many situations, including sharing sites with other team members or when you need to switch computers. Sites are saved as XML files, and all settings from the Site Definition dialog box are retained.

1) Choose Site › Manage Sites and select the Lights of the Coast site in the Manage Sites dialog box. Click the Export button.

TIP *To export the current site, you can click the context menu on the Files panel (Macintosh) and choose Site > Export.*

The Export Site dialog box opens, in which you can name the file and specify the location to save the exported site.

2) Save the Exported Site file in a location outside of your Lights of the Coast site root folder.

The site is saved with the .ste extension. Do not delete or change this extension.

Conversely, you can use the Site Import function to import a site into Dreamweaver. To do so, choose Site > Import; then use the Import Site dialog box to find and select the site. You will be prompted to select a Local Root Folder. You can only import sites that have been exported from Dreamweaver as XML files with the .ste extension. The Export and Import features transfer settings from the Site Definition only; files are not transferred along with the site settings. To keep or include files in the transfer, you need to transfer your root folder with all your files to the new location in addition to exporting the site. If you are using the Local/Network remote access option, you may need to update the path to the remote folder in the imported site.

ENABLING CONTRIBUTE COMPATIBILITY

Macromedia Contribute is a program that is used primarily by nontechnical users, such as content editors who may have little or no experience creating, editing, or managing Web sites. Contribute gives Web developers the ability to share the responsibility for editing and updating your site with a team while maintaining control over the design, style, code, and structure of the site. As the administrator of a Web site, you can set a variety of options to control the site, including setting user access to specific sections of the site on an individual basis and specifying style sheets (covered in Lesson 6) and templates (covered in Lesson 8) for content editors to use.

NOTE *A 30-day trial version of Contribute 2.0 is included on the CD-ROM that accompanies this book for both Macintosh and Windows. A trial version can also be downloaded from Macromedia's Web site.*

1) In the Manage Sites dialog box, select the Lights of the Coast project site in the list and click the Edit button.

The Site Definition for Lights of the Coast dialog box opens.

2) Click the Advanced tab if it is not already selected. Choose Contribute in the Category list and click the Enable Contribute compatibility box.

NOTE *If Design Notes and Check In/Out are not both enabled prior to enabling Contribute, a message appears to inform you that working with Contribute requires the Design Notes and Check In/Out features of Dreamweaver to be enabled. Click OK to enable both.*

426

Continuing to set up Dreamweaver to administer a Web site that uses Contribute requires access to the remote server on which the Web site is located, and the Contribute program must be installed on the same computer as Dreamweaver. Because you may not have access to a remote server while you complete this lesson, the following information concerning the use of Dreamweaver and Contribute is presented as reference material only:

* Site root URL: The full URL of the Web site that you are setting up to administer should be typed in this text field in the Contribute section of the Site Definition dialog box. (The Advanced tab of the Site Definition dialog box should be active.) After typing in the URL, click the Test button to verify that Dreamweaver can connect to the site you specified.

* Administration: The Administer Site in Contribute button opens Contribute and allows you to set the administrative settings, such as controlling access to the site. For this to function, the Macromedia Contribute program must be installed on your computer.

All other settings and options for administering a Contribute site are set in Contribute.

3) Select the Remote Info category and uncheck the Enable file check in and check out box. Click OK in the Site Definition dialog box and Done in the Manage Sites dialog box.

Because you are not creating the Lights of the Coast project site with a team, the Check In/Out feature is not necessary. The rest of this book assumes that you have Check In/Out disabled.

CREATING SERVER CONNECTIONS

You can set up quick connections to remote servers to transfer files without going through the process of defining a site. Using a Dreamweaver site, such as the one that you initially set up in Lesson 1 and have been working with throughout this lesson, gives you access to a great deal of site-management features. Server connections using FTP or RDS (Remote Development Services) do not provide access to the Dreamweaver site-management features that have been covered in this lesson.

1) Choose Computer (Macintosh) or Desktop (Windows) from the Show menu on the Files panel. Collapse Macintosh HD (Macintosh) or My Computer (Windows) if it is open. Right-click or Control-click (Macintosh single button mouse) the FTP & RDS Servers item in the Files panel list and select Add FTP Server.

The Configure Server dialog box opens.

TIP *You can also access the Configure Server dialog box by choosing Site > Manage Sites, clicking the New button, and choosing FTP & RDS Server from the menu that appears.*

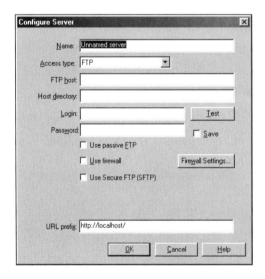

Many of the options available here are similar to those that are available in the Remote category of the Site Definition dialog box.

2) If you do not have access to an FTP server you can click the Cancel button.

Because you may not have access to a remote server while you complete this lesson, the following information is presented as reference material only:

• Description: A name or brief description of the server to which you are creating a connection.

- Access type: You can choose FTP or RDS. FTP is most common and the one that is described here. The RDS option should be selected only when you are connecting to a server that is running ColdFusion.

- FTP host: The host name of your Web server (such as macromedia.com).

- Host directory: The directory on the remote site in which documents visible to the public are stored (also known as the **site root**).

- Login: Your login name on the server.

- Password: Your password on the server. If you deselect the Save checkbox, you are prompted for a password when you connect to the remote site.

WHAT YOU HAVE LEARNED

In this lesson, you have:

- Performed site-management functions within the Files panel, including creating new files, renaming files, and moving files (pages 388–397)

- Created a site map, viewed it horizontally and vertically, used it to manage your files, and learned how to save the site map as an image (pages 397–399)

- Customized the Files panel and edited the columns (pages 399–401)

- Used the Update Files dialog box to ensure that your paths and links stay correct when you moved files (pages 402–406)

- Learned the difference between a local site and a remote site, how to use local/network and FTP to connect to servers, and how to define and edit both kinds of sites (pages 406–411)

- Set up a connection to a local/network folder as your remote site (pages 410–415)

- Copied files to and from a remote site using the Select Newer Local command to save time (pages 411–415)

- Enabled cloaking to prevent certain file types from being uploaded or downloaded (pages 415–419)

- Used the Check In/Out options for collaboration (pages 419–423)

- Attached a design note to a file, edited design notes, and learned to use them to share information with team members and keep track of file status and versions (pages 423–425)

- Learned how to export a Dreamweaver site and how to import the site definition to transfer site settings from one computer to another (pages 425–426)

- Learned how to administrate Macromedia's Contribute to work with a people who may not know Dreamweaver, such as content editors (pages 426–427)

- Learned how to create quick server connections to transfer files without setting up a Dreamweaver site (pages 428–429)

accessibility and testing

LESSON 13

Up to this point in the lessons, you have tested Web pages by previewing them in a browser, usually when you completed an exercise. As you built individual pages or sections, you had a chance to see how those pages looked and make modifications as needed. Before making a site available to the public or to your intended audience, however, you should go further and test your entire site. Take the extra time to be sure that you've worked out all the potential problems. If you have access to a testing server—a remote server on which you can test your site without making it publicly available—it's a good idea to load the site onto that server and access the pages from all computer types and from as many versions of browsers as you can find. Test the pages under real user conditions. If you think a majority of your users will be using a dial-up modem, make sure that you use a dial-up modem to test the speed at which the pages load. If you are the primary Web developer, have others test your pages.

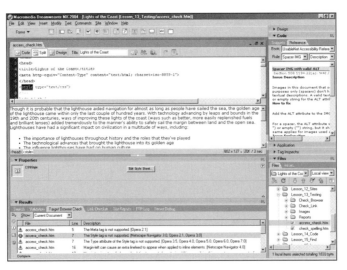

In this project, you will use Dreamweaver to test Web pages for accessibility. You will also test the links in your project site and use reports to determine how your site is functioning and what browsers, if any, may have problems accessing your site.

Watch how other people try to navigate your site and then consider the usability: Is the site intuitive and functional? Make sure to test every link and fix any broken ones. Remember that not all users think alike—try to prepare for the unexpected as you check the entire site. Analyze which possible paths a visitor might take. Make a list of potential tasks your viewers might perform (searching for and buying an item, looking for contact information, and so on), and go step-by-step through what those visitors will need to do to complete the task.

Ideally, you should not wait to begin the testing process until the Web site is finished. By starting the testing process early and incorporating it as a part of the production process, you can catch and solve problems quickly. If you wait until the end, after you've put hours or weeks of work into your site, it is possible that you might catch an error that will require a great deal of time to fix throughout the site. If you can discover such problems early on, you can address them and save yourself and your Web team a great deal of time.

On any site, large or small, the task of thorough testing can be daunting. You've worked hard on the content and the design, but if users get frustrated because of broken links, pages that don't work in their browsers, or pages that are large and very slow to load, you've lost them. In this lesson, you will learn how to use Dreamweaver in your testing process by running reports on your site to find out whether the pages are compatible with certain browsers. You'll also learn how to check links throughout the site and test for accessibility.

WHAT YOU WILL LEARN

In this lesson, you will:

- Test your site for browser compatibility
- Test the links in your site
- Create site reports
- Check for orphaned files
- Check spelling

APPROXIMATE TIME

This lesson should take about one half hour to complete.

LESSON FILES

Media Files:

Lesson_13_Testing/Images/…(all files)

Starting Files:

Lesson_13_Testing/…(all files)

GENERATING SECTION 508–COMPLIANT CODE

Section 508 is an amendment to the Rehabilitation Act of 1973, which requires Federal agencies to account for the needs of people with disabilities when developing, procuring, maintaining, or otherwise using electronic and information technology. The goal is to ensure that all users have an equal opportunity to access the content made available through technology such as the Internet. Section 508 defines the standards that are necessary for those who have disabilities to be provided with comparable information and services as those available to non-disabled users. Although Section 508 is not forced upon the private sector, it is important for all Web sites to adhere to the practice of creating compliant code wherever possible for many reasons. Disabilities ranging from poor or failing eyesight to color blindness or even total blindness affect a significant portion of the population—and therefore, your audience.

One solution is to create an alternative, text-only page for every page of content on your site. Although this solution provides appropriate and functional pages that can be specifically tailored to the needs of the disabled, it may not be feasible or even necessary for every site (particularly given issues of the kinds of content and services offered, the amount of space available, time and resources needed to create additional pages, and increased requirements for site maintenance). There are a number of solutions you can work into your pages without creating a duplicate site and with no degrading visual impact on your page designs. Dreamweaver provides you with an easy way to incorporate such solutions to create Section 508–compliant Web pages through the use of elements in the code such as alternative text, descriptions, and summaries. You already used a number of these features: You inserted an accessible image in Lesson 3; you inserted accessible tables in Lesson 5; and you created accessible forms in Lesson 10. You can also insert other objects with accessibility attributes.

TIP *To turn accessibility options on or off, choose Dreamweaver > Preferences (Macintosh) or Edit > Preferences (Windows) and select Accessibility from the list of categories.*

TESTING FOR ACCESSIBILITY

You can run reports on pages within your sites to determine how well they stack up in terms of compliance with accessibility standards.

1) Open access_check.htm from the Lesson_13_Testing folder. Choose Site › Reports.
The Reports dialog box opens.

2) Select Current Document from the Report on menu. Click to check the Accessibility box in the HTML Reports section. Leave all other options unchecked and click the Run button.

THE ACCESSIBILITY BOX IN
THE HTML REPORTS SECTION

A list of results displays in the Site Reports tab of the Results panel. Each item indicates the filename of the document in which it was found—which in this case is the current document, access_check.htm—along with the line number where the item can be found in the code and a brief description of the item.

CLICK TO COLLAPSE RESULTS PANEL

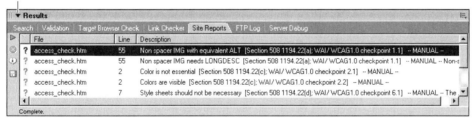

3) Select the third item in the list, which begins with "Color is not essential." Click the More Info icon on the left side of the Results window.

MORE INFO

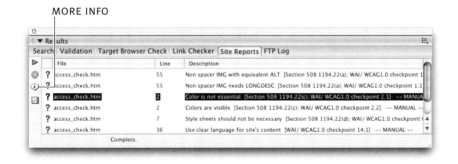

433

A more detailed description appears in the Reference panel, located in the Code panel group. This description gives you specifics about the particular accessibility rule in question, as well as suggestions of methods that can make your pages more accessible.

TIP *Color, brightness, and contrast are important elements to consider when building your Web site. Monitor displays often vary dramatically; typically, Windows screens tend to be considerably darker than Macintosh screens. You can test your pages by using different settings to calibrate your monitor. Using a variety of monitors to test your page is also helpful.*

Dreamweaver provides you with a number of books in the Reference panel through which you can learn more about the code used to create Web pages. The UsableNet Accessibility Reference provides you with a quick way to get a thorough explanation of the many standards created by Section 508.

TIP *As with all panels, you can resize the Reference panel. Enlarging it may help you to read the content. When the panel is reduced, it can be hard to read the information it contains.*

4) Verify that UsableNet Accessibility Reference is selected on the Book drop-down menu at the top of the Reference panel. From the Rule menu on the Reference panel, choose Spacer IMG with Valid ALT.

RULE MENU

The description of the selected accessibility standard appears in the Reference panel. Displayed in green just above the text description is the specific location of this accessibility standard in Section 508. The description gives you information about the necessity of using the proper alternative text for all spacer and decorative (non-essential) images used. You learned to specify the alternative attribute of images in Lesson 3; in the same lesson you used the <empty> option available in the Alt menu on the Property inspector for spacer images and other similar images that serve only a graphical, aesthetic purpose—that is, they do not convey vital information to the visitor.

5) Close (Macintosh) or collapse (Windows) the Results panel and the access_check.htm file.

The Reference panel will be particularly helpful for developing accessible Web sites after you start working directly in the code, as you will learn in Lesson 14.

CHECKING BROWSER COMPATIBILITY

Many of the elements that you can add to your Web pages work only in the later versions of browsers. CSS and layers, for example, are supported only in 4.0 or later browsers. Before making a site available to the public, you should test your pages so you have a chance to fix any errors and be sure your audience can view the pages as you intend them to be seen. To develop an accessible site, you can identify target browsers and design your pages with those browsers in mind. If you know or suspect that a significant number of your users are still using Netscape Navigator 3.0, for example, you want to test your pages in that browser. If your pages are geared toward people who may be using hand-held devices, readers, or ways other than standard browsers to access your pages, you should test your site with those devices and software applications.

In this exercise, you will use Dreamweaver to test the HTML in your pages against a browser profile and determine whether or not that browser supports the code in your page. You can run a browser check on a saved file, a folder, or the entire site. Dreamweaver only reports the errors—it does not make any changes to your files. To make your site compatible, you need to take into account the errors reported by Dreamweaver and modify the pages in your site accordingly until you come to an acceptable solution. What is acceptable may vary from site to site and depends on your intended audience.

1) Open the check_browser.htm file from the Lesson_13_Testing/Check_Browser folder.

In the following steps, you will run a target browser check on this file.

2) Click the Check Target Browser menu on the Document toolbar and choose Show All Errors.

TIP *You can also choose File > Check Page > Check Target Browsers.*

CHECK TARGET BROWSER

Whenever you open a document, Dreamweaver automatically scans the page, checking for browser errors. The Check Target Browser icon on the Document toolbar changes depending on whether any errors have been detected: If there are no errors but possibly warnings and informational messages), it displays a green checkmark. If errors are found, it displays a yellow warning icon.

The Target Browser Check tab of the Results panel opens.

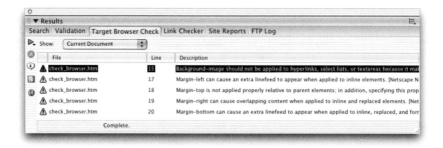

In the Results panel, errors are indicated by red octagons with exclamation marks in white. Warnings are represented by yellow triangles with exclamation marks in black. Errors are signals that there is something wrong with the code that will cause browser

436

errors or other serious viewing problems. Warnings also signal potential display problems, although they are of a less serious nature and generally do not impact the display or functionality of a page as much as an error might. You may also see informational messages appear in the Results panel—these generally alert you to code that while it may not be supported in a particular browser, it is simply ignored.

In this case, there are no errors found in the check_browser.htm document, but there are five warnings.

3) Choose Settings from the Check Target Browser menu on the Document toolbar and choose 3.0 from the Netscape Navigator version menu to check that browser against the page; then click OK.

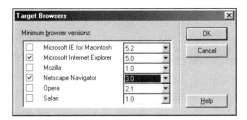

The Check Target Browser icon on the document toolbar now displays the yellow triangle, warning you that portions of the document are incompatible with one of the browsers Dreamweaver is set to check the page against.

The Results panel refreshes and displays the error(s) associated with the document.

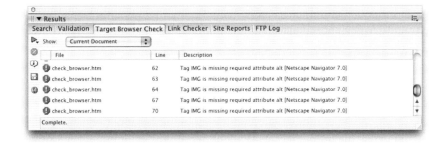

TIP *If the Results panel does not refresh, close it and choose Show All Errors from the Check Target Browser menu on the document toolbar.*

4) Double-click the Style tag error that is displayed at the top of the Results panel.

TIP *You may have to scroll up in the Results panel to find the Style tag error, which is the first error.*

When you double-click an error, Dreamweaver lets you know exactly where that error occurs. The document window switches to Split view, and the <style> tag is highlighted in the code. The problematic code is also underlined with red squiggly lines (it may be hard to see the color when the code is selected). Only errors are indicated in the code by these red lines—warnings and informational messages appear only in reports and the results panel. This option can be extremely helpful when you are trying to correct errors in your documents.

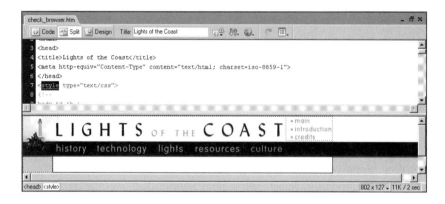

In this case, you do not need to make any modifications because the 3.0 version of Netscape simply ignores this tag. This item is considered an error and not a warning because even though the tag will be ignored, the lack of support can potentially cause display problems, or unexpected results. When developing your Web pages, it is best to test your pages to be sure that any code or elements that are not supported in certain browsers degrade or fail gracefully. When a behavior "fails gracefully" it will not produce any errors or warning in the browser (although you may still see errors and warnings in Dreamweaver); the browsers will simply ignore those elements that they do not support. If an error does appear in the browser, you may want to modify your page accordingly, to develop an alternative that does not produce a visible error.

5) Choose Settings from the Check Target Browser menu on the Document toolbar and check the Opera box to include the Opera browser in the Browser check. Click OK.
The Results panel now displays several additional errors that can be found in various versions of Opera, a popular alternative browser.

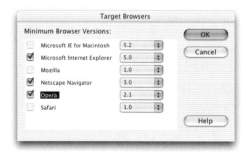

NOTE *Dreamweaver uses browser profiles to check your document for errors. Information on supported tags, attributes, and elements—as well as warnings, error messages, and tag substitute suggestions—can be included in browser profiles. You can create or add profiles for browsers that are not included in this list (such as WebTV and mobile phone browsers) by using a browser profile that has already been developed or by creating one yourself. You can find additional browser profiles on the Dreamweaver Exchange Web site, which is covered in Lesson 17.*

6) Click the Browse Report icon on the left side of the Results dialog box. Review the information presented in the browser; then switch back to Dreamweaver.

BROWSE REPORT

A detailed report is now displayed in a browser window. A list of target browsers indicates the number of errors and warnings that are found for each browser version in the list.

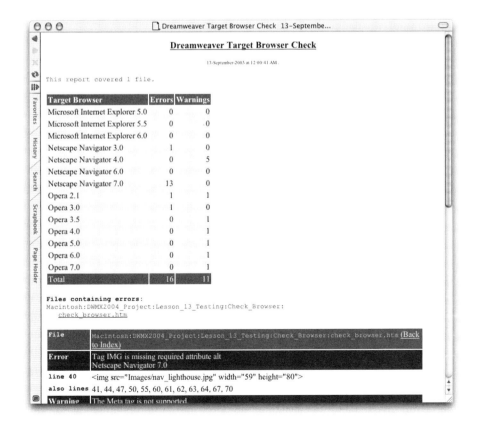

Target Browser	Errors	Warnings
Microsoft Internet Explorer 5.0	0	0
Microsoft Internet Explorer 5.5	0	0
Microsoft Internet Explorer 6.0	0	0
Netscape Navigator 3.0	1	0
Netscape Navigator 4.0	0	5
Netscape Navigator 6.0	0	0
Netscape Navigator 7.0	13	0
Opera 2.1	1	1
Opera 3.0	1	0
Opera 3.5	0	1
Opera 4.0	0	1
Opera 5.0	0	1
Opera 6.0	0	1
Opera 7.0	0	1
Total	16	11

The Check Target Browser feature runs when you open a document and when you manually run the test by choosing Show All Errors from the Check Target Browser menu. The icon on the document toolbar is not continuously updated as you work.

7) Use the Files panel to select the Check_Browser folder in Lesson_13_Testing. Click the Check Target Browser menu, which is indicated by the green arrow in the upper left corner of the Target Browser Check tab. Choose Check Target Browsers for Selected Files/Folders in Site from the Check Target Browsers menu.
On the Macintosh, the Check Target Browser menu/button will appear to be highlighted after you select the Check Target Browsers for Selected Files/Folders in Site option—you will need to click the button to run the check. On Windows, the check is automatically run after you make your Selection—you do not need to click it again.

TIP *You do not have to make a selection from the Show menu on the Results panel— Dreamweaver automatically switches to Site Report when you choose Check Target Browsers for Selected Files/Folders in Site.*

CHECK TARGET BROWSER MENU

▼ Results			☰
Search	Validation	Target Browser Check	Link Checker	Site Reports	FTP Log	Server Debug
⊳ Show:	Current Document ▼		
	File	Line	Description
ⓘ	check_browser.htm	7	The Style tag is not supported. [Netscape Navigator 3.0, Opera 2.1, Opera 3.0]
⚠	check_browser.htm	7	The Type attribute of the Style tag is not supported. [Opera 3.5, Opera 4.0, Opera 5.0, Opera 6.0, Opera 7.0]
⚠	check_browser.htm	15	Background-image should not be applied to hyperlinks, select lists, or textareas because it makes them unusable. I...
⚠	check_browser.htm	17	Margin-left can cause an extra linefeed to appear when applied to inline elements. [Netscape Navigator 4.0]
Complete.			

The test runs and a report displays in the Target Browser Check Tab of the Results dialog box.

There are differences in the way your site displays in every browser version. You may have to make trade-offs in the way the pages appear. Certain JavaScript routines, for example, produce error messages in browsers that do not support them; other JavaScript routines simply do not work, and the visitor may never know it. To reach the widest audience possible, you want to create a Web site that is error-free for older browsers. It is far better for visitors to miss certain features than to have error messages appear. If your audience uses a wide variety of browsers, you may want to make sure that the navigation of your pages does not rely on features that may not be supported in older browsers, (or provide alternative pages for those who are either not using the latest versions, or who may be using drastically different Internet applications).

8) Choose Settings from the Check Target Browser menu on the Document toolbar and choose 4.0 from the Netscape Navigator version menu and uncheck the Opera box.

TIP *You can also select Settings from the Check Target Browser menu on the Results panel.*

The Check Target Browser settings are now returned to the original Dreamweaver default settings. When deciding which browsers to target, consider the latest browser trends and your target audience. After your site is available to the public, you can continue to assess what your target browsers are by using Web site statistics and programs that gather and evaluate that information to find out what browsers your visitors are using the most. You may need to talk with your Web host, service provider, or system administrator for more information.

Many Web designers test their pages in multiple versions of Netscape, Explorer, and other browsers. It is a good idea to have multiple versions of browsers on your computer for this reason.

You can close any open files.

CHECKING LINKS IN YOUR SITE

It is not uncommon for a Web designer to add, delete, or change the filenames of pages in a site during the development process. It can be easy to overlook pages that link to deleted or renamed files and that have not been updated. It can be very frustrating for visitors to receive the "404: File Not Found" error message, indicating that a page is missing when they click a link.

In this exercise, you will use the Check Link feature to find those missing links. Dreamweaver can only verify links to files within the site. External links are listed, but it is up to you to test those links and make sure that the external links are valid URLs.

1) Open links.htm from the Check_Link folder in the Lesson_13_Testing folder. Choose File > Check Page > Check Links.

The Link Checker tab of the Results dialog box opens. Broken Links should be selected by default when you run Check Links; any broken links are displayed in the Broken Links column. If Broken Links is not selected, choose it from the Show menu.

In this exercise, only one broken link is displayed in the list.

SHOW MENU

TIP *You can also use the keyboard shortcut Shift+F8 to open the Link Checker report window.*

2) Click the name of the file to which the broken link points: none.html.

The filename highlights, and a folder icon appears to the right of the broken link.

3) Replace none.html by typing *culture.htm* **in its place; then press Return (Macintosh) or Enter (Windows).**

You can also click the folder icon and browse to the correct file to link to.

If there were any other broken references to the same file, a dialog box would open, asking if you want to fix the other references as well. Clicking Yes will fix all the references to the file.

NOTE *You can also check files or folders by selecting them in the Files panel and clicking the Files panel group context menu, and choosing File > Check Links. On the Macintosh, the Files panel group may be called the Assets panel group, due to a bug explained in Lessons 1 and 12. If you want to view the document or fix the links by using the Property inspector, double-click the filename in the Link Checker window to open the file. You used the context menu with the Files panel in Lesson 12.*

You can save and close this file and leave the Results panel open.

CHECKING FOR ORPHANED FILES

In the process of creating a Web site, you build new files as well as revise and replace old ones. Throughout the development phase, you may develop multiple versions of certain files or end up disregarding other files entirely. An orphaned file is one that is included with the site files, but is not used on your site. These files may be HTML files that have no links pointing to them, or images that haven't been used on any pages.

1) In the Files panel, select the local root folder for your project Web site.

To run an Orphaned files report, you must first run a link check on the entire site.

2) Click the Link Checker tab of the Results dialog box and verify that Broken Links is selected in the Show drop-down menu. Click the Check Links icon (the green arrow) and choose Check Links For Entire Site from the Check Links menu.

Macintosh users will need to click the now highlighted Check Links menu/button to start the link checking process. The process will start on Windows immediately after the Check Links for Entire Site option is selected.

The Results panel status bar indicates that Dreamweaver is checking the site. When the process is done, a large list appears in the dialog box. The Results panel status bar displays a summary of the report.

CHECK LINKS

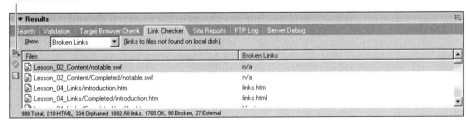

3) From the Show menu, choose Orphaned Files.

A list of orphaned files appears in the dialog box.

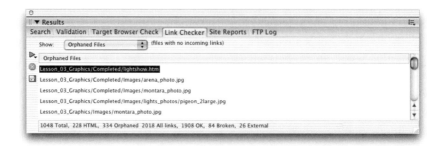

4) Close (Macintosh) or Collapse (Windows) the Results panel.

Deleting orphaned files can reduce the amount of disk space used by your site. It is particularly helpful to perform regular maintenance on large sites. Identifying and removing all orphaned files can have a great impact on the size of your site.

When deleting orphaned files, be sure to thoroughly review the list of files. There may be necessary files that are needed on your site that are not linked to or used in any other file.

For this exercise, do not delete any of the orphaned files listed. The files in the "Lights of the Coast" project site are needed for completion of this book's lessons, and some may appear to be orphaned files.

GENERATING REPORTS FOR A SITE

While testing your site, you can compile and generate reports on several HTML attributes by using the Reports command, which lets you check several options, including searching for untitled documents and redundant nested tags. You can run reports on a single document, a folder, or the entire site to help you troubleshoot and find potential problems before publishing your site.

1) Select the Reports folder in the Lesson_13_Testing folder in the Files panel. Click the Files panel group context menu and choose Site > Reports.

NOTE *On the Macintosh, the Files panel group may be called the Assets panel group, as explained in Lessons 1 and 12.*

The Reports dialog box opens.

2) Choose Selected Files In Site from the Report on menu. Leave all the options in the Workflow area unchecked. Check all the options in the HTML Reports area except for Accessibility.

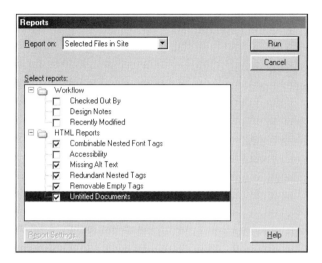

The Workflow options are most useful when you are collaborating with a Web team and need to quickly see who has checked files out and what design notes have been created. The Check In/Out and Design Notes features were covered in Lesson 12.

The HTML Reports options check for combinable nested font tags, accessibility, missing alt text, redundant nested tags, removable empty tags, and untitled documents.

You can choose to run reports on the current document, an entire local site, selected files in a site, and a specific folder.

3) Click Run to create the report.

A list of results displays in the Results panel. In this case, Dreamweaver alerts you that the relocation.htm document has not been given a title.

4) Click Save Report on the lower left corner of the Results panel and save the report in the Lesson_13_Testing folder.

All reports are saved as XML files with the .xml file extension.

The Reports command lists problems in your pages, but does not fix them.

TIP *After running the reports, you can use Clean Up HTML on any open documents by choosing Commands > Clean Up HTML. This command fixes many, but not all, of the problems found in the site report. A dialog box appears with a number of items you can choose to have Dreamweaver remove: empty tags, redundant nested tags, non-Dreamweaver HTML comments, Dreamweaver HTML comments, and specific tags. You can also choose to combine nested <font> tags when possible (if <font> tags are used in your pages) and to show the log upon completion. The log gives you a detailed list of the changes that were made to the document. More information about this feature will be given in Lesson 14 when you work with the code.*

CHECKING SPELLING

Correct spelling is an important aspect of the appearance of your Web site. Dreamweaver can check the spelling of text in your Web pages, much like a word processor such as Microsoft Word.

1) Open the check_spelling.htm file in the Lesson_13_Testing folder. Choose Text › Check Spelling.

The Check Spelling dialog box opens with the word "onlly" selected. A list of suggested words with similar spellings appears. Select "only" from the list and click the Change button.

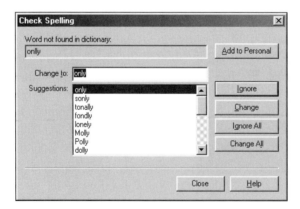

You can save and close the check_spelling.htm document and close the Results panel by clicking the Results panel context menu and choosing Close panel group.

WHAT YOU HAVE LEARNED

In this lesson, you have:

- Discovered the requirements for creating accessible Web pages and how Dreamweaver can help (pages 432–435)

- Used browser profiles to test individual pages, folders, or an entire site for browser compatibility and find out whether there are any errors or unsupported tags (pages 435–441)

- Tested the links in your pages to quickly find any broken links within your site (pages 441–442)

- Checked for and viewed a list of orphaned files (pages 443–444)

- Created site reports to find common problems in your site such as redundant nested tags and untitled documents (pages 444–446)

- Checked and fixed the spelling in a document (page 446)

editing
the code

You can gain more control over many of the elements on your Web pages after you become familiar with the code used to create those pages and how to edit that code or even write it from scratch (otherwise known as hand coding). Dreamweaver does a great deal of work for you, saving you time by creating the code in the background while you visually design your pages. However, Dreamweaver is a great deal more than just a visual editor. It provides an extensive array of tools and resources for hand coding and code editing. These features enable advanced programmers to make precise modifications, troubleshoot their documents, and make use of the most recent progress in code development—even if those advances go beyond what is available in Dreamweaver. The ability to introduce items that Dreamweaver may not recognize and the level of control that you have over the code makes for a

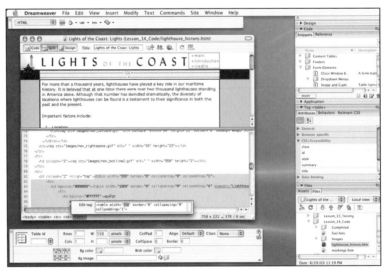

In this lesson you will work directly with the code, using features such as Snippets and the Quick Tag Editor to speed up the process.

very flexible program that you can use while staying up-to-date in the rapidly changing world of Web development. Even as a beginner, you can make use of these code features and use Dreamweaver's code tools and resources to learn about the code. You can use Dreamweaver to work with a variety of different code languages including JavaScript, ColdFusion, ASP, JSP, XML, and more. In this lesson, you will work with HTML (Hypertext Markup Language).

In this lesson, you will learn to edit the code and make use of many of the tools that will enable you to create code by hand. This lesson is intended to give you a basic introduction to the extensive code-editing features available in Dreamweaver—a thorough and advanced exploration of these tools is outside the scope of this book.

To see examples of the finished pages for this chapter, open lighthouse_history.htm, fuel.htm, and markings.htm from the Lesson_14_Code/Completed folder.

WHAT YOU WILL LEARN

In this lesson, you will:

- Learn to switch document views
- Use the Code view to edit HTML
- Create meta tags and HTML comments
- Use the Tag Selector
- Use the Quick Tag Editor
- Use snippets
- Clean up HTML
- Clean up Word HTML

APPROXIMATE TIME

This lesson should take approximately one hour to complete.

LESSON FILES

Media Files:

Lesson_14_Code/Images/…(all files)

Starting Files:

Lesson_14_Code/lighthouse_history.htm
Lesson_14_Code/markings.htm
Lesson_14_Code/fuel.htm

Completed Project:

Lesson_14_Code/Completed/lighthouse_history.htm
Lesson_14_Code/Completed/markings.htm
Lesson_14_Code/Completed/fuel.htm

449

SWITCHING DOCUMENT VIEWS

As you develop your pages, you may need to view the source code generated by Dreamweaver. Perhaps a stray line break or other unseen character is ruining the effect you are trying to achieve, but you can't locate it in the document window. By looking at the HTML source code, however, you can find and remove the line break easily.

Dreamweaver gives you three options for viewing your documents: Design view, which shows all the objects (text, images, tables, and so on) that you have added to your page; Code view, which shows only the HTML source code; and Split view, a combination of both Code and Design views. In the following exercise, you'll look at each of these views.

1) Open the lighthouse_history.htm document from the Lesson_14_Code folder.

The document toolbar is displayed at the top of the document window on the Macintosh and above the document window as its own panel in Windows.

SHOW CODE VIEW
SHOW CODE AND DESIGN VIEWS
SHOW DESIGN VIEW
THE DOCUMENT TOOLBAR
REFRESH DESIGN VIEW
VIEW OPTIONS

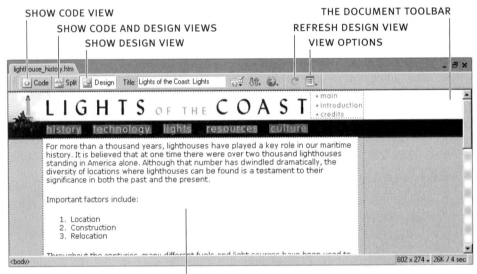

THE DOCUMENT WINDOW IN DESIGN VIEW

TIP *If the document toolbar is not visible, choose View > Toolbars > Document.*

2) Click the Code button in the toolbar.

TIP *You can also choose View > Code to switch to Code view.*

In Code view, you don't see the visual elements of the Web page as they would appear in a browser window. Instead, you see the HTML code in a text editor. The document toolbar contains the following code-related controls:

- Refresh Design View: This feature updates the Design view (the visual representation of your page) to reflect any changes you make in Code view while using Split view.

- View Options: This menu provides options that adjust the display of Code view. You can add line numbers for each line of code, enable wrapping to eliminate horizontal scrolling and make the code easier to view, and so on. You can customize any of these options by choosing Dreamweaver > Preferences (Macintosh) or Edit > Preferences (Windows) and selecting the Code Format category.

THE DOCUMENT WINDOW IN CODE VIEW

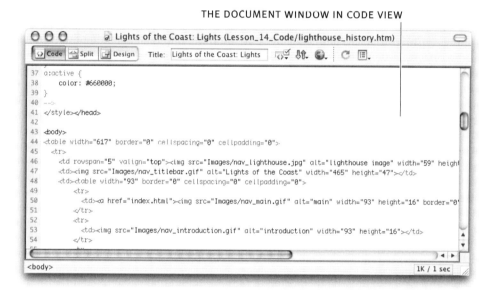

NOTE *You can also open the Code inspector, which gives you the same options and controls as Code view. The difference is that the inspector opens in a separate window. Some developers use two monitors and place the Code inspector on one screen to simultaneously view the code as they work in the Design view of the document window. This serves a function similar to the Split view, while giving more room for each view. To open the Code inspector, choose Window > Code Inspector or press the F10 key.*

3) Click the Split button in the document toolbar.

TIP *You can also switch to Split view by choosing View > Code and Design.*

THE DOCUMENT
WINDOW IN SPLIT VIEW

DRAG THE BORDER TO RESIZE
THE CODE AND DESIGN PANES

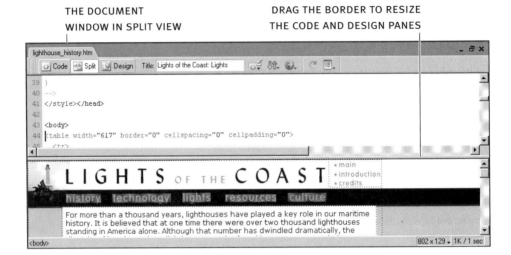

In this view, you can see both the design and the code that creates the page. You can resize the HTML pane by dragging the border between the design and HTML panes. To change the location of the HTML pane, click the View Options button in the toolbar and choose Design View on Top from the menu. This menu also contains other options for adjusting the view, including rulers, visual aids, and the grid.

4) Click the Design button in the toolbar.

TIP *You can also choose View > Design to switch to Design view.*

Your document window changes to Design view, which shows you all the visual elements of your page approximately as they will appear in the browser. As in the other document views, you can access several view options through the toolbar.

EDITING HTML IN CODE VIEW

You can edit code by hand, and Dreamweaver will not overwrite those changes. If a change is made that appears to be wrong, however, Dreamweaver will highlight it to call the code to your attention. There may be many times when you need to adjust the code by hand, as demonstrated in the following steps.

1) In the lighthouse_history.htm document, place the insertion point in the first paragraph, beginning with "For more than a thousand years..." and click the right-most `<table>` tag in the Tag selector—the third from the left.

The nested table is now outlined with a thick black line to indicate that it is selected.

2) Switch to Split Code and Design view. Find the beginning of the table in the code. It should appear as follows:

```
<table width=100% border="0" cellspacing="0" cellpadding="6">
```

Because the table is selected in the Design view of the document window, the corresponding code in the Code view is also highlighted. To find the opening table tag, look to the beginning of the selection in the Code view.

This table doesn't have a summary describing the purpose of the table. When you insert a table, there are a number of accessibility features available, including the option to create a summary for the table. However, after a table has been inserted, you can't add a summary unless you do so through the code or the Tag inspector.

3) In the Code view pane, place the insertion point just before the › character at the end of the opening table tag.

TIP *The Code view pane displays with a heavy line around the edges of the pane (Macintosh) or a highlighted margin (Windows) to indicate that it is active.*

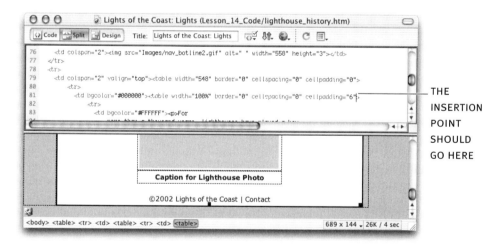

To learn more about any of the HTML tags that you see in Code view, you can choose a tag from the Tag menu at the top of the Reference panel, which is located in the Code panel group. For example, selecting TABLE from the Tag menu presents you with information about the <table> tag. An additional menu, located to the right of the Tag menu, indicates that the information presented about the <table> tag is a description of that HTML tag. You can use this menu to learn more about the attributes that are related to the <table> tag. For instance, you could choose

453

summary from this menu to learn more about the summary attribute that you are creating in this exercise.

NOTE *You can read introductory information about the O'REILLY HTML Reference by using the Book menu at the top of the Reference panel to select a different book. Then use the Book menu to select the O'REILLY HTML Reference again, which causes the HTML reference material to open up to the introductory information, without any tags selected.*

4) In the Code view pane, press the spacebar and type *summary="Lighthouses have played a key role in our maritime history. This section covers lighthouse history. "* **Click in the Design view pane to refresh the document.**

TIP *You can also click the Refresh button that appears on the Property inspector after you make a change to the code.*

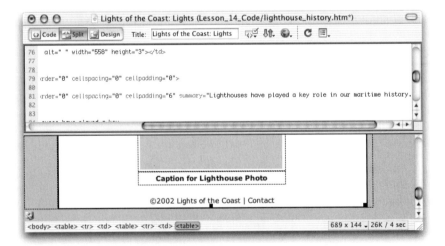

A Code Hints menu may appear as you type in the Code view—you'll work with this menu later in this lesson.

If you make a mistake while editing HTML code, Dreamweaver does not correct the mistake. Dreamweaver does have a feature called Highlight Invalid HTML (which is off by default) that will highlight in bright yellow the code that appears to be invalid. You have to make the corrections yourself. This feature is one of Dreamweaver's advantages, known as **RoundTrip HTML**. The fact that Dreamweaver does not change the code is important because there may be times when Dreamweaver comes across code that appears to be invalid that you used for a reason. For instance, you can add special tags that your Web server recognizes but that are not standard HTML. Dreamweaver leaves them alone. The Invalid Markup highlight appears only in Dreamweaver and does not affect what is seen in the browser. The Property inspector informs you that the selection is Invalid Markup, and lists the problematic tag, along with additional information concerning why the code is invalid and a suggestion for how to remedy the problem.

You can turn the Invalid Markup highlight on or off in the Code view by choosing View > Code View Options > Highlight Invalid HTML. You cannot turn the Design view highlight of Invalid Markup off.

Although you won't see any outward sign of the change that you made, the page is now more accessible. You can add summary tags or otherwise edit code when you need to make a change that is not provided for within Dreamweaver's visual interface.

NOTE *You can also right-click or Control-click (Macintosh single button mouse) on a tag in the Code view pane to pull up the context menu and then choose Edit Tag. The Tag Editor dialog box will open and give you a number of categories and options for editing the tag. The number of categories and options depend on the tag selected.*

ADJUSTING NEW WINDOW PLACEMENT

You learned how to control the attributes of new windows in Lesson 11 with the Open Browser Window behavior. By editing the HTML in Code view, you can also control the placement of those windows.

1) Preview the lighthouse_history.htm document in your primary browser. Click the fuel cells link in the paragraph below the numbered list.

A new browser window opens with the definition of fuel cells. You created new windows like this one using the Open Browser window to select the fuel.htm file, but you had no control over the exact placement of the window. You can control the placement by adding certain parameters to the JavaScript code to place the window in an exact location on the visitor's screen.

2) In the lighthouse_history.htm document, look in the Code view pane for the code that opens the new browser when the visitor clicks the fuel cells link.

TIP *You can find the code by placing the insertion point in the linked "fuel cells" text in the Design view pane—the corresponding code in the Code view pane will automatically become selected. It should be on line 101 in the Code view pane.*

You'll see some code like this:

```
<a href="#" onClick="MM_openBrWindow('fuel.htm','definition',
'scrollbars=yes,width=300,height=100')">fuel cells</a>
```

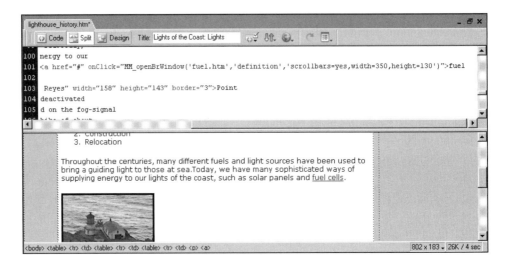

3) After the value of the height parameter, type , (a comma) and the following code: *screenX=0,screenY=0,top=0,left=0.*

Be sure to type the comma and code after the numeric value of 100 and before the single apostrophe. Do not include any spaces.

The screenX and screenY parameters are for Netscape 4.0 and later; they position the window at the top and left side of the screen. The top and left parameters are for Internet Explorer 4.0 and later; they do the same thing as screenX and screenY. Using a parameter of 0 places the new window at those coordinates—in the top-left corner of the screen.

The resulting code should look like this:

```
<a href="#" onClick="MM_openBrWindow('fuel.html','definition',
'scrollbars=yes,width=300,height=100,
screenX=0,screenY=0,top=0,left=0')">fuel cells</a>
```

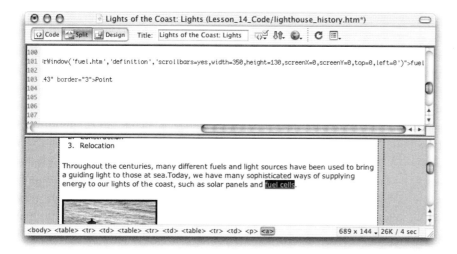

4) Save your page and test it in the browser.

The new window displays at the top and left side of your screen.

TIP *You should close the fuel cells definition window that you viewed earlier before previewing your page.*

5) Change all four parameters to *300*, and see the difference when you view the page in the browser.

The new window displays in a different position.

When defining the placement of a new browser window, be careful not to position the window too far down or too far to the right. Users who have smaller monitors might not be able to see your window if the coordinates place the window outside the dimension of their screen.

META TAGS AND COMMENTS

You can insert certain elements into your code that are not displayed in a browser, but are nonetheless important to the document. Meta tags and HTML comments are two examples of these kinds of elements. **Meta tags** are used for many purposes: They identify and describe documents, provide copyright information, identify the authors or creators, redirect visitors to different pages, control the appearance of the document summary in some search engines, as well as affect ranking within search engines. **HTML Comments** are used to make notes in the code, to indicate or explain the use of a particular section of code, or to disable a portion of the document without actually deleting the code.

1) Choose View > Head Content.

457

The Head Content area appears right above the Design view pane, which is where icons will appear for items that are located in the head of your document, between the <head> and </head> tags. At this point, the items contained in this area include icons for the title of the document, the <meta> tag with the http-equiv attribute, and the portions of JavaScript that are required to appear in the head of the document.

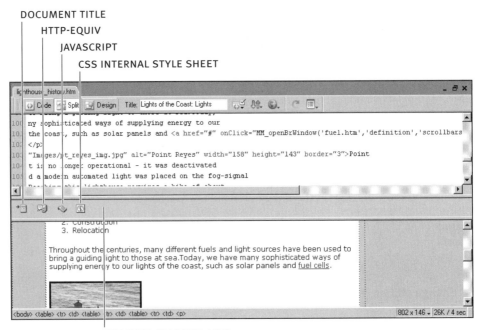

DOCUMENT TITLE
HTTP-EQUIV
JAVASCRIPT
CSS INTERNAL STYLE SHEET

THE HEAD CONTENT AREA

TIP *As you click the icons in the head pane, the corresponding code for those items will highlight in the Code view pane.*

You must be in either Design view or Split view to view this head content area. If you are in Code view, the View > Head Content option is unavailable. For this exercise, you should use Split view.

2) Click the View Options button on the document toolbar and choose Design View on Top. From the same View Options menu, verify that the line numbers option is turned on. Place the pointer over the bar that separates the Design and Code views. When the pointer turns into a line with double arrows, click and drag the bar upward to enlarge the Code view and shrink the Design view.

You can now see the head content near the top of your document window, just above the Design view pane. You also now have only a minimal amount of the Design view pane showing, and you can easily see the corresponding code in the Code view when selecting the head area icons.

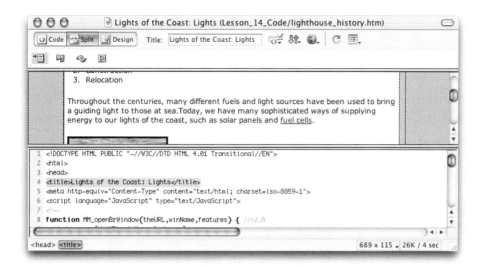

3) In the Code view pane, place the insertion point at the end of line 4, which contains the title of the document, just after the `</title>` **tag, and then press Return (Macintosh) or Enter (Windows). Select the HTML category on the Insert bar; choose Description from the Head menu.**

HTML CATEGORY OF THE INSERT BAR

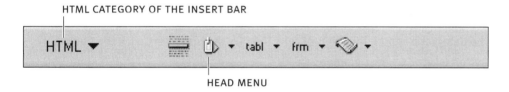

HEAD MENU

The Description dialog box opens with a text field in which you can type a description of your page. The description meta tag, used to give a brief synopsis to identify your page, is included in search results displayed by some search engines. Adding the description meta tag to your pages is an important part of site promotion.

4) Type *Learn how lighthouses have played a key role in maritime history.* **Click OK.**

Descriptions should be short—200 characters or fewer. Most search engines have a cut-off; anything more than their limit will not be used. A good description is a very short, concise indication of the contents of the document.

5) The insertion point should now be at the end of line 5. Press Return (Macintosh) or Enter (Windows) and choose Keywords from the Head menu in the HTML category of the Insert bar. Type *lighthouses, maritime history, lens, keepers, fuel cells* **into the Keywords text field. Click OK to close the Keywords dialog box and insert the keywords into your document.**

TIP *If the insertion point is already on a blank line (line 6), you do not need to press Return (Macintosh) or Enter (Windows).*

When developing a list of keywords, you can separate individual words or phrases by commas. Do not repeat the same keyword or phrase over again—using "lighthouse lighthouse lighthouse lighthouse" as a keyword list is considered spamming because of the repetition of the word "lighthouse." Keywords should be representative of what is on your page and also be words that are actually used on your page.

6) Enlarge the Design view pane of your document window by moving the bar between the Design view and the Code view. Place the cursor at the beginning of the paragraph containing the fuel cells link. On the Insert bar, click the Comment button located on the Common tab.

COMMENT

The Comment dialog box opens.

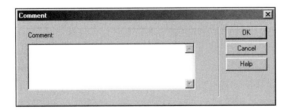

An HTML comment is text that is placed in the code for developers that the browsers do not display. Comments are not visible to the visitors of your site—unless they look at the source code of your document.

7) Type `Lightsource Information` **and click OK.**

You may see a message informing you that you will not see the element unless the Invisible Elements visual aid is turned on, and the preference setting for this element is on. If this alert appears, click OK to close the message after reading it.

The Comment icon appears in the document window and `<!--Lightsource Information -->` is inserted into the code. To see comment icons in the document window, choose Dreamweaver > Preferences (Macintosh) or Edit > Preferences (Windows), select the Invisible Elements category and check the Comments box.

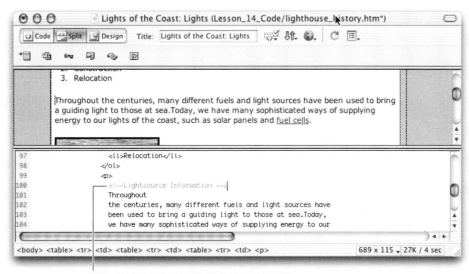

THE COMMENT IN THE CODE VIEW PANE

TIP *If the Comment icons are visible in the document window (follow steps above to make them visible) you can select the Comment icon to edit the comment in the Property inspector.*

Comments are often used to mark sections of code to indicate the function of that code or to make note of copyright information on certain scripts or other content.

NOTE *CSS (Cascading Style Sheet) comments are different from standard HTML comments. A CSS comment would appear as |*Comment*| in a style sheet. You can insert either single-line or multi-line CSS comments by selecting the desired comment type from the Comments folder on the Snippets panel and clicking the Insert button.*

8) Choose View > Head Content to remove the checkmark next to the Head Content view option.

The Head area disappears. The rest of this book assumes that you have the Head Content view option turned off.

461

USING THE TAG SELECTOR

The Tag Selector enables you to jump quickly through a hierarchy of HTML tags, depending upon what is active, or selected, in the document window. This tool begins with the <body> tag and outlines the structure of the tags to the selection. This process can be very useful for quickly selecting an item, particularly if it is one that may be difficult to select in the document window.

1) In the lighthouse_history.htm file, click anywhere inside the white cell of the nested table that contains the text and images for this page.

Nested tables are particularly hard to select in the document window. You can't easily grab the border of a nested table, especially if the borders are defined as 0. The first step in doing so is to place the cursor at a point in the hierarchy of the HTML code that is after the desired table tags.

2) Using the Tag Selector at the bottom of the document window, right-click or Control-click (Macintosh single button mice) the <table> tag that is second from the right (the middle <table> tag).

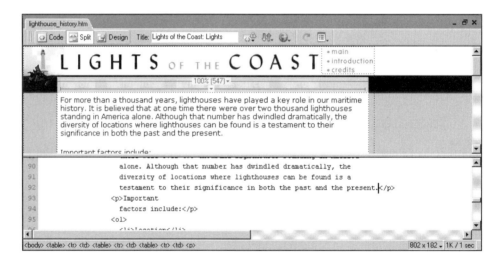

This <table> tag corresponds to the table that creates the outline effect. This table is the wrong size. The width is 548 pixels, but it should be 558 pixels. The cell padding value is also wrong, which is causing the black outline that should be around the white area to not appear.

You worked a little bit in the previous lessons with the Tag Selector. The more familiar you get with the hierarchy of HTML code, the easier it will be to move immediately to the point in the code that you need. The Tag Selector menu gives you additional control and quick access to the tags in the HTML.

3) In the menu that appears, choose Edit Tag.

A small Edit Tag box appears near the Tag Selector with a text field containing the <table> tag and the attributes contained within that tag. In the text field, you should see the following:

```
<table width="548" border="0" cellspacing="0" cellpadding="0">
```

4) In the Edit Tag box, change the width to 558 pixels and the cell padding to 1.

The resulting code should appear as follows:

```
<table width="558" border="0" cellspacing="0" cellpadding="1">
```

5) Press Return (Macintosh) or Enter (Windows).

The changes that you defined are now made to the document, and the Edit Tag box disappears.

EDITING CODE WITH QUICK TAGS

Quick Tags give you the ability to rapidly insert HTML tags. This is especially important when you are writing code by hand because it will help to speed up the process. There are three ways to edit HTML with the Quick Tag Editor. You can insert new HTML code, edit an existing tag, or wrap a new tag around the current selection.

1) In the lighthouse_history.htm document, place the insertion point between the image of the lighthouse and the text beginning with "Point Reyes" in the Design view. Click the Quick Tag Editor button near the upper right corner of the Property inspector.

QUICK TAG EDITOR

QUICK TAG EDITOR BUTTON

CODE HINTS MENU

The Quick Tag Editor opens in the Insert HTML mode because the insertion point was in the document window and there was nothing selected. For the Quick Tag Editor to appear in the Insert HTML mode, the cursor must be in the Design view of the document window as if you were going to insert an object.

The Insert HTML Quick Tag Editor opens as a box with a text field and a hints menu that you can scroll through to choose a tag. You will need to pause and wait for the Code Hints menu to appear.

2) Scroll through the list of tags in the hints menu, find and double-click br. Press Return (Macintosh) or Enter (Windows).

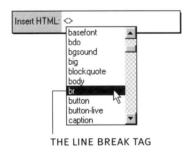

THE LINE BREAK TAG

The selection br is the break tag, and it will appear between the < and > characters in the Quick Tag text field when you double-click it. After pressing Return (Macintosh) or Enter (Windows), the break will be inserted into the document window at the place the insertion point was located.

The text is now on a line directly below the image.

NOTE *You can also perform more extensive code edits by typing directly into the text field; as you do so, Dreamweaver will automatically make corrections to the code for you.*

3) In the Design view of the document window, select the image of the lighthouse and click the Quick Tag Editor button on the Property inspector.

The Quick Tag Editor opens in the Edit Tag mode because you had an object in the document selected. The path to the image is initially selected in the Quick Tag text field.

4) Press the Tab key to move from the path of the image to the next attribute. Keep pressing the Tab key until you reach the numeric width attribute. Change the width by typing *143* (so it is the same dimension as the height). Keep pressing Tab until the number *3*, which defines the border, is highlighted. Change the border of the image by typing *1*. Press Return (Macintosh) or Enter (Windows) to apply the changes.

Each time you press Tab, the Quick Tag Editor applies the change you just made (if any) and jumps you to the next attribute.

TIP *You can move the Quick Tag Editor to a different position by clicking and dragging the left corner.*

CLICK HERE AND DRAG TO MOVE THE EDIT TAG BOX

THE EDIT TAG TEXT FIELD OF THE QUICK TAG EDITOR

The width of the image has changed to 143, and the border of the image has now changed from 3 pixels to 1 pixel.

5) With the image of the lighthouse still selected, click the Quick Tag Editor button on the Property inspector. Press Command+T (Macintosh) or Ctrl+T (Windows) to cycle through the three different Quick Tag options until you get the Wrap Tag mode. Each time you Press Command+T (Macintosh) or Ctrl+T (Windows) the Quick Tag Editor switches to a different mode.

> **TIP** *Depending on what you have selected in the document, the Quick Tag Editor may open in either Edit Tag mode or in Wrap Tag mode. For example, if you select text, the Quick Tag Editor will open in Wrap Tag mode. If you want a different mode, use Command+T (Macintosh) or Ctrl+T (Windows) to select a different option.*

6) Choose div from the Quick Tag Editor menu. Press the spacebar and type _a_. Wait for the Code Hints menu to appear and then double-click align. When the Code Hints menu appears after `align=""` **is inserted into the text field, double-click center. Press Return (Macintosh) or Enter (Windows) to apply the changes to the code.**

THE QUICK TAG EDITOR INDICATING THAT
IT IS CURRENTLY IN WRAP TAG MODE

The lighthouse image is now centered. The tags `<div align="center">` and `</div>` have been placed around the image.

> **NOTE** *If you were to select a tag in the Tag selector and press Delete (Macintosh) or Backspace (Windows), the tag and everything it contains would be deleted. However, if you want to remove just the tag while leaving the contents intact, you can right-click or Control-click (Macintosh single button mice) and choose Remove Tag.*

MAKING USE OF CODE HINTS

While you are working in Code view, you can make use of Code Hints to speed up the process of writing code, as you have been doing while working with the Quick Tag Editor. As you begin to write code, the Code Hints list appears. This list is a scrolling menu with a large number of tags that you can use to complete nearly any tag or tag attribute that you may be typing. This exercise is an example of how to use the Code Hints for inserting an email link. You learned to insert email links in the Design view in Lesson 4.

1) In the Design view pane of the lighthouse_history.htm document, place the insertion point in front of the word "Contact" at the bottom of the document, located just after the copyright information.

The Code view pane displays that portion of the code. You see a static cursor located right in front of the word "Contact" in the code.

2) In the Code view pane, click in front of the corresponding word "Contact" in the code.

The Code view pane is now active, as indicated by the heavy line around the border of the pane (Macintosh) or the highlighted margin (Windows).

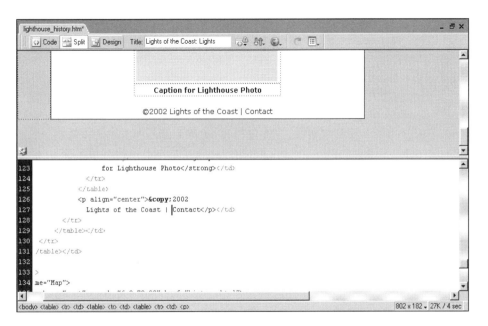

3) Type < in front of the word "Contact."

The < character indicates the start of a tag. The Code Hints menu appears with a list of tags that you can choose from.

NOTE *You can access the Code Hints preferences by choosing Edit > Preferences and selecting the Code Hints category. The options allow you to turn off Auto Tag Completion (enabled by default) and turn off Code Hints (also enabled by default). The Delay slide allows you to set how long Code Hints waits before displaying a list of options. The Menus list box lets you specify the tags to include in the list of tags that appear in the Code Hints list.*

467

4) Double-click a, the first tag in the list, to insert the tag and then press the spacebar.

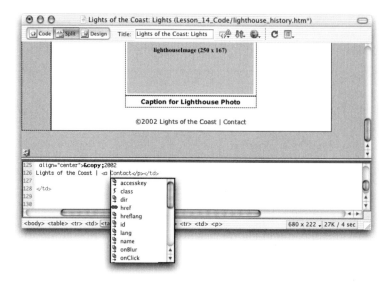

The a tag is inserted into the Code view and the Code Hints list pops up again.

5) Scroll down in the list until you find href, the fourth item in the list; double-click to insert it in the document.

Dreamweaver has inserted href="" into the code, which indicates a link. The cursor is automatically placed between the quotes, and the Code Hints list pops up again with a browse link that pulls up the Select File dialog box if clicked. In this exercise you are creating an email link, so you won't use the browse box to select a file.

6) Inside the quotes, type *mailto:* **followed by your email address.**

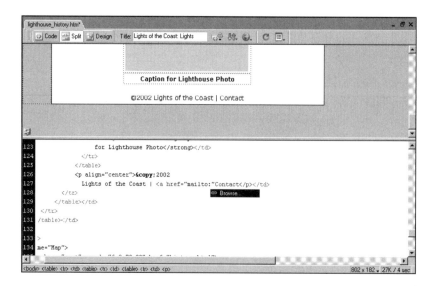

The cursor now appears just outside the ending quote after `mailto:` in the code.

7) Use the right arrow key to move to the right once so the insertion point is just outside of the quote; then type the > character.

Your email address now appears in the code defining the email link, and Dreamweaver has inserted a closing </a> tag.

8) Double-click the word "Contact" in the Code view; click and drag it between the open and end tags. Click back in the Design view pane when you finish and save the lighthouse_history.htm file.

Your code should look like this:

```
<a href="mailto:YourEmailAddress">Contact</a>
```

The Design view pane will refresh when you click in it or press the Refresh button on the Property Inspector.

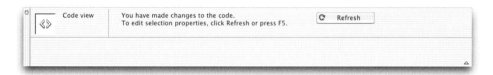

NOTE *Dreamweaver includes many tools for code editing that give users precise control over the development of code. You can store information on standard and custom tags using the Tag Library Editor. This new tool gives you the ability to modify current tags and import new tags into the already extensive database of tags that is integrated in Dreamweaver. Tags are set up in a system of libraries; each library is specific to a different type of code (HTML, CFML, ASP, and so on). You can add or delete libraries. The individual libraries each contain a number of tags for which you can edit the Tag Format: Line Breaks, Contents, and Case. The Preview text field displays the tag according to the options you set. Each tag contains a number of attributes that can be customized as well. Choose Edit > Tag Libraries to open the Tag Library Editor. Use caution when adding, modifying, or deleting tag libraries, tags, and tag attributes. This dialog box is best for advanced Dreamweaver users who have a thorough understanding of the code they want to alter.*

USING SNIPPETS

In Dreamweaver you can store portions of code, called **snippets**, so that they can be reused easily. There are a certain number of predefined snippets provided in Dreamweaver that you can use, or you can create your own snippets from comments, JavaScript routines, portions of code, and other sources. Snippets are particularly useful for code that needs to be used repetitively throughout a site, like an email address or a link. In this way, they are similar to library items (covered in Lesson 7);

469

however, unlike library items, snippets do not update throughout a site when you make changes to the original snippet. You can either place a snippet directly into the code or have it wrap around a selection.

1) Open the fuel.htm document and place the insertion point after the last word in the fuel cells definition: "energy." Press Return (Macintosh) or Enter (Windows).

In the following steps, you will insert a predefined Dreamweaver snippet on the new paragraph line at the bottom of the table.

2) Open the Code panel group and select the Snippets tab. Open the Form Elements folder on the Snippets tab and select the Close Window Button snippet. Click Insert at the bottom of the Snippets panel. Save the fuel.htm document.

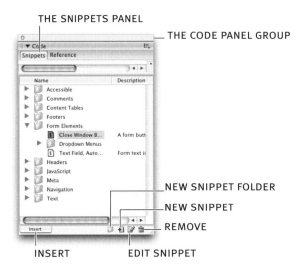

THE SNIPPETS PANEL

THE CODE PANEL GROUP

NEW SNIPPET FOLDER

NEW SNIPPET

REMOVE

INSERT

EDIT SNIPPET

This snippet creates a button that the visitor can click to close the window. When you use pop-up menus, it is helpful to include a button that allows the visitor to close the window quickly and easily.

TIP *You can also drag the snippet to the point in the document where you want it to be placed.*

3) In the lighthouse_history.htm document, select the table at the bottom of the page that contains the placeholder image and corresponding caption.

This table is an example of one that might be used throughout a Web site such as the "Lights of the Coast" project site for images and corresponding captions. By creating a snippet that contains this table, you no longer have to re-create the same code every time you want to include an image and caption combination. You can just insert the snippet quickly and easily. Another advantage is the consistency that

470

comes from using a snippet—you can use a standard look and layout for the image and caption combinations.

4) Click the New Snippet button at the bottom of the Snippets panel.

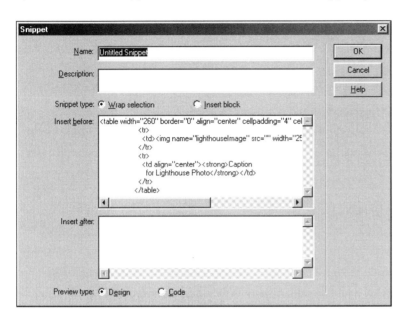

The Snippet dialog box opens.

TIP *You can also delete and modify snippets by selecting them and clicking the Edit Snippet or Remove buttons at the bottom of the Snippets panel. You can create folders to organize your snippets by clicking the New Snippet Folder button.*

5) Type *Image and Caption Table* **in the Name text field. Type** *Table layout for lighthouse images needing captions* **in the Description text field. Select Insert Block for Snippet Type and select Design for Preview Type. Click OK.**

The snippet is created and now appears in the Snippets panel. You can now insert this snippet into a document whenever you need it by selecting it in the Snippets panel and either dragging it to your document or clicking the Insert button on the Snippets panel.

6) Test your new snippet by deleting the original table at the bottom of lighthouse_history.htm and replacing it with the new snippet by selecting the Image Caption Table snippet button in the Snippets panel and clicking the Insert button. Replace the placeholder image with pt_arena.jpg from the Lesson_14_Code/ Images folder and replace the caption with *View from the Point Arena Lighthouse.*

Keep the names and descriptions of your snippets as short as possible. The first column in the Snippets panel displays the icons and names; the second column displays the descriptions. You can roll over a description to see the full description pop up.

NOTE *You can organize your snippets by dragging them into different folders, creating folders and renaming folders—much like how you work with files in the Files panel. You can also create keyboard shortcuts for your snippets. Access the Keyboard Shortcuts dialog box from either the context menu on the Code panel group or Dreamweaver > Keyboard Shortcuts (Macintosh) or Edit > Keyboard Shortcuts (Windows). To create shortcuts for snippets, choose Snippets from the Commands menu, select a snippet from the list of snippets and click the plus (+) button to add a shortcut for the selected item, (follow the Dreamweaver prompts to create a new set if necessary) and press a key combination. The combination of keys pressed will appear in the Press key text field.*

USING CLEAN UP HTML

Throughout the process of creating an HTML document, you may wind up with empty or redundant tags, unnecessary or improperly nested tags, and more problems with the HTML code in your document. Using the Clean Up HTML command gets rid of nearly all of these problematic instances. It is recommended that you run the Clean Up HTML command whenever you finish a page or site.

1) In the lighthouse_history.htm document, choose Commands > Clean Up HTML.

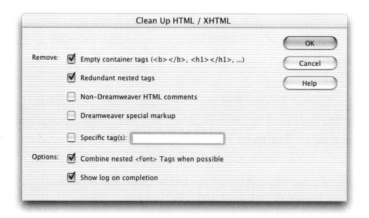

The Clean Up HTML/XHTML dialog box opens. By default, the first two options under the Remove section are checked, and both options under the Options section are checked. The choices in the dialog box are as follows:

- **Remove Empty container tags** (`<strong></strong>`, `<h1></h1>`, …): Empty tags such as the example `<strong></strong>` (where there is nothing between the open bold and end bold tags) given in this dialog box can occur as you format text; particularly when you format, edit, reformat, and so on. The more you work on a document, the more likely it is to have these kinds of nested tags. These tags may not cause problems in the browser, but they do take up space and make it harder to read through the code if you are editing in Code view. This option is checked by default.

- **Remove Redundant nested tags:** When you have a duplicate set of tags inside of a set of tags that do the same thing, the inner set of tags is redundant because the outside set has already made the definition. As you work in a document, redundant nested tags can occur. If this box is checked, Dreamweaver removes all instances of a set of duplicate tags because they are unnecessary. This option is checked by default.

- **Remove Non-Dreamweaver HTML comments**: Any comments that have not been inserted by Dreamweaver are removed if this box is checked, including comments that have been inserted while using Dreamweaver. Dreamweaver HTML Comments are those that are created by Dreamweaver in order to mark certain objects such as the `<!--#BeginEditable "lighthouse" -->` comment that signifies the editable region "lighthouse" in a template (templates were covered in Lesson 8). This option is unchecked by default.

- **Remove Dreamweaver special markup**: Dreamweaver creates a number of tags that are not standard HTML. These tags include items (such as `<mm:libitem>`, which signifies a library item) that indicate to Dreamweaver how specific objects should be handled. Only Dreamweaver recognizes this markup; browsers ignore it. Use caution when checking this box because it causes all tags related to library items, templates, and tracing images to be removed. If this is done, you can no longer update the page using those features. This option is unchecked by default.

- **Remove Specific tag(s)**: This text field allows you to instruct Dreamweaver to remove particular tags. If you want to remove multiple tags at the same time, separate the tags with commas. This option is unchecked by default.

- **Combine Nested** `<font>` **Tags when possible:** If your document uses `<font>` tags, these tags may become nested as you format text in your documents. For example, you might wind up with something that looks similar to this:

```
<font size="-1"><font face="Verdana, Arial, Helvetica, sans-serif"> <font color="#336633">Lights of the Coast</font></font></font>
```

The three sets of font tags in this example can be combined into one `<font>` and `</font>` set, making the code much cleaner and leaner:

```
<font size="-1" face="Verdana, Arial, Helvetica, sans-serif" color="#336633">_Lights of the Coast</font>
```

This option is checked by default.

473

NOTE *The <font> tag is deprecated in HTML 4.0—that is, it may become obsolete in future versions of HTML. Styles sheets are recommended for text formatting instead.*

- **Show Log on Completion:** The log lets you know what items Dreamweaver was able to clean up. This option is checked by default.

NOTE *You can run this command on both HTML and XHTML documents. When cleaning up XHTML, you will have different options available to you.*

2) Leave the default options selected and click OK.

Dreamweaver runs Clean Up HTML and displays a dialog box with a log of what was cleaned up. In some cases, there may not be anything to clean up.

3) Click OK to close the log. Save and close the lighthouse_history.html and fuel.htm documents.

Running Clean Up HTML helps to make your code as clean and free of errors as possible. It can potentially help decrease the file size and browser loading time for your document.

NOTE *To further optimize the code in your documents, you can run Validate Markup to examine the code for tag and syntax errors by choosing File > Check Page > Validate Markup or selecting the Validation tab in the Results window and clicking the Validate button (the green triangle on the left). Any errors found will be displayed in the Results dialog box.*

WORKING WITH MICROSOFT WORD HTML

Web page content can come from a variety of sources. Clients or colleagues might send material in a Microsoft Word file. If the format of the Word document is fairly simple, you can use the copy-and-paste method to import your text into Dreamweaver. If the Word document has formatting such as bullets or tables, you may want to save the document as a Web page (choose File > Save As Web Page in Word 97 or later) and open the resulting HTML file in Dreamweaver. Word inserts a great number of unnecessary tags, however. You can clean up this code in Dreamweaver in one step. The tags that Dreamweaver removes are required to display the page in Word, but are not needed in HTML or a browser.

1) Open the markings.htm file from the Lesson_14_Code folder.

This HTML file was saved from a Word 2001 document.

2) Choose Commands > Clean Up Word HTML.

The Clean Up Word HTML dialog box opens.

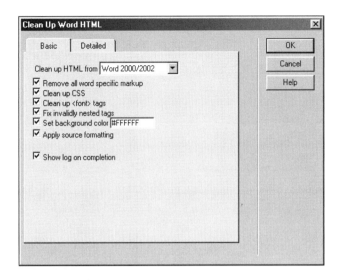

Dreamweaver attempts to determine which version of Word was used to create the HTML. If Dreamweaver cannot determine the version, you need to choose the correct version from the menu.

The dialog box has two tabs, Basic and Detailed, with several options to check for each. For this exercise, use the default setting (all options checked).

The options on the Basic tab are as follows:

- Remove all Word-specific markup

- Clean up CSS

- Clean up <font> tags

- Fix invalidly nested tags

- Set background color

- Apply source formatting

- Show log on completion

The Detailed tab contains additional options to remove all Microsoft Word-specific markup and clean up CSS.

3) All the boxes should be checked. Click OK. Click OK again to close the dialog box after reviewing the changes Dreamweaver made when cleaning up the file. Save the file.

Dreamweaver displays a dialog box listing all the changes that it made.

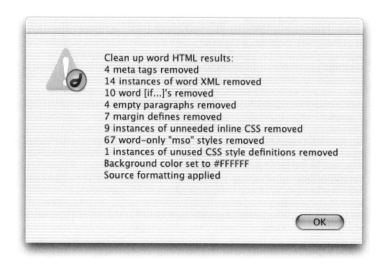

PRINTING FROM CODE VIEW

There are many times when it can be difficult to view code on a computer screen. Dreamweaver allows you to print out the code, a useful feature that can allow you to simply work on a hard copy or share with team members. You will need to have a printer connected to your computer to complete this exercise.

1) In the markings.htm file, choose File > Print Code.

As long as you have a printer connected to your system you can print by clicking the Print button after specifying the printing options such as number of copies and page numbers.

NOTE *You can't print the Design view from within Dreamweaver. If you need to have a printout of the Web page as it will look in a browser, preview the page in a browser, and print it from the browser.*

2) You can close the markings.htm file.

WHAT YOU HAVE LEARNED

In this lesson, you have:

- Switched document views and edited the HTML in Code view (pages 450–452)

- Edited HTML code by hand using split Code and Design view (pages 452–455)

- Changed the location of a new browser window by adding x and y coordinates to the code (pages 455–457)

- Inserted keyword and description meta tags (pages 457–461)

- Used the Tag Selector to quickly edit tags (pages 462–463)

- Inserted and edited code using Quick Tags and Code Hints (pages 464–469)

- Created and inserted code using snippets (pages 469–472)

- Ran the Clean Up HTML command to streamline code (pages 472–474)

- Imported a Word HTML file and used Clean Up Word HTML to remove unnecessary tags (pages 474–476)

- Learned how to print the HTML code (page 476)

using find and replace

LESSON 15

The Find and Replace feature in Dreamweaver provides you with a powerful searching tool. You can search the current document, a specified folder, or an entire site. The extensive options enable you to search for text or HTML tags, or even limit your search to certain attributes within HTML tags. After you find what you are looking for, you can modify or replace it. The Find and Replace feature can save a lot of time when you need to make massive changes to a document or an entire site.

In this lesson, you will use the Find and Replace feature to make a wide variety of changes to several documents. You will use the Find and Replace feature to apply

In this project, you will use find and replace to change words in this document. You will also adjust the formatting attributes of text in this document by using find and replace to automate the process of linking to an external style sheet and applying a custom style to text.

CSS styles and attach external style sheets to a number of documents all at once. You'll find and replace text, change text formatting, learn to save your searches to use at a later time, find dates, and replace names.

To see examples of the finished pages for this lesson, open women.htm and ca_lights.htm from the Lesson_15_Find/Completed folder.

WHAT YOU WILL LEARN

In this lesson, you will:

- Find and replace text
- Find text within HTML tags
- Use the Find and Replace feature to apply a custom style
- Use the Find and Replace feature to attach external style sheets
- Save and reuse your search settings
- Search for patterns in text
- Find variations of a name

APPROXIMATE TIME

This lesson should take about one half hour to complete.

LESSON FILES

Starting Files:

Lesson_15_Find/women.htm
Lesson_15_Find/ca_lights.htm
Lesson_15_Find/highlight_query.dwr
Lesson_15_Find/light_style.css

Completed Project:

Lesson_15_Find/Completed/…(all files)

SEARCHING YOUR DOCUMENT

In this exercise, you will perform a simple search to find and replace words in the text of a document.

1) Open the women.htm file from the Lesson_15_Find folder. Place the insertion point at the end of the header "Women of the Lights."

This document refers to "lite house keepers" throughout the text, when it should actually be "lighthouse keepers." You'll replace that text in this exercise.

2) Choose Edit > Find and Replace.

The Find and Replace dialog box opens.

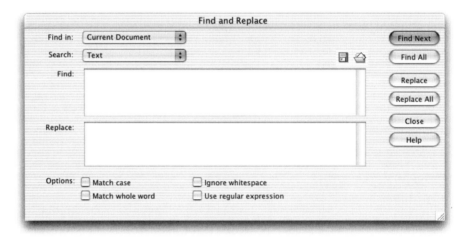

3) In the Find in menu, choose Current Document. In the Search menu, choose Text. In the Find text field, type *lite house keepers*. **In the Replace text field, type** *lighthouse keepers*. **Uncheck the boxes for four options (Match case, Match whole word, Ignore whitespace, Use regular expression).**

TIP *Selecting a portion of text before opening the Find and Replace dialog box automatically causes the selected text to appear in the Search For text field.*

Find in Current Document searches the entire document. This option can be used only from a single document while it is open. The Find in menu also has five additional options:

- **Selected Text:** Searches what you have selected in the current document.
- **Open Documents:** Searches all files that are open.

- **Folder:** Allows you to browse to select a folder and search all the contents of that folder.

- **Selected Files in Site:** Searches files you have selected in the site panel.

- **Entire Current Local Site:** Searches the active site.

There are four options at the bottom of the Find and Replace dialog box:

- **Match case:** Limits the search to the exact case of the words. If the Match Case box is checked, a search looks only for content that exactly matches the capitalization you used in the Find text field.

- **Match whole word:** Matches only complete words.

- **Ignore whitespace:** Ignores all spaces—if this is checked and you are searching for two words, Dreamweaver also finds all instances in which those two words have additional spaces between them.

- **Use regular expression:** Provides patterns to describe character combinations in the text. Use this option to select sentences that begin with "The" or attribute values that contain a number.

4) Click Find Next.

The first occurrence of the phrase after the insertion point is highlighted.

5) Click Replace.

The phrase is changed to "lighthouse keepers," and the next occurrence of the phrase is highlighted.

TIP *When replacing text in your document, it is recommended that you click Replace first and check the new text to make sure you typed the correct information in the Replace field. Use Replace All after you verify the search criteria.*

6) Click Find All.

The results of the search are found and displayed in the Results panel—three more instances of the text for which you searched. Double-clicking an item in this list highlights the instance in the document window. Using the Find All option allows you to review all instances of the text.

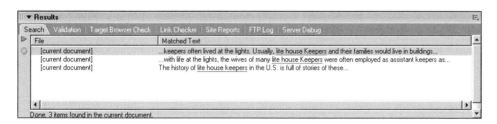

7) Click the green arrow on the left of the Results panel.

The Find and Replace dialog box opens again.

Dreamweaver remembers the settings from your most recent search. If you close and reopen the dialog box, the text and options you set the last time the dialog box was open are still there. The Find text field should contain "lite house keepers" and the Replace text field should contain "lighthouse keepers."

8) Now click Replace All on the Find and Replace dialog box.

The Find and Replace dialog box automatically closes after it finishes searching for and replacing text. The status bar of the Results panel reports the number of items found and replaced in your document.

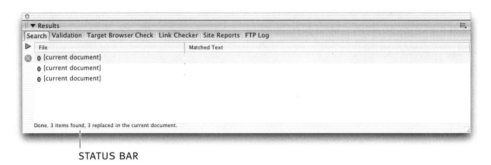

STATUS BAR

9) Click the context menu in the upper right corner of the Results panel and choose Clear Results; then close the Results panel (Macintosh) or collapse the Results panel (Windows). Save the women.htm document.

Leave this file open for the next exercise.

REMOVING HTML TAGS

The women.htm file contains <font> tags. As explained in Lessons 2 and 6, the <font> tag has been deprecated in HTML 4.0—it may become obsolete in the future. Although it is still supported by browsers, CSS (covered in Lesson 6) is the recommended way to style text. In documents such as women.htm, which were created using previous versions of Dreamweaver, you cannot access some CSS document attributes with the existence of the <font> tag in that document.

If you were to open a document that uses <font> tags, the Property inspector would list only the Appearance, Title/Encoding, and Tracing Image categories. The Links and Headings categories use CSS to set the attributes and are not available until the <font> tags are removed. The link colors and background color or images will be available in the Appearance section, although they will be set as attributes of the <body> tag.

482

The <font> tag is one type of local formatting. In CSS, local formatting overrides any internal or external styles—if you want to apply CSS styles, the local formatting needs to be removed. In older versions of Dreamweaver, local formatting was applied using the Property inspector to define the text attributes with <font> tags. For new documents in Dreamweaver MX 2004, the default formatting applied with the Property inspector is CSS-based. When you open documents such as this one, which use <font> tags, the Property inspector uses the <font> tags to edit and define text formatting.

In this exercise, you will use the Find and Replace feature to remove the HTML <font> tag.

1) In the women.htm document, choose Edit > Find and Replace to open the Find and Replace dialog box. The Find in menu should be set to Current Document. Change the Search menu selection to Specific Tag.

TIP *You can also use the shortcut Ctrl+F (Windows) or Command+F (Macintosh) to open the Find and Replace dialog box.*

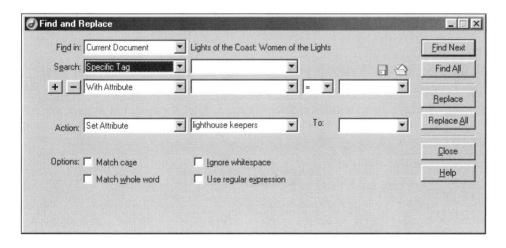

Choosing Specific Tag allows you to search Dreamweaver for a certain tag. The dialog box changes to reflect this search method. A set of options to choose from is displayed to narrow the search and look for tags with specific attributes.

**2) Select font from the list of HTML tags in the Tag menu, located to the right of the
Search menu.**

You can also type tags (without the < > brackets) in the Search For text field instead
of using the menu.

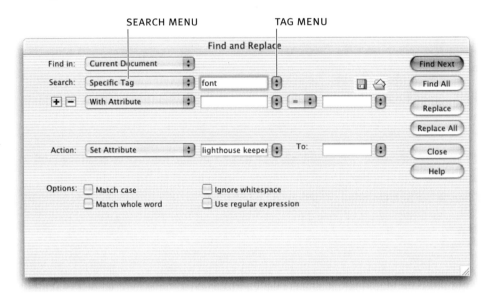

**3) Click the minus (–) button to remove the tag modifier option. Choose Strip Tag
from the Action menu and uncheck all four boxes in the Options area.**

Because you are going to entirely remove the <font> tags, the modifiers are not needed.

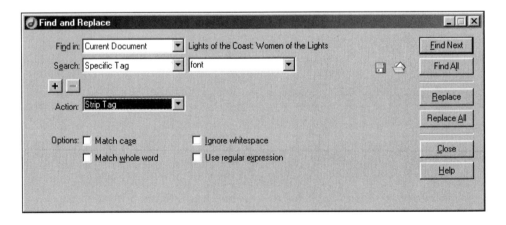

NOTE *You can continue to add additional modifiers by clicking the plus sign (+) button. Several menus and text fields appear that allow you to make very specific selections. You can use these menus and text fields to limit your searches and find unique occurrences of a tag or a tag with a specific attribute. The additional options here include a number of qualifiers for attributes, including the ability to search for a tag with or without a specific attribute, a tag that contains or doesn't contain a specific attribute, or an attribute that is inside or not inside of the specified tag. The tag modifiers give you the ability to choose a specific attribute that can be used with the selected tag; to select whether the attribute should be equal to (=), less than (<), greater than (>), and not equal to (!=); and a place to set a value for the desired attribute. The options in the menus vary depending upon the tag and attribute that you have selected.*

4) Click the Replace All button.

All <font> tags within the document are removed.

The Find and Replace dialog box closes automatically. The Results panel contains details on what was replaced, or in this case deleted, from the document. If the Results panel does not open automatically, Macintosh users can choose Window > Results to open the panel that was closed in the previous exercise, and Windows users can expand the panel that was collapsed in the previous exercise. For Windows users, the collapsed panel is located beneath the Property inspector.

TIP *Windows users can click the white arrow on the thin bar located just above the Property inspector to reduce both the Property inspector and Results panel at the same time. Click this button again at the bottom of the Dreamweaver interface to expand the panels located in that area again.*

THE RESULTS PANEL PROVIDES DETAILS ON THE FIND AND REPLACE RESULTS

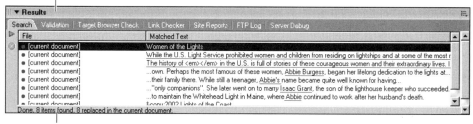

THE STATUS BAR SHOWS A SUMMARY OF THE RESULTS

5) Click the context menu in the upper right corner of the Results panel and choose Clear Results. Close the Results panel (Macintosh) or collapse the Results panel (Windows). Save the women.htm document.

Leave the women.htm file open for the next exercise.

485

USING FIND AND REPLACE TO ATTACH EXTERNAL STYLE SHEETS

In Lesson 6, you created an external style sheet and attached that style sheet to another document. The steps to add a style sheet to a document are not difficult, but they can be time-consuming if you need to attach a style sheet to multiple pages or an entire site. By using the Find and Replace feature, you can accomplish that task in a matter of minutes.

In this exercise, you attach the external style sheet light_style.css to multiple pages.

1) In the women.htm document, click Split button on the Document toolbar.

The document window now shows both Code and Design views.

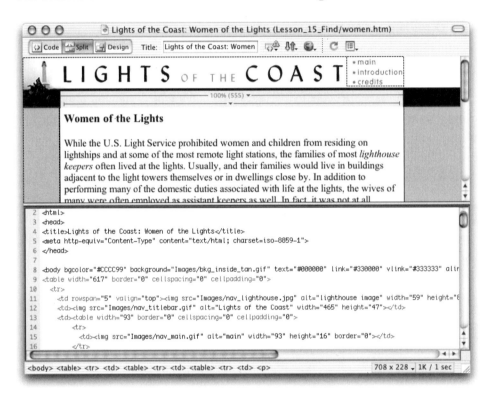

2) In the Code view, find the body tag near the top of the document. Select and delete all the attributes of the <body> **tag.**

To remove the attributes of the <body> tag, you need to remove the following code that appears between <body and > (Do not delete <body or the >):

```
bgcolor="#CCCC99" background="Images/bkg_inside_tan.gif" text="#000000"
link="#330000" vlink="#333333" alink="#660000" leftmargin="0" topmargin="0"
marginwidth="0" marginheight="0"
```

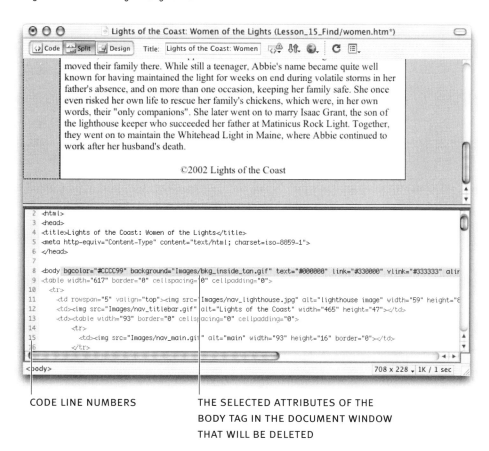

CODE LINE NUMBERS

THE SELECTED ATTRIBUTES OF THE
BODY TAG IN THE DOCUMENT WINDOW
THAT WILL BE DELETED

TIP *Use the code line numbers on the left side of the Code view panel to find line 8, which contains the <body> tag. As an alternative to selecting the attributes, you can click the line number to select all the code on that line and then type* **<body>** *to replace the tag—but you will need to delete the </body> tag that Dreamweaver automatically inserts. You can use Command+Z (Macintosh) or Ctrl+Z (Windows) immediately after Dreamweaver inserts the </body> tag to remove it.*

This document uses attributes of the <body> tag to define the appearance of the page. If you are using external style sheets—which you will learn to attach using the Find and Replace feature later in this lesson—these attributes override the formatting defined in the style sheet. If an external style sheet were attached to this page and specified a different background image, this page would not use the updated background; it would continue to use the one you see now because the formatting is local and overrides the style sheet.

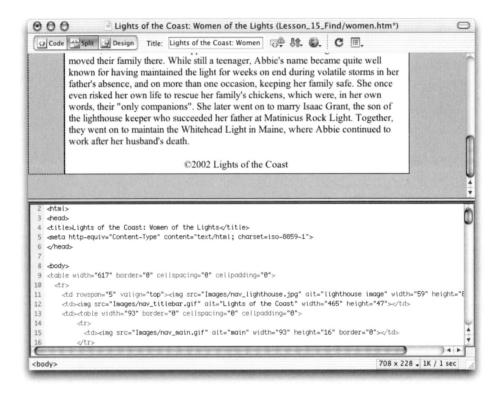

The code on line 8 should now be <body> and include no spaces.

3) Press the Refresh button on the Property inspector.

The Design view refreshes, showing that the background, link, and margin attributes of the <body> tag have been removed.

4) Choose Edit > Find and Replace.

The Find and Replace dialog box opens with the same settings that were used in the previous exercise.

5) The Find in menu should be set to Current Document. Set the Search menu to Source Code. Type </head> **in the Find text field. In the Replace text field, type the following code:** <link href="light_style.css" rel="stylesheet" type="text/css"></head>

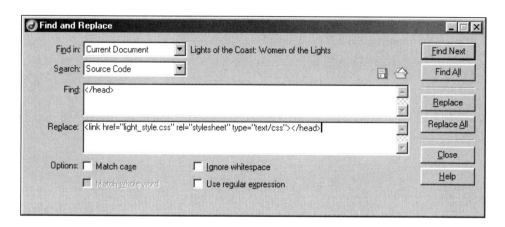

NOTE *The* <link> *tag specifies that the style sheet is attached by linking it to the document, which is the recommended way to attach the first style sheet (as opposed to the import method of attaching style sheets—both methods were covered in Lesson 6). The location of the style sheet is specified by* href="light_style.css", *the relationship between the current document and attached stylesheet is defined by* rel="stylesheet", *and the output header* type="text/css" *specifies the kind of content through the MIME (Multipurpose Internet Mail Extensions) type, allowing browsers that do not support style sheets to ignore the link tag.*

When you use the Attach Style Sheet icon, Dreamweaver adds the <link> tag within the <head> tag. You are using find and replace to search for the end head (</head>) tag and then add the <link> tag before it by replacing it with the <link> tag followed by a </head> tag.

NOTE *To get a new line when you are within the Replace text field, press Shift+Return (Macintosh) or Shift+Enter (Windows). Using the Return or Enter key alone activates the Find Next button in the dialog box. Because the* </head> *tag is usually on a different line, you might want to place a line break in the code before the* </head> *tag—this is not a*
 (break); it is simply a new line in the code.

6) All the Options should be unchecked. Click the Find Next button.
The first document in the folder in which Dreamweaver finds the </head> tag opens in Code view. Dreamweaver selects the </head> tag.

7) Click Replace.

Dreamweaver makes the replacement, and the Find and Replace dialog box indicates that there was one item found and replaced in the document.

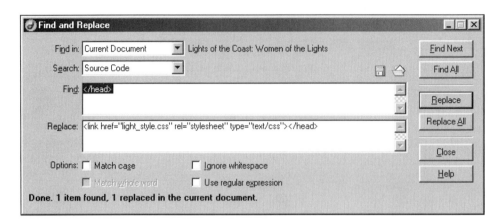

8) Change the Find in menu selection to Folder, and click the folder icon to the right of the text field that appears to the right of the Find in menu.

The Choose Search Folder dialog box opens.

9) Locate the Files folder in the Lesson_15_Find folder. On Macintosh, select the Files folder and click Choose. In Windows, open the Files folder and click Select.

There are two HTML documents in the Files folder that need to have the external style sheet attached. Neither document in the Files folder uses <font> tags, so you don't need to use the Find and Replace feature to strip the <font> tag from the documents as you did with women.htm.

10) Click the Find Next button.

Dreamweaver opens the first document in the folder in which it finds the </head> tag. The document is opened in Code view with the </head> tag selected.

The link to the style sheet that is in the code you typed in the Replace text field is a document-relative link. Because the link is simply the name of the file, the browser looks for the CSS file inside the same folder that the keepers.html and life.html files are located in. For the demonstration purposes of this exercise, there is a duplicate of the light_style.css file inside the Files folder. In your own sites, however, it is recommended that you not duplicate external style sheets in this manner because if you make a change in one, the documents that draw on a duplicate of that style sheet do not reflect the changes unless the duplicate is also updated. To link documents in different folders to the same CSS file, you may want to use site-root relative links, which ensure that no matter where the HTML documents are located, they still link to the correct CSS file. Site-root relative links were covered in Lesson 4.

11) Click the Replace button.

Dreamweaver makes the replacement; then automatically finds the next document in the folder containing the source code that it is searching for and opens it in Code view with the </head> tag selected.

12) Click Replace. Close the Find and Replace dialog box and close (Macintosh) or collapse (Windows) the Results panel if it is open. Save and close keepers.html and life.html documents.

NOTE *You may not see the change applied to the background in either document until you close the Find and Replace dialog box and either click in the document window or click the Refresh button as you may be prompted to do by the Property inspector.*

The style sheet is now attached to both documents. You can save all open documents. Leave the women.htm file open for the next exercise and close the other documents.

APPLYING CUSTOM STYLES WITH FIND AND REPLACE

Now that you have removed the <font> tags and attached an external style sheet, you can apply a custom CSS style to text in the women.htm document. In this exercise, you will use the Find and Replace feature to locate the text in the code and apply the HTML tags for the custom style.

1) In the women.htm document, select the first occurrence of the word "keepers" in the body text. Select the boldcolor custom style from the Style menu on the Property inspector to apply it to the selected text.

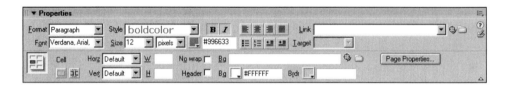

The text changes to reflect the bold and brown attributes that are defined by the custom style.

2) Choose Edit > Find and Replace. Select Current Document from the Find in menu and select Source Code from the Search menu. Type *keepers* **in the Find text field if it is not already there.**

> **TIP** *If you select text before you open the Find and Replace dialog box, that specific text appears in the Find text field.*

The dialog box changes to reflect the Source Code search method.

3) Leaving the Find and Replace dialog box open, look at the HTML for the custom style you just applied in step 2.

You should see <span class="boldcolor">keepers</span>.

4) Copy the HTML in the Code view beginning with <span class="boldcolor"> **and ending with** </span>.

You may need to move the Find and Replace dialog box if it is in your way.

> **TIP** *You can also click inside the word keepers in the Code view, click the <span.boldcolor> tag in the Tag Selector, and then use Command+C (Macintosh) or Ctrl+C (Windows) to copy the code. You must click inside the Code view first to make the Code view active.*

492

You must have the Code view active to copy the HTML along with the text; otherwise, you get just the text and no HTML code. You should now have `<span class="boldcolor">keepers</span>` selected.

5) Return to the Find and Replace dialog box. Paste the HTML code you copied in step 5 into the Replace text field. All four options should be unchecked.

TIP *Use Command+V (Macintosh) or Ctrl+V (Windows) to paste the code into the Replace text field.*

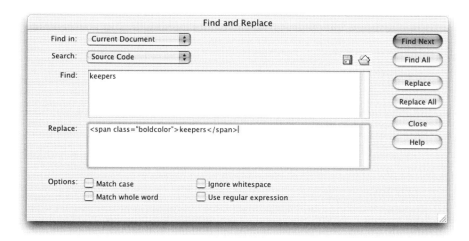

The code `<span class="boldcolor">keepers</span>` replaces all instances of the word "keepers" in the women.html document—the styled word will replace the un-styled words.

6) Click Find Next to select the next occurrence of the word "keepers." Click Replace to change the text and add the HTML. Verify that the change is correct. Click Replace All to change all occurrences in your document.
The Property inspector lets you know that changes have been made to the code. After you click OK, the document refreshes and the changes are visible.

All instances of the "keepers" are now formatted with the boldcolor CSS style. Using the Find and Replace feature to apply styles in this way can save you a lot of time. You may need to click in the document window or click the Refresh button if you are prompted to do so by the Property inspector to see the changes appear in the document window.

The Find and Replace dialog box closes automatically.

When using this method, you need to be certain that there no occurrences of the word that you are replacing (in this case, it is "keepers") in the code anywhere but in the text. If any images were named "keepers," or if "keepers" were part of a pathname, you would have problems with your code. When in doubt, use the Replace button rather than the Replace All button so you can double-check the item to be replaced.

7) Open (Macintosh) or Expand (Windows) the Results panel if it is not already open. Click the context menu in the upper right corner of the Results panel and choose Clear Results; then close (Macintosh) or collapse (Windows) the Results panel. Save the women.htm document.

TIP *If you do not see the Results panel, you can open it and view the results of the Find and Replace function by choosing Window > Results.*

Look back to the first occurrence of "keepers" where you manually applied the custom style. You should see that now you have two <span> tags applied to this text because the Find and Replace feature added the extra tag. Although the word appears to display properly in Dreamweaver, you need to remove the extra tag. You can manually remove the second set of tags in Code view, or you can choose Commands > Cleanup HTML (covered in Lesson 14). When using the Cleanup HTML command, make sure the Remove Redundant Nested Tags option is selected in the Cleanup HTML dialog box and click OK. Dreamweaver removes the extra <span> tags.

Macintosh Users: You can close the women.htm document.

Windows Users: You should leave the women.htm document open.

SAVING AND REUSING YOUR SEARCH CRITERIA

You might want to save your search criteria for other documents in your site, especially with complex searches. Saved search criteria, known as **queries**, are usually saved in the Configuration/Queries folder inside the Dreamweaver folder by default. They can, however, be saved in different places.

In this exercise, you will save your search query in the Lesson_15_Find folder.

NOTE *Macintosh users do not need to open a document to use the Find and Replace feature. Windows users, however, must have a document window open to use Find and Replace. Windows users should have the women.htm file open for this exercise.*

1) Choose Edit > Find and Replace. Click the Save Query icon in the Find and Replace dialog box.

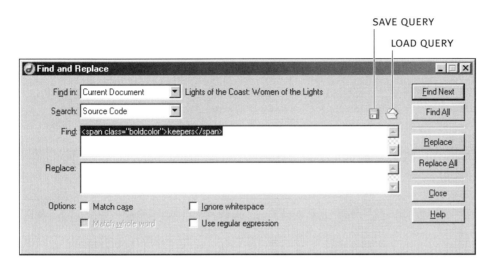

SAVE QUERY

LOAD QUERY

The Find and Replace dialog box has the same settings that were used in the last exercise to attach the light_style.css style sheet to documents.

The Save Query icon looks like a floppy disk icon. This option makes it possible for you to save and reuse complex searches.

2) In the Save Query to File (Macintosh) or Save Query (Windows) dialog box, locate and open the Lesson_15_Find folder; then type *addStyle* **in the File Name text field and click Save.**

Find queries have a .dwq extension; Replace queries have a .dwr extension. The extension is automatically added for you upon saving the query. The default location for the file to be saved is in the Queries folder inside the Configuration folder. The Configuration folder is located in the Dreamweaver program folder.

Now that you have saved the addStyle query, it is available to you any time you need to run the same Find and Replace function in other documents.

TIP *To save your own searches, set up your search and test it. Then follow steps 1 and 2 in this exercise.*

3) Click the Load Query icon in the Find and Replace dialog box.

The Load Query icon looks like an open folder icon next to the disk icon.

You now load a new Query that has already been saved for you.

495

4) In the Load Query (Windows) or Load Query from File (Macintosh) dialog box, locate and open the highlight_query.dwr query in the Lesson_15_Find folder.

This query looks for "keeper" and adds the highlight custom style from the external style sheet you just added to the files in the folder.

5) Leaving the Find and Replace dialog box open, use the Files panel to select keepers.html and life.html in the Files folder. In the Find and Replace dialog box, choose Selected Files in Site From the Find in menu.

TIP *Use the Shift key to select multiple contiguous files and use the Command key (Macintosh) or Ctrl key (Windows) to select multiple noncontiguous files.*

Dreamweaver uses the search criteria you loaded from the highlight_query on both documents selected in the Site window.

NOTE *You can Shift-click to select contiguous files, or Command-click (Macintosh) or Ctrl-click (Windows) each filename to select noncontiguous files in the Site window.*

6) Click the Replace All button to make the changes in the selected files.

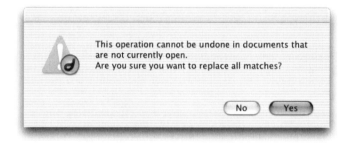

You can click OK in the dialog box informing you that this operation cannot be undone in documents that are not currently open. The Find and Replace dialog box closes automatically when done.

7) Click the context menu in the upper right corner of the Results panel and choose Clear Results. Close (Macintosh) or collapse (Windows) the Results panel.

Both keepers.html and life.html are updated to include the highlight custom style on any "keeper" text. Windows users can close the women.htm file.

SEARCHING AND REPLACING WITH REGULAR EXPRESSIONS

Regular expressions are control characters that describe character combinations or patterns in text. For example, if you want to find all occurrences of years from 1700–1799, the pattern is "17" followed by any combination of two numbers from 0–9. You can use a number of special characters to define the search pattern. For example, the backslash (\), dollar sign ($), and question mark (?) are all special characters. When using regular expressions, it is important to know these characters; if you are looking for such special characters in your text, you need to precede the character with a backslash to indicate it is part of the character search and not used as a special character.

Appendix A contains a table with all the special characters, regular expressions, and their meanings.

In this exercise, you will use patterned searches in a document.

1) Open the ca_lights.htm file in the Lesson_15_Find folder, place the insertion point at the beginning of the document and choose Edit > Find and Replace.

TIP   *You can also use Command+F (Macintosh) or Ctrl+F (Windows) to open the Find and Replace dialog box.*

The Find and Replace dialog box opens.

2) Select Current Document in the Find in menu. Set the Search menu to Text. Check the Use regular expression option box.

Notice that Ignore whitespace is disabled or grayed-out when you select Use regular expression.

NOTE   *The Ignore whitespace option, when selected, treats all whitespace as a single space for the purposes of matching. For example, with this option selected, "this text" matches "this text" but not "thistext." This option is not available when the Use regular expression option is selected; you must explicitly write your regular expression to ignore whitespace. Note that P and BR tags do not count as whitespace.*

3) In the Find text field, type *17\d\d.*

Be sure to type backslashes (\), not forward slashes (/), when you enter 17\d\d into the text field.

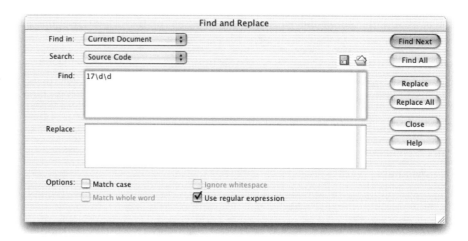

The first search looks for all years from 1700–1799. The ca_lights.htm file contains a list of years that are mostly after the 1800s. In this exercise, you will draw attention to the few years in the 1700s by applying the bold attribute to any year from 1700–1799. You want to skip the other years such as 1821 or 1901. To search for any number between 0–9, you use \d (known as a wildcard) as the search pattern. Because you want to limit the search to only the 1700 years, you are preceding the pattern character with the explicit text "17." See Appendix A for more regular expressions to use for search patterns.

TIP *To distinguish decimal numbers from years—19.09 for example—when searching in the document, include a period in your search. A period is also a special character, so you need to precede it with a backslash in your search.*

4) Click the Find Next button.
Dreamweaver selects the first year (1783) in the document window. You may need to move the Find and Replace dialog box to see the selection.

5) Continue to click the Find Next button several times to see what gets selected.
Any years in the 1800s or 1900s are not selected because they don't match the exact pattern.

6) In the Find and Replace dialog box, change the Search menu selection to Source Code.

In the following steps, you use the strong tags (<strong> and </strong>) to bold the dates. However, if you were to type **<strong>17\d\d</strong>** in the Replace text field, the text in the document window would be changed to 17\d\d—it would literally change the numbers in the year to \d. Instead, you need to isolate the search as a pattern by surrounding the pattern that you are searching for in parentheses.

7) In the Find text field, insert a left parenthesis before the text and a right parenthesis after the text, like this: *(*17\d\d*)*.

The parentheses create the first pattern.

8) In the Replace text field, type <strong>$1</strong>.

To reference the pattern you created in the previous step, you use $1 in the Replace text field. Surrounding this symbol with tags for bold formatting causes the bold tags to be added around the results of the first pattern search. If you were to create several patterns, the next pattern, as indicated by the parentheses, would be referenced in this text field with $2 and so on in a sequential manner.

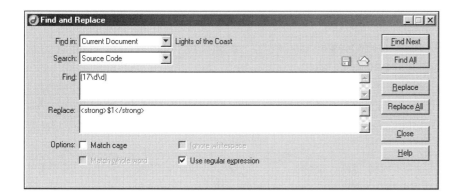

9) Click the Find Next button and then click the Replace button.

The bold tags are placed around the year in the Code Inspector. Click in the document window to see the results.

10) Click the Replace All button to find and replace all occurrences in the document. Save the ca_lights.htm document. Click the context menu in the upper right corner of the Results panel and choose Clear Results. Close (Macintosh) or collapse (Windows) the Results panel.

TIP *To view and clear the results, Macintosh users need to open the Results panel if it is not already open by choosing Window > Results.*

Leave this file open for the next exercise.

FINDING VARIATIONS IN A NAME

You can also look for variations in a name. For example, some of these lighthouses are located in California, but the name of the state is written in various formats throughout the page: ca, Ca, california, and California. You want to make the format consistent and change it to California.

1) In the ca_lights.htm document, place the insertion point at the top of the document and choose Edit > Find and Replace. Set the Find in menu selection to Current Document and the Search menu selection to Text. Type *C\w* built* **in the Find text field.**

The \w searches for any alphanumeric character after the C, and the asterisk means you want to find any number of alphanumeric characters. Adding "built" limits the search even further by causing Dreamweaver to search for instances that match C\w* and that are followed by the word "built." For instance, "C\w* built" finds "Ca built," "California built," and other variations of the character 'C' followed by any number of alphanumeric characters and the word "built." If you were to leave off "built," the search would also find items such as "Cape" and "Cabrillo" in the document.

2) In the Options, make sure Match case is unchecked. Only the Use regular expression box should be checked.

If Match case were selected, the search would be limited to finding only words that begin with an uppercase C. In this exercise, you want to find both the uppercase and lowercase instances of California, so you are leaving Match case unchecked.

3) In the Replace text field, type *California built*. **Place the insertion point at the beginning of the text in the document window. Click the Find Next button to find the first occurrence of a variation of California and then click Replace to change it.**

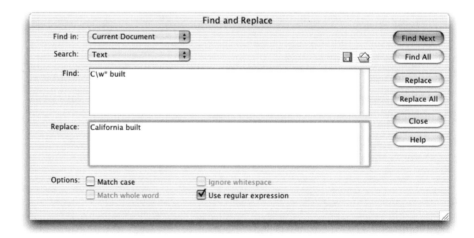

The first version of the state name is found in this document and replaced with California.

Dreamweaver selects the second instance of a "c" followed by "built": "chusetts built." You don't want to change this one because it is not a version of the CA state name.

4) Click the Find Next button. Continue to replace all the remaining versions of the CA state name. Save the ca_lights.htm document.

You can close this document and the Results panel.

WHAT YOU HAVE LEARNED

In this lesson, you have:

- Found and replaced text using detailed options to quickly modify a document (pages 480–482)
- Found text within HTML tags and learned how to change it using the Find and Replace feature (pages 482–485)
- Used the Find and Replace feature to attach external style sheets to multiple pages within a site (pages 486–491)
- Used the Find and Replace feature to quickly apply a custom style to a document (pages 492–494)
- Saved your search settings for later use and loaded saved queries (pages 494–496)
- Searched for patterns in text using regular expressions to find specific text such as dates and names (pages 497–499)
- Found multiple variations of a name and replaced them with one version (pages 500–501)

creating layers

LESSON 16

A **layer** is a rectangular container for HTML content that you can position at an exact location in the browser window. Layers can contain a wide variety of elements: text, images, tables, and even other layers. Anything you can place in an HTML document you can also place in a layer. Layers are especially useful for placing elements atop each other or making them overlap. Layers are supported by 4.0 or later browsers only. They can control layout and appearance when used in combination with CSS, and they provide interactivity when used in combination with behaviors.

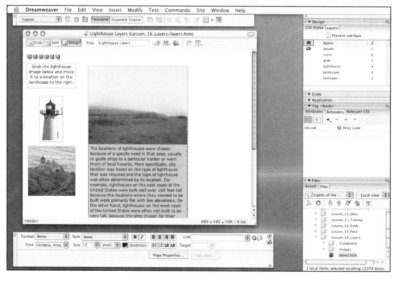

In this project, you will create layers, place text and images in them, move them to exact locations on the page, and change their properties.

In this lesson, you will learn several ways to create layers in Dreamweaver. You will draw a layer on the page to the size you want and place a layer on the page using a predetermined width and height. You will learn to modify layer attributes including size, placement, and visibility. You will also convert your layers to tables to make it possible for users with older browsers to view your pages.

To see an example of the finished page, open layers.htm from the Lesson_16_Layers/Completed folder.

WHAT YOU WILL LEARN

In this lesson, you will:

- Create layers

- Name layers

- Modify layer sizes and locations

- Use layers to control content on your page

- Change the stacking order of layers

- Nest and unnest layers

- Change layer visibility

- Set rulers and grids

- Use a JavaScript fix for a Netscape bug

- Make pages designed with layers compatible with earlier browsers

APPROXIMATE TIME

This lesson should take about one hour to complete.

LESSON FILES

Media Files:

Lesson_16_Layers/Images/…(all files)

Starting Files:

Lesson_16_Layers/layer.htm

Completed Project:

Lesson_16_Layers/Completed/layers.htm
Lesson_16_Layers/Completed/layers_table.htm
Lesson_16_Layers/Completed/transparent.gif

CREATING LAYERS

There are several different ways to create a layer. The method you choose may depend on how you plan to use the layer and where you want to place it. In this exercise, you will create several layers and insert content into them.

1) Open layers.htm from the Lesson_16_Layers folder. Switch to the Layout category on the Insert bar and verify that the Standard button is selected.

NOTE *You should be using Design view for this lesson.*

Standard view is the default, and the Standard button on the Insert bar will be highlighted to indicate that it is active. You must be in the Standard view to create a layer.

THE LAYOUT CATEGORY OF THE INSERT BAR

DRAW LAYER   STANDARD VIEW

2) Click the Draw Layer button in the Layout category of the Insert bar. Move the pointer into the document window; then click and drag to create a new layer on the right side of the page.

The pointer changes to a crosshair (+) when you move the pointer into the document window. After you drag and release the pointer to create the layer, a rectangle appears to display the new layer.

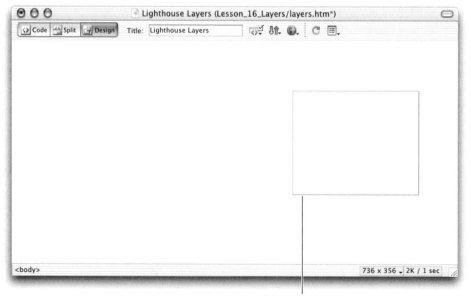

A LAYER IN THE DOCUMENT WINDOW

3) Choose Dreamweaver > Preferences (Macintosh) or Edit > Preferences (Windows). Select the Invisible Elements category and check the Anchor points for layers box. Click OK.

ANCHOR POINTS FOR LAYERS OPTION

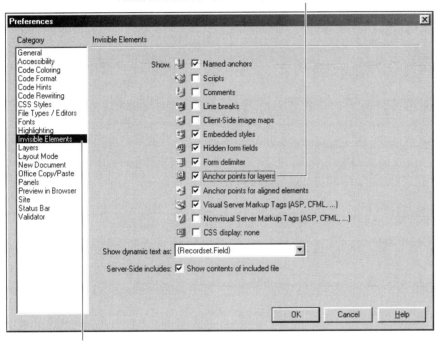

INVISIBLE ELEMENTS CATEGORY ON THE PREFERENCES DIALOG BOX

You should now see a layer marker at the top left of the document window. It appears blue when it is selected and yellow when it is not selected.

NOTE *You can use the layer marker for selecting the layer, but if your layer is positioned at the top left of the document window, the marker could get in the way and may appear to shift the position of the layer. This shift happens only in the document window; when the page is viewed in the browser, all elements will be in their correct positions. Turn the markers off temporarily by using View > Visual Aids > Invisible Elements. A checkmark next to the command in the menu indicates the option is on.*

By default, the layer code is inserted at the top of the page, just after the <BODY> tag. The <DIV> tag is used to create layers because it is the most common and allows the largest possible audience to be able to view your layers. Dreamweaver uses the <DIV> tag to create layers that use absolute positioning to determine the placement of the layer in relation to the top and left sides of the browser window. The <DIV> tag is a block-level element. A block-level element is a container that structures portions of your page—it begins on a new line, or a new block. Other block-level elements include <P> (paragraph) and <UL> (unordered list). Block-level elements can contain other block-level elements as well as inline elements. Inline elements usually contain only text and other inline elements, and are used within block elements—they do not create new blocks or lines. Some examples of inline elements include <SPAN> (span),
 (line break) and <A> (anchors, otherwise known as links).

NOTE *Dreamweaver recognizes several additional tags that can be used to create layers (<SPAN>, <LAYER>, and <ILAYER>), but it does not provide the option to use these tags to create layers. The <SPAN> tag, which is an inline element, uses relative positioning to determine the placement of the layer depending upon the position of other elements around it. The <LAYER> and <ILAYER> tags were supported only in Netscape Navigator 4. Netscape no longer supports these tags, and Internet Explorer has never supported them. The Design view does not render or display these types of layers, although it does insert a layer marker for the layer.*

4) Position the pointer over the border of the layer. When the pointer turns into a hand (Macintosh) or a four-headed arrow (Windows), click to select the layer.
When the pointer rolls over the lines that indicate the border of the layer, the lines turn red to indicate that you can select the layer.

The layer is now shown with a square tab at the top left. This tab is the layer selection handle. The black squares on the borders of the layer are sizing handles.

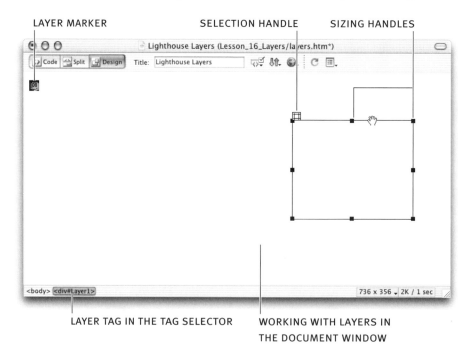

LAYER MARKER   SELECTION HANDLE   SIZING HANDLES

LAYER TAG IN THE TAG SELECTOR   WORKING WITH LAYERS IN THE DOCUMENT WINDOW

5) Place the insertion point inside the layer. Insert a table into the layer with the following attributes: 1 row, 1 column, 300 pixels wide, a border of 0, cell padding of 5, cell spacing of 0, no header, no caption and no summary. Open locations.txt from the Lesson_16_Layers/Text folder, copy all the text, and paste it into the table you created inside the layer.

TIP *The Layout category of the Insert panel contains an insert Table button.*

The layer expands if necessary to accommodate the table and the text that table now contains. Layers expand to show you all of their content unless you change the overflow setting in the Property inspector.

6) Place the insertion point in the document outside the layer. Click the Draw Layer button and draw a small second layer on the left side of the page. Insert the PMlight70.gif image from the Lesson_16_Layers/Images folder, into the layer.
The layer expands if necessary to the dimensions of the image. The layer does not change size if it is larger than the image.

TIP *To draw multiple layers continuously without clicking Draw Layer more than once, hold down Command (Macintosh) or Ctrl (Windows) as you draw the first layer. You can continue to draw new cells until you release the modifier key.*

If the insertion point is within a layer when you insert the layer, the new layer is nested inside the other layer.

TIP *Be aware that nested layers can cause problems in older browsers.*

At this point, your document should look similar to the example shown here.

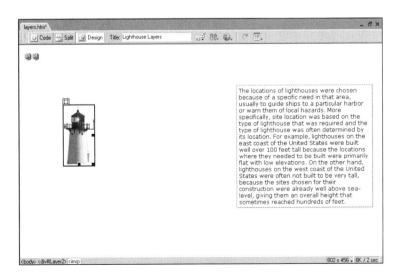

7) Place the insertion point in the document outside the first and second layers and choose Insert > Layout Objects > Layer. Insert the rocks-ocean.jpg image from the Lesson_16_Layers/Images folder into the layer.

The layer appears in the upper left corner of the document window with the default width and height specified by the layer preferences.

A third layer marker appears after the first two markers to show where the layer code has been inserted. At this point, the third layer may partially obscure the layer markers and portions of the other layers.

8) Click in the document window outside of the existing layers to deselect the layer you inserted in the previous step. Drag the Draw Layer icon from the Insert bar into the document window and drop it outside the existing layers. With the insertion point inside of the new layer, insert the landscape.jpg image from the Lesson_16_Layers/Images folder into the layer.

A fourth layer with the default width and height is created in the document window, over top and offset slightly to the right of the last layer you created, similar to the following example. After you insert the layer, the insertion point will automatically be in that layer.

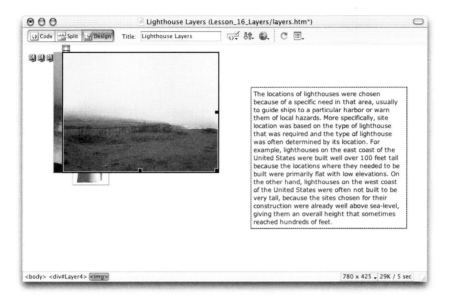

Figure showing Dreamweaver window titled "Lighthouse Layers (Lesson_16_Layers/layers.htm*)" with text:

The locations of lighthouses were chosen because of a specific need in that area, usually to guide ships to a particular harbor or warn them of local hazards. More specifically, site location was based on the type of lighthouse that was required and the type of lighthouse was often determined by its location. For example, lighthouses on the east coast of the United States were built well over 100 feet tall because the locations where they needed to be built were primarily flat with low elevations. On the other hand, lighthouses on the west coast of the United States were often not built to be very tall, because the sites chosen for their construction were already well above sea-level, giving them an overall height that sometimes reached hundreds of feet.

9) Save the layers.htm document.

Leave this file open for the next exercise.

NAMING LAYERS

Dreamweaver assigns generic names automatically in a numeric order: Layer1, Layer2, etc. These names are not very descriptive, especially when you create complex pages with multiple layers. It's best to get in the habit of giving your layers short descriptive names.

1) Choose Window > Layers to open the Layers panel.

TIP *You can also bring up the Layers panel by opening the Design panel group and clicking the Layers panel tab.*

The Layers panel, located in the Design panel group, gives you a list of the layers on the page. You can use this panel to select a layer, name a layer, change the layer's visibility, change the stacking order, or select multiple layers on the page. When you create a layer the new layer is placed at the top of the list on the Layer panel before other layers, if there are any—layers are listed in descending order. If the layer is hidden or placed off the page, using the Layers panel and layer markers may be the only methods for selecting the layer.

If the insertion point is inside a layer, that layer's name appears in bold on the Layers panel and the selection handle appears in the document window to indicate that the layer is active but not selected.

The four layers you just created are named Layer1, Layer2, Layer3, and Layer4.

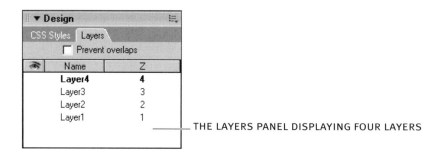

THE LAYERS PANEL DISPLAYING FOUR LAYERS

2) Double-click the Layer1 layer in the Layers panel, type *textlayer* **for the layer name, and press Return (Macintosh) or Enter (Windows). Double-click the Layer2 layer in the panel, type** *lighthouse*, **and press Return (Macintosh) or Enter (Windows). Don't change the name for the Layer3 layer. Double-click the Layer4 layer in the panel, type** *landscape*, **and press Return (Macintosh) or Enter (Windows).**

Do not use spaces or special characters (including the underscore character) for layer names. A layer name must be unique—don't assign the same name to more than one layer or to a layer and another element such as a graphic. It is a good idea to use a consistent naming scheme for all layer names.

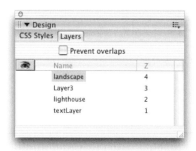

You can also type the name in the Layer ID text field on the Property inspector if the layer is selected.

As you assign names to the layers, they become selected in the document window. A selected layer appears to be in front of the other layers. You can click in the document window, outside of all the layers, to deselect a selected layer.

3) Save the layers.htm document.

Leave this file open for the next exercise.

MODIFYING LAYERS

After you create a layer, you might want to add a background to it, move it around, or resize it. One of the advantages of using layers is that you can place them in precise locations on the page. You can use the Property inspector and type in values for placement, and you can align layers to other layers. You need to select a layer first before you can make any modifications to it. There are several methods for selecting a layer—the method you use may depend on the complexity of your layout.

1) In the layers.htm document window, position the pointer over the border of the textlayer layer and click the border line when the pointer turns into a hand (Macintosh) or a crosshair with arrows (Windows) and the border turns red.

NOTE *If no layers are selected, Shift-clicking inside a layer selects it, whereas simply clicking inside a layer places the insertion point in the layer and activates it, but does not actually select the layer itself. You can select multiple layers by Shift+clicking other layers. Additional ways to select a single layer are to click the yellow layer marker that represents the layer's marker in the document window, the layer's tag in the Tag selector, or the name of the layer in the Layers panel.*

The layer becomes selected, and square black sizing handles appear around the layer. The name of the selected layer in the Layers panel is highlighted.

The Property inspector changes to reflect options for the selected layer. To see all properties, click the expander arrow in the lower right corner of the Property inspector.

NOTE *To delete a layer, select it and press Delete (Macintosh) or Backspace (Windows).*

2) Resize the textlayer layer by typing *320px* for the width in the W text field on the Property inspector and pressing Return (Macintosh) or Enter (Windows).

In the Property inspector, the W and H text fields display the specified width and height of the layer. Resizing a layer changes these values. The default unit of measurement is px (pixels).

NAME OF THE SELECTED LAYER (ALSO KNOWN AS LAYER ID)

WIDTH TEXT FIELD

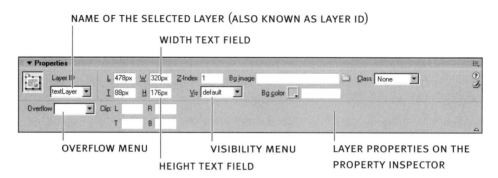

OVERFLOW MENU   VISIBILITY MENU   LAYER PROPERTIES ON THE PROPERTY INSPECTOR

HEIGHT TEXT FIELD

You can also resize the layer by dragging any of the sizing handles.

TIP *To resize the layer one pixel at a time using the keyboard, select the layer and press Option+right-arrow key (or any arrow) for Macintosh or Ctrl+right-arrow key (or any arrow) for Windows. To resize the layer by the current grid increment, press Shift+Option+right-arrow key (or the arrow for the direction that you want the layer to expand in) for Macintosh or Shift+Ctrl+right-arrow key (or the arrow for the direction that you want the layer to expand in) for Windows. See the Grid and Ruler Settings exercise later in this lesson to learn how to set the grid increment.*

As you learned while inserting the text and images earlier in this lesson, layers expand to fit their content. When the content of the layer exceeds the specified size, the original values for width and height will be overridden. The Overflow setting on the Property inspector controls how layers behave when this occurs. There are four Overflow options: visible, hidden, scroll, and auto. Visible, the default option, increases the size of the layer, expanding the layer down and to the right as much as is needed for all the layer's contents to be visible. Hidden maintains the size of the layer and clips any content that doesn't fit without providing scroll bars. Scroll adds scroll bars to the layer, whether or not the contents exceed the layer's size. Auto makes scroll bars appear only when the contents of the layer exceed its boundaries. You may need to click the expander arrow on the Property inspector to make these options visible.

You can also set the clipping area to specify the part of the layer that is visible. The clipping area can be smaller, larger, or the same size as the layer. Use the Property inspector to define the visible area by typing values in all four Clip text fields: L (left), T (top), R (right), and B (bottom). Any content outside of the clipping area is hidden. This setting is available with all four Overflow options.

3) With the textlayer layer still selected, type *350px* **in the L text field and** *50px* **in the T text field on the Property inspector. Select the landscape layer and type** *25px* **in the L text field and** *100px* **in the T text field.**

Be sure to select the landscape layer—and not the image that it contains—before trying to modifying the left (L text field) and top (T text field) distance properties for the landscape layer in the Property inspector.

The layer position can be off the page if the values in L and T are set to negative numbers. You might do this if you want to animate the layer and want it initially placed off the page. You will animate layers in Lesson 16.

LEFT TEXT FIELD

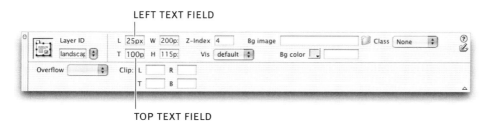

TOP TEXT FIELD

Be sure to use the L and T text fields on the top half of the Property inspector. Do not use the Clip text fields for this step. The L text field on the top half of the Property inspector defines the space between the layer and the left side of the browser window. The T text field on the top half of the Property inspector defines the space between the layer and the top side of the browser window.

You can also drag the selection handle or border of the selected layer to move it to a different location on the page. To move a layer from the keyboard one pixel at a time, select the layer and use the arrow keys. Hold the Shift key and press an arrow key to move the layer by the current grid increment.

4) Select the lighthouse layer in the layers panel and drag the layer selection handle in the document window down on the page so the layer appears farther down the page, below the landscape layer. Select the Layer3 layer and drag it farther down the page, below the lighthouse layer.

TIP *When dragging Layer3, pausing the layer over top of the bottom edge of the document window causes the document to scroll upward, giving you the space you need for the layer at the bottom of the window.*

When layers are hiding other layers that appear below them, you need to use the layers panel or the layer markers to select a hidden layer that you want to modify. You can also adjust the order in which layers are overlaid (their stacking order), as demonstrated in the next exercise.

Your document now looks similar to the example shown here.

5) Select the textlayer layer. In the Property inspector, click the Bg Color box and select pale tan or type *#CCCC99* **into the text field.**

BACKGROUND IMAGE

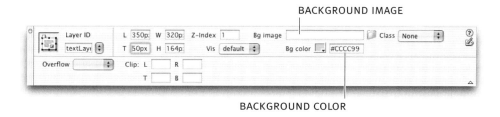

BACKGROUND COLOR

The background of the layer changes to pale tan.

There are two options for the backgrounds of layers:

- **Bg Image:** Specifies a background image for the layer. Type the path for the image in the text field or click the folder icon to select a source image. The background of a layer might not display in all browsers.

- **Bg Color:** Specifies a background color for the layer. Leave the text field blank or choose the default no color (the empty color swatch with a red line through it) at the top of the color menu to specify transparency.

When using either option, test your pages in all browsers—the results may not be what you expect, depending on the content of the layer. In this case, you have text in the layer. When viewed in the browser, the size of the text can vary greatly depending upon the visitor's browser and system, particularly if the text size is relative. The text may exceed the defined length of the layer, in which case the background may be either too big or too small. To avoid this, you can assign the pale tan color to the background of the table instead. Another way to solve the problem is to use CSS to define an absolute size for the text, and then set the size of the layer accordingly.

6) Select the landscape layer; then press and hold down the Shift key while selecting the textlayer layer by clicking the border of that layer.

TIP *You can also hold down the Shift key and click the layer name in the Layers panel to select multiple layers.*

515

Because multiple layers are selected, the most recently selected layer appears with solid black handles—the other layer has outlined handles.

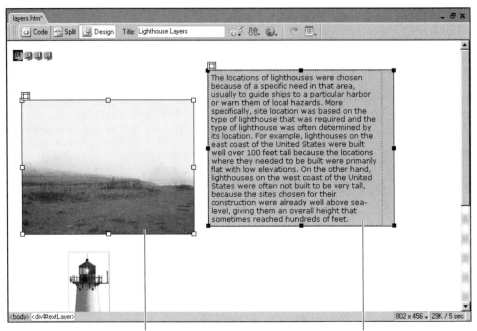

THE LAYER SELECTED FIRST   MOST RECENTLY SELECTED LAYER

NOTE *To resize multiple layers at once, select two or more layers in the document and choose Modify > Align > Make Same Width or Make Same Height. The first selected layers change to the width or height of the last selected layer. You can also enter width and height values in the Property inspector to apply the values to all selected layers.*

7) Choose Modify > Align > Top.

When you choose an alignment option, all the selected layers are aligned to the position of the last layer selected. The alignment options in this menu also include Left, Right, and Bottom.

The tops of the textlayer and landscape layers are now aligned to each other.

8) Save the document.

Leave this file open for the next exercise.

CHANGING THE STACKING ORDER OF LAYERS

You can use either the Property inspector or the Layers panel to change the stacking order of layers by adjusting the z-index of each layer. The **z-index** determines the order in which layers are drawn in a browser. A layer with a higher z-index number appears to be laid atop layers with lower z-index numbers. Values can be positive or negative. This is particularly useful when you have overlapping layers and you need to specify which layer(s) will be atop others. It is also possible for more than one layer to have the same z-index number, in which case the layer that appears in the code first appears on top.

1) In the layers.htm document, select the lighthouse layer and drag it upward until it partially overlaps the landscape layer. Preview your page in the browser.

The PMlight70.gif image that you inserted into this layer was created with a transparent background and saved in the GIF image format, which supports transparency. While the lighthouse layer is selected, it appears over the landscape layer and you can see the effect of the transparency. However, after you click off of the layer, the landscape layer appears to be overlapping the lighthouse because the landscape layer has a higher z-index value.

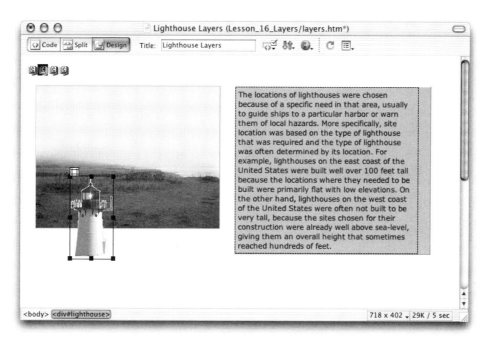

In the following steps of this exercise, you will adjust the stacking order of the layers to make the lighthouse layer appear above the landscape layer.

2) Select the landscape layer in the Layers panel and drag it downward in the list. Stop dragging and release the layer when a thin black line appears between the lighthouse and textlayer layers in the Layers panel.

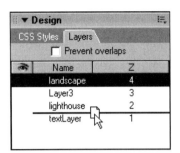

You will see the changes applied in the Layers panel—the landscape layer now appears between the lighthouse and textlayer layers. The z-index numbers on the layers panel also change automatically. It can be easier to change the stacking order when you move layers in the Layers panel than it would be to change the z-index values yourself via the Property inspector because Dreamweaver automatically changes the z-index values.

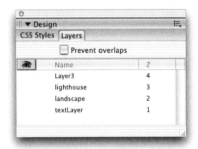

The landscape layer's z-index text field located on the Property inspector has changed from 4 to 2.

3) Select the lighthouse layer and move it up in the document window, positioning it so that the lighthouse image appears to be on the ground near the cliff in the landscape image.

Your document now looks similar to the example shown here.

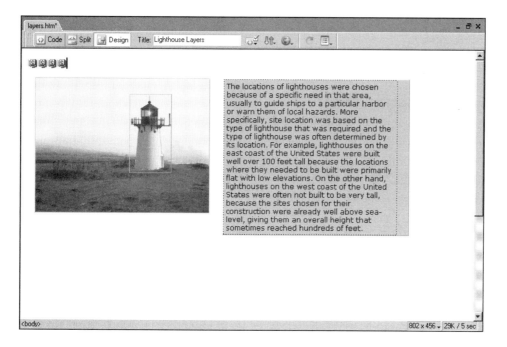

Save this file and leave it open for the next exercise.

NESTING AND UNNESTING LAYERS

Nesting is a way to group layers together. A nested layer moves with its parent layer and inherits the parent's visibility. There may be times when you want to nest or unnest a layer, and this exercise demonstrates that process. Be cautious; the results may be unreliable because nested layers may not display correctly in all browsers. If you do choose to nest layers, test your pages with your target browsers to be sure the result is what you expect. Testing was covered in Lesson 13.

NOTE *The top (T) and left (L) values in the Property inspector for a nested layer are relative to the parent layer, not the top left corner of the page. T and L specify the location of the layer from the top left corner of the page or parent layer.*

1) In the layers.htm document, use the Layers panel to select the Layer3 layer and drag it over the textlayer layer while pressing Command (Macintosh) or Ctrl (Windows). Release Layer3 when it is over top of the textlayer.

In Windows, a solid outline will appear around the textlayer name as you drag Layer3 over it. There is no visual indication on the Macintosh.

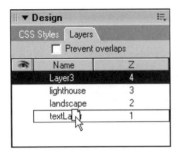

TIP *Don't release when the area between the layers is highlighted—doing so changes the stacking order of the layers instead of nesting the layers.*

In the Layers panel, the Layer3 layer appears indented below its parent layer, textlayer. Next to the textlayer layer is a downward-pointing triangle (Macintosh) or a minus sign (–) button (Windows) that allows you to see the nested layer. You can collapse this view by clicking the triangle (Macintosh) or minus sign (Windows) to display only the parent layer with a triangle pointing to the right (Macintosh) or a plus sign (+) button (Windows). You can click the plus sign or triangle again to show the list of nested layers. The position of the Layer3 layer in the document window shifts to be directly beneath the textlayer layer because the left value of the Layer3 layer is now relative to its parent layer, textlayer.

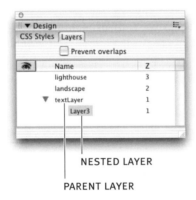

NESTED LAYER

PARENT LAYER

In the document window, the layer icon representing the nested Layer3 layer appears at the top of the textlayer layer, just above the table. The space created by this icon is seen in Dreamweaver only if you have visual aids enabled. The icon is not seen in (nor does it take up space in) the browser window.

520

If you preview the layers.htm file in several different browsers, you may notice differences that occur in the display of layers. In the older Netscape Communicator 4.75, the background color of the textlayer layer extends to encompass the Layer3 layer, and the lighthouse layer is displayed in the upper left corner of the browser window. In Internet Explorer 5, the lighthouse layer displays in the correct position, but the background color of the textlayer does not extend to encompass Layer3. The display varies depending on the system visitors' operating systems and browsers.

NOTE *You can also create a layer within an existing layer by selecting Draw Layer on the Insert bar and drawing the layer within an existing layer. For this to work, the Nest when created within a layer box must be selected in Preferences. To change the Layer Preferences, choose Dreamweaver > Preferences (Macintosh) or Edit > Preferences (Windows) and select the Layers category.*

2) On the Layers panel, select the nested Layer3 layer and drag it above the textlayer layer so a thin black line shows just above the textlayer layer.

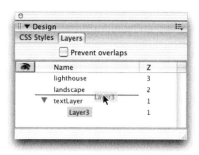

The nesting of a layer is removed, and the layer no longer appears indented in the Layers panel. The Layer3 layer is now moved back to its original location in the document window and appears above the textlayer in the Layers panel.

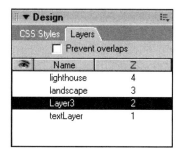

3) Save the layers.htm document.
Leave this file open for the next exercise.

CHANGING LAYER VISIBILITY

You can change layer visibility to show or hide a layer, which can be useful when using layers to add user interactivity. You may need to change the visibility of a layer if you are creating dynamic content that displays in response to user interaction.

1) Select the Layer3 layer in the layers.htm document. Click once in the Visibility column on the left side of the Layers panel to change the visibility of that layer.

A closed eye icon will appear in the column on the Layer3 row to indicate that the visibility has been changed to hidden.

HIDDEN

TIP *To change the visibility of all layers at once, click the eye icon at the top of the column.*

There are three visibility options on the Layers panel: inherit, visible, and hidden.

- Inherit uses the visibility property of the layer's parent. For this option, there is no icon displayed in the visibility column.

- Visible displays the layer contents, regardless of the parent's value. For this option, there is an open eye icon displayed in the visibility column.

- Hidden displays the layer content as transparent, regardless of the parent's value. If you set a layer to hidden, the layer markers and the Layers panel may be the only ways for you to select that layer. For this option, there is a closed eye icon displayed in the visibility column. Even though you have set the Layer3 layer to hidden, you still see scroll bars because hidden layers take up the same space as if they were visible.

On the Property inspector, there is a fourth visibility option: Default does not specify a visibility property, but most browsers interpret this as inheriting the parent's value.

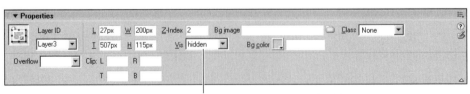

LAYER VISIBILITY OPTIONS ON
THE PROPERTY INSPECTOR

NOTE *Choose Dreamweaver > Preferences (Macintosh) or Edit > Preferences (Windows) and select the Layers category to set the default visibility for new layers.*

2) Save the layers.htm document and preview it in the browser.

When the Layer3 layer is selected in Dreamweaver, you can see it in the document window. When it is not selected, the layer disappears, making the document window look just as it does in the browser.

When you preview the file, notice that the browser window continues to scroll past the end of the text because of the hidden Layer3 layer.

3) Select the Layer3 layer in the Layers panel and choose Edit › Clear (Macintosh) or press Backspace (Windows).

TIP *Pressing Delete may not work with the Layers panel on the Macintosh. You can choose Edit > Clear, or remove the layer from the document window instead.*

Leave this file open for the next exercise.

SETTING GRID AND RULER OPTIONS

When you work with layers, you might want to use grids and rulers as visual guides for the placement of layers on your page.

1) In the layers.htm document, choose View › Grid › Show Grid.

The grids display in the document window. A checkmark next to the command indicates that the option is on.

2) Choose View › Grid › Snap To Grid.

This option turns snapping on or off. A checkmark next to the command indicates that the option is on. When this option is on, the layers snap to the grid lines when you move them close.

3) Select the lighthouse layer; then press the Shift key and select the landscape layer. Use the landscape layer selection handle to move them to the right so that four of the grid boxes are showing between the edge of the document window and the left edge of the landscape layer and one grid box is showing between the top edge of the document window and the top edge of the landscape layer.

The landscape layer appears to be on top of the lighthouse layer while you move them because you selected the landscape layer last—you can see that they are both selected in the Layers panel because both layer names are highlighted. After you click off of the layers in a blank area of the document window, the lighthouse layer appears above the landscape layer again.

The landscape layer will have snapped to the grid line. If you click in the document window to deselect both layers, select only the landscape layer; the L value should now be 200px. You may be able to see the faint gray border of the landscape layer just to the left of the grid line in the document window when it is deselected. The layer is actually aligned exactly with the grid line, even though the border appears to be 1 pixel to the left of the grid line; the 1-pixel gray layer border that you see is a Dreamweaver visual aid that does not display in the browser.

TIP *You can change the grid setting by choosing View > Grid > Grid Settings. The Edit Grid dialog box appears, in which you can change the color, set the spacing value and units (pixels, inches, or centimeters), and switch the grid display to lines or dots. The grid can be useful when you need to align layers.*

4) Choose View > Rulers > Show.

The rulers display in the document window. A checkmark next to the command indicates that the option is on. The units for rulers can be changed by choosing View > Rulers > Pixels, Inches, or Centimeters. A checkmark next to a unit of measure indicates which one is set.

5) Select the textlayer layer and move it just below the landscape layer, aligning it along the same grid line on the left side. Change the width of the textlayer layer to 300px.

The background color of the textlayer layer should touch the landscape layer. This may be difficult to see in the document window because the layer borders visual aid is turned on. Using the arrow keys help you match up the top edge of the textlayer layer with the bottom edge of the landscape layer.

6) Preview the page in the browser. If necessary, adjust the T value of the textlayer layer on the Property inspector or adjust the vertical orientation of the textlayer layer using the up and down arrow keys so there is no white space between the landscape layer and the background color of the textlayer layer.

You can also temporarily turn off the layer borders visual aid by choosing View > Visual Aids > Layer Borders. The rest of this lesson assumes that you have the layer borders visual aid turned on.

The zero point is the point where the horizontal and vertical rulers intersect. The default location for the zero point is the upper left corner of the page, where the top and left sides of the page meet. You can set the zero point to a different location by clicking in the square between the vertical and horizontal rulers, dragging the zero point downward and to the right and then releasing. When the zero point is moved to a point inside the document, you see negative values appear upward and to the left of the zero point. Choose View > Rulers > Reset Origin to reset the zero point.

Your document should now look similar to the example shown here.

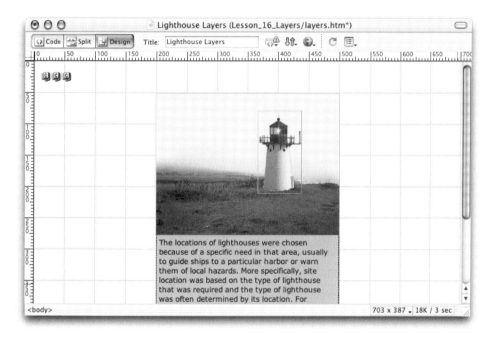

NOTE *If the tan background of the textlayer does not continue to the edge of the image below the table and you see white space near the bottom of the table, you can either set the background of the table to the same tan color or you can increase the height of the layer.*

7) Turn off the Grid, Snap to Grid, and Ruler options.

TIP *Choose View > Grid > Show Grid to remove the checkmark and hide the grid. Use the same method to remove the checkmarks for the Snap to Grid (View > Grid > Snap to Grid) and Ruler options (View > Rulers > Show).*

The rest of the book assumes that you have the grid turned off. You can either turn off the rulers or leave them on. Save this file and leave it open for the next exercise.

USING THE DRAG LAYER BEHAVIOR

Layers can be combined with behaviors to enable your visitors to interact with your page. The Drag Layer behavior makes it possible for the visitor to grab a layer in the browser window and move it to a different spot on the page. This is a great way to create interactive games or teaching tools with elements that can be moved by the user.

1) Place the insertion point in the text that is in the textlayer layer. Click the `<table>` tag in the Tag Selector at the bottom of the document window. Press the right arrow key once to move the insertion point after the table and insert the rocks-ocean.jpg image.

The rocks-ocean.jpg image that you used previously in Layer3 is now in the textlayer, just below the table containing the text.

2) Select the lighthouse layer. Set the width of the lighthouse layer to *70px*, the height to *131px*, the left value to *50px*, and the top value to *140px*. Create a layer just above the lighthouse layer. Name it *grab* and type the following inside the layer: *Grab the lighthouse image below and move it to a location on the landscape to the right.* **With the insertion point in the new text, click the Align Center button on the Property inspector.**

You adjusted the dimensions of the lighthouse layer to make it exactly the same size as the image it contains: 70 pixels wide by 131 pixels high. The new grab layer should not overlap any other layers.

Your document should now look similar to the example shown here.

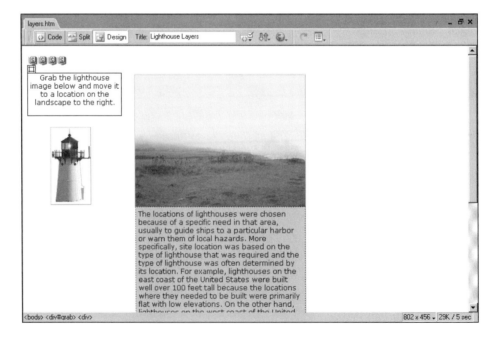

It is a good practice to let your visitors know when an item can be moved. Now that you've included text to let the visitor know the lighthouse image is draggable, you can apply the behavior.

3) Click the <body> **tag in the Tag Selector at the bottom of the document window to select it.**

The Drag Layer behavior cannot be applied directly to a layer, so you will apply it to the document's <body> tag.

NOTE *You can also apply the Drag Layer Behavior to other tags, such as link* <a href>, *which can be either inside or outside of a layer.*

4) In the Behaviors panel, click the plus sign (+) button and select the Drag Layer action from the Actions drop-down menu.

TIP *The Behaviors panel is located in the Tag Inspector panel group. Behaviors were covered in Lesson 11.*

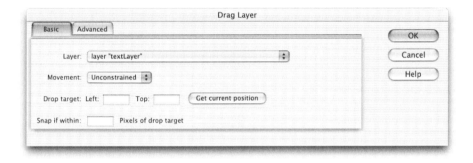

The Drag Layer dialog box appears with the Basic tab active.

NOTE *The Drag Layer action is not available if you have a layer selected. If it is grayed-out, you should make sure that the* <body> *tag is selected.*

5) Select layer lighthouse from the Layer menu and choose Constrained from the Movement menu.

Four text fields appear to the right of the Movement drop-down menu: Up, Down, Left, and Right.

6) Type 70 **in the Up text field,** 22 **in the Down text field,** 0 **in the Left text field, and** 390 **in the Right Text field. Leave the text fields for Drop Target and Snap if Within blank.**

527

The coordinates allow the visitor to place the lighthouse only within the area of the landscape image. The amount of allowable movement is relative to the original position of the lighthouse layer. You are restricting the visitor to moving the lighthouse only 70 pixels upward of where it is now, only 22 pixels downward, and so forth.

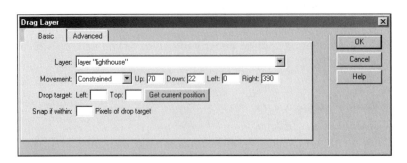

NOTE *If you had chosen Unconstrained from the Movement menu, the visitor could move the lighthouse image anywhere on the page.*

You can use the Constrain option to control the direction and amount of pixels in which the visitor can drag a layer. You can restrict the visitor to moving the layer only in a horizontal direction by setting the Up and Down text fields to 0 so that the image could not be moved up or down. Likewise, you can restrict movement to a vertical direction by the Left and Right text fields to 0.

NOTE *If you have a target area where you want the visitor to place the layer, you can specify that location by typing into the Drop Target text fields the left and top values that the layer should have in its target position into the Drop Target text fields. You can make it easier for a visitor to place the layer in the target location by causing the layer to snap to the target location if the layer is moved within the range of pixels that you specify; use the Snap if Within text field to set the snap-to range.*

7) Click OK. Save the file and preview it in the browser.

Test the movement of your lighthouse image by trying to move it. Notice that you can move it only within the region specified by the numeric values you entered in step 6. This behavior may not work in all browsers.

NOTE *The Advanced tab in the Drag Layer dialog box allows you to specify an area of the image as a handle that the visitor can use to grab and move the layer. It also gives you control over what happens to the z-index of the layers when the layer is moved. You also have the option to call additional JavaScripts while the layer is moving, when the layer is dropped, or when the layer snaps to the target. The Drag Layer behavior gives you the ability to create a more interactive experience for the visitor.*

USING THE SHOW-HIDE LAYERS BEHAVIOR

You can use the Show-Hide Layers behavior to control a layer's visibility and have that visibility change based on the visitors' actions.

1) Create a new layer below the lighthouse image, name it *reyes*, **and place the pt_reyes_img.jpg image inside it. Create a second new layer below the new layer and image. Name it** *details* **and type the following in the new layer:** *Reaching the Point Reyes Lighthouse requires a hike of about half a mile and a descent of over 300 steps.*

Your document should look like the following example.

2) Set the visibility of the details layer to hidden by selecting the layer and choosing hidden from the Vis menu on the Property inspector. Click outside the layer in the document window to deselect it.

TIP *You can also set the visibility of the layer by clicking in the Visibility column to show the closed eye icon that indicates the layer is designated as hidden. Clicking on the visibility icon in the column for any given layer will change the visibility for that layer.*

The details layer now disappears.

3) Select the pt_reyes_img, type # into the Link text field on the Property inspector, and press Return (Macintosh) or Enter (Windows). With the image still selected, click the plus sign (+) button in the Behaviors panel (located in the Tag Inspector panel group) to add a behavior. Choose Show-Hide Layers from the behaviors menu.

The Show-Hide Layers dialog box appears with a list of the layers on the page.

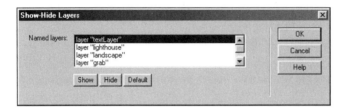

4) Select the details layer from the Named Layers list and click the Show button. Click OK to close the Show-Hide Layers dialog box.

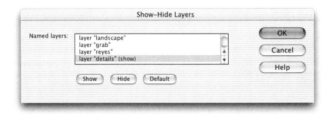

When you click the Show button, (show) is displayed next to the details layer in the list on the Show-Hide Layers dialog box.

5) In the Behaviors panel, click the Event menu and choose <A> onMouseOver from the Event menu.

This behavior is now triggered when the visitor rolls over it. Selecting events for behaviors was covered in Lesson 11.

6) Save the layers.htm file and test it in the browser.

Leave this file open for the next exercise.

CONVERTING LAYERS TO TABLES

Layers can be an easy way to design your page; however, your audience may be limited because not all browsers support layers. Although most current browsers will support layers, earlier browsers display layer contents without any positioning and without any control as to the placement. If you decide to design your page using layers, you may want to convert the layers to a table to provide an alternate page for those viewers with browsers that do not support layers. Test you pages in different browsers and see what your audience is using to help determine if you want to provide an alternative page. After you have converted the layers to a table, you can switch to Layout view to complete any design changes. You can then use the Check Browser behavior to redirect users based on their browser version.

The following exercise shows you how to convert layers, but the recommended method of creating tables is using Layout view to draw tables and table cells or Standard view to create tables (as you did in Lesson 5).

A few restrictions apply when you're converting layers to tables: You can't have nested layers, and the layers can't overlap. If these conditions exist, Dreamweaver displays an alert and does not create the table. You also cannot convert a single layer or a group of layers to a table while leaving other layers as layers—the entire page and all the layers that it contains will be converted to a table.

1) In the layers.htm document, choose File > Save As and type *layers_table.htm* **in the Save As (Macintosh) or File name (Windows) text field. Save the file in the Lesson_16_Layers folder.**

The layers in this document will be converted and replaced with a single table.

NOTE *The conversion to a table removes the layer names.*

2) Click in the document window. On the Layers panel, check the Prevent Overlaps box.

PREVENT OVERLAPS

Overlapping layers cannot be converted to a table. If you select this option before you begin drawing layers, Dreamweaver prevents the layers from overlapping. After the Prevent Overlaps box is checked, you might want to test it by trying to move the lighthouse layer over the landscape layer. By using the Prevent Overlaps option, you can move layers as close as possible to other layers.

If you already have layers that overlap, checking the Prevent Overlaps checkbox does not move those layers. You have to move them to stop them from overlapping.

3) Select the ‹body› tag in the Tag Selector, select the Drag Layer behavior in the Behaviors panel, and click the Remove Event button. Select the pt_reye_img image in the document window, select the Show-Hide Layers behavior in the Behaviors panel, and click the Remove Event button.

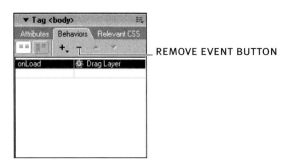

REMOVE EVENT BUTTON

When you use behaviors that apply to or are intended to affect layers, those behaviors are no longer be necessary after you convert the layers to a table. Such behaviors should be removed to keep your document clean, free of errors and unnecessary code, and reduce the file size.

4) Choose Modify > Convert > Layers to Table.
The Convert Layers to Table dialog box opens with a number of options:

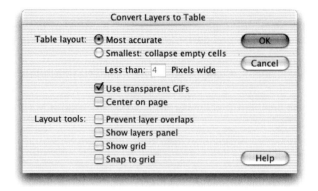

- Most Accurate creates a table cell for every layer plus any additional cells that are necessary to preserve the space between layers.

- Smallest: Collapse Empty Cells specifies that the layers' edges should be aligned if they are positioned within the specified number of pixels. If this option is selected, the resulting table may have fewer empty rows and columns.

- Use Transparent GIFs fills the last row of the table with transparent GIFs, which ensures that the table displays the same way in all browsers. When this option is selected, you cannot edit the resulting table by dragging its columns. When this option is deselected, the resulting table does not contain transparent GIFs, and its appearance might vary slightly in different browsers.

- Center on Page centers the resulting table on the page. If this option is deselected, the table is left-aligned.

- Layout Tools allows you to set any desired layout or grid options.

5) Keep the default settings of Most Accurate and Use Transparent GIFs. Click Center on Page and click OK.

If you have any layers that overlap, you get a warning dialog box, informing you that Dreamweaver cannot convert the layers to a table. If this happens, go back to your document and make sure that none of the layers overlap.

Any hidden layers are deleted. After you convert your layers to a table, you can make any necessary adjustments to the table.

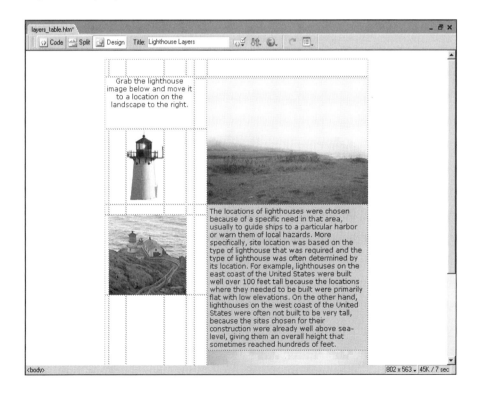

NOTE *You can also convert a table to layers by choosing Modify > Convert > Tables to Layers while in Standard view. The Convert Tables to Layers dialog box opens, and you can select the desired options and then click OK. Empty cells in the table are ignored and not converted to layers. Any content on the page outside the table is converted to a layer.*

USING THE NETSCAPE RESIZE LAYER FIX

Netscape 4.*x* versions have a problem with layers that occurs when the user resizes the browser window: The layer changes its shape when the browser window is resized, which can cause problems with the page. You can fix this problem by inserting the Netscape Resize Layer Fix JavaScript code into your document whenever you use layers. The JavaScript code fixes the Netscape 4.x problem and does not affect other browsers.

Dreamweaver will automatically add the Netscape Resize Fix when you create a layer in a document. When you delete all layers from a document you should run this command and remove the code if the script is still in your document. Because you converted from layers to a table in the previous exercise, you'll remove the script now because it is no longer needed.

1) In the layers_table.htm document, choose Commands > Add/Remove Netscape Resize Fix.

In the Add/Remove Netscape Resize Fix dialog box that opens, you can either add or remove the JavaScript code, depending on whether or not the script is in the document. The code causes the page to reload if the user resizes the browser window. Dreamweaver adds this code to your page automatically. If it is not in a page that uses layers, you can add it easily with this dialog box.

2) Click Remove.

TIP *If Dreamweaver automatically removed the script for you, you can skip this step.*

The Netscape Resize Fix JavaScript code is removed from the page

3) Save the layers_tables.htm document.

You can close this file.

WHAT YOU HAVE LEARNED

In this lesson, you have:

- Created layers by drawing them in the document window and by inserting default presized layers (pages 504–509)

- Named layers to keep track of them in the Layers panel (pages 509–511)

- Selected single and multiple layers, modified their sizes and locations, and aligned them relative to each other (pages 511–516)

- Used layers to control the placement and display of content on your page (pages 511–516)

- Changed the stacking order of layers to specify the order in which they display from top to bottom (pages 517–519)

- Nested and unnested layers to understand how layers can work in groups or become nested accidentally (pages 519–523)

- Set rulers and grids to help when moving layers on the page (pages 523–525)

- Combined layers with behaviors to let users interact with your pages (pages 526–531)

- Changed layer visibility to hide and show entire layers (pages 529–530)

- Made pages designed with layers compatible with earlier browsers by converting the layers to a table (pages 531–533)

- Learned to insert or remove a JavaScript to remedy a Netscape bug that causes viewing problems with layers (pages 534–535)

extending
dreamweaver

LESSON 17

Dreamweaver was designed to be extensible. As a result, you can expand Dreamweaver's capabilities through the use of *extensions*—pieces of software that can be added to increase the functionality of the program. There are several different kinds of extensions, ranging from simple HTML objects to more complex JavaScript commands. The Dreamweaver Extension Manager is used to install, manage, and remove extensions.

You can create new behaviors and extensions for use in Dreamweaver yourself or you can obtain extensions created by others from the Dreamweaver Exchange Web site. There are a wide range of extensions available on Macromedia's Dreamweaver Exchange, ranging from ones that you can buy to freeware-style scripts. In this lesson, you will use extensions that have been provided for you on the CD that accompanies this book.

In this project, you will customize Dreamweaver with extensions that will enable you to increase the functionality of forms as well as insert elements such as calendars and placeholder text.

In addition to creating and making use of extensions, you can also customize Dreamweaver by creating your own objects and customizing the Insert bar. You can also customize your workspace by reorganizing the panels you learned to work with in Lesson 1, and by adjusting Dreamweaver's preferences that you've worked with throughout the book.

To see examples of the finished pages for this lesson, open events.htm and lights_form.htm from the Lesson_17_Customize/Completed folder.

WHAT YOU WILL LEARN

In this lesson, you will:

- Add extensions using the Extension Manager
- Use new extensions
- Create your own objects

APPROXIMATE TIME

This lesson should take about one hour to complete.

LESSON FILES

Starting Files:

Lesson_17_Customize/events.htm

Lesson_17_Customize/lights_form.htm

Lesson_17_Customize/copyright.htm

Lesson_17_Customize/copyright.gif

Extensions:

*Lesson_17_Customize/Extensions/
    Calendar204.mxp*

*Lesson_17_Customize/Extensions/
    flevToggleChecks111.mxp*

*Lesson_17_Customize/Extensions/
    Lorem_andMore1_2.mxp*

*Lesson_17_Customize/Extensions/
    Superscript.mxp*

Completed Project:

Lesson_17_Customize/Completed/events.htm

Lesson_17_Customize/Completed/lights_form.htm

Lesson_17_Customize/Completed/copyright.htm

INSTALLING EXTENSIONS

Extensions are installed into Dreamweaver using the Extension Manager, a separate program that is installed along with Dreamweaver. In this exercise, you will install several extensions that have been provided for you on the CD-ROM that accompanies this book.

1) Choose Commands > Manage Extensions.

The Macromedia Extension Manager folder is usually installed in the same folder as the Macromedia Dreamweaver MX 2004 folder. The default installation location will be inside your Applications (Macintosh) or Program Files > Macromedia (Windows) folders.

The Extension Manager enables you to install extensions, remove extensions, find out more information about an installed extension, and prepare your own extensions. It also provides a convenient way to bring up the Dreamweaver Exchange Web site, through which you can find more extensions.

THE MACROMEDIA EXTENSION MANAGER MANAGES EXTENSIONS FOR
DREAMWEAVER AS WELL AS OTHER MACROMEDIA PRODUCTS

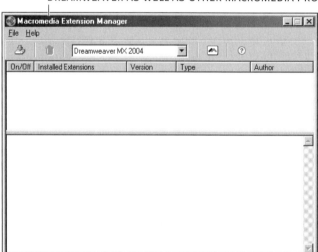

2) Choose File > Install Extension in the Extension Manager.

TIP *For Windows users, the File menu is located at the top of the Macromedia Extension Manager dialog box. Windows users can also click the Install New Extension button on the dialog box toolbar (the toolbar does not appear on the Macintosh version of Dreamweaver).*

The Install Extension (Macintosh) or Select Extension to Install (Windows) dialog box opens.

538

3) Locate and open the Extensions folder in the Lesson_17_Customize folder. Select Calendar204.mxp from the list of extensions and then click Choose (Macintosh) or Install (Windows).

Dreamweaver will begin to install the extension.

Macintosh Users: If the extensions are grayed out in the Install Extension dialog box and you cannot select the extension, you need to quit Dreamweaver, locate the Lesson_17_Customize/Extensions folder in the Finder and double-click the Calendar204.mxp file to install the extension. The Extension Manager will automatically open and begin the installation process—you can continue on to step 4.

4) A dialog box opens with licensing and disclaimer information. After you have read the material provided, click Accept to continue with the installation.

If the extension has been developed by a third party, its licensing information (if any) appears at the bottom of the dialog box.

If you click Decline, the extension is not installed.

If you already have another version of the extension installed—or another extension with the same name—the Installer will ask if you want to remove the one already installed. If you click Yes, the previously installed extension is removed and the new extension is installed. If you click No, the installation is cancelled, leaving the existing extension in place.

If the installer doesn't encounter any problems, it displays a message to inform you that the extension has been successfully installed.

TIP *Some extensions will take longer to install than others. There may appear to be a lag or pause in the installation process.*

5) Click OK.

The Macromedia Extension Manager displays the extension name, version number, type, and author. A description appears for the selected extension that gives details concerning what the extension does as well as the location of the extension in Dreamweaver. For example, the description for the Calendar extension informs you that the Calendar object can be accessed from either the Objects palette or the Calendar menu item in the Insert menu. Older extensions such as this one may have outdated descriptions that refer to interface elements in prior versions of Dreamweaver—the Objects palette is now known as the Insert bar. Extensions listed on the Dreamweaver Exchange indicate which version of Dreamweaver they were written for. Some older extensions work fine with newer versions of the program, whereas others may cause problems. If you encounter any difficulties after installing an extension, you should remove it.

TIP *You can check the boxes in the On/Off column to temporarily disable extensions. This may help to determine if errors are related to specific extensions. A checkmark in a box indicates that the corresponding extension is currently installed.*

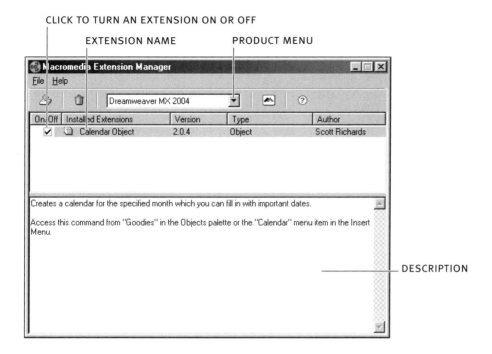

DESCRIPTION

6) Repeat steps 2 through 5 to install the following extensions:

- flevToggleChecks111.mxp
- Lorem_andMore1_2.mxp
- Superscript.mxp

Macintosh Users: If you are unable to install extensions by choosing File > Install Extension in the Extension Manager, double-click the extension file in the Finder (as described in step 3). You can leave the Extension Manager open as you do so—you do not need to quit.

As you go through the installation process for each extension, the installation results dialog box may inform you that you need to restart Dreamweaver.

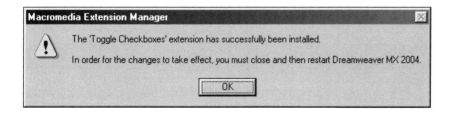

The Macromedia Extension Manager now displays a list of the extensions you have installed.

NOTE *If you are connected to the Internet, you can obtain more extensions from the Dreamweaver Exchange by choosing File > Go To Macromedia Exchange while you are in the Extension Manager. The Dreamweaver Exchange will open in your default browser. You must be a member of macromedia.com to download, submit, or review extensions—it is a free membership. You can sign up and log in at the Dreamweaver Exchange home page. Macromedia provides the Dreamweaver Exchange Web site as a repository for all kinds of extensions. When you download extensions from the Dreamweaver Exchange, the Extension Manager automatically opens and begins the installation process after the download is complete for Macintosh users. Windows users have to open the downloaded file or follow the install process described in this exercise. Macromedia creates some extensions, whereas third parties create other extensions.*

7) Choose Extension Manager > Quit Extension Manager (Macintosh) or File > Exit (Windows) to close the Extension Manager. Quit and restart Dreamweaver.
It is a good practice to always restart Dreamweaver after installing extensions (just as you would restart your computer after installing a program). When you restart Dreamweaver, you can use the new extensions. Extensions may not be available until the program is restarted.

Dreamweaver MX 2004 has changed dramatically from Dreamweaver MX and Dreamweaver 4. Although many of the extensions that were used in Dreamweaver 4 still work in Dreamweaver MX 2004, not every extension will. Some extensions may cause errors in Dreamweaver MX 2004. If you find this to be the case, just remove the problematic extension. If you run into a problem, you can test your extensions by turning them off.

> **NOTE** *To remove an extension, choose File > Remove Extension from the Extension Manager. Select an extension from the list of installed extensions and confirm that you want to remove the extension by clicking Yes in the confirmation dialog box. Only extensions that appear in the list can be removed with the Extension Manager. If you manually installed an extension, you need to manually remove it. Restart Dreamweaver for the changes to take effect.*

USING THE CALENDAR EXTENSION

The Calendar extension provides a quick way to insert calendars on your Web pages. Calendars can be useful on sites, such as when you need to post schedules and event information for your visitors.

Dreamweaver Extension: Calendar Object, V2.0.4

Extension Developer: Scott Richards

Developer URL: http://www.macromedia.com

1) Open events.htm in the Lesson_17_Customize folder and place the insertion point on a new paragraph line at the bottom of the document, beneath the existing page content. Choose Insert > Calendar.

> **TIP** *You can also choose the Goodies category on the Insert bar and click the Insert Calendar button. The Goodies category was created when you installed the Calendar extension.*

TOP LEFT

The Insert Calendar dialog box opens.

2) Leave the options set to their defaults and click OK.

Your page now displays a calendar for the current month. You can make a number of choices for your calendar in the dialog box, such as selecting different months and years, choosing format options for the days and months, or specifying a style sheet to control the appearance of the calendar.

The calendar table uses the percentage-based measurement—it is 95 percent of the window size. You can modify the size, if necessary, by selecting the table and adjusting the properties as you learned to do in Lesson 5.

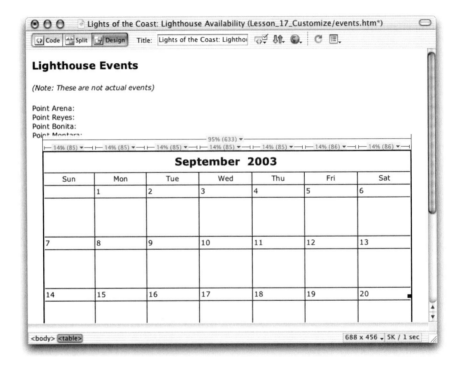

Leave this file open for the next exercise.

USING THE SUPERSCRIPT EXTENSION

This extension enables you to apply superscript for date abbreviations such as st, th, nd, and rd. When your text includes a date, such as November 1st, the "st" abbreviation is usually formatted as superscript. The Superscript extension makes it quick and easy to apply superscript formatting.

Dreamweaver Extension: Superscript Package, V1.1.1

Extension Developer: Tamara Jackson

Place the insertion point just to the right of the "Point Bonita:" text. Press the spacebar, type *Guided Walk, Aug 3* **and then choose Insert > Superscript > Superscript – rd.**

The date abbreviation is inserted with superscript formatting.

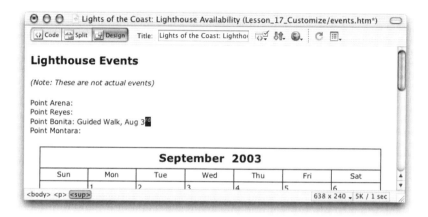

NOTE *Another extension with a similar purpose is available on the Dreamweaver Exchange Web site—Instant Subscripts and Superscripts, which allows you to insert both subscripts and superscripts.*

You can save and close the events.htm document.

USING THE TOGGLE CHECKBOXES EXTENSION

This extension is a behavior that automatically checks or unchecks all the checkboxes in a particular group, which can be useful in long lists of options on forms. Forms were covered in Lesson 7.

Dreamweaver Extension: Toggle Checkboxes, V1.1.1

Extension Developer: Marja Ribbers-de Vroed, FlevOOware

Developer URL: http://www.flevooware.nl/dreamweaver

1) Open lights_form.htm from the Lesson_17_Customize folder. Place the insertion point at the end of the text Point Montara and press Return (Macintosh) or Enter (Windows).

The Toggle Checkboxes extension lets you provide your visitors with a quick way to select all the checkbox options in this form.

2) Insert a button by clicking the Button button in the Forms category of the Insert Bar. In the Input Tag Accessibility Attributes dialog box, choose No label tag, leave the Position option at the default and leave the Access Key and Tag Index text fields blank. Use the Property inspector to change the name to *all* **and the Label to** *Check All*. **Choose None from the Action options in the Property inspector.**

BUTTON

The default action for buttons in Dreamweaver is Submit Form. Applying the Toggle Checkboxes behavior to a button that uses the Submit Form action will cause errors in the browser—be sure to change this option to None.

BE SURE TO CHOOSE NONE FOR
THE ACTION OF THE BUTTON

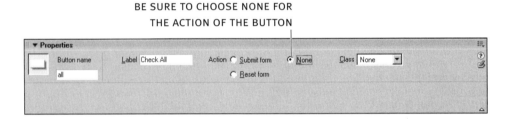

3) Select the Check All button and choose FlevOOware › Toggle Checkboxes from the Add Behavior menu on the Behaviors panel in the Tag inspector.

The Toggle Checkboxes dialog box opens.

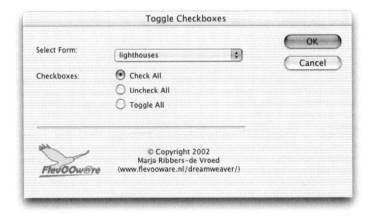

4) Make sure that lighthouses is selected in the Select Form menu and choose Check All from the Checkboxes options. Click OK to apply the behavior.

The Toggle Checkboxes behavior is applied to the Check All button. The Toggle Checkboxes behavior will apply to all checkboxes in the form.

5) Repeat steps 2 through 4 to create a button to uncheck all the boxes. Use *none* **for the button name,** *Uncheck All* **for the button label and choose Uncheck All in the Toggle Checkboxes dialog box when applying the behavior.**

The Toggle Checkboxes behavior is applied to the Uncheck All button. Preview your page in the browser and test the new Check All and Uncheck All buttons.

USING THE LOREM AND MORE EXTENSION

Earlier in this book (Lesson 3), you used the placeholder image object. When creating Web pages, you may also need to use placeholder text. The Lorem and More extension provides you with a quick way to insert such text.

Dreamweaver Extension: Lorem and More, V1_2

Extension Developer: David Powers

Developer URL: http://www.computerbookshelf.com

1) Place the insertion point in the top cell of the nested table, the cell just above the one that contains the checkbox list.

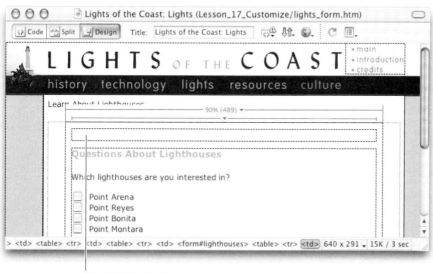

PLACE THE INSERTION POINT HERE

The insertion point should be in the cell just above the "Questions About Lighthouses" text.

2) Click the Lorem and More button in the Common category of the Insert bar.

The Lorem and More dialog box opens.

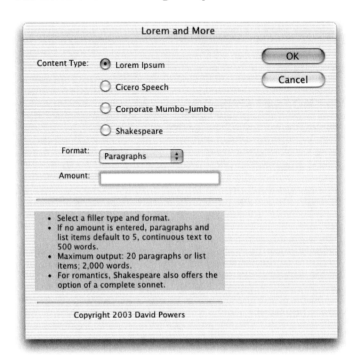

3) For this exercise the Content Type should be Lorem Ipsum. Type _1_ into the Amount text field, leave the Format menu at the default selection of Paragraphs and press OK.

The number that you type into the Amount text field indicated the number of paragraphs that should be inserted. Your document should now look like the following example.

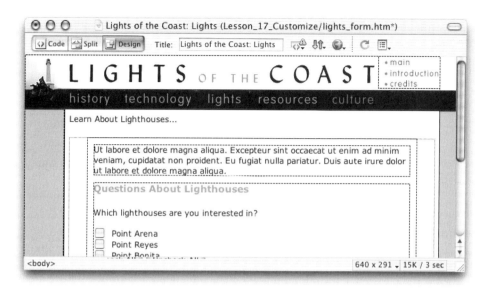

Using the Format menu on the Lorem and More dialog box, you can specify whether the placeholder text should be in a paragraph, continuous text, or a list (unordered or numbered).

You can save and close the lights_form.htm document.

CREATING A SIMPLE OBJECT

The Insert bar is divided into a number of categories, each of which corresponds to a folder within the Dreamweaver Program Folder. The Insert bar is an easy way to insert HTML elements that you use regularly into your pages. All the objects included in the Insert bar can be modified to suit your needs. Using only some basic HTML, you can create an object for use in all your documents.

NOTE *The example in this exercise is a simple copyright line that could also be created as either a library item (covered in Lesson 8) or as a snippet (covered in Lesson 14) to serve similar, although not identical, functions. Some items (such as those that you may want to update at a later time) work better as library items, whereas others work best as snippets, and still others are most useful as objects in the Insert bar (such as objects that you will use many times, in many different sites). It depends on the purpose of the object or code you are creating and how you want to access it. Library items were covered in Lesson 7, and snippets were covered in Lesson 14.*

1) Use the Finder (Macintosh), My Computer (Windows) or Windows Explorer (Windows), to locate Dreamweaver's Configuration > Objects > Goodies folder. The following instruction will help you locate the folder for your operating system.

In the Goodies folder, you'll see an HTML file and a GIF image file for the Calendar object that is in the Goodies category, which was created when you installed the extension. Other extensions may use a JavaScript file ending with the .js extension. Earlier in this lesson, you installed the Lorem and More extension, which placed the Lorem and More object into the Common category on the Insert bar. You can see the Common folder in the Objects folder as well.

A basic way to create a new object in the Insert bar is to create an HTML file that contains the object and a corresponding GIF file that serves as the object's icon. The HTML file and the GIF can then be placed into an appropriate folder inside of Dreamweaver's Objects folder, as you will do in this exercise.

If you are working in a multi-user environment such as Macintosh OS X, Windows NT, Windows 2000, or Windows XP, you have your own Configuration folder. This allows each user to have a different setup on the same computer.

Macintosh Users: The default location of your Configuration folder is Macintosh > Users > Your Username > Library > Application Support > Macromedia > Dreamweaver MX 2004 > Configuration. You can make modifications for all users by editing the main Configuration folder, which is located at Macintosh > Applications > Macromedia Dreamweaver 2004 > Configuration.

NOTE *When you first install Dreamweaver on a Macintosh, there will not be an Objects folder in the individual user Configuration folders as described above. The Objects folder will be created when extensions that install icons into the Insert bar are installed or when you modify the Favorites category of the Insert bar. The Goodies folder, for example, was created when you installed the Calendar extension. Object folders inside the individual user Configuration folders only contain additional objects. The default objects contained in the Insert bar are located in the Objects folder of the main program configuration folder, which is usually installed in Macintosh > Applications > Macromedia Dreamweaver 2004.*

Windows Users: If you have a single user setup, the default location of your Configuration folder is C: > Program Files > Macromedia > Dreamweaver MX 2004 > Configuration folder. If you have a multi-user setup, the default location of your own Configuration folder is C: > Documents and Settings > user > Application Data > Macromedia > Dreamweaver MX 2004 > Configuration folder.

550

2) Open the copyright.htm document in the Lesson_17_Customize folder.

This document contains a copyright, a horizontal rule, and a date that updates automatically when the document is saved (all these elements were covered in Lesson 2). The document does not have a title.

3) Click the Code button on the document toolbar to view the HTML. Delete everything in the document except for the following:

```
<hr align="center" width="90%" size="1" noshade>
<div align="center">&copy; 2003 | Modified:
<!--#BeginDate format:fcAm1 -->
Monday, August 25, 2003
<!--#EndDate --></div>
```

In Code view, your document looks like the example that follows.

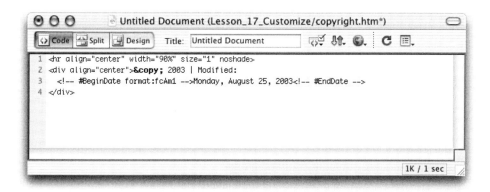

4) Save your file and quit Dreamweaver.

After you have prepared the HTML file, you need to create an icon to represent the object you are creating. The icons used by Dreamweaver are GIF files. In this exercise, an icon has already been created for you and is located in the Lesson_17_Customize folder. When you create new objects, the icon and the corresponding HTML document should both have the same names, although their extensions will be different.

NOTE *To create your own icons for the Insert bar, create an 18 × 18-pixel GIF image in an image-editing program such as Macromedia Fireworks. Make sure that the name of the GIF file is the same as the name of your HTML file.*

5) Select the copyright.htm and copyright.gif files. Copy them both into Dreamweaver's Configuration > Objects > Goodies folder and restart Dreamweaver. Create a new HTML document and choose the Goodies category on the Insert bar.

TIP *You located the Configuration > Objects > Goodies folder in step 1 of this exercise.*

When you open a new document and switch to the Goodies portion of the Insert bar after Dreamweaver restarts, you can see the copyright icon in the Goodies category of the Insert bar. The name of the HTML file is the name of the menu item.

THE COPYRIGHT OBJECT IN THE GOODIES CATEGORY

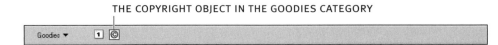

The Goodies category was created when you installed extensions earlier in this lesson. At the start of this exercise, the Goodies tab had only one object in it—that object is defined by the files you see for the Calendar extension in the Goodies folder. Because the Goodies category already exists and has only one object in it, you'll place the copyright object there. The categories on the Insert bar are specified in the insertbar.xml file, which contains information about the order of categories and objects. Objects that are not listed in the insertbar.xml file are given lower priority, being displayed after those that are listed. Folders that are not specified in the insertbar.xml file are ignored; they do not display on the Insert bar.

NOTE *Please be aware that the files that are contained within the Configuration folders in the Dreamweaver application folder are essential files; these files are central to the Dreamweaver program. You should be very careful when modifying, deleting, or adding to these files and folders—do so only if you intend to customize Dreamweaver and are familiar with the code and file structures. If you plan to make changes to files such as the insertbar.xml file, make backup copies first. There is a Configuration_ReadMe.htm file in the Configuration folder of the Dreamweaver application folder with more information on the Configuration files. If you have installed multiple versions of Dreamweaver on your computer, you may see an older and unnecessary Configuration folder called Configuration-1 if you have not completely uninstalled or deleted the program.*

6) Switch to Design view, place the insertion point in the new document and click the new Copyright icon in the Goodies category of the Insert bar.

The horizontal rule, copyright line, and modified date are all inserted in your page.

You can close this file without saving it.

552

ADVANCED CUSTOMIZATION

Up to this point in the lessons, you worked with a wide variety of Dreamweaver's toolbars and panels. In Lesson 1, you learned how to arrange the toolbars and panels by rearranging their order within existing panel groups, moving them to different panel groups, creating new panel groups, and docking and undocking panel groups. You worked with the Dreamweaver Preferences throughout the book. In this lesson, you learned how to install extensions as well as create your own objects.

There are many other things that you can do to customize Dreamweaver to suit your needs. Other possibilities include, but are not limited to, changing FTP Mappings to specify file extensions and file creators; customizing the Dreamweaver menus by adding, removing, changing, or moving menu items; changing the keyboard shortcuts; customizing default documents; customizing browser profiles; and creating your own extensions.

Use caution when making changes to any of the Dreamweaver program files; advanced customization is best done by those with a thorough understanding of HTML, JavaScript, and the structure of the Dreamweaver program.

WHAT YOU HAVE LEARNED

In this lesson, you have:

- Added extensions to expand Dreamweaver's capabilities using the Macromedia Extension Manager (pages 538–543)

- Learned where to find more extensions (page 542)

- Used new extensions to create a calendar, superscript text, and a toggle check box function; and to insert placeholder text (pages 543–549)

- Created a new object and placed it into the Insert bar (pages 549–553)

regular expressions

APPENDIX A

Regular expressions describe patterns that you can use to search code and text. Searching with regular expressions is covered in Lesson 15. The following table lists the special characters that are used in regular expressions, descriptions of their meanings, and examples of their matches.

Type	Description	Example
^	Beginning of input or line.	**^T** matches "T" in "This good earth," but not in "Uncle Tom"
$	End of input or line.	**h$** matches "h" in "teach," but not in "teacher"
*	The preceding character zero or more times	**um*** matches "um" in "rum," "umm" in "yummy," and "u" in "huge"
+	The preceding character one or more times.	**um+** matches "um" in "rum" and "umm" in "yummy," but nothing in "huge"
?	The preceding character at most once.	**st?on** matches "son" in "Johnson" and "ston" in "Johnston" but nothing in "Appleton" or "tension"
.	Any single character except newline.	**.an** matches "ran" and "can" in the phrase "bran muffins can be tasty"
x|y	Either x or y.	**FF0000|0000FF** matches **"FF0000"** in **BGCOLOR="#FF0000"** and **"0000FF"** in **FONT COLOR="#0000FF"**
{n}	Exactly n occurrences of the preceding character.	**o{2}** matches "oo" in "loom" and the first two o's in "mooooo," but nothing in "money"
{n,m}	At least n and at most m occurrences of the preceding character.	**F{2,4}** matches **"FF"** in **"#FF0000"** and the first four Fs in **"#FFFFFF"**

Type	Description	Example
[abc]	Any one of the characters enclosed in the brackets. Specify a range of characters with a hyphen (for example, **[a-f]** is equivalent to **[abcdef]**.	**[e-g]** matches "e" in "bed," "f" in "folly," and "g" in "guard"
[^abc]	Any character not enclosed in the brackets. Specify a range of characters with a hyphen (for example, **[a-f]** is equivalent to **[abcdef]**.	**[^aeiou]** initially matches "r" in "orange," "b" in "book," and "k" in "eek!"
\b	A word boundary (such as a space or carriage return).	**\bb** matches "b" in "book," but nothing in "goober" or "snob"
\B	Anything other than a word boundary.	**\Bb** matches "b" in "goober," but nothing in "book"
\d	Any digit character. Equivalent to **[0-9]**.	**\d** matches "3" in "C3PO" and "2" in "apartment 2G"
\D	Any nondigit character. Equivalent to **[^0-9]**.	**\D** matches "S" in "900S" and "Q" in "Q45"
\f	Form feed	
\n	Line feed	
\r	Carriage return	
\s	Any single white-space character, including space, tab, form feed, or line feed.	**\sbook** matches "book" in "blue book," but nothing in "notebook"
\t	A tab.	
\w	Any alphanumeric character, including underscore. Equivalent to **[A-Za-z0-9_]**.	**b\w*** matches "barking" in "the barking dog" and both "big" and "black" in "the big black dog"
\W	Any nonalphanumeric character. Equivalent to **[^A-Za-z0-9_]**.	**\W** matches "&" in "Jake & Mattie" and "%" in "100%"

macintosh shortcuts

APPENDIX B

Keyboard shortcuts can speed up the process of developing your site, making it quicker and easier to work with design and code elements as well as site management functions. You can add, remove, or modify Dreamweaver's keyboard shortcuts by choosing Dreamweaver > Keyboard Shortcuts to open the Keyboard Shortcuts dialog box.

MENU SHORTCUTS

DREAMWEAVER MENU

Command	Shortcut
Preferences	Command+U
Hide Dreamweaver	Command+H
Quit Dreamweaver	Command+Q

FILE MENU

Command	Shortcut
New	Command+N
Open	Command+O
Open in Frame	Shift+Command+O
Close	Command+W
Close All	Shift+Command+W
Save	Command+S
Save As...	Shift+Command+S
Print Code	Command+P
Preview in Primary Browser	F12
Preview in Secondary Browser	Command+F12
Check Links	Shift+F8
Validate Markup...	Shift+F6

EDIT MENU

Command	Shortcut
Undo	Command+Z or Option+Delete
Redo	Command+Y or Shift+Command+Z
Cut	Command+X or Shift+Delete
Copy	Command+C
Paste	Command+V
Clear	Delete
Copy HTML	Shift+Command+C
Paste HTML	Shift+Command+V
Select All	Command+A
Select Parent Tag	Command+[
Select Child	Command+]
Find and Replace	Command+F
Find Again	Command+G
Go to Line	Command+,
Show Code Hints	Control+Space
Indent Code	Shift+Command+.
Outdent Code	Shift+Command+,
Balance Braces	Command+'

VIEW MENU

Command	Shortcut
Switch Views	Control+`
Refresh Design View	F5
Live Data*	Shift+Command+R
Head Content	Shift+Command+H
Table Mode > Expanded Tables Mode	F6
Table Mode > Layout Mode	Command+F6
Visual Aids > Hide All	Shift+Command+I
Rulers > Show	Option+Command+R
Grid > Show	Option+Command+G
Grid > Snap to Grid	Option+Shift+Command+G
Plugins > Play	Option+Command+P
Plugins > Stop	Option+Command+X
Plugins > Play All	Option+Shift+Command+P
Plugins > Stop All	Option+Shift+Command+X
Hide/Show Panels	F4

*Command is not included in the View Menu.

INSERT MENU

Command	Shortcut
Tag...	Command+E
Image	Option+Command+I
Media > Flash	Option+Command+F
Media > Shockwave	Option+Command+D
Table	Option+Command+T
Named Anchor	Option+Command+A
HTML > Special Characters > Line Break	Shift+Return
HTML > Special Characters > Non-Breaking Space	Shift+Command+Space
Copyright Character (©)*	Option+G
Template Objects > Editable Region	Option+Command+V

*Command is not included in the Insert Menu.

MODIFY MENU

Command	Shortcut
Page Properties	Command+J
Quick Tag Editor	Command+T
Make Link	Command+L
Remove Link	Shift+Command+L
Table > Select Table	Command+A
Move to the Next Cell*	Tab
Move to the Previous Cell*	Shift+Tab
Table > Merge Cells	Option+Command+M
Table > Split Cell	Option+Command+S
Table > Insert Row	Command+M
Table > Insert Column	Shift+Command+A
Table > Delete Row	Shift+Command+M
Table > Delete Column	Shift+Command+-
Table > Increase Column Span	Shift+Command+]
Table > Decrease Column Span	Shift+Command+[
Align > Left	Shift+Command+1
Align > Right	Shift+Command+3
Align > Top	Shift+Command+4
Align > Bottom	Shift+Command+6
Align > Make Same Width	Shift+Command+7
Align > Make Same Height	Shift+Command+9

*Command is not included in the Modify Menu.

TEXT MENU

Command	Shortcut
Indent	Option+Command+]
Outdent	Option+Command+[
Paragraph Format > None	Command+0
Paragraph Format > Paragraph	Shift+Command+P
Paragraph Format > Heading 1	Command+1
Paragraph Format > Heading 2	Command+2
Paragraph Format > Heading 3	Command+3
Paragraph Format > Heading 4	Command+4
Paragraph Format > Heading 5	Command+5
Paragraph Format > Heading 6	Command+6
Align > Left	Option+Shift+Command+L
Align > Center	Option+Shift+Command+C
Align > Right	Option+Shift+Command+R
Align > Justify	Option+Shift+Command+J
Style > Bold	Command+B
Style > Italic	Command+I
Check Spelling	Shift+F7

COMMANDS MENU

Command	Shortcut
Start Recording	Shift+Command+X

SITE MENU

Command	Shortcut
Get	Shift+Command+D
Check Out	Option+Shift+Command+D
Put	Shift+Command+U
Check In	Option+Shift+Command+U
Check Links Sitewide	Command+F8

WINDOW MENU

Command	Shortcut
Insert	Command+F2
Properties	Command+F3
CSS Styles	Shift+F11
Layers	F2
Behaviors	Shift+F3
Snippets	Shift+F9
Reference	Shift+F1
Databases	Shift+Command+F10
Bindings	Command+F10
Server Behaviors	Command+F9
Components	Command+F7
Files	F8
Assets	F11
Tag Inspector	F9
Results	F7
History	Shift+F10
Frames	Shift+F2
Code Inspector	F10
Hide/Show Panels	F4
Next Document	Command+`
Previous Document	Shift+Command+`

HELP MENU

Command	Shortcut
Using Dreamweaver	F1
Using ColdFusion	Command+F1
Reference	Shift+F1

CODE SHORTCUTS

Command	Shortcut	Command	Shortcut
Select Parent Tag	Command+[	Character Select Left	Shift+Left
Select Child	Command+]	Character Select Right	Shift+Right
Balance Braces	Command+'	Select to Page Up	Shift+PgUp
Select All	Command+A	Select to Page Down	Shift+PgDn
Bold	Command+B	Move Word Left	Command+Left
Italic	Command+I	Move Word Right	Command+Right
Copy	Command+C	Select Word Left	Command+Shift+Left
Find and Replace	Command+F	Select Word Right	Command+Shift+Right
Find Next	Command+G	Move to Start of Line	Home
Paste	Command+V	Move to End of Line	End
Cut	Command+X	Select to Start of Line	Shift+Home
Redo	Command+Y	Select to End of Line	Shift+End
Undo	Command+Z	Move to Top of File	Command+Home
Print Code	Command+P	Move to End of File	Command+End
Switch to Document	Command+`	Select to Start of File	Command+Shift+Home
Delete Word Left	Command+Delete	Select to Start of File	Command+Shift+End
Select Line Up	Shift+Up	Snippets	Shift+F9
Select Line Down	Shift+Down		

FILES PANEL MENUS

FILE MENU

Command	Shortcut
New File	Shift+Command+N
New Folder	Option+Shift+Command+N
Rename	F2
Preview in Primary Browser	F12
Preview in Secondary Browser	Command+F12
Check Links	Shift+F8

EDIT MENU

Command	Shortcut
Cut	Command+X
Copy	Command+C
Paste	Command+V
Duplicate	Command+D
Select All	Command+A

VIEW MENU

Command	Shortcut
Refresh	F5
Show/Hide Link	Shift+Command+Y
View as Root	Shift+Command+R
Show Page Titles	Shift+Command+T
Site Files	F8
Site Map	Option+F8

SITE

Command	Shortcut
Get	Shift+Command+D
Check Out	Option+Shift+Command+D
Put	Shift+Command+U
Check In	Option+Shift+Command+U
Check Links Sitewide	Command+F8
Link to New File	Shift+Command+N
Link to Existing File	Shift+Command+K
Change Link	Command+L
Remove Link	Shift+Command+L

windows
shortcuts

APPENDIX C

Keyboard shortcuts can speed up the process of developing your site, making it quicker and easier to work with design and code elements as well as site management functions. You can add, remove, or modify Dreamweaver's keyboard shortcuts by choosing Edit > Keyboard Shortcuts to open the Keyboard Shortcuts dialog box.

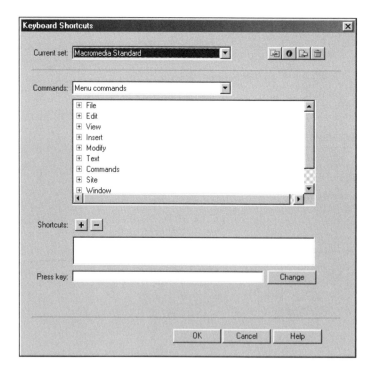

Menu Shortcuts

FILE MENU

Command	Shortcut
New	Ctrl+N
Open	Ctrl+O
Open in Frame	Ctrl+Shift+O
Close	Ctrl+W
Close	Ctrl+Shift+W
Save	Ctrl+S
Save As	Ctrl+Shift+S
Print Code	Ctrl+P
Preview in Primary Browser	F12
Preview in Secondary Browser	Ctrl+F12
Check Links	Shift+F8
Validate Markup	Shift+F6
Exit	Ctrl+Q

EDIT MENU

Command	Shortcut
Undo	Ctrl+Z
Redo	Ctrl+Y
Cut	Ctrl+X
Copy	Ctrl+C
Paste	Ctrl+V
Copy HTML	Ctrl+Shift+C
Paste HTML	Ctrl+Shift+V
Select All	Ctrl+A
Select Parent Tag	Ctrl+[
Select Child	Ctrl+]
Find and Replace	Ctrl+F
Find Next	F3
Go to Line	Ctrl+G
Show Code Hints	Ctrl+Space
Indent Code	Ctrl+Shift+›
Outdent Code	Ctrl+Shift+‹
Balance Braces	Ctrl+'
Preferences	Ctrl+U

VIEW MENU

Command	Shortcut
Switch Views	Ctrl+'
Refresh Design View	F5
Live Data*	Ctrl+Shift+R
Head Content	Ctrl+Shift+W
Table Mode > Expanded Tables Mode	F6
Table Mode > Layout Mode	Ctrl+F6
Visual Aids > Hide All	Ctrl+Shift+I
Rulers > Show	Ctrl+Alt+R
Grid > Show Grid	Ctrl+Alt+G
Grid > Snap to Grid	Ctrl+Shift+Alt+G
Plugins > Play	Ctrl+Alt+P
Plugins > Stop	Ctrl+Alt+X
Plugins > Play All	Ctrl+Shift+Alt+P
Plugins > Stop All	Ctrl+Shift+Alt+X
Hide/Show Panels	F4

*Command is not included in the Modify menu.

INSERT MENU

Command	Shortcut
Tag	Ctrl+E
Image	Ctrl+Alt+I
Media > Flash	Ctrl+Alt+F
Media > Shockwave	Ctrl+Alt+D
Table	Ctrl+Alt+T
Named Anchor	Ctrl+Alt+A
Special Characters > Line Break	Shift+Enter
Special Characters > Non-Breaking Space	Ctrl+Shift+Space
Template Object > Editable Region	Crtl+Alt+V

MODIFY MENU

Command	Shortcut
Page Properties	Ctrl+J
Quick Tag Editor	Ctrl+T
Make Link	Ctrl+L
Remove Link	Ctrl+Shift+L
Table > Select Table	Ctrl+A
Move to the Next Cell*	Tab
Move to the Previous Cell*	Shift+Tab
Table > Merge Cells	Ctrl+Alt+M
Table > Split Cell	Ctrl+Alt+S
Table > Insert Row	Ctrl+M
Table > Insert Column	Ctrl+Shift+A
Table > Delete Row	Ctrl+Shift+M
Table > Delete Column	Ctrl+Shift+-
Table > Increase Column Span	Ctrl+Shift+]
Table > Decrease Column Span	Ctrl+Shift+[
Align > Left	Ctrl+Shift+1
Align > Right	Ctrl+Shift+3
Align > Top	Ctrl+Shift+4
Align > Bottom	Ctrl+Shift+6
Align > Make Same Width	Ctrl+Shift+7
Align > Make Same Height	Ctrl+Shift+9

*Command is not included in the Modify menu.

TEXT MENU

Command	Shortcut
Indent	Ctrl+Alt+]
Outdent	Ctrl+Alt+[
Paragraph Format › None	Ctrl+0
Paragraph Format › Paragraph	Ctrl+Shift+P
Paragraph Format › Heading 1	Ctrl+1
Paragraph Format › Heading 2	Ctrl+2
Paragraph Format › Heading 3	Ctrl+3
Paragraph Format › Heading 4	Ctrl+4
Paragraph Format › Heading 5	Ctrl+5
Paragraph Format › Heading 6	Ctrl+6
Align › Left	Ctrl+Shift+Alt+L
Align › Center	Ctrl+Shift+Alt+C
Align › Right	Ctrl+Shift+Alt+R
Align › Justify	Crt+Shift+Alt+J
Bold	Ctrl+B
Italic	Ctrl+I
Check Spelling	Shift+F7

COMMANDS MENU

Command	Shortcut
Start Recording	Ctrl+Shift+X

SITE MENU

Command	Shortcut
Get	Ctrl+Shift+D
Check Out	Ctrl+Shift+Alt+D
Put	Ctrl+Shift+U
Check In	Ctrl+Shift+Alt+U
Check Links Sitewide	Ctrl+F8

WINDOW MENU

Command	Shortcut
Insert	Ctrl+F2
Properties	Ctrl+F3
CSS Styles	Shift+F11
Layers	F2
Behaviors	Shift+F3
Snippets	Shift+F9
Reference	Shift+F1
Databases	Ctrl+Shift+F10
Bindings	Ctrl+F10
Server Behaviors	Ctrl+F9
Components	Ctrl+F7
Files	F8
Assets	F11
Tag Inspector	F9
Results	F7
History	Shift+F10
Frames	Shift+F2
Code Inspector	F10
Hide/Show Panels	F4
Next Document	Ctrl+`
Previous Document	Ctrl+Shift+`

HELP MENU

Command	Shortcut
Using Dreamweaver	F1
Using ColdFusion	Ctrl+F1
Reference	Shift+F1

Code Shortcuts

Command	Shortcut	Command	Shortcut
Select Parent Tag	Ctrl+Shift+[	Delete Word Left	Ctrl+Backspace
Select Child	Ctrl+Shift+]	Delete Word Right	Ctrl+Del
Balance Braces	Ctrl+'	Move to Page Up	Page Up
Select All	Ctrl+A	Move to Page Down	Page Down
Bold	Ctrl+B	Select to Page Up	Shift+Page Up
Italic	Ctrl+I	Select to Page Down	Shift+Page Down
Copy	Ctrl+C	Move Word Left	Ctrl+Left
Find and Replace	Ctrl+F	Move Word Right	Ctrl+Right
Find Next	F3	Select Word Left	Ctrl+Shift+Left
Paste	Ctrl+V	Select Word Right	Ctrl+Shift+Right
Cut	Ctrl+X	Move to Start of Line	Home
Redo	Ctrl+Y	Move to End of Line	End
Undo	Ctrl+Z	Select to Start of Line	Shift+Home
Print Code	Ctrl+P	Select to End of Line	Shift+End
Switch to Document	Ctrl+`	Move to Top of File	Ctrl+Home
Select Line Up	Shift+Up	Move to End of File	Ctrl+End
Select Line Down	Shift+Down	Select to Start of File	Ctrl+Shift+Home
Character Select Left	Shift+Left	Select to End of File	Ctrl+Shift+End
Character Select Right	Shift+Right	Snippets	Shift+F9

Files Panel Menus

FILE MENU

Command	Shortcut
New File	Ctrl+Shift+N
New Folder	Ctrl+Shift+Alt+N
Rename	F2
Delete	Del
Check Links	Shift+F8
Exit	Ctrl+Q

EDIT MENU

Command	Shortcut
Cut	Ctrl+X
Copy	Ctrl+C
Paste	Ctrl+V
Duplicate	Ctrl+D
Select All	Ctrl+A

VIEW MENU

Command	Shortcut
Refresh	F5
Show/Hide Link	Ctrl+Shift+Y
View as Root	Ctrl+Shift+R
Show Page Titles	Ctrl+Shift+T
Site Files	F8
Site Map	Alt+F8

SITE MENU

Command	Shortcut
Get	Ctrl+Shift+D
Checkout	Ctrl+Shift+Alt+D
Put	Ctrl+Shift+U
Check In	Ctrl+Shift+Alt+U
Check Links Sitewide	Ctrl+F8
Link to New File	Ctrl+Shift+N
Link to Existing File	Ctrl+Shift+K
Change Link	Ctrl+L
Remove Link	Ctrl+Shift+L

index

577

file structure for, 127–128, 389

generating reports for, 444–445

keeping track of colors used in, 60

launching, 387

managing/maintaining, 386–387.
  See also Files panel

moving to another computer,
  425–426

naming, 14

planning, 10–11

repeating items throughout, 240–241

testing, 430–447

uploading to remote site, 411–415

using forms in, 316–317. *See also*
  forms

using template for, 257. *See also*
  templates

viewing subset of, 399–400

Web standards, 228

weight declarations, style, 223

Window menu, 28, 559, 565

Window Size menu, 179–180

windows

controlling placement of, 455–457

opening new browser, 373–375

options for viewing, 28

Windows, Microsoft

and ASCII text files, 40–41

and font sizes, 56

and .htm/.html extension, 21

and image placeholders, 91

keyboard shortcuts, 562–567

options for viewing documents, 28

and Redo command bug, 52

screen resolution, 215

system requirements, 5

workspace options, 8

Windows NT, 22

Word, Microsoft, 41, 150, 474–476

word wrap. *See* wrapping text

**words, inserting multiple spaces
  between**, 43

workspaces

options for Windows/Macintosh, 8

switching between, 8

World Wide Web Consortium, 228

Wrap menu, 331

wrapping text, 88–89, 159, 331

X

XHTML, 20

XML, 20, 425

Z

z-index values, 517–518

zero point, 525

real world. real training. real results.

Get more done in less time with
Macromedia Training and Certification.

Two Types of Training

Roll up your sleeves and get right to work with authorized training
from Macromedia.

1. Classroom Training

   Learn from instructors thoroughly trained and certified by
   Macromedia. Courses are fast-paced and task-oriented to get
   you up and running quickly.

2. Online Training

   Get Macromedia training when you want with affordable, interactive online
   training from Macromedia University.

Stand Out from the Pack

Show your colleagues, employer, or prospective clients that you
have what it takes to effectively develop, deploy, and maintain dynamic
applications–become a Macromedia Certified Professional.

Learn More

For more information about authorized training or to find a class near you,
visit **www.macromedia.com/go/training1**

LICENSING AGREEMENT